Behaviour for Learning

Behaviour for Learning offers teachers a clear conceptual framework for making sense of the many behaviour management strategies on offer, allowing them to make a critical assessment of the appropriateness and effectiveness of these in the classroom, and assisting them to promote closer links between 'behaviour' and 'learning'. Now in a fully updated second edition, the book focuses on how teachers can provide a safe and secure setting where positive relationships are fostered, placing increased emphasis on learning behaviours that contribute to pupils' cognitive, social and emotional development.

The book is full of practical approaches that can help teachers support pupils to achieve, relate to others and develop behaviours that characterise self-esteem, confidence and resilience. It includes chapters covering:

- relationship with the curriculum, relationship with self and relationship with others;
- whole-school approaches and the school behaviour policy;
- reframing special educational needs;
- dealing with more challenging behaviour;
- transitions.

This second edition also includes an updated emphasis on the links between mental health, behaviour and relationships in schools, and reflects Department for Education advice for school staff, changes to the National Curriculum and the new SEND Code of Practice.

Through the application of the Behaviour for Learning framework, the book encourages teachers to address the needs of pupils who exhibit behavioural difficulties, whilst still pursuing excellence in teaching and learning for all pupils. It is a compelling and essential read for all trainees and practicing teachers, CPD coordinators and other professionals working with children in schools.

Simon Ellis is a Senior Lecturer in the Faculty of Education at Canterbury Christ Church University, UK. He currently teaches on the Masters in Education programme and the National Award for SEN Coordination course. He also regularly provides input on Behaviour for Learning to a range of the University's initial teacher education programmes. Simon has previously worked as a Key Stage 3 National Strategy Behaviour and Attendance consultant and a local authority Behaviour Support Service manager.

Janet Tod is Emeritus Professor of Education at Canterbury Christ Church University, UK. She led the Teacher Training Agency (TTA) funded Evidence for Policy and Practice Information (EPPI) review 'A systematic review of how theories explain learning behaviour in school contexts' (Powell and Tod 2004) that produced the Behaviour for Learning conceptual framework which is now used in a range of teacher education programmes. She is a qualified speech therapist and a British Psychological Society (BPS) chartered educational and clinical psychologist.

Behaviour for Learning

Promoting Positive Relationships in the Classroom

2nd Edition

Simon Ellis and Janet Tod

Routledge
Taylor & Francis Group

LONDON AND NEW YORK

Second edition published 2018
by Routledge
2 Park Square, Milton Park, Abingdon, Oxon, OX14 4RN

and by Routledge
711 Third Avenue, New York, NY 10017

Routledge is an imprint of the Taylor & Francis Group, an informa business

© 2018 Simon Ellis and Janet Tod

First edition published by Routledge 2009

British Library Cataloguing-in-Publication Data
A catalogue record for this book is available from the British Library

Library of Congress Cataloging-in-Publication Data
A catalog record has been requested for this book

ISBN: 978-1-138-29306-9 (hbk)
ISBN: 978-1-138-29307-6 (pbk)
ISBN: 978-1-315-23225-6 (ebk)

Typeset in Bembo
by Wearset Ltd, Boldon, Tyne and Wear

Contents

Figures

Tables

Preface to the second edition

We are grateful to Routledge for giving us the opportunity to write a second edition of this book. When we wrote the first edition in 2009 the Behaviour for Learning approach was still relatively new, having developed from a conceptual framework presented in a systematic review of literature (Powell and Tod 2004). Since then we have had the opportunity to provide input on Behaviour for Learning to many more groups of teachers and others. From these experiences we have developed improved ways of introducing the overall approach and explaining the key principles.

As might be expected, policy and guidance for both education generally and behaviour in schools has changed over the past nine years. This edition has been thoroughly updated to reflect this. In addition to policy updates, we have drawn on a range of other literature published since 2009 relevant to the Behaviour for Learning approach.

One of the most significant changes in policy and guidance has been an increased emphasis on children's mental health. To reflect this we have separated the 'Relationship with self and relationship with others' chapter from the 2009 edition into two discrete chapters. To make space for this we have removed the 'Learning from history' chapter that opened the first edition. Although there is no longer a discrete chapter on this topic, we continue to believe that it is important to recognise that the way in which school-based learning is conceptualised within policy and guidance influences the learning behaviours schools prioritise and the type of relationship with the curriculum that is expected. It is interesting to note, for example, that when we wrote the 2009 edition we incorporated a quote predicting that by 2020 'ways of knowing' would be 'more important than familiarity with particular bodies of knowledge' (Newby 2005: 299). In this edition we refer to a National Curriculum that seeks to provide pupils with 'an introduction to the essential knowledge that they need to be educated citizens (DfE 2014a: 6).

In this edition we have included appendices containing strategies and lists of learning behaviours in order to provide readers with some practical support and ideas when implementing the Behaviour for Learning approach.

We recognise that a wide range of readers will access this book, including beginning teachers, experienced teachers, middle and senior leaders and tutors on Initial Teacher Education or Masters programmes. Whatever your role and reason for accessing it, we hope this new edition makes a valuable contribution to your thinking and practice.

Acknowledgements

This book is based on work that developed from a research project commissioned by the Teacher Training Agency (TTA), and managed at Canterbury Christ Church University. The original research project (Powell and Tod 2004) was conducted following the procedures developed for systematic review by the Evidence for Policy and Practice Information and Coordinating Centre (EPPI–Centre), http://eppi.ioe.ac.uk/cms/.

We would like to express our thanks to those involved in the original EPPI review and also to our colleagues at the University, students and teachers who have contributed to our thinking in the 14 years since the publication of that research.

The views represented in this book are those of the authors and are not intended to represent the views or policies of any particular body.

Abbreviations

ADHD	Attention Deficit Hyperactivity Disorder
ASD	Autism Spectrum Disorder(s)
ATL	Association of Teachers and Lecturers
BESD	Behaviour, Emotional and Social Development
BFL	Behaviour For Learning
BPS	British Psychological Society
CACE	Central Advisory Council for Education
CESE	Centre for Education Statistics and Evaluation
DCSF	Department for Children, Schools and Families
DES	Department of Education and Science
DfE	Department for Education
DfEE	Department for Education and Employment
DfES	Department for Education and Skills
EBD	Emotional and Behavioural Difficulties
EEF	Education Endowment Foundation
EPPI-Centre	Evidence for Policy and Practice Information and Co-ordinating Centre
ICT	Information and Communication Technology
IDP	Inclusion Development Programme
IPRN	Initial Teacher Education Professional Resource Network
ITT	Initial Teacher Education
NASEN	National Association for Special Educational Needs
NASUWT	National Association of Schoolmasters Union of Women Teachers
NFER	National Foundation for Educational Research
NQT	Newly Qualified Teacher
Ofsted	Office for Standards in Education, Children's Services and Skills
PE	Physical Education
PECS	Picture Exchange Communication System
PRU	Pupil Referral Unit
PSHE	Personal, Social and Health Education
QCA	Qualifications and Curriculum Authority
QTS	Qualified Teacher Status
REMs	Reciprocal Effects Models
SDQ	Strengths and Difficulties Questionnaire
SEAL	Social and Emotional Aspects of Learning
SEL	Social and Emotional Learning
SEMH	Social, Emotional and Mental Health

SEN	Special Educational Needs
SENCO	Special Educational Needs Coordinator
SEND	Special Educational Needs and Disability
SLCN	Speech, Language and Communication Needs
SpLD	Specific Learning Difficulty
TA	Teaching Agency
TDA	Training and Development Agency
TTA	Teacher Training Agency

Introduction

This book expands upon a conceptual framework that emerged from a systematic literature review (Powell and Tod 2004) funded by the Teacher Training Agency (TTA). The framework is now well established, having been tried and tested with teachers, trainees and tutors.

We acknowledge there is already a plethora of books, guidance and support material available to trainees, teachers and tutors in relation to pupil behaviour. This text does not seek to replace these but we consider it to be different in several ways

It builds on teachers' existing expertise

Teaching as a profession promotes learning, normally in group contexts and conditions. The Behaviour for Learning approach builds on this area of expertise as a route to improving behaviour in the classroom. As such the key theme of this book is the explicit linking of learning and behaviour, via the term 'learning behaviour'. The use of this term will hopefully serve to reduce perceptions that 'promoting learning' and 'managing behaviour' are separate issues for teachers (Powell and Tod 2004). Teachers and schools already have experience in using a range of existing behaviour management techniques. This book does not seek to replace such approaches but in Chapters 8, 9 and 10 examines ways in which such management techniques may be enhanced via the Behaviour for Learning approach.

It provides a way of evaluating the efficacy of behaviour management strategies

Through the use of the term 'learning behaviour', pupil progress in *learning* provides a relevant indicator against which to measure the efficacy of school-based *behaviour* management strategies. Strategies, approaches or interventions are therefore selected based on awareness of their likely contribution to the development of learning behaviour and evaluated against their actual impact.

It promotes the development of learning relationships

A core feature of the Behaviour for Learning approach is that it places emphasis on the relationships that underpin learning and behaviour in school contexts. It endorses the view that learning and behaviour are influenced by the quality of relationships that characterise classroom interactions. These relationships are changing, interdependent and reciprocal, and as such do not lend themselves to any one quick-fix set of strategies. However, teachers and others can prepare for – and pupils can contribute positively to – these relationships.

Within classroom contexts the three core relationships identified from the original research (Powell and Tod 2004) and underpinning this book are:

- relationship with others;
- relationship with self;
- relationship with the curriculum.

It explicitly recognises and utilises the interdependence of the cognitive, social and emotional aspects of learning and behaviour

The three Behaviour for Learning relationships reflect the social, emotional and cognitive factors that influence pupil behaviour and learning. Although in school contexts pupils' relationship with the curriculum is seen as a priority and teachers are able to draw upon extensive curriculum guidance in this area, it is clear that for some pupils improving their relationship with the curriculum will require attention to their relationship with self and/or their relationship with others.

It adopts a proactive approach to behaviour management

The Behaviour for Learning approach does not seek to pathologise individual pupil behaviour or place blame on teachers. This book adopts a proactive approach to behaviour management, placing an emphasis on supporting teachers to identify and develop the learning behaviours that are relevant to *all* pupils.

It recognises diversity, delay and difference within individuals in group contexts

This book accepts that a teacher is involved in the process of responding to the often complex needs of individual pupils and therefore has to make multiple decisions in non-routine situations (Haggarty 2002). It places emphasis on the fact that contexts and conditions of the classroom, designed for groups, will be experienced differently by individuals. In asking teachers to consider how their behaviour management strategies are experienced by individuals, it is anticipated that teachers will become more confident in supporting pupils with diverse needs, including those with special educational needs (SEN).

It is realistic in its aims

The book is honest in accepting that it does not seek to provide a solution to the range of behaviour problems that trainees and teachers encounter or fear. This is an unrealistic pursuit given that individual pupils interpret, experience and make sense of classroom events from their own personal perspective. However, the Behaviour for Learning conceptual framework that underpins this book enables teachers to make informed choices from the ever-growing plethora of behaviour management strategies and approaches available.

Ways of using this book

This book sets out an approach to pupil behaviour based on a conceptual framework that may be unfamiliar to many readers. As such it necessarily combines exploratory and explanatory content related to underpinning concepts alongside sections that relate familiar existing practices to these concepts.

As with many educational texts it is more likely that many readers will home in on particular chapters, dependent on their time, need and experience. Readers will note from Chapter 2 that there are three broad levels of use of the Behaviour for Learning approach. These are:

- day-to-day use;
- core use;
- extended use.

Day-to-day use

At whole-school and class levels, teachers need to provide contexts and conditions that promote the development of learning behaviours through a focus on learning and teaching. Essentially, the priority is to promote learning behaviour and protect and enhance the three Behaviour for Learning relationships that underpin its development. This requires the teacher to keep a watchful eye on the three relationships and look for opportunities through the curriculum, the behaviour they model and their routine interactions with pupils to develop learning behaviours. Readers who seek to improve their understanding at this level of practice will be best directed towards Chapter 2, followed by Chapters 8, 9 and 10. This will provide a working understanding of the Behaviour for Learning approach and its relationship to more conventional behaviour management approaches.

Core and extended use

For many pupils, it will suffice simply to focus on the general learning behaviours necessary to develop in learners at their age and stage of development, while keeping a watchful eye on the effect of any practice on the three relationships. However, the flexible nature of the behaviour for learning approach means that, when this is not sufficient, it can be applied in a more systematic way as an assessment and planning tool for groups and specific individuals whose behaviour causes particular concern. At the level of *core use* the teacher would seek to achieve positive change by developing one or two target learning behaviours. This would involve identifying strategies and approaches that have the potential to contribute to the development of these learning behaviours. The strategies and approaches are likely to be recognisable as cognitive, social and/or emotional in their focus. At the level of *extended use* a teacher may consider that the current problematic behaviour results from a significant weakness in one or more of the three relationships. Learning behaviours remain important but the focus would shift to strengthening one or more of three Behaviour for Learning relationships. Chapters 3, 4, 5, 6 and 7 provide detailed coverage of the concepts underpinning the Behaviour for Learning approach and aim to support readers in understanding its application in relation to specific individuals whose behaviour is a cause for particular concern.

Our own thinking with regard to the Behaviour for Learning approach has developed, and continues to develop, through our face-to-face teaching in contexts that allow for discussion and critical debate with practitioners. Writing a book necessarily involves communicating with practicing teachers and tutors through the more limited medium of the written text. In producing a book format we would hope that this text will provide the necessary content and impetus for active engagement with fellow trainees, school colleagues, mentors and tutors. Such engagement will allow readers to activate this book and apply it to their own practice-based concerns and professional development.

The chapters

Chapter 1 seeks to locate the Behaviour for Learning approach within a broad national context in which there is an ongoing concern regarding behaviour in schools. It explores the nature of the concern and examines the ways in which policy makers have sought to understand and respond to it. Policy and guidance has typically attempted to balance a concern for both discipline and control with a need for pastoral support and nurture. Despite reassurances (e.g. Ofsted 2005) that the vast majority of children and young people enjoy learning, work hard and behave well, behaviour in schools has continued to remain a concern with regard to its negative impact on pupils' learning, the effect on the recruitment and retention of teachers and the wider implications for society.

Chapter 2 argues that the traditional separation of learning and behaviour is not only conceptually flawed but is ultimately unhelpful to those who seek to improve behaviour and raise achievement in schools. The chapter examines the limitations of an exclusive focus on behaviour management. Central to this chapter is the introduction of the Behaviour for Learning conceptual framework that underpins the Behaviour for Learning approach. The key terminology within the framework is explored and the three levels of use (day-to-day, core and extended) are explained. A case study ('Steven') is provided that illustrates how a Behaviour for Learning stance changes both the approach to tackling behaviour issues and way in which the efficacy of any behaviour strategy employed by the teacher is evaluated.

Chapter 3 focuses exclusively on 'learning behaviours'. This term is used to represent the fusion of learning and behaviour that is a central theme of this book. The chapter seeks to maintain a view that promoting positive behaviours is more effective than seeking to stop negative behaviours. In order to support teachers to identify particular behaviours, this chapter draws on relevant literature as a source for descriptors and definitions. This critical review of learning behaviours allows readers access to the meaning and the utility of the term in school contexts.

Chapter 4 sets the scene for working within a framework that roots classroom practice within the building and maintenance of positive relationships. Teachers are familiar with the term 'relationship' and have experience of relationships. This chapter builds on this knowledge to explicitly consider what is meant by a relationship in the context of the Behaviour of Learning approach. The use of this term recognises the dynamic interactions and interdependence that make up the activity and purpose of the classroom.

The chapter steers readers towards an understanding of how a focus on relationships may not necessarily change what they are doing in the classroom but will change their thinking and in so doing will allow them to develop increasing confidence in their choice and evaluation of strategies.

Chapter 5 focuses specifically on 'relationship with the curriculum'. In so doing it explores what it means to have a relationship with something that is inanimate but nonetheless mirrors what we experience in human relationships. If, for example, we experience success and enjoyment, this usually leads to positive approaches to relationships; whereas failure is more likely to lead to relationships characterised by a cycle of negativity, such as a will to disrupt or harm the relationship. This chapter draws on literature to consider what it might mean in practice to have a positive relationship with the curriculum. It directs attention towards factors that should then influence choice of strategies that will support the building and maintenance of a positive relationship with the curriculum.

Chapter 6 focuses specifically on 'relationship with self', exploring what is meant by this term when used in the context of the Behaviour for Learning approach. We critically explore a number of widely used constructs relating to 'self' that have been developed to both explain and address individual differences in behaviour. These include self-esteem, self-efficacy attributional style and locus of control. Consideration is given to how such constructs can support teachers in selecting strategies that will support the building and maintenance of a positive relationship with self.

Chapter 7 focuses specifically on 'relationship with others'. This is likely to be the more familiar of the three Behaviour for Learning relationships as most teachers would accept that teaching is a social activity as well as recognise that pupils will need to relate to their peers when learning alongside them within a classroom. The chapter considers what is meant by the term 'relationship with others' when used in the context of the Behaviour for Learning approach. We critically consider the teacher–pupil relationship, peer relationships, social learning behaviours and the issue of bullying and highlight the implications for developing pupils' relationship with others.

Chapter 8 considers whole-school approaches to behaviour and the role of the school behaviour policy in defining and maintaining this. The chapter initially considers some of the implications for the development of a whole- school approach to behaviour if a Behaviour for Learning perspective is adopted. Whole-school behaviour policies are then critically examined in relation to their capacity to promote learning behaviour and protect and enhance the three relationships that underpin its development.

Chapter 9 focuses on the contexts and conditions for developing learning behaviour within the classroom. It considers teacher behaviours, the role of rules and routines, preparing for predictable occurrences, planning with learning behaviour in mind, effective use of positive feedback and organisation of the physical environment.

Chapter 10 focuses on what are commonly known as 'positive correction' techniques. It is recognised within this chapter that there will be occasions when teachers need to correct or re-direct pupils. A number of familiar positive correction strategies are outlined and discussed in the context of their potential to address the behaviour while also protecting the three Behaviour for Learning relationships.

Chapter 11 deals with more challenging behaviour. It initially considers procedures for exiting a pupil from the classroom in a manner that minimises the risk of compromising one or more of the behaviour for learning relationships. The remainder of chapter looks at behaviour that is motivated by anger. The nature and dynamics of anger are explored. The assault cycle (Breakwell 1997) is presented as a means by which a pupil's behaviour in an angry incident can be understood. Each stage of the assault cycle is discussed in the context of the implications for the teacher's priorities. The issue of physical intervention is considered in the context of its potential impact on relationships and the need for appropriate follow up procedures.

Chapter 12 is concerned with those individual learners who may experience particular difficulties, delay or difference in developing the relationships that underpin their learning in school contexts. These learners are likely to include, but are not necessarily restricted to, those who are described as having special educational needs (SEN). Using the examples of dyslexia, Autism Spectrum Disorders (ASD) and Social, Emotional and Mental Health (SEMH) difficulties, the chapter reframes special educational needs in terms of the Behaviour for Learning conceptual framework. The chapter seeks to look at provision in terms of supporting the development of meaningful relationships from the perspective of the individual and, in so doing, aims to support teachers in making informed choices from the plethora of available strategies.

Chapter 13 covers transitions. The focus is on four specific transition points: Foundation Stage to Year 1, Year 2 to Year 3, primary to secondary school, and Key Stage 3 to Key Stage 4. These transitions are considered from the perspective of identifying risks to the three Behaviour for Learning relationships and the practices that can help to reduce these.

We hope you enjoy reading this book and experience a positive impact on your thinking, learning and teaching and above all on the experience and behaviour of individuals in your class.

Chapter 1

Behaviour in schools

Introduction

Behaviour in English schools is frequently portrayed as a problem by policy makers (e.g. DfES 2005a; DfE 2010) and one that needs to be addressed. The existence of a problem and the need for action is reinforced by equally frequent media comment (e.g. Halpin and Blair 2005; Whitehead and Riches 2005; Harris 2015; Glaze 2016). Such reporting has served to place behaviour in schools in the public domain and establish it as a topic of public interest and concern. Successive governments have commissioned reports (e.g. DES 1989; DfES 2005b; Bennett 2017) and published guidance (e.g. DfE 1994a; DfES 2003a; DCSF 2009; DfE 2016a) designed to assist schools in developing effective behaviour policies. In the search for a solution to the perceived problem, there have also been repeated calls to strengthen initial teacher training (e.g. DfE 2010; DfE 2012a; Carter 2015) based on a belief that beginning teachers do not enter the profession with sufficient knowledge, skills and understanding in relation to behaviour management.

This chapter seeks to locate the Behaviour for Learning approach within a broad national context in which there is ongoing concern regarding behaviour in schools. It explores the nature of the concern and examines the ways in which policy makers have sought to understand and respond to it.

Examining the concern

The true extent of the problem of behaviour in schools is difficult to gauge (Bennett 2017). The Education White Paper *Educational Excellence Everywhere* (DfE 2016b) reported that 81 per cent of teachers and senior leaders said behaviour in their schools was good or very good. Until relatively recently there has also been a consistent message from Ofsted that 'the great majority of children and young people enjoy learning, work hard and behave well' (Ofsted 2005: 3), contradicting the more common, if not necessarily accurate, view of a decline in standards of behaviour. Indeed, in its Annual Report for 2010/11, Ofsted (2011) judged pupils' behaviour to be good or outstanding in 87 per cent of schools inspected between 1 September 2010 and 31 August 2011. The 2012/13 Annual Report from Ofsted (2013) did not differ significantly in its general message but made more regular reference to the problems of low level behaviour in a small minority of schools. A report, *Below the Radar: Low-Level Disruption in the Country's Classrooms* (Ofsted 2014a) was later published. The title alone, through its reference to 'the country's classrooms', conveyed the impression of a widespread issue. The report drew on evidence from inspections of nearly 3,000 maintained schools and academies conducted between January and early July 2014 and from 28 unannounced inspections of schools where behaviour was previously judged to require improvement, as well as survey data from teachers. This report appeared to contradict Ofsted's own official statistics published elsewhere the same year that indicated that, out of 21,104 schools inspected, 19,458 were judged to be good or better in relation to the behaviour and safety of pupils based on their most recent inspection (Ofsted 2014b).

Teachers' own opinions may, of course, provide an indicator of the reality. These, however, are far from conclusive. Despite 60 per cent of respondents in the 2012 National Foundation for Educational Research (NFER) Teacher Voice Survey feeling that negative pupil behaviour was driving teachers out of the profession, 95 per cent felt that behaviour was acceptable or better in their own schools (NFER 2012). It seems from these percentages that there was a perception that behaviour was having a negative effect on colleagues *somewhere* within the teaching profession but, at the level of the day-to-day experience of the individual respondent, it was not perceived as a major concern. The apparent discrepancy may partly be explained by availability bias. This is a term used to describe a natural tendency to give weight to what comes to mind most easily. The question 'To what extent do you agree that in your opinion, negative pupil behaviour is driving teachers out of the profession?' (NFER 2012: 9) does not particularly invite consideration of personal experience as evidence, and it may be that respondents based their answer on information available to them in the form of the widely reported view (e.g. DfE 2010; McCorkell and Greig 2010) regarding the effect of behaviour on teacher retention. It is possible to speculate that if the question had asked directly whether the respondent, or a teacher they knew, was contemplating leaving the profession due to pupil behaviour the response may have been different. However, the Teacher Support Network's 2010 Behaviour Survey (Teacher Support Network 2010) did ask a question regarding teacher retention that focused on personal experience. Just over 70 per cent of respondents indicated that poor pupil behaviour had, at some point, caused them to consider leaving the profession. This survey was based on a smaller sample of just over 350 teachers: the NFER survey was completed by just over 1,600 teachers from 1,269 schools (NFER 2012).

These apparent discrepancies between the popular views of behaviour in schools and some of the evidence reflect the House of Commons Education Committee's (2011) dilemma that because opinions varied so much about the nature or extent of a problem it was difficult to say to what extent the problem existed or even if there was one. The Committee had to concede that it was unable 'to come to any evidence-based or objective judgment on either the state of behaviour in schools today or whether there has been an improvement over time, as some people believe' (House of Commons Education Committee 2011: 3).

In his independent review of behaviour in schools, Bennett (2017: 15) remarks on the 'striking contrast between data gathered from school leaders or school inspectors, and the experiences of front line teachers and students'. Bennett (2017: 15) speculates on the reason, suggesting that as the stakes for school leaders are high, 'it is natural for the most positive interpretation of one's school to be presented publicly, especially in circumstances of external inspection'. Interpreting Bennett's (2017) more careful consideration of this issue, the *Mail Online* ran with the simpler headline, 'The badly behaved pupils kept hidden from Ofsted: Heads cover up problems by removing troublesome students from school premises during inspections' (Harris 2017). This is perhaps indicative of a discourse on behaviour in schools so firmly established that explanations for the lack of evidence confirming a problem are sought rather than questioning whether, in reality, the problem actually exists.

While there may be useful sociological debates to be had about changing patterns of behaviour in schools over the years, a simple assumption that it is worse now is likely to be unproductive. Changes in pupil behaviour occur within the broader changing social, cultural and educational context; if there ever was a 'golden age' where pupils showed unquestioning obedience and never challenged authority, attempting to reclaim this would be unrealistic. Though Bennett (2017) concludes there is enough evidence to suggest there is a problem with behaviour in schools, it is important to remember that both the Steer Report (DfES 2005b) and the Elton Report (DES 1989) were also commissioned in response to national concerns about this problem. Going back further, the Newsom Report (CACE 1963), explaining its motivation for seeking head teachers' views on behaviour, stated:

> Since young people are often under fire these days over matters of behaviour we asked the heads to write to us fully and frankly about general standards of conduct, and about the forms of discipline used in school and, as far as they knew, at home.
>
> (CACE 1963: 60)

Some head teachers contributing to the Newsom Report were reportedly 'bitterly angry about the harm done to secondary schools by grossly exaggerated accounts of indiscipline – which often make it difficult to recruit staff' (CACE 1963: 61). If there is a problem with behaviour in schools it seems that it is an enduring one rather than new and unprecedented. The Elton Report's observation from 1989 that '[b]ad behaviour is not a new problem, nor is it confined to England and Wales' (DES 1989: 65) seems just as relevant today.

It is not our intention or wish to attempt to diminish the significance for individual teachers or their schools of the pupil behaviour they currently encounter; rather, we are raising the issue that policy makers may be perpetually attempting to respond to a problem for some as though it is a problem for all. The Steer Report, itself commissioned in the wake of apparent growing concern about behaviour, noted that 'whilst the overall principles of good practice are well established, it is clear that not all school leaders nor all school staff are effectively implementing that practice' (DfES 2005b: 5). This would seem to indicate that there is little new to discover about the management of pupil behaviour. Policy makers should perhaps stop trying to 'crack' behaviour and heed the advice from the Elton Report that 'any quest for a single, dramatic remedy, such as a major piece of new legislation, would be futile' (DES 1989: 64). There may still be value in government seeking to produce guidance that identifies common features of good practice, but there needs to be appropriate recognition that 'schools vary enormously in their demographics, economic circumstances, staff composition, histories, premises, location and multiple other variables' (Bennett 2017: 12). These differences mean that 'the wholesale import of ideas and strategies from alien school circumstances would be ill considered' (Bennett 2017: 12).

The importance attached to whole-school approaches

The influential Elton Report (DES 1989: 54) was triggered by 'public concern about violence and indiscipline in schools and the problems faced by the teaching profession

today'. It was a wide-ranging enquiry regarding discipline in schools and used information from teachers and schools to form its views and make recommendations. Taking
account of research by Rutter *et al.* (1979) and similar work by Mortimore *et al.* (1988)
looking at primary schools, the Elton Report (DES 1989) framed pupil behaviour as a
school improvement issue. Reflecting themes from this research, the Elton Report
challenged the assumption that 'different home backgrounds' (DES 1989: 88) could
explain differences in the standards of learning and behaviour or in the 'overall school
atmosphere' (DES 1989: 88). The suggestion was that these 'differences had something
to do with what went on in the schools themselves' (DES 1989: 88).

The Elton Report (DES 1989) represented a major shift with regard to the management of behaviour in schools by encouraging a move towards whole- school approaches
to behaviour and discipline (Hallam and Rogers 2008). The underlying premise was
that pupils' behaviour could be influenced by all the major features and processes of a
school, including 'the quality of its leadership, classroom management, behaviour
policy, curriculum, pastoral care, buildings and physical environment, organisation and
timetable and relationships with parents' (DES 1989: 89–90)

The Elton Report advocated that schools adopt what it termed 'a healthy balance
between punishments and rewards' (DES 1989: 99), based on its finding that 'some
schools appear to have more punitive regimes than others, and that punitive regimes
seem to be associated with worse rather than better standards of behaviour' (DES 1989:
99). Though the reference to rewards and punishments reflected a perspective on
behaviour rooted in behaviourism, the Elton Report (DES 1989), like the majority of
schools at the time and today, did not adopt a purely behaviourist approach. It coupled
a belief in the use of rewards to encourage good behaviour and sanctions to discourage
misbehaviour with an acknowledgement of the central influence of the teacher–pupil
relationship, a stressing of the importance of personal and social education and recognition of the pastoral role of teachers and the need for parental involvement. In many
ways, the Elton Report (DES 1989) can be seen as providing the blueprint for the
general approaches to behaviour in schools that have been reiterated in subsequent
guidance and that form the basis for most schools' current practice.

The belief in the importance of a whole-school approach to behaviour was reflected
in the first set of materials published when the Behaviour and Attendance strand of the
Key Stage 3 National Strategy was introduced in 2003. The content of the Core Day 1
Behaviour and Attendance materials (DfES 2003b) provided schools with materials to
lead training in relation to behaviour and an audit (DfES 2003c) to enable them to
evaluate the whole-school behaviour policy and develop an action plan based on the
outcome. The audit was a dominant element within the Core Day 1 training presented
by local behaviour and attendance consultants. The intention was that schools would
conduct an initial audit of ten areas and use the data gathered to identify priorities to
investigate further using the in depth audit booklets. From this in depth auditing the
school would then develop an action plan. The ten areas were:

- leadership and management;
- everyday policies: rewards, sanctions and the promotion of positive behaviour;
- dealing with consistently poor behaviour;
- bullying;
- pupil support systems;
- classroom behaviour;

- out of class behaviour;
- curriculum;
- attendance;
- links with partners and other agencies.

The broad range of areas covered was indicative of the government's view on the aspects of school activity that impact on behaviour and was effectively an endorsement of the Elton Report's (DES 1989) views regarding the importance of a whole-school approach. Throughout the audit and the Core Day 1 materials (DfES 2003b) as a whole there was a strong focus on changes at a policy level that would impact on the Elton Report's 'low level disruption' (DES 1989: 67), rather than guidance on how to deal with the most challenging incidents.

During the 2004–2005 period there was once again a flurry of media interest (e.g. Revel 2004; Halpin and Blair 2005; Whitehead and Riches 2005) in behaviour in schools. A further high profile example of media interest in behaviour at this time was provided by Channel 4's documentary *Undercover Teacher* (Channel 4 2005) screened in July 2005. In the documentary a science teacher with two years' teaching experience carried out undercover filming while working in three secondary schools in London and Leeds. In setting these media concerns in context, it is interesting to note that, while not a cause for complacency, particularly at secondary level, evidence from Ofsted inspections conducted in 2003–2004 did not indicate a national picture of classroom chaos. The data gathered showed that 'behaviour was good or better in 90% of primary schools, 68% of secondary schools and 80% of special schools and PRUs' (Ofsted 2005: 3).

The Steer Report, *Learning Behaviour: The Report of the Practitioners' Group on School Behaviour and Discipline* (DfES 2005b), sought to review the current situation in schools and make recommendations for the way forward. The Practitioners' group had a remit to 'advise on how good practice found in so many schools can be spread and embedded to the benefit of others' (DfES 2005b: 6) and 'consider whether anything further needed to be done by policy makers to assist teachers and schools in their task, and what more might be done to engage parents' support' (DfES 2005b: 6). In responding to this remit, the Practitioners' group came up with some 147 recommendations. In section 2 entitled 'Principles and practice: What works in schools?' the Steer Report (DfES 2005b) outlined ten aspects of school practice that, when effective, contribute to the quality of pupil behaviour. These were:

- a consistent approach to behaviour management, teaching and learning;
- school leadership;
- classroom management, learning and teaching;
- rewards and sanctions;
- behaviour strategies and the teaching of good behaviour;
- staff development and support;
- pupil support systems;
- liaison with parents and other agencies;
- managing pupil transitions;
- organisation and facilities.

The majority of these areas not only reflected the content of the Key Stage 3 Behaviour and Attendance audit (DfES 2003c) but are also identifiable in the Elton Report, produced 16 years earlier. The Steer Report (DfES 2005b: 5) openly acknowledged that the core message from the Elton Report (DES 1989) 'about the need for a coherent whole school approach to promoting behaviour that is based on good relationships between all members of the school community', still held true

In Tom Bennett's independent review of behaviour in schools (Bennett 2017), the importance of a whole school approach was again highlighted, with considerable emphasis placed on the leadership and management of the school. In the report, Bennett (2017) was able to set out features that were most routinely encountered in the schools visited, or described by school leaders in the interviews conducted. In summary, these were:

- committed headteachers, with high levels of focus, ambition, mission, altruism and tenacity;
- strong management teams with a balance of aptitudes, employed in areas that suited those aptitudes;
- a clear and detailed sense of purpose and strategy;
- a robust, firm communication of that purpose and strategy to all members of the school community;
- consistency between all staff and students about cultural and academic norms;
- close attention to detail and thoroughness in the execution of school policies and strategies;
- well-advertised, repeatedly demonstrated routines in every aspect of civil and academic conduct;
- a commitment to staff development with the concomitant expectation that staff reciprocate by contributing their best efforts;
- highly visible members of the school leadership team were a normal part of the public life of the school;
- behaviour policies that were made a continual focus in every aspect of school strategy and planning;
- a commitment to every student's wellbeing and success, despite the challenges they may present;
- a focus by senior staff on supporting the most challenging students appropriately.

Like previous reports (DES 1989; DfES 2005b), Bennett's (2017) findings would suggest that a range of whole school factors can positively or negatively influence pupil behaviour. Therefore, if the aim is to secure better standards of behaviour across the school population as a whole the priority would seem to be to focus on these factors. It seems that, finely tuned, these factors can contribute to the realistic aim of promoting good behaviour among the majority and reducing misbehaviour (DES 1989). Attending to such factors represents a strategic, proactive approach and is an alternative to responding reactively by continually trying to identify new ways to address misbehaviour.

The types of substantial reports so far considered (DES 1989; DfES 2005b; Bennett 2017) serve to provide general direction for the way in which schools view and respond to pupil behaviour. Separate guidance is typically produced by central government to support schools in developing whole school behaviour policies and approaches. Circular 8/94 (DfE 1994a) and its successor DfES (2003a) were quite slim documents but *School Discipline and Pupil Behaviour Policies* (DfES 2007a) was a more substantial volume. This was repackaged (DCSF 2009) two years later with the cartoon style cover that by this time graced most Department for Children, Schools and Families (DCSF) guidance. Running to a total of 63 pages, it represented a considerable contribution to the more than 600 pages of guidance on school discipline in place by the time the (Conservative–Liberal Democrat) coalition government (2010–2015) came into office in May 2010 (DfE 2011a). *School Discipline and Pupil-Behaviour Policies* (DCSF 2009) covered the statutory power to discipline introduced in the Education and Inspections Act 2006 as well as including a range of other guidance that aimed to help schools understand their overall legal powers and duties with regard to establishing a school behaviour policy and disciplining pupils. It provided general advice on good practice regarding rules, rewards and sanctions as well as more specific, detailed advice on certain key sanctions such as the use of detentions and the confiscation of pupils' property. Perhaps the most distinctive feature of this guidance was the inclusion of material intended 'to help schools take account of a range of individual pupil needs when developing and implementing their behaviour policies' (DCSF 2009: 44). The advice focused primarily on pupils with SEN or disabilities, but also referred to 'certain other groups defined by Ofsted as "at risk" within the education system' (DCSF 2009: 44). The implication was that, just as schools might personalise or differentiate learning, they might sometimes have to respond differently to individuals in relation to behaviour.

In 2012 the coalition government issued *Behaviour and Discipline in Schools: A Guide for Head Teachers and School Staff* (DfE 2012b). A notable feature of policy and guidance produced by the coalition government and the subsequent Conservative government is the regular issuing of updated versions. The use of online documents rather than publishing in paper form allows minor changes to be made, previous versions to be removed or archived and the document to be republished with a new publication date and the same title. Within this book we refer primarily to the 2016 version of *Behaviour and Discipline in Schools: Advice for Headteachers and School Staff* (DfE 2016a) except where highlighting a particular difference in an earlier version.

The guidance on behaviour and discipline in schools produced by the coalition government and the subsequent Conservative government has primarily concerned itself with the law, providing 'an overview of the powers and duties for school staff' (DfE 2016a: 3) and leaving individual schools 'to develop their own best practice for managing behaviour in their school' (DfE 2016a: 3). In contrast to the extensive guidance provided by *School Discipline and Pupil-Behaviour Policies* (DCSF 2009), the advice on this topic primarily comprised of a re-statement of the ten key aspects of school practice identified within the Steer Report (DfES 2005b) that, 'when effective, contribute to improving the quality of pupil behaviour' (DfE 2016a: 5). The brevity of *Behaviour and Discipline in Schools: Advice for Headteachers and School Staff* (DfE 2016a) reflected a move by central government to significantly reduce the quantity of nationally produced guidance on discipline that schools were expected to access (DfE 2011a).

A noticeable change in government guidance (DfE 2016a) has been the use of the term 'good behaviour' in place of 'acceptable behaviour' that was used in *School Discipline and Pupil-Behaviour Policies* (DCSF 2009). Our presumption is that this was intended to convey higher aspirations, suggesting more than the achievement of just a minimum acceptable standard.

Faith in rules, rewards and sanctions to secure positive behaviour

For many years, national policy and guidance has encouraged a framework for managing behaviour in schools based on rules, rewards and sanctions. For example, the Elton Report stated: 'We consider that the best way to encourage good standards of behaviour in a school is a clear code of conduct backed by a balanced combination of rewards and punishments within a positive community atmosphere'. (DES 1989: 99). Subsequent guidance has typically reinforced this message. For most schools, rules, rewards and sanctions tend to form the operational core of their behaviour policies and for most readers these are likely to represent the aspect of the policy's application with which they are most directly involved during their day-to-day practice. Within the last Labour government's *School Discipline and Pupil-Behaviour Policies* (DCSF 2009), two sections entitled 'Promoting and rewarding good behaviour' and 'Punishing poor behaviour – use of disciplinary sanctions' made it clear there was an expectation that rewards and sanctions would form a central part of a school's policy.

Although a much briefer document than its 2009 counterpart, current guidance on behaviour and discipline in schools (DfE 2016a) suggests that, in developing the behaviour policy, the head teacher should reflect on rewards and sanctions along with the nine other key aspects of school practice the Steer Report (DfES 2005b) had suggested contribute to improving the quality of pupil behaviour. In light of past recognition (e.g. DCSF 2009) of the need for a balance between rewards and sanctions, and the recommendation of the 5:1 ratio in favour of the former, an interesting feature of the current government's guidance (DfE 2016a) is the lack of any suggestion of the rewards a school might use but a list of nine possible sanctions. A further indication of acceptance that rules, rewards and sanctions are key tools in managing behaviour is the requirement in the Teachers' Standards that teachers use 'praise, sanctions and rewards consistently and fairly' (DfE 2011b: 8–9). Guidance intended to improve teacher training for behaviour also suggests trainees should 'know how to apply rewards and sanctions to improve behaviour' (TA 2012: 2).

In terms of the national perspectives on behaviour, it is interesting to note that the 2014 version of *Behaviour and Discipline in Schools: Advice for Headteachers and School Staff* (DfE 2014b) was launched in the immediate wake of press coverage (e.g. *Guardian* 2014) of Secretary of State Michael Gove's wish for a return to 'traditional' punishments for school misbehaviour. In reality, many items on the list of suggested sanctions in the guidance (DfE 2014b) reflected a range that schools have been accustomed to using for some time and had previously featured in the Labour government's guidance (DCSF 2009). Of particular note, however, were those that were given greatest prominence in the reporting of the apparent return to 'traditional' punishments, namely, litter-picking, running around the field and writing lines. The suggested sanction of 'extra physical activity such as running around a playing field' (DfE 2014a: 8) was removed from a later version of the guidance (DfE 2016a) after pressure from members of the sporting community (e.g. Jude 2014) and others due to concern over the portrayal of sport and exercise as a punishment. Viewed from the similar perspective that typically teachers are trying to encourage positive attitudes to writing, we might question why 'the setting of written tasks as punishments, such as writing lines or an essay' (DfE 2016a:8) remains. The premise behind the proposed return to 'traditional' punishments is interesting in light of the Elton Report's suggestion that '[s]chools which put too much faith in punishments to deter bad behaviour are likely to be disappointed' (DES 1989: 98).

Skills in behaviour management

The term 'behaviour management' is an established part of the discourse on behaviour in schools, appearing no less than 19 times in the Steer Report (DfES 2005b) and five times in the DCSF (2009) guidance document *School Discipline and Pupil-Behaviour Policies*. Current guidance for head teachers and school staff on behaviour and discipline in schools (DfE 2016a), reiterating advice from the Steer Report (DfES 2005b), identifies a consistent approach to behaviour management as the first of ten 'key aspects of school practice that, when effective, contribute to improving the quality of pupil behaviour' (DfE 2016a: 5). Though the current professional standards (DfE 2011b: 12) do not use the term, they do require teachers to 'manage behaviour effectively'. Additional guidance intended to improve teacher training in relation to behaviour sets out 'the knowledge, skills and understanding that trainees will need in order to be able to manage their pupils' behaviour' (TA 2012: 1). An internet search using the term 'behaviour management' will produce a plethora of texts and websites on the subject, as well as numerous consultants and training providers. Though a regularly used term, defining the specific teacher activities that represent behaviour management can prove difficult. As the guidance documents considered in this section demonstrate, the range of teacher activities that contribute to the promotion and maintenance of positive pupil behaviour in the classroom is wide. A problem sometimes is that the use of the term in some government documents (e.g. DfE 2010) alongside expressions of concern regarding behaviour in school leads to the perception that behaviour management solely relates to strategies for establishing control over disruptive pupils.

Significantly, in the context of the themes of this book, the Elton Report (DES 1989) did not use the term 'behaviour management' and instead referred to 'classroom management'. 'Group management skills' were viewed as a component of 'classroom management'. 'Classroom management' represented a wider concept than 'behaviour management' and included the teacher's knowledge of the subject being taught and the ability to plan and deliver a lesson which flowed smoothly and held pupils' attention (DES 1989). Group management skills, the Elton Report suggested, included 'the ability to relate to young people, to encourage them in good behaviour and learning, and to deal calmly but firmly with inappropriate or disruptive behaviour' (DES 1989: 67). The practical nature of much of the content of the Elton Report was exemplified by the inclusion of messages that emerged from the literature regarding good practice. The Elton Report advised that teachers should:

- Know their pupils as individuals. This means knowing their names, their personalities and interests and who their friends are.
- Plan and organise both the classroom and the lesson to keep pupils interested and minimise the opportunities for disruption. This requires attention to such basics as furniture layout, grouping of pupils, matching work to pupils' abilities, pacing lessons well, being enthusiastic and using humour to create a positive classroom atmosphere.
- Be flexible in order to take advantage of unexpected events rather than being thrown off balance by them.
- Continually observe or 'scan' the behaviour of the class.

- Be aware of, and control their own behaviour, including stance and tone of voice.
- Model the standards of courtesy that they expect from pupils.
- Emphasise the positive, including praise for good behaviour as well as good work.
- Make the rules for classroom behaviour clear to pupils from the first lesson and explain why they are necessary.
- Make sparing and consistent use of reprimands. This means being firm rather than aggressive, targeting the right pupil, criticising the behaviour and not the person, using private rather than public reprimands whenever possible, being fair and consistent, and avoiding sarcasm and idle threats.
- Make sparing and consistent use of punishments. This includes avoiding whole-group punishment, which pupils see as unfair. It also means avoiding punishments that humiliate pupils by, for example, making them look ridiculous. This breeds resentment.
- Analyse their own classroom management performance and learn from it. This is the most important message of all.

(DES 1989: 71–2)

Circular 8/94 (DfE 1994a) built on the recommendations from the Elton Report (DES 1989), providing guidance to schools on developing whole school policies on behaviour and discipline. It noted that in classrooms in the most successful schools:

- Procedures are clearly understood regarding pupil discussion, participation in lessons, movement in class, the way in which work is handed in, and what pupils should do when tasks are completed.
- Explanations are clear.
- Work requirements of pupils are clearly set out, and progress is monitored carefully.
- Clear instructions are given so that activities run smoothly.
- Misbehaviour is handled quickly and calmly so that the pace of a lesson is not lost and further disruption is minimized.
- Teachers have developed good listening skills, and react appropriately to pupils' responses.
- Work set is appropriate to pupils' abilities.
- Clear goals are set for each work activity and all pupils understand them before an activity begins.
- Lessons start and end on time.
- Classrooms are suited to a particular activity as far as possible.
- Seating arrangements are suitable. These will often be dictated by the activity, but particular attention should be paid to the location of the more troublesome pupils and those easily distracted.
- External interruptions are minimised wherever possible.
- Necessary materials for a given activity are available.

(DfE 1994a: 14)

A salient point to note from the list from Circular 8/94 (DfE 1994a) in particular is that many of the points relate to the organisation and management of the learning environment rather than what we might think of as behaviour management.

Many of the elements of good practice identified by the Elton Report (DES 1989) and Circular 8/94 (DfE 1994a) have subsequently been expanded upon in numerous classroom management texts (e.g. Hook and Vass 2002; Dix 2007; Rogers 2007, 2011) and are enduring features of accepted good practice.

Reflective Exercise 1.1

Consider the advice given above in the 11 bullet points from the Elton Report (DES 1989) and 13 bullet points from Circular 8/94 (DfE 1994a).

- To what extent do you adhere to these principles in your practice?
- To what extent do these principles represent sound advice for twenty-first-century classrooms?
- Is there anything else that you would add to this list?

The Key Stage 3 National Strategy Behaviour and Attendance materials provided an indication of what, at the level of national guidance, was seen as important in managing behaviour. The Core Day 1 (DfES 2003b) and Core Day 2 (DfES 2004a) training materials presented identical lists of strategies based on the work of Australian writer and educational consultant, Bill Rogers (e.g. 1997, 2002). In the former they were included in a section entitled 'Effective classroom management' and in the latter under the heading, 'Developing staff skills to support behaviour'. Rogers has, over many years (e.g. Rogers 1990, 1997, 2011; Rogers and MacPherson 2008), written on the subject of behaviour management, placing particular emphasis on teacher language. The presentation of this list of strategies twice in the Key Stage 3 National Strategy materials would suggest that the DfES saw some value in Rogers' focus on the language of behaviour management. We cover these strategies as well as a number of others in Chapter 10.

Expanding further on the use of teacher language, the DfES suggested that 'most interventions should take the form of positive actions that fit somewhere on a continuum from positive reinforcement through to positive correction' (DfES 2004a: 54). The suggestion was that 'staff should aim for a proportion of intervention equivalent to five positive types of reinforcement used for every one corrective action' (DfES 2004a: 54). This, of course, reflected the Elton Report's (DES 1989) emphasis on establishing a positive ethos. The attempt to apply a ratio (5:1) needs perhaps to be questioned as it does not take account of factors such as whether the pupil attaches significance to the approval of the person providing positive reinforcement and how they interpret and experience the positive reinforcement provided. Nevertheless, it helped to reinforce the view that the emphasis needed to be on the positive if schools were to address the Elton Report's concern that 'in some schools a pupil can only get attention in one or other of two ways – by working well or behaving badly' (DES 1989: 99).

In its revised set of Teachers' Standards (DfE 2011b) the coalition government expanded on the familiar focus in the two previous sets (DfES/TTA 2002; TDA 2007) on acting as a role model, knowing a range of behaviour management strategies and establishing and maintaining a framework for classroom discipline. Under the broad requirement to 'Manage behaviour effectively to ensure a good and safe learning environment' the document specified that teachers should:

- Have clear rules and routines for behaviour in classrooms, and take responsibility for promoting good and courteous behaviour both in classrooms and around the school, in accordance with the school's behaviour policy.
- Have high expectations of behaviour, and establish a framework for discipline with a range of strategies, using praise, sanctions and rewards consistently and fairly.
- Manage classes effectively, using approaches which are appropriate to pupils' needs in order to involve and motivate them.
- Maintain good relationships with pupils, exercise appropriate authority, and act decisively when necessary.

(DfE 2011b: 12)

The additional guidance (TA 2012) produced in 2012 to supplement the new Teachers' Standards was developed by the government's then expert advisor on behaviour, Charlie Taylor. This covered eight broad areas:

- personal style;
- self-management;
- reflection;
- school systems;
- relationships;
- classroom management;
- more challenging behaviour;
- theoretical knowledge.

The significance of this document was its explicit recognition that managing behaviour involved a broad range of interacting factors. Though there is reference to knowledge of generic behaviour management systems and techniques, this is set within a broader context of teacher behaviours and attributes. There is a clear underlying message that the successful management of behaviour relies on far more than a set of strategies to draw upon when pupils misbehave. The DfE (2011c) document *Getting the Simple Things Right: Charlie Taylor's Behaviour Checklists* also provided an indication of how behaviour management was understood by government at this time. The advice for teachers is shown in Table 1.1

A conclusion we can draw from much of the policy and guidance considered in this section of the chapter is that behaviour management needs to be understood as encompassing more teacher activities than just the use of primarily verbal strategies to either reinforce positive behaviour or correct unwanted behaviour and the application of rewards and sanctions. The lists included above from the Elton Report (DES 1989), Circular 8/94 (DfE 1994a) and Charlie Taylor (DfE 2011c; TA 2012) all extend into the consideration of factors related to the organisation and management of the learning environment and general issues of teaching and learning.

A growing concern with emotional health and wellbeing

As the Elton Report (DES 1989:111) noted, the 'tradition in British schools is for teachers to combine academic, disciplinary and welfare functions'. It is the integration of these functions, the report claims, that makes 'knowing and educating the "whole"

Table 1.1 Advice for teachers from Charlie Taylor's behaviour checklist

Classroom	Pupils	Teaching	Parents
• Know the names and roles of any adults in class. • Meet and greet pupils when they come into the classroom. • Display rules in the class – and ensure that the pupils and staff know what they are. • Display the tariff of sanctions in class. • Have a system in place to follow through with all sanctions. • Display the tariff of rewards in class. • Have a system in place to follow through with all rewards. • Have a visual timetable on the wall. • Follow the school behaviour policy.	• Know the names of children. • Have a plan for children who are likely to misbehave. • Ensure other adults in the class know the plan. • Understand pupils' special needs.	• Ensure that all resources are prepared in advance. • Praise the behaviour you want to see more of. • Praise children doing the right thing more than criticising those who are doing the wrong thing (parallel praise). • Differentiate. • Stay calm. • Have clear routines for transitions and for stopping the class. • Teach children the class routines.	• Give feedback to parents about their child's behaviour – let them know about the good days as well as the bad ones.

Source: (DfE 2011c).

pupil possible' (DES 1989: 111). The Elton Report (DES 1989) recognised the role of pastoral support within school and also went as far as suggesting that 'initial teacher training establishments should introduce their students to basic counselling skills' (DES 1989: 114). However, in most schools, unless pupils demonstrated a particular need for support, the development of social, emotional and behavioural skills tended to rely on the combination of rules, rewards and sanctions, some teaching primarily through Citizenship and Personal, Social and Health Education (PSHE) and the behaviour modelled by peers and teachers.

The launch of Social and Emotional Aspects of Learning (SEAL) materials (DfES 2005c) through the Primary National Strategy reflected a significant a change from this approach. This comprehensive set of materials represented an attempt to teach social, emotional and behavioural skills systematically. The primary SEAL materials included staff development activities, curriculum materials for Reception through to Year 6, materials for small groups and materials for work with parents. The primary SEAL curriculum was based on a series of themes that were repeated each year. These are shown in Table 1.2.

The model (see Figure 1.1) advocated for using the SEAL materials was based on the 'waves' model that featured in other DfES guidance materials (e.g. DfES 2002a, 2005d).

The approach was underpinned by the premise that *all* pupils required the teaching of social, emotional and behavioural skills. In addition, there were some pupils for whom small-group or individual interventions would be necessary.

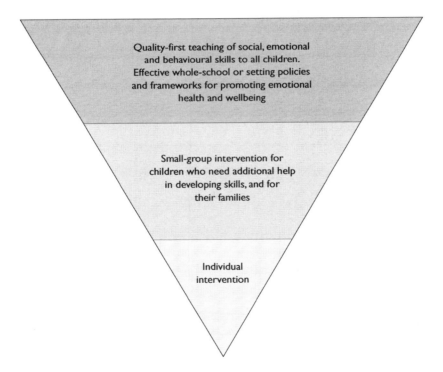

Figure 1.1 SEAL provision.

Source: © Crown copyright [2005] Department for Education and Skills (from DfES 2005c).

Table 1.2 Primary SEAL themes

Theme number and time of year	Theme title	Key social and emotional aspects of learning addressed
1. September–October	New beginnings	• **Empathy** • Self-awareness • Motivation • Social Skills
2. November–December	Getting on and falling out	• **Managing feelings** • Empathy • Social skills
3. One to two weeks in the autumn term (to coincide with national anti-bullying week in November)	Say no to bullying	• **Empathy** • Self-awareness • Social skills
4. January–February	Going for goals!	• **Motivation** • Self-awareness • Self-awareness
5. February–March	Good to be me	• **Managing feelings** • Empathy
6. March–April	Relationships	• **Self-awareness** • **Managing feelings** • Empathy
7. June–July	Changes	• **Motivation** • **Social skills** • Managing feelings

Source: © Crown copyright [2005] Department for Education and Skills (from DfES 2005c).

Note
The bold text indicates the main social and/or emotional aspect of learning targeted through the theme.

Though SEAL had been a dominant element within the Primary National Strategy since the original behaviour and attendance pilot materials were launched, it was not until 2007 that secondary SEAL materials (DfES 2007b) were launched through the Secondary National Strategy (formerly the Key Stage 3 National Strategy). The fourth set of Core Day training materials (DfES 2005e) within the Key Stage 3 National Strategy Behaviour and Attendance strand had previously emphasised the importance of whole school approaches to the development of pupils' emotional health and wellbeing. The Core Day 4 pack included a short guidance document for senior leaders and a book of training materials. This was packaged with *Promoting Emotional Health and Wellbeing through the National Healthy Schools Standards* (DoH/DfES 2004) which was already available to schools. Its inclusion here helped to connect strands of policy and conveyed an important message that emotional health and wellbeing was not just linked to behaviour and attendance issues and should be a concern for all schools.

The secondary SEAL materials differed significantly from their primary counterparts. Materials were only initially produced for Year 7, designed to build on the approaches and themes of primary SEAL. The guidance booklet (DfES 2007b) simply encouraged schools to consider how these could be extended into Years 8 and 9. Materials were subsequently produced for Years 8 and 9 based around three themes:

- Learning to be Together, focusing on social skills and empathy.
- Keep on Learning, focusing on self-awareness and motivation.
- Learning about Me, focusing on managing feelings.

The Year 7 materials also included an introductory theme designed for use as part of a school's programme to support pupils through the process of transfer from primary to secondary education.

In terms of the development of central government thinking, the emphasis placed on emotional health and wellbeing (e.g. DoH/DfES 2004) and the social and emotional aspects of learning was indicative of the adoption of a more psychological perspective on behaviour. The explicit recognition through the chosen title of SEAL that learning involved not only cognitive but also social and emotional aspects reflected the holistic priorities of *Every Child Matters* (Treasury Office 2003; DfES 2004b), and in particular its focus on emotional health and wellbeing. Such a policy direction was not without its critics. Ecclestone and Hayes (2009) have argued that too much emphasis has been placed on 'therapeutic education', which they define as any activity focusing 'on perceived emotional problems and which aims to make educational content and learning processes more "emotionally engaging"' (Ecclestone and Hayes 2009: x). Their perception and concern was that emotional competence, emotional literacy and wellbeing were increasingly being seen as the most important outcomes of education.

Reflective Exercise 1.2

Ecclestone and Hayes (2009) have been critical of schools' engagement with activities that they consider to represent 'therapeutic education'. The SEAL initiative is one such activity. Consider the following quotes:

- Social and emotional skills are the skills of making positive relationships with other people, of understanding and managing ourselves and our own emotions, thoughts and behaviours. If people have these skills they can then respond to the emotions and behaviour of others, in ways that are in the best long-term interest of themselves and others (DfES 2007b: 4).

- Feelings, emotions and relationships are the core of our personal lives. They are an intimate part of us. The Centre [for Confidence and Well-Being] believes that any initiative which suggests that government departments, schools and teachers should micromanage young people's feelings is Orwellian and a good enough reason on its own to say we have to drop this idea altogether (Craig 2007: 5).
- The ultimate aim of much emotional literacy work is to help produce more socially-minded citizens, who see the benefit of participating in social and community processes, increased levels of social capital (a feeling of belonging to a community), a more flexible, resilient and effective workforce, and a reduction in violence and crime. Ultimately emotional literacy should also make communities better places to live, with higher levels of tolerance, understanding, care, compassion and citizenship (Weare 2004: 15–16).
- Formally teaching children from 3–18 about their emotions or how to calm themselves, for example, has never been done before in the systematic, year-on-year way SEAL suggests. We have no idea whether this will be beneficial or not (Craig 2007: 3).
- An overload of emotional awareness can lead to paralysing introspection, self-centredness, and/or dwelling on or getting stuck in a difficult mood rather than trying to deal with it (Weare 2004: 32).
- Children are learning from an early age that life, with all its trivial and serious tribulations, mundane and difficult low moments, 'sucks', and requires an array of 'therapeutic support workers' in the form of peer-buddies, theatre educators, teachers trained in various therapeutic approaches, life coaches and mentors, or specialist counsellors. Therapeutic education elevates everyday feelings of uncertainty, vulnerability, discomfort or lack of confidence and depicts them as 'treatable' (Ecclestone and Hayes 2009: 155).

1 Which of these quotes most closely reflect your own perspective?
2 What arguments would you use to defend your perspective?
3 Do any of the quotes raise an alternative perspective you had not previously considered?
4 What arguments would you make against the quotes you disagree with?

With the demise of the National Strategies and subsequent government messages emphasising the importance of a National Curriculum that outlines 'a core of knowledge in the traditional subject disciplines' (DfE 2010: 42) there is no reason to anticipate that more SEAL resource materials will be produced centrally. The focus in policy and guidance has now shifted from the development of emotional intelligence through SEAL to a concern to address children and young people's mental health needs. It is a concern in part motivated by recognition that in international comparisons children in England fared particularly poorly in terms of their feelings and perceptions of themselves and their feelings about their life at school (Children's Society 2015). In addition, some other alarming statistics on mental health problems in children and young people have been published. The National Children's Bureau (Weare 2015: 2) noted that, '1 in 10 children and young people have a clinically diagnosed mental health disorder and/or emotional and behaviour problems (often the same children) and around one in seven has less severe problems that interfere with their development and learning.' It was also reported that, in 2014, there was a 43 per cent rise in the number of young people who admitted attempting suicide; self-harm and eating disorders were also a growing problem (Weare 2015).

In its document *Mental Health and Behaviour in Schools*, the DfE (2016c: 4) sought to clarify the responsibilities of schools, and offer guidance on how they might support 'a child or young person whose behaviour – whether it is disruptive, withdrawn, anxious, depressed or otherwise – may be related to an unmet mental health need'. It was presented as support to schools in responding to the recommendation in *Behaviour and Discipline in Schools: Advice for Headteachers and School Staff* (DfE 2016a) that schools should consider whether continuing disruptive behaviour might be a result of unmet educational or other needs. The guidance (DfE 2016c) contained four sections:

- promoting positive mental health;
- identification;
- interventions;
- referral and commissioning.

The guidance made clear that schools had a responsibility to promote positive mental health in all pupils and could do a lot to provide non-specialist support and intervention for pupils exhibiting particular difficulties in this area. There was an expectation that schools would engage with other services to develop the quality of this provision through, for example, training for staff or advice and guidance on resources and interventions. It was recognised, however, that other services would need to be accessed to provide targeted and specialist support from statutory services, as well as voluntary and community sector organisations.

A recently published Green Paper, *Transforming Children and Young People's Mental Health Provision*, has expressed the government's intention to 'ensure that a member of staff in every primary and secondary school receives mental health awareness training' (DfE 2017a: 5). Illustrating what this training might include, the Green Paper refers to an already available programme developed 'to provide teachers and frontline professionals working with young people the skills and confidence to spot common signs and triggers of mental health issues, as well as the knowledge and confidence to help' (DfE 2017a: 27).

In the context of our preceding consideration of the government response to the putative problem of behaviour in schools, the emphasis on emotional intelligence through SEAL – and subsequently the focus on mental health – can be seen as reflecting a distinct strand in national policy and guidance. SEAL and the focus on mental health reflect an overt concern with addressing the emotional factors underpinning the behaviour, whereas much of the other national guidance on behaviour in schools has placed emphasis on the development of 'a strong behaviour policy to support staff in managing behaviour' (DfE 2016a: 30), based primarily on the use of rules, rewards and sanctions.

Behaviour as a special educational need

Circular 8/94 (DfE 1994a) referred to earlier in this chapter was issued to provide general guidance on pupil behaviour and discipline in schools. At the same time, a separate Circular was issued entitled *The Education of Children with Emotional and Behavioural Difficulties* (DfE 1994b). Its existence as a separate document reinforced the view that there was a distinct group of pupils whose behaviour required provision that was 'additional to, or otherwise different from' (DfE 1994c: 5) the standard combination of rules, rewards, sanctions and pastoral support typically available in schools as described in Circular 8/94 (DfE 1994a). Emotional and Behavioural Difficulties (EBD) was one of eight different types of special educational needs referred to in the first SEN Code of Practice (DfE 1994c). Circular 9/94 (DfE 1994b) attempted to define this category in terms of pupils who exhibited a level of emotional or behavioural difficulty that was beyond sporadic naughtiness or moodiness but not sufficiently severe to be classed as mental illness.

The problematic aspect of attempting to define 'emotional and behavioural difficulties' (EBD) was that, although the term related the difficulty to the individual pupil, there was a strong contextual element that determined both the degree to which the problems manifested themselves and whether these problems warranted categorising the pupil as having EBD. The DfE (1994b: 9) suggested that: 'Perceptions of whether a child's behaviour constitutes an emotional and behavioural difficulty are likely to differ according to the context in which it occurs as well as the individual teacher's management skills, tolerance levels, temperament and expectations.' This raised the issue of the relative nature of EBD; in one school, with one teacher, a pupil might be considered to have EBD whereas in another school with another teacher the difficulties may be less pronounced or even non-existent. The influence of context on identification of a pupil as having EBD was further reflected in the DfE's (1994b: 8) observation that,

> Schools vary widely in the extent to which they successfully help children overcome their difficulties and the extent to which they either create, minimise or exacerbate the levels of disruption or distress associated with emotional and behavioural difficulties.... [The school] may, through appropriate action, be able to keep the difficulty within manageable limits or even prevent it developing in the first place.

In Circular 9/94 (DfE 1994b) the DfE combined language that located the need firmly within the pupil (e.g. 'their difficulties') with a message that in some cases schools themselves were the determining factor in whether a pupil had an emotional and behavioural difficulty. This highlighted the issue that a pupil's emotional and behavioural difficulty needed to be understood as an interaction or relationship between factors related to the individual and factors related to the environment.

Just as the Underwood Report (Ministry of Education 1955) had done almost 40 years earlier when trying to define the then official category of 'maladjusted', Circular 9/94 produced an extensive list of behaviours that might be exhibited by a pupil who had an emotional and behavioural difficulty. It stated:

> Their behaviour may be evident at the personal level (for example through low self-image, anxiety, depression or withdrawal; or through resentment, vindictiveness or defiance); at the verbal level (for example the child may be silent or may threaten, or interrupt, argue or swear a great deal); at the non-verbal level (for

example through clinginess, or truancy, failure to observe rules, disruptiveness, aggression or violence); or at the work skills level (for example through an inability or unwillingness to work without direct supervision, to concentrate, to complete tasks or to follow instructions).

(DfE 1994b: 7–8)

Given the extensive nature of this list, it could be argued that every child has an emotional and behavioural difficulty of some kind at some point in their development. This is a point the DfE (1994b) acknowledged and attempted to address through the suggestion that: 'Whether or not a child has emotional or behavioural difficulties will depend on the nature, frequency, persistence, severity or abnormality and cumulative effect of the behaviour, in context, compared to normal expectations of a child of the age concerned' (DfE 1994b: 8).

The revised SEN Code of Practice (DfES 2001) referred to just four broad areas of need. Emotional and behavioural difficulties was replaced with the term 'behaviour, emotional and social development' (BESD), though 'difficulty' was often used in place of 'development' in common usage. In places within the text the term 'emotional and behavioural difficulties' was still used when describing those pupils whose needs fell within the category of BESD. The revised Code of Practice (DfES 2001) did not differ significantly from Circular 9/94 (DfE 1994b) and the first Code of Practice (DfE 1994c) in how this area of need was defined. In defining who might fall into the new category, it referred to:

Children and young people who demonstrate features of emotional and behavioural difficulties, who are withdrawn or isolated, disruptive and disturbing, hyperactive and lack concentration; those with immature social skills; and those presenting challenging behaviours arising from other complex special needs.

(DfES 2001: 87)

A trigger for taking 'additional or different action to enable the pupil to learn more effectively' (DfES 2001: 52) was that they presented 'persistent emotional or behavioural difficulties which are not ameliorated by the behaviour management techniques usually employed in the school' (DfES 2001: 53). In terms of contributing to consistency in identification of BESD between schools, this was a potentially problematic piece of guidance. The implication was that failing to respond positively to the behaviour management techniques usually employed in the school revealed something about the pupil's level of needs. However, it needs to be recognised that this could equally reveal something about the range and quality of the behaviour management techniques employed.

The Special Educational Needs and Disability (SEND) Code of Practice (DfE/DoH 2015) replaced BESD with Social, Emotional and Mental Health (SEMH) difficulties. The 2011 SEN Green Paper (DfE 2011d) had previously explained that the rationale for this change was that the term 'behavioural, emotional and social difficulties' placed too great an emphasis on the presenting behaviour. The change in terminology reflected a desire to 'ensure that assessments of SEN and any assessments of children displaying challenging behaviour, by any professional, identify the root causes of the behaviour rather than focus on the symptoms' (DfE 2011d: 70). Despite the renaming of the category, the SEND Code of Practice (DfE/DoH 2015) provides a similarly broad list to its predecessors (DfE 1994c; DfES 2001) of pupils who might fall within it. It states:

> Children and young people may experience a wide range of social and emotional difficulties which manifest themselves in many ways. These may include becoming withdrawn or isolated, as well as displaying challenging, disruptive or disturbing behaviour. These behaviours may reflect underlying mental health difficulties such as anxiety or depression, self-harming, substance misuse, eating disorders or physical symptoms that are medically unexplained. Other children and young people may have disorders such as attention deficit disorder, attention deficit hyperactive disorder or attachment disorder.
>
> (DfE/DoH 2015: 98)

The Code of Practice makes clear that '[p]ersistent disruptive or withdrawn behaviours do not necessarily mean that a child or young person has SEN' (DfE/DoH 2015: 96) and encourages schools to undertake 'an assessment to determine whether there are any causal factors such as undiagnosed learning difficulties, difficulties with communication or mental health issues' (DfE/DoH 2015: 96). There is also recognition that wider social issues might represent an underlying cause in the suggestion that: 'If it is thought housing, family or other domestic circumstances may be contributing to the presenting behaviour a multi-agency approach, supported by the use of approaches such as the early help assessment, may be appropriate' (DfE/DoH 2015: 96).

Looking beyond the presenting behaviour is commendable but the emphasis on identifying a root cause, despite considerable face validity, may be problematic in some cases. In this book we emphasise the need to understand the meaning or purpose of the behaviour for the individual as this plays an important role in informing strategy/intervention choice; but this is not the same as saying it is always necessary to identify the root cause. At a practical level, identifying the root cause may not always be possible given the adaptive behaviours that pupils develop in response to their own unique and individual experiences. The reported efficacy of some cognitive-behavioural and solution-focused approaches would also suggest that knowing the cause is not necessarily a prerequisite to identification of the solution (Ellis et al. 2012).

Current indications are that the change in category and the guidance provided on identification is resulting in fewer pupils being identified as having a social, emotional and mental health difficulty than were identified previously as having behaviour, emotional and social difficulties. National statistics (DfE 2011e) indicate that in 2010 22.5 per cent of pupils with SEN were identified as having BESD as their primary need. In 2016 16.3 per cent of pupils with SEN were identified as having SEMH as their primary need (DfE 2017b). The obvious point to make is that, while proportionally fewer pupils are being identified, there is no reason to assume there are fewer pupils proportionally in the education system exhibiting the behaviour, emotional and social difficulties that previously led schools and teachers to identify them.

Reflective Exercise 1.3

As the preceding text has outlined, pupils who exhibit patterns of behaviour that are considered to warrant classification as a special educational need will fall into the category of social, emotional and mental health difficulties. Consider these questions:

- How might the categorisation as 'SEMH' affect the teacher's expectations of the pupil?
- How might the categorisation as 'SEMH' affect the teacher's perceptions of their responsibilities in relation to the pupil with this label?
- How might the categorisation as 'SEMH' affect the teacher's confidence and perceptions of competence in relation to the pupil with this label?

Conclusion

The true extent to which pupil behaviour and classroom climate are issues within English schools is difficult to gauge (Bennett 2017). As this chapter has indicated, there is a popular and enduring perception that there is a problem. The media undoubtedly exerts an influence over this perception but, arguably, policy makers, in responding to the public concern fuelled by the media portrayal with promises of action, play a reinforcing role. Ofsted's annual reports have consistently presented a relatively positive picture of standards of behaviour nationally, though more recently, in the Annual Report 2012–2013 and the subsequent publication *Below the Radar: Low-Level Disruption in the Country's Classrooms* (Ofsted 2014a), concerns have been expressed. As Bennett (2017) has pointed out, the general positivity of Ofsted reports (e.g. Ofsted 2005, 2011, 2013) is, to some extent, at odds with some of the findings from teacher surveys.

As the consideration of a range of documents in this chapter has demonstrated, within national policy and guidance there is recognition of the importance of a whole-school approach to behaviour. An effective whole-school approach fulfils an important role in maintaining a stable, safe and predictable environment in which every pupil can benefit from the learning opportunities on offer. A school's behaviour policy is a key document defining its approach to behaviour. Specific guidance documents (e.g. DfES 2003a; DCSF 2009; DfE 2016a) have supported schools in developing their behaviour policies. The concern for policy makers and individual schools is typically those pupils who do not respond as expected to the combination of rules, rewards and sanctions that usually form the operational core of a behaviour policy.

The term 'behaviour management' is regularly used in policy and guidance documents to describe a particular area of a teacher's professional activity. As a working definition, we could interpret behaviour management as referring to the use of primarily verbal strategies to either reinforce positive behaviour or correct unwanted behaviour, coupled with appropriate application of rewards and sanctions. This may be a useful conceptualisation for beginning teachers and training providers in defining a particular set of skills that can be learned and developed. However, ultimately it needs to be recognised that there are many other factors related to the organisation and management of the learning environment and teaching and learning that exert an influence over classroom behaviour.

The common characteristic of the focus on whole-school approaches to behaviour and the emphasis on the development of skills in behaviour management is the attention given to the adult's side of the relationship with the pupil. There is an implicit assumption that if, with the help of national policy and guidance, the school or the individual teacher can come up with the 'right' set of strategies then a predictable response can be assured from the pupil. A key message within this book is that pupils experience and interpret strategies and approaches as individuals and this determines their response. It is possible to make some reasonable predictions about how many pupils will experience, interpret and respond to our strategies and approaches but it would be naïve to expect all pupils' experience, interpretation and response to be the same.

The SEAL curriculum (DfES 2005c, 2007b) represented a significant development in encouraging schools to look in a systematic way at how social, emotional and behavioural skills could be developed rather than assuming that these would simply be 'caught' by virtue of being within a school environment. This development indicated recognition at the level of national policy and guidance that developing and maintaining positive patterns of behaviour in pupils may require more than the traditional combination of rules, rewards and sanctions. The relatively recent (e.g. DfE 2016c) emphasis on children and young people's mental health represents an understanding that 'continuing disruptive behaviour might be a result of unmet educational or other needs' (DfE 2016c: 4) which, by implication, might not be ameliorated by the measures described in general guidance on behaviour in schools (e.g. DfE 2016a). It is undoubtedly important that teachers can recognise 'common signs and triggers of mental health issues' (DfE 2017a: 27), know to whom concerns should be referred and understand the implications of a pupil's particular mental health issue for teaching, learning and the teacher–pupil relationship. However, the suggestion of the need for training that provides teachers with 'the knowledge and confidence to help' (DfE 2017a: 27) once they notice the signs of an emerging or worsening mental health issue may raise some questions regarding the boundaries of a teacher's professional role. It is salient to recall that, when suggesting initial teacher training providers introduced trainee teachers to basic counselling skills and their value, the Elton Report recognised that 'teachers are not social workers or psychotherapists' (DES 1989: 114). The extent to which a classroom teacher should, and feasibly can, intervene to address a mental health issue is an area for continued debate.

Some pupils' behaviour continues to be categorised as a special educational need. Though the category title has changed over the years and we are currently using the term 'social, emotional and mental health difficulties' (DfE/DoH 2015), this is still a difficult group of pupils to define. Descriptions encompass those who exhibit challenging, disruptive or disturbing behaviour through to those who present as withdrawn or isolated. In many ways we are still struggling with the same issue previously identified by the Ministry of Education (1955: 23) when trying to determine who fell into the category of 'maladjusted': 'It is only possible to say tentatively that certain modes of behaviour or habits fall outside the limits of the normal or are incompatible with a state of adjustment'. In defining a distinct group of pupils whose behaviour represents a special educational need the risk is that it creates the impression, first, that there might be different learning priorities for these pupils and, second, that specialist teaching approaches are necessary to address these. Once a pupil is identified as having such a need, the teacher may feel that the teaching and learning agenda with which they are familiar is – or should be – supplanted by a less familiar agenda based on the traditions of special education, psychology, social work and counselling.

As Chapter 12 explains in more detail, the Behaviour for Learning approach does not seek to make a distinction between non-specialist and specialist approaches. Instead, we suggest it is more helpful to think in terms of a continua of teaching approaches ranging from strategies that represent adaptations to standard practice through to those that could be deemed 'specialist', due either to the requirement for specialist knowledge to implement them and/or the high level of adaptation necessary to incorporate them into class teaching. The conceptual framework that underpins the Behaviour for Learning approach is intended to enable all teachers to recognise the social, emotional and cognitive factors influencing behaviour and to use this knowledge to plan and implement adaptations to standard practice, interventions and support, drawing on additional expertise available in the school and from external agencies where necessary.

As this chapter has demonstrated, it is possible to identify a number of consistent themes within national policy and guidance, over recent years, related to behaviour in schools. The development of this policy and guidance has typically taken place against the influencing background of ongoing concern regarding standards of discipline in schools. There have also been some important changes in emphasis and priorities within this policy and guidance. For example, there is now a more explicit focus on pupils' mental health and within guidance on SEN (DfE/DoH 2015) there is an expectation that schools will look beyond the presenting behaviour when attempting to determine whether a pupil has a social, emotional or mental health difficulty.

The next chapter introduces the conceptual framework that underpins the Behaviour for Learning approach. It is offered as a durable, flexible framework that is not susceptible to changes in policy and guidance. Learning behaviour and three relationships (with self, with the curriculum, with others) that underpin its development will have enduring relevance to learning in schools and other group settings. The Behaviour for Learning approach enables teachers to both understand pupil behaviour and select and evaluate strategies based on clear, consistent criteria.

Chapter 2

The Behaviour for Learning approach

Reframing behaviour management

Introduction

As we considered in the previous chapter, behaviour management is a familiar, commonly used term. An internet search using the term 'behaviour management' will produce a plethora of texts and websites on the subject, as well as numerous consultants and training providers. There are also regular calls (e.g. DfE 2010, 2012a; Carter 2015) to strengthen initial teacher training in response to findings from some surveys (e.g. NASUWT 2012; NFER 2012) that suggest that teachers feel insufficiently prepared to manage behaviour. A former government expert adviser on behaviour, Charlie Taylor, suggested that the greatest fear trainee teachers had was that they would not be able to manage behaviour, and pupil behaviour was one of the main reasons why teachers leave the profession (DfE 2012a). Behaviour management is, therefore, a well-established phrase within the discourse on behaviour in schools. Policy makers and others continue to express considerable confidence in the potential for improved knowledge, skills and understanding in behaviour management to address the types of concerns explored in Chapter 1. As a phrase 'behaviour management' has a respectable, quasi-professional tone and its provenance is rarely explored.

This chapter invites you to consider critically the limitations of a focus on behaviour management when narrowly construed to mean a set of methods used to establish and maintain control over pupils' behaviour. We then introduce the Behaviour for Learning approach, offering this as an alternative perspective that reframes behaviour management in terms of promoting learning behaviour. The key elements of the Behaviour for Learning conceptual framework are described and its practical application is considered.

The separation of learning and behaviour

A popular text on behaviour management begins: 'Behaviour management: if you get it right, your life is easy, you're free to do what you're meant to do, which is of course to teach!' (Cowley 2003: xiii).

In some respects, Cowley is right: there are undoubtedly some ways of responding to pupil behaviour that are less effective than others and either escalate the situation or lead to the teacher becoming embroiled in an extended disciplinary interaction at the expense of the pace and flow of the lesson. Both outcomes get in the way of the teacher's core focus, which is the promotion of learning. However, taken literally, Cowley's comment presents behaviour management and the promotion of learning as distinct elements of the teacher's role; if the teacher can do the first, then they will be free to do the second. It is a perspective that has insufficient regard for the influence on pupil behaviour of a number of factors over which the teacher has some control.

The implication of an emphasis on behaviour management is that there is a discrete set of skills that can be learned by the teacher. In itself, this notion is not a problem and may even have some value in challenging any assumption that skills in behaviour management are a natural gift (DES 1989). The problematic element is when these skills are seen as a distinct aspect of the teacher's role without due recognition of the influence of factors such as the curriculum, teaching approaches and the teacher–pupil relationship. It is noteworthy that the lists of strategies from government publications (DES 1989; DfE 1994a; DfE 2011c) presented in Chapter 1 encompass strategies and approaches beyond those we might categorise under the heading of behaviour management. Ofsted has also noted a link between behaviour and the quality of teaching, commenting,

> Where teaching does not meet pupils' needs or does not engage pupils sufficiently they can lose attention, demonstrate poor attitudes to learning and eventually interrupt the learning of others. In these cases teaching can then focus too much on continually managing low-level disruption at the expense of providing interesting and relevant opportunities for pupils to learn.
>
> (Ofsted 2011: 59)

Assuming Ofsted's (2011) attribution of cause to be correct, the priority in such situations would seem not to be working on becoming better at behaviour management 'in order to do what you're meant to do, which is of course to teach!' (Cowley 2003: xiii) but to strengthen the quality of teaching. Even government advice intended to strengthen the coverage of behaviour in initial teacher training prefaced its description of the knowledge, skills and understanding that trainees need in order to be able to manage their pupils' behaviour with the message,

> It is important to note that good teaching is the most effective way to get good behaviour. Teachers who plan and teach dynamic, stimulating lessons based on sound assessment and excellent subject knowledge are likely to experience fewer difficulties with behaviour.
>
> (TA 2012: 1)

Yet in highlighting the link between the quality of teaching and pupil behaviour there is the risk that we, Ofsted (2011) and the Teaching Agency (TA 2012) are guilty of '… the pious platitude that provided you have spent enough time preparing your lessons properly, you will never have discipline problems' (Wheldall and Glynn 1989: 2). The challenge, we would suggest, is to live with the complexity rather than dealing in truisms and part truths. The influential Elton Report was clear that: 'Reducing misbehaviour is a realistic aim. Eliminating it completely is not' (DES 1989: 65). The implication is that inevitably, however well planned and executed the lesson, there will be times when a teacher will need to respond to unwanted behaviour. There are some principles and practices that, if learned and rehearsed, can allow teachers to deal swiftly and effectively with behaviour more often and with more pupils. It would be professionally foolhardy not to develop capacity in this area. However, in acknowledging this, it should not lead us to neglect the potentially powerful influence of the curriculum, teaching and learning approaches and the pupil–teacher relationship in securing more positive behaviour within the classroom.

Differences in how we think about learning and behaviour

If we look at the phrase 'behaviour management', it neatly encapsulates both the purpose and success indicator of any strategy undertaken:

- The purpose is to manage behaviour.
- The indicator of success is that behaviour is managed.

The focus on achieving compliance as the primary purpose of behaviour management reflects and potentially reinforces differences in how we think about learning and behaviour. Reflective Exercise 2.1 provides an opportunity to consider some of the differences that may currently exist.

Reflective Exercise 2.1

Answer these questions in relation to *learning*:

- What indicators of progress do you look for?
- What methods do you use to assess progress?

Answer these questions in relation to *behaviour*:

- What indicators of progress do you look for?
- What methods do you use to assess progress?

You may find from Reflective Exercise 2.1 that progress in learning is measured in a variety of ways ranging from informal observation through to national tests. Indicators may have been in the form of *increases* and *mastery*. However, when thinking about progress in behaviour you may have found a blurring of the distinction between *methods* and *indicators* and identified things such as reductions in referrals to senior members of staff, receiving less sanctions, causing less disruption, being able to remain in class and perceptions of changes in attitude. Overall, you may have found that when thinking about behaviour the emphasis was generally on *reduction* or *cessation*.

It is also useful to reflect on how we view mistakes in learning compared to mistakes in behaviour. Porter (2007) makes the distinction shown in Table 2.1.

Table 2.1 Possible differences in how errors in learning and errors in behaviour are viewed

Academic errors	Behavioural errors
Errors are accidental.	Errors are deliberate.
Errors are inevitable.	Errors should not happen.
Errors signal the need for teaching.	Errors should be punished.
Students with learning difficulties need modified teaching.	Students with behavioural difficulties need punishment.

Source: Porter 2007.

Not only are we inclined to see errors as inevitable in learning, we may even see them as essential. Indeed, Ofsted once commented in guidance to inspectors on making judgements based on samples of work that: 'Pupils' work that is always marked right is almost certainly too easy' (Ofsted 2003: 78). We rarely apply a similar line of thinking in relation to behaviour. The interpretation of behavioural errors shifts the focus away from a teaching and learning agenda to one that emphasises the ascription of motive (i.e. 'deliberate'), dealing with aberrations, limiting and sanctioning.

Why is the separation of learning and behaviour a problem?

Some readers at this point may have accepted the academic argument that there is a separation between learning and behaviour, but may be questioning whether in practice this presents any problem. The problem lies in the priorities this separation creates and the implications of these priorities for the selection and evaluation of strategies and approaches. This issue is explored in Reflective Exercise 2.2.

Reflective Exercise 2.2

Think about the quote from the start of this chapter:

'Behaviour management: if you get it right, your life is easy, you're free to do what you're meant to do, which is of course to teach!'

(Cowley 2003: xiii)

Now consider this scenario:
The teacher has already noticed Lauren, a Year 6 pupil, turn around a number of times to talk to some pupils sitting behind her. She does it again and she giggles loudly, as do those she is talking to.
   Three different teachers respond to this situation:

Teacher A: 'Lauren, facing this way, thanks.'
Lauren dutifully faces the front and does not turn around again for the duration of the lesson.

Teacher B: 'Lauren, facing this way, thanks.'
Lauren briefly glances in the teacher's direction when she hears her name but continues to turn around and talk. This pattern continues for the remainder of the lesson.

Teacher C: 'Lauren, stand up (Lauren stands up). Would you like to tell the rest of the class what it is that's so interesting? (Lauren is silent.) Come on, I'm sure it was fascinating. We're all waiting to hear.'
   Lauren sits down sheepishly and remains quiet for the rest of the lesson. The rest of the class are noticeably quieter too.
   Which of these teachers *got it right*?

If we are just interested in stopping behaviour then Teachers A and C both *got it right*. Hopefully, however, you feel at least a little uncomfortable with Teacher C's approach, as, although it works at the level of stopping behaviour, in terms of their relationship with Lauren it has probably been detrimental. It has also modelled to

Lauren and any observers that in a power relationship it is acceptable for the dominant party to embarrass the other in front of their peers. Teacher A used an appropriate strategy that we would fully endorse. The teacher *got it right*. Let's look now at Teacher B. It is the same strategy as that used by Teacher A. Did they still *get it right*? If the definition of *getting it right* is that the teacher is free to teach, then presumably Teacher B did not as the behaviour still continued.

Two problems begin to emerge. First, the limited evaluation criterion of stopping the behaviour makes the teacher a hostage to fortune because it is impossible to plan and predict every pupil's response in every situation. With no better criteria by which to judge the efficacy of the chosen strategy, Teacher B is in this position. Lauren did not comply, therefore was the strategy flawed? Would it be better to try Teacher C's approach next time? If we link judgements about the efficacy of a strategy simply to pupil compliance we inevitably embark on a futile, never-ending journey to find the perfect strategy because no strategy, whatever its good practice credentials, will be effective with every pupil. Second, as professionals, teachers cannot be satisfied with an *end justifies the means* outlook. They need to be able to select strategies based on ethicality and compatibility with both the school's stated core values and principles and the wider national policy agenda (e.g. DfE 2016c, 2017a) concerned with pupils' emotional health and wellbeing.

The continued separation of behaviour and learning within thinking and practice would seem to leave teachers in a position where they are able to achieve increasing confidence and competence in their main area of expertise (i.e. that of promoting learning) but continue to seek security in the area of behaviour management through a search for more and more strategies. A plethora of strategies and approaches to pupil behaviour is already included in books, past and present government guidance documents, publications by professional associations and websites. In addition, teachers are likely to have access to the advice of colleagues within their own schools as well as from a wider network, including, for example, other schools in the same multi-academy trust or input from external agencies. The Behaviour for Learning approach is based on the premise that teachers need the means by which to select effectively from the range of materials related to pupil behaviour already available. Teachers need to be able to make informed professional decisions about the contribution any new approach or package could potentially make to the development of behaviours necessary for learning.

'Be independent, use your initiative and take risks – but only when I say'

A number of developments in policy and guidance (e.g. Treasury Office 2003; DfES 2004b, 2005c, 2007b; DfE 2016c), over the years have placed teachers in a role where, in addition to traditional responsibilities related to improving academic learning, they are required to secure a range of holistic outcomes and develop transferable skills through the curriculum. This expanded remit introduces tensions and incongruities. Many teachers would, for example, endorse the importance of promoting collaborative learning. Corrie (2002) compared this priority with what she termed 'cooperative behaviour' (Table 2.2).

Corrie (2002) sought to illustrate the potential for these two sets of behaviours to result in incongruent messages being received by certain pupils. The behaviours Corrie includes under the heading of 'cooperative' are essentially about *compliance*. There are

Table 2.2 Collaborative learning and cooperative behaviours

Collaborative learning	*Cooperative (with teacher) behaviour*
Pupils:	Pupils:
• Interact with peers/adults to construct knowledge, often in small groups. • Interact with others by posing questions, negotiating meanings, problem solving, constructing creative solutions. • Use materials and equipment with others in creative ways. • Are risk takers who pursue their interests and build on their strengths and competencies with others.	• Complete the teacher's set tasks by working independently. • Speak when the teacher gives permission. • Answer the teacher's questions, following the class rules for doing so. • Follow the teacher's instructions quickly, quietly and with little deviation expected. • Follow the rules and routines of the classroom.

Source: adapted from Corrie 2002: 33.

some inherent contradictions when we manage for basic compliance and seek strategies to achieve this in isolation from our loftier priorities in relation to learning – involving the promotion of qualities such as independence, risk-taking, resourcefulness, resilience and persistence.

The teaching profession has moved over the years from a traditional transmission-based model of teaching where the teacher transmitted the knowledge they held and allowed pupils to practice and refine their knowledge and skill (Corrie 2002), often through a very limited range of pedagogic approaches. Yet where behaviour is concerned, little of this sophistication is displayed. Rewards and sanctions are still the mainstay and the evaluation of the efficacy of any approach rarely extends beyond short-term, pragmatic consideration of whether it stops the behaviour. Strategy selection in relation to pupil behaviour tends to be based on ideology, common sense or school-based experience rather than evaluated effectiveness (Olsen and Cooper 2001). This is despite considerable recent emphasis (e.g. Goldacre 2013; Nelson and O'Beirne 2014) on evidence based and evidence informed practice in the field of education generally.

Whole-school policies provide a degree of coherence and consistency for the majority of pupils and ensure that teachers make decisions about the strategies they employ within an agreed framework. However, for those pupils who do not respond to such approaches, schools and teachers may feel they have little to draw on beyond a 'trial and error' use of existing behaviour management strategies. It is hoped that the Behaviour for Learning approach outlined in this chapter provides an alternative, representing a means of developing strategies based on appropriate assessment, a coherent framework and a supporting knowledge base (Powell and Tod 2004).

The Behaviour for Learning approach: An alternative perspective

The term 'behaviour for learning' has found considerable popularity, probably because it captures the idea that schools should have a focus on learning and that in order for pupils to learn together in relatively large groups there needs to be a reasonable standard of behaviour. However, there is no shared understanding of the term 'behaviour for learning' and it is used to describe a variety of approaches. The use of the term in this book refers specifically to a conceptual framework that developed from a systematic literature review commissioned by the Teacher Training Agency (TTA) and conducted by Powell and Tod (2004), together with a team of colleagues from Canterbury Christ Church University. The overall aim was to inform initial teacher training tutors about the theoretical underpinnings of learning behaviour in school contexts in order to enhance initial teacher training in relation to behaviour management. The central concern was that the review should contribute to training that allowed trainees to reflect upon the *purpose* of behaviour management. The team held the view that the fostering of learning behaviour or 'behaviour for learning' was the foundation for effective behaviour management, and argued that this represented a contrast with the more common perception that behaviour management is solely concerned with establishing control over disruptive pupils. The use of the terms 'learning behaviour' and 'behaviour for learning' was intended to reduce the perception that 'promoting learning' and 'managing behaviour' were separate issues for teachers (Powell and Tod 2004).

The Behaviour for Learning approach offers an alternative way of thinking about pupil behaviour that addresses some of the problems outlined above that are associated with a focus on behaviour management. The remainder of this chapter presents and explains the key components of the Behaviour for Learning conceptual framework that emerged from the original EPPI-Centre review (Powell and Tod 2004). These components are then expanded upon in Chapters 3–7.

The Behaviour for Learning conceptual framework

The Behaviour for Learning approach is underpinned by the conceptual framework depicted in Figure 2.1.

The term 'learning behaviour' is placed at the centre of the triangle, indicating that the promotion of learning behaviour provides a shared aim for teachers and others with responsibility for providing appropriate learning experiences for children and young people. Within the Behaviour for Learning approach, an identified learning behaviour provides the focus for assessment, intervention and positive change.

The triangle surrounding the term 'learning behaviour' is used to indicate that the development of learning behaviour is influenced by *social*, *emotional* and *cognitive* factors. We sometimes refer to this triangle as the 'triangle of influence'. Explicitly recognising the influence of social, emotional and cognitive factors allows learning behaviour to be explored and addressed through the three relationships (with self, others and the curriculum) experienced by the individual within the classroom. The arrows that surround the triangle represent the dynamic nature of learning and reflect the reciprocal influence that these social, emotional and cognitive factors have on the development of learning behaviour.

The terms 'access', 'engagement' and 'participation' in the diagram are used to reflect the essential components of effective inclusion in group settings. These act as a reminder that the learner should not be viewed as a passive recipient of the disciplinary frameworks and learning opportunities available within the classroom and the school. The experience of the pupil is placed at the heart of effective practice.

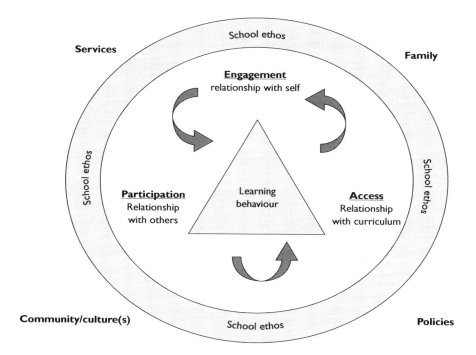

Figure 2.1 The Behaviour for Learning conceptual framework.
Source: adapted from Powell and Tod 2004.

The circle surrounding the triangle of influence, entitled 'school ethos', as well as the terms that lie outside this circle, acknowledge that the development of learning behaviours takes place in a broader context that itself exerts an influence.

The overall purpose of the Behaviour for Learning conceptual framework is to encourage teachers to focus on what learning behaviour they need to develop in order to replace or reduce the problematic behaviour a pupil currently exhibits. The framework's acknowledgement that behaviours have a cognitive, social and emotional component provides a means by which teachers can select the most appropriate strategies and evaluate their efficacy.

What is 'learning behaviour'?

A learning behaviour can be thought of as a behaviour that is necessary in order for a person to learn effectively in the group setting of the classroom. Some examples are provided in Appendix 1. The use of the term 'learning behaviour' within the EPPI review (Powell and Tod 2004) encompassed a deliberate double meaning. The first meaning, applying *learning* as a verb, in the same way as we might talk about learning French or learning the piano, captured the idea that it is necessary for pupils to *learn* behaviour. In other words, it should not be assumed that pupils will enter the school or move to a new phase of their school careers with a specific set of behaviours already learned. Instead, the teacher needs to recognise the learning behaviours it is necessary to develop in order for the pupil to succeed as they move through the different phases of their education. The second meaning used the word *learning* as an adjective describing a particular type of behaviour, in the same way as we might, for example, refer to a behaviour as *disruptive* or *off task*.

The Behaviour for Learning approach is based on the premise that there are particular behaviours necessary for learning and it is therefore important for teachers to think consciously about how they create opportunities to develop these learning behaviours. Reflective Exercise 2.3 invites you think a little more about what we mean by a learning behaviour.

Reflective Exercise 2.3

Think about what you have learned since the subtitle above, *What is 'learning behaviour'*? You have probably learned something from this and are now in a position where you could tell another person about the dual meaning of the phrase learning behaviour.

1   What skills did you use to learn something from this text?
2   Are there different or additional skills that you would have used if, instead of reading it, somebody was explaining this to you?
3   Are there different or additional skills that you would have used if, instead of reading it, somebody was explaining this to you while you were in the company of others?
4   What additional or different skills might be necessary if you were discussing with others what you had learned from the text?
5   If you were unclear about the meaning of part of the text what skills would you draw on if you were reading it alone? Are these different to the skills you would use in the situations described in 2, 3 or 4?

There are behaviours as a learner that you need to be able to perform in order to learn, and there are some differences between those required to learn individually and those required to learn within groups. As an experienced learner, in your responses to Reflective Exercise 2.3 you may have neglected certain elements because they have largely become automated; you learned them at a young age and you no longer have to give them any conscious thought. In situations 3 and 4, for example, a range of social skills are involved that as adult learners we take for granted. It is for this reason that the EPPI-Centre review (Powell and Tod 2004) retained a strong focus on learning in group settings, acknowledging that even when pupils are required to learn individually they typically do it in the company of others, and this requires certain behaviours that may be different to those employed if learning alone.

Within Reflective Exercise 2.3 the focus was on *skills*, but when thinking about learning behaviours this is only half of the picture. For example, what made you pick up this book in the first place and how did you keep yourself motivated to continue – even through any difficult bits or in the face of other competing demands? This introduces the notion that learning behaviour involves both skills and *dispositions* (Carr and Claxton 2002). This is discussed in more detail in Chapter 3.

The three relationships that underpin the promotion of learning behaviour

Classrooms are places characterised by individual teachers seeking to 'manage' groups of diverse individuals in order to promote learning. Within this context, interactions, influences and outcomes are complex. By focusing on three relationships – with self, with others and with the curriculum – the Behaviour for Learning framework seeks to unpick this complexity in order to allow teachers to make sense of and address problematic behaviour while maintaining a focus on learning.

Reflective Exercise 2.4 provides an opportunity to use your own experiences as a learner in school as a means of developing a working understanding of the three Behaviour for Learning relationships and their link with the development of learning behaviour.

Reflective Exercise 2.4

Think about your own learning at school and recall a lesson in which you behaved well – or, if you prefer, one in which you did not behave so well.

- How interested and capable were you in the subject being taught?
- How well did you get on with your teacher and with peers in the class?
- How were you feeling emotionally in this specific lesson?

The factors explored in Reflective Exercise 2.4 reflect, respectively, the three Behaviour for Learning relationships. These are:

- relationship with the curriculum (predominantly cognitive);
- relationship with others (predominantly social);
- relationship with self (predominantly emotional).

We use the term 'relationship' to reflect the dynamic reciprocity that is inherent in curricular, social and personal experiences. To illustrate what we mean by this, if we return to your recollections from your own schooldays, you can probably recall that your interest in the subject, how well you got on with your teacher and with peers in the class and how you felt emotionally were influenced by factors such as:

- the way the particular teacher presented the lesson;
- the types of tasks and activities set by the teacher;
- your perception of how the teacher viewed you as a learner and as a person;
- how the teacher related to you and your classmates;
- who you were with when you were learning.

Therefore, although you are likely to have brought to your school-based learning various influencing skills, dispositions and previous experiences, your interest in the subject, how well you got on with your teacher and with peers in the class and how you felt emotionally were also influenced for better or worse by a range of contextual variables. The Behaviour for Learning approach does not leave the interaction between these elements to chance. The class teacher aims to be aware of the effect on the pupil's behaviour of these variables, and to work positively with the pupil to foster the development of learning behaviour. Care would be taken to avoid any practice that would have a predictable negative impact on either the three relationships or the development of learning behaviour. In cases where an individual's behaviour causes particular concern, due to its intensity, persistence and resistance to change through the influence of the behaviour management techniques usually employed, the teacher can use the conceptual framework more systematically as a problem–solving and planning tool.

Behaviour management: Necessary but not sufficient?

We are not suggesting that teachers do not need a toolkit of strategies at their disposal to use within the classroom. Our view is that this is necessary, but not sufficient. This is illustrated through the following case study.

Case Study 2.1

A Year 9 teacher is taking a middle-ability English group. They are studying Shakespeare's *Much Ado About Nothing*. The first activity is based on a worksheet that requires pupils individually to use a dictionary to look up a set of words from a passage from the play and copy down the meanings. Once all the words have been found, the pupils then have to complete a cloze procedure, writing the words in the correct space in the passage. Most pupils get on with this. A number of pupils wander around the room for no obvious task-related purpose. Others talk about non-task related matters. A few call out remarks across the room to others. The teacher circulates, stopping to help various pupils or address the more overt behaviours.

After about 20 minutes the teacher attempts to take some feedback from the group. Only one or two put their hands up and they are asked to answer. Most of the others are not listening. The situation is not helped by the table arrangement which has the pupils grouped in fours, leading to a significant number facing away from the teacher.

The teacher's professional integrity means that while she recognises that providing the pupils with structured activities such as the cloze procedure used here can maintain behaviour at a reasonably acceptable level, pupils are missing out on so much that the subject has to offer. For this reason, she has valiantly, but with a little trepidation, planned a role-play exercise as the next activity.

Knowledge of some behaviour management strategies would undoubtedly be useful in the situation described in Case Study 2.1. An injection of some of Bill Rogers (e.g. Rogers 2011) strategies into this teacher's repertoire would provide a way of directing the wanderers to their seats and of dealing with the extraneous chatter and calling out. A class reward scheme to which individuals contribute may provide the teacher with a tool with which to motivate pupils to behave. A more decisive use of the school's system of warnings, leading to sanctions, may help curb some of the excesses of some members of the group. Use of different questioning techniques may lead to pupils perceiving there to be a greater risk of being asked and consequently to greater attentiveness when the teacher attempts to take feedback.

We would want teachers to be thinking about these aspects of their practice, but we would also want them to have a clear reason as to *why* they are applying these techniques, which extends beyond simply freeing the teacher to teach. In Case Study 2.1, the teacher's trepidation was based on a realistic prediction, informed by the pupils' performance in more structured activities such as the cloze procedure, that the role-play would be difficult. A behaviour management focus may encourage the pursuit of a robust enough set of techniques to *control* behaviour during the role-play. In contrast, a Behaviour for Learning focus places attention on the teacher's original appraisal of the situation, looking at the learning behaviours exhibited in the structured activities in comparison to those necessary to take part in the planned role-play. The teacher needs to ask questions in relation to the learning behaviour at whole-class level:

- What can the pupils do now unaided?
- What can pupils do now with support?
- What do the pupils need to learn to do next?
- How can I, through my subject teaching, develop this learning behaviour?

This sort of thinking is regularly applied in relation to learning, but less so in relation to behaviour. Within this thinking process, behaviour management is relegated to its rightful place as a description of a particular set of techniques *integrated within* the extensive range of techniques teachers use to promote learning.

The Behaviour for Learning approach promotes a view that even in situations where it is necessary to stop or limit behaviour, this can be done with a focus on learning behaviour. There will be occasions when pupils talk out of turn, distract or interfere with others, fail to comply with instructions, answer back and engage in other behaviours identified by the Elton Report (DES 1989) and, more recently, Ofsted (2014a) as low-level disruption. Teachers undoubtedly need to be familiar with and skilled at using a range of strategies to address these issues as part of their repertoire in order to facilitate learning in group settings. Our suggestion is not that 'knowledge of generic behaviour management systems and techniques' (TA 2012: 1) is unnecessary. We view the typical strategies associated with behaviour management as tools a teacher would draw on, selected from the far broader array of other professional tools at their disposal, that have the potential to promote the behaviours necessary for effective learning in the classroom.

The strength of the Behaviour for Learning approach is that it does not seek to prescribe a range of strategies to respond to such behaviours; rather it encourages teachers to harness the plethora of strategies currently available, while always keeping a critical eye on two constant questions:

- Does the strategy have the potential to promote, or at least not undermine, the promotion of learning behaviour?
- Does the strategy have the potential to promote, or at least not undermine, the three relationships that underpin the development of learning behaviour?

Even in an immediate management situation, the teacher should aspire through their verbal and non-verbal communication to ensure that they do not do anything that undermines the three relationships or promotes what we might term a 'negative' learning behaviour. Strategies that, for example, are intended to cause fear or embarrassment, may superficially work in the sense that the class is quiet, but they may promote alienation, resentment, reticence, an unwillingness to take risks in learning and a preoccupation with remaining unnoticed by the teacher.

Is the Behaviour for Learning approach just another version of 'positive behaviour management'?

'Positive behaviour management' is a generic phrase used to describe a range of strategies and approaches that are delivered in a particular way. Typically, the teacher frames any corrections positively and places emphasis on recognising and acknowledging 'good' behaviour. Though the central purpose is usually the management of behaviour there is also likely to be an accompanying intention to achieve this without damage to the teacher–pupil relationship or to the pupil's emotional wellbeing. From this description it should be clear that there is a relationship between 'positive behaviour management' and the Behaviour for Learning approach, but they are not the same. It is perhaps easiest to understand this relationship if we think about positive behaviour management strategies as *one* of a range of tools available to support the teacher in promoting learning behaviour.

Table 2.3 highlights the distinctions between the types of positive behaviour management approaches (e.g. Hook and Vass 2002; Rogers 2011) that many readers will already be familiar with and Behaviour for Learning.

In highlighting these distinctions there is no intention to criticise or devalue either the term 'positive behaviour management' or the practices that ensue from this perspective. Quite to the contrary, we fully endorse this approach. It is important however for readers to understand the distinctions between positive behaviour management and Behaviour for Learning if they are to appreciate the conceptual framework within this book as more than rebranding.

The conceptual framework that is central to the Behaviour for Learning approach allows teachers to explore and understand the determinants of learning behaviour and to make sense of, and evaluate, the efficacy of the plethora of strategies available.

We are not advocating that the phrase 'behaviour management' is abandoned; indeed, we will use it on occasions throughout this book. Instead we are encouraging readers to think more about the extent to which their management of behaviour is integrated into their promotion of learning.

While we hope readers will increasingly think and talk in terms of learning behaviour and Behaviour for Learning, we would encourage more than a superficial rebranding. It requires a conceptual shift rather than just the replacement of any reference to behaviour management or managing behaviour in policy or teacher language with the term Behaviour for Learning.

Practical application of the Behaviour for Learning conceptual framework

In practically applying the Behaviour for Learning framework it is initially useful to think in terms of the three levels of use depicted in Figure 2.2, though in practice we would not consider there to be a rigid distinction between core and extended use, just a shift in emphasis.

Some readers who were teaching at the time will recognise the obvious parallels with the waves model set out in a range of National Strategy documents (e.g. DfES 2002a, 2005d, 2006) produced during the Labour Government's administration (1997–2010). In our three-tiered model there is recognition that it is neither necessary nor feasible to adopt a highly individualised approach for most pupils. For all members of the class, the

Table 2.3 Key differences between positive behaviour management and Behaviour for Learning

Positive behaviour management	Behaviour for Learning
'Positive behaviour management' is a generic term for a range of strategies and approaches that are delivered in a particular way. Positive behaviour management is well known and used in many schools.	Behaviour for Learning is based on a conceptual framework developed from a 2004 EPPI review (Powell and Tod 2004) and as such is still relatively new.
In practice, positive behaviour management strategies discussed in this book – *if* applied in the spirit and manner intended by their authors – are likely to be compatible with Behaviour for Learning principles.	Behaviour for Learning encourages the use of a range of existing positive behaviour management strategies but requires that they are evaluated against the extent to which they promote learning behaviour.
Positive behaviour management does not *necessarily* demand a concern with anything other than achieving compliance – albeit through positive means.	While accepting that compliance may be necessary, Behaviour for Learning explicitly demands the systematic evaluation of a strategy's efficacy against its contribution to the development of learning behaviour.
Positive behaviour management often evaluates in terms of the reduction or absence of behaviour (e.g. less calling out).	Behaviour for Learning always evaluates in terms of an increase in or presence of learning behaviour.
Positive behaviour management has regard for, but is not based upon recognition of, the social, emotional and cognitive aspects of learning.	The promotion of learning behaviour is based on the interdependence of the social, emotional and cognitive aspects of learning.
Positive behaviour management places emphasis on preserving positive interactions with pupils through strategy and language use.	Behaviour for Learning places emphasis on the need to balance the three key relationships and to avoid promoting any one of these to the detriment of another.
Positive behaviour management places value on a repertoire of good practice strategies.	Behaviour for Learning endorses the need for a toolkit of strategies but explicitly acknowledges that no one set of strategies will 'work' for all pupils. Individuals inevitably experience and interpret the strategy in different ways – whatever its good practice credentials. A teacher using the Behaviour for Learning approach is constantly alert to this.

teacher's priority will be to ensure that their standard classroom practice reflects the principles of the Behaviour for Learning approach. For some pupils achieving change may require a more explicit focus on the development of specific learning behaviours. In a few cases, unwanted behaviours may be pervasive and so the development of target learning behaviours may require intervention that specifically addresses underlying social, emotional or cognitive factors through strengthening one or more of the three relationships. Each tier of use is outlined below.

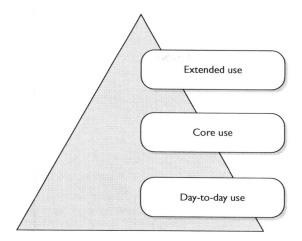

Figure 2.2 Different levels of use of the Behaviour for Learning approach.
Source: Ellis and Tod 2015.

Day-to-day use

In day-to-day practice the priority is to promote learning behaviour and protect and enhance the three Behaviour for Learning relationships that underpin its development. This requires the teacher to keep a watchful eye on the three relationships and look for opportunities through the curriculum, the behaviour they model and their routine interactions with pupils to develop learning behaviours. In addition, the teacher would intuitively vary practice based on knowledge of particular groups and individuals, drawing on the principles of the Behaviour for Learning approach. The teacher might, for example, use the 'social' appeal of group work to develop motivation for a less popular subject, or provide more support when pupils are required to undertake an activity that draws on emerging rather than well-established learning behaviours.

Applied at the day-to-day use level, the Behaviour for Learning approach has the potential to inform what Schon (1983) described as reflection-in-action and reflection-on-action. Whilst the teacher is engaged in the act of classroom teaching they can use the principles of the Behaviour for Learning approach as a reference point to guide their actions. After the event, they can reflect on whether any actions taken were consistent with these principles. We would also suggest that there is an earlier stage when, in planning their teaching, including possible responses to predictable classroom behaviours, the teacher can consider the compatibility of intended actions with the principles of the Behaviour for Learning approach. In reflecting on proposed or used strategies, the teacher is always required to consider:

1   the effect on the development of learning behaviour;
2   the effect on the three relationships within the conceptual framework.

In both cases, the effect of the strategy or approach should not be negative. The teacher should be able to identify either a neutral or (ideally) a positive effect.

From the description of the day-to-day use of the Behaviour for Learning approach, it should be evident that we are suggesting a wider application than just a means of selecting and evaluating strategies to respond to misbehaviour. Reflecting the intention to maintain links between learning and behaviour, we view it as a way of thinking that should be applied to all aspects of school practice, including curricular approaches, assessment procedures, SEN interventions, pastoral systems and the management of behaviour.

Chapters 8, 9 and 10 provide support in thinking about day-to-day use of the Behaviour for Learning approach.

Core use

In the case of some pupils, it may be that the development of one or more learning behaviours appears to be the priority. Through careful observation the teacher will have recognised that if these specific behaviours were developed then there would be a significant positive effect on the pupils' behaviour in school. Core use of the model makes use of a clear, sequential process based on four key questions/steps:

1   What is the learning behaviour that I need to promote?
2   What can I do through standard practice, adaptations to standard practice, targeted interventions and/or support in order to promote the identified learning behaviour?
3   Can I do this on my own or do I need help? What help or support do I need?
4   What are my evaluation criteria? What are the assessable indicators that would show progress had been made in promoting this learning behaviour?

Because the purpose is to promote learning behaviour, progress is always judged against its development. It is important, therefore, to be clear at step 1 about the target learning behaviours and at step 4 about assessable indicators. Often the assessable indicators will simply be the learning behaviours identified at step 1, but it is important to be open to the possibility that there may be other, unanticipated indicators that evidence progress in this area. This is particularly true if the target learning behaviour is a disposition rather than a skill. If attempts to develop the target learning behaviours are not having the intended effect, it can be useful when planning at step 2 to consider the balance between social, emotional and cognitive/curricular oriented strategies used so far. This may reveal an underused or alternative route to bringing about behavioural change.

Extended use

For most pupils it will suffice to follow the sequence of steps outlined above. For a few pupils, through careful observation, the teacher will have recognised that the individual has developed a *repertoire*, *range* and *frequency* of problematic behaviours that cluster around one or more of the Behaviour for Learning relationships. The pervasive nature of these behaviours may require intervention that specifically addresses underlying social, emotional or cognitive factors through strengthening one or more of the *learning relationships*. The learning behaviours remain important, with the sequence of questions becoming:

1   What is the relationship that I need to promote for learning in a group setting?
2   Is it better for the individual pupil if I focus directly on the target relationship or seek to develop it via one of the other two relationships?
3   Is there a relationship area that I feel more confident or competent to work in initially?
4   Which cluster of learning behaviours (or specific significant learning behaviour) do I need to promote in order to have a pervasive, positive effect on the relationship?
5   What can I do through standard practice, adaptations to standard practice, targeted interventions and/or support to promote the targeted relationship?
6   What positive skills and dispositions does the pupil bring to this relationship?
7   What professional and personal knowledge, skills and understanding can I contribute to this relationship?
8   Do I need any additional advice, guidance and support from within my school or from multi-agency partners?
9   What are my evaluation criteria? What are the assessable indicators that would show progress had been made in promoting the target relationship?

When applying the framework in its 'extended' form the teacher is seeking to strengthen one (or more) of the three relationships. However, the learning behaviours identified in answer to Question 4 are important to consider when responding to Question 9. Success in promoting the target relationship is likely to be indicated by the emergence of some or all of the learning behaviours identified in response to Question 4. This should not restrict recognition of other indicators of progress made by the pupil that were not previously identified by the teacher but are, nonetheless, relevant in demonstrating improvements in the target relationship.

Planning for the individual using the Behaviour for Learning conceptual framework

When starting to use the Behaviour for Learning framework to plan for individuals it is useful to consider whether to approach the particular case through either core or extended use questions in order to provide a clear structure. However, it is important to understand the difference between core and extended use as a gradual shift in emphasis from a focus on the learning behaviours to a focus on one or more of the three relationships rather than a clearly demarcated division. The learning behaviours the pupil exhibits give an indication of the quality of their relationships with self, the curriculum and others; so there is a fluidity and flexibility in the real life application of the Behaviour for Learning framework that conceptualisation as two distinct tiers cannot fully convey. The following case study (Table 2.4) illustrates this more flexible application of the Behaviour for Learning framework.

The commentary accompanying the case study demonstrates how a Behaviour for Learning approach takes us from an initial focus on reducing disruptive behaviour to one which seeks to promote more positive learning behaviours. Emphasis is placed on the Behaviour for Learning relationships as experienced by the pupil. This allows us to identify and select strategies to personalise a response, based on an awareness of the individual's level of social, emotional and cognitive development.

Table 2.4 Case study with a Behaviour for Learning commentary

Pen picture: Steven, Year 6 (age 11)	*Behaviour for Learning commentary*
Steven regularly distracts others. This often takes the form of irritating pieces of behaviour such as poking, taking equipment without asking and trying to talk to other pupils when they are engaged in an activity and clearly don't want to be interrupted. He can also disrupt teacher input to the class by calling out. The comments that he calls out are usually related to the subject but their frequency is disruptive and irritating to others. Some of the other pupils have started to say, 'Shut up, Steven', in these and other situations when his behaviour becomes irritating. Steven often takes this as an affront and will either answer the pupil back aggressively or complain loudly, e.g. 'S/he told me to shut up'. As well as distracting others, he is easily distracted and may play with objects such as rubbers or sharpeners or other small items.	• Frequency is an issue and is impacting negatively on his relationship with others. • Is he choosing not to behave or does he lack the necessary behaviour in his repertoire? • What is the purpose of the behaviour for him?
Verbally Steven is very able – in fact some staff say he has 'the gift of the gab' in reference to the long-winded excuses he uses to try to talk himself out of the frequent trouble he gets into. On a one-to-one basis some staff describe him as 'charming'.	• He does seem to be able to form relationships with some others. • Do I need to know more about who and under what conditions?
Steven seldom appears totally absorbed in a lesson and doesn't appear to have a favourite subject. He shows some interest in practical Science activities, but finds it difficult to work with others as he tries to dominate.	• This could point to a relationship with the curriculum issue.
When he does receive praise for a good piece of work it seems that Steven deliberately then spoils it, either by throwing it away, scribbling on it or rubbing and crossing out large chunks of what he has done. He shows a similar reaction when praised for behaviour – it is as though he wants to reject any positive recognition.	• The rejection of praise could point to a relationship with self issue.

Pen picture: Steven, Year 6 (age 11)	*Behaviour for Learning commentary*
Steven is good at recalling facts verbally but is slow to produce written work. The reason for this seems to be because he distracts himself and others, as when required to complete work on his own at break time he can do it quickly and to a reasonable standard.	• Verbal recall of facts is a useful learning behaviour. • He can do the work alone – this could be a relationship with peers issue.
Organisationally Steven is chaotic – regularly losing things, not having the right equipment to hand and forgetting/ignoring the standard conventions for setting out work. His parents report that he is much the same at home – very *laissez-faire* in his attitude, not really taking care of his possessions or taking any responsibility for organising himself.	• Learning behaviour is not evident in the area of personal organisation. • The problem doesn't only occur in one context – so it suggests he lacks the skills. • Are we sure about the 'will' aspect?
Steven is good at PE and most games, which attracts some admiration from his peers. However, he is not a 'team player', so although his prowess impresses others they soon become irritated with him.	• His relationship with one particular curriculum area is good, but his relationship with other pupils is an issue.
Socially it is difficult to make a judgement about Steven's popularity among his peers. He is able to get others to join in conversations, often at inappropriate times, but he doesn't seem to have any close friends and often appears isolated at break times. He appears to like the idea of having one or two best friends but these friendships rarely last as he cannot accept that his 'best' friends might also want to associate with others or pursue other interests. This has led to some major 'fall-outs', including physical altercations. The most notable occasion was last term when he was excluded for three days after giving another pupil a black eye.	• This presents as a relationship with others issue, but we would need to be aware that this could also indicate an underlying relationship with self issue. • The learning behaviours needed to mix with others *and* protect self emotionally are not evident.

From the thinking and analysis set out in Table 2.4 we can progress to synthesis. The analysis appears to indicate that:

1   Steven has some relevant learning behaviours:
    a   good verbal memory;
    b   good grasp of language;
    c   ability to defend his position verbally and avoid punishment;
    d   listening (the comments he calls out are usually subject–related);
    e   initiates social interaction.
2   Steven does not have sufficiently well–developed learning behaviours in the areas of:
    a   personal organisation;
    b   peer relationships, though he is marginally better with adults;
    c   collaborative working;
    d   self–regulation;
    e   empathy;
    f   ignoring distractions;
    g   responding to criticism from peers;
    h   accepting praise.
3   Steven has skills that are only evident in some contexts:
    a   relating to adults;
    b   completion of work when alone.

Let's assume that from this analysis we decide that personal organisation is the issue we want to prioritise. Without the analysis we might simply move into a system of rewards for bringing the right equipment and some form of consequence when it is forgotten. The analysis and synthesis leads us to a more personalised, sophisticated response that is planned in relation to social, emotional and cognitive relationships.

The key issue that emerges is that aged 11, and with secondary transfer looming, Steven is using insufficient planning in many aspects of his life. The area of difficulty does not just relate to what we might term *cognitive* planning; there are issues to address in relation to *emotional* and *social* planning. The overall aim is to provide him with a range of strategies for planning at which he can succeed. He can then experience the benefits of this and in so doing increase his motivation to take responsibility for his own planning. Based on the analysis and synthesis we could implement the following strategies in the three areas.

Cognitive planning (relates to 'relationship with curriculum')

- Implement a strategy that makes a link for Steven between days of the week and equipment he needs. Depending on his known preferences this might be in electronic form (e.g. lists on his phone) or in physical form. For example, he could be provided with open top plastic drawers labelled with days of the week at home in which he can place the items he needs for the next day – this could be developed into a written planner in preparation for secondary transfer.
- Provide opportunities to state to an adult the equipment he needs for the task in advance, with a view to promoting 'out loud' self-talk at first and moving towards silent self-talk.

- Provide a personal timetable, which could be visual, to allow self-monitoring.
- Use rule-reminders in response to calling out in class.
- Attach a personal reminder to his desk of the rules for asking for help or making a verbal contribution to the lesson.
- Provide opportunities to work with peers on a curriculum-based task that makes limited social and emotional demands, e.g. a collaborative Science activity with teacher-defined roles for each member of the group.

Emotional planning (relates to 'relationship with self')

- *Planning and rehearsing responses to criticism*
  Rehearsal can be depersonalised initially through, for example, the use of role-play, stories and examples from TV. The purpose of this strategy is to develop a disposition that allows for criticism to be an accepted, though not always pleasant, part of human interaction. We cannot seek to avoid it forever but what matters is our response to it.
- *Planning and rehearsing responses to praise*
  Rehearsal can be depersonalised initially through the use of role-play, stories, examples from TV, etc.
- *Planning for reward and failure*
  The traditional reward system is unlikely to be effective as Steven already appears to have a fear of failure. For him a reward based on total success may simply represent another potential source of failure. Therefore, in looking at the strategies that target personal organisation, our emphasis would not be on rewarding him for bringing the right equipment, but for telling us when the system has worked and when it did not. In this way we are giving him the message that there is information in failure that can positively inform future learning.

Social planning (relates to 'relationship with others')

- Use role-play as a means to rehearse social situations that require communication with others. The purpose is to develop and practise the *skills* involved in communication in a safe social context.
- Use comic strip conversations (Gray 1994a) to aid understanding of social situations. Typically, this involves drawings of stick people to depict a particular social situation. In Steven's case this might be when a friend wants to play a game with someone else. Taking this example, stick people would be drawn to represent Steven and the friend. Speech bubbles and thought bubbles would then be used to distinguish between what the friend actually says and what Steven *believes* they might be thinking. Steven's own responses in this social situation can also be explored. In his speech bubble there might be a verbally aggressive phrase, but in his thought bubble there might be phrases that indicate that he feels rejected or vulnerable.

Although these strategies are designed with Steven in mind, the planning, involving visual timetables, rule reminders and planners, would be appropriate for the whole group. The difference for Steven is in the way his response is assessed through the development of appropriate learning behaviours. He may also require a more individualised approach involving discussion as to the purpose behind the strategies and the contribution expected from him.

Conclusion

As this chapter has outlined, the Behaviour for Learning approach is underpinned by a conceptual framework that is intended to encourage a focus on the purpose and *outcomes* of behaviour management. It invites a shift in thinking away from a concern with stopping unwanted behaviour towards the promotion of effective learning behaviours.

We fully acknowledge the complexity inherent within definitions of learning and its associated cognitive, affective and social behaviours. The Behaviour for Learning conceptual framework seeks to address this complexity through identifying three core relationships relevant to the development of learning behaviours in school settings. Each relationship impacts on the other and the use of an apparently simple visual model belies, in some ways, the complexity and dynamism of those relationships. Together, the different elements that make up the Behaviour for Learning conceptual framework contribute to an overall perspective on pupil behaviour summarised in Table 2.5.

Table 2.5 The Behaviour for Learning perspective on behaviour

Formulation
- The Behaviour for Learning approach is based on the view that successful learning in a group setting, such as a school, requires the development of a range of 'Product' (curricular)-centred learning behaviours, Participation (social)-centred learning behaviours and Person (emotional)-centred learning behaviours.
- Learning behaviours may be skills or dispositions.
- Learning behaviours are seen as being influenced by the pupil's relationship with self (predominantly emotional factors), relationship with others (predominantly social factors) and relationship with the curriculum (predominantly cognitive/curricular factors).
- Both positive and problematic behaviour can be explained in terms of the learning behaviours the pupil currently exhibits and understood by reference to the emotional, social and cognitive factors associated with one or more of the three relationships.

Identification and Assessment
Assessment focuses on the learning behaviours exhibited by the pupil and what these indicate about the quality of each of the three relationships. In the case of pupils causing concern, the unwanted behaviours currently exhibited can either be used directly to define the alternative positive learning behaviours that need to be developed or as indicators of one or more of the three relationships it would be beneficial to strengthen.

Intervention
Intervention (standard practice, adaptations to standard practice, targeted interventions and/or support) is based on the premise that change can be achieved by developing positive learning behaviours. In some cases unwanted behaviours may be pervasive and the development of positive learning behaviours may require intervention that specifically addresses underlying social, emotional or cognitive factors through strengthening one or more of the three relationships.

Evaluation
The impact of standard practice and any adaptations to standard practice, targeted interventions and/or support is based on the emergence of identified target learning behaviour(s).

This chapter represents only a basic grounding in the Behaviour for Learning approach. It has sought to provide a working understanding of key elements within the Behaviour for Learning conceptual framework sufficient to support initial changes in thinking and practice. The next five chapters explore the key elements in more detail, contributing to a deeper understanding of learning behaviour and the three relationships that underpin its development.

Chapter 3

Learning behaviour

Introduction

As described in the previous chapter, the Behaviour for Learning approach presented in this book is based on a conceptual framework (Powell and Tod 2004) that links learning and behaviour, via the term 'learning behaviour'. The use of this term is deliberate in that it seeks to promote the view that 'promoting learning' and 'managing behaviour' should not be seen as separate issues for teachers. This is important given that teachers typically regard the promotion of learning as a core aim of their profession. How 'behaviour' fits with that aim is of crucial importance, with some viewing the *control* of behaviour as a necessary prerequisite for school learning to occur, while others see the curriculum and classroom as a medium through which children and young people develop the social skills and individual responsibility needed for lifelong learning.

The phrase 'learning behaviour' itself is not new and has been used previously by writers such as Day and Libertini (1992), Norwich (1994) and Norwich and Rovoli (1993), as well as White and Mitchell (1994) whose work we refer to later in this chapter. The terms 'learning behaviour' and 'behaviour for learning' have now slipped almost effortlessly into educational discourse. For example, the Steer Report (DfES 2005b) incorporated the term 'learning behaviour' into its title, Key Stage 3 National Strategy training materials (DfES 2003b) identified a set of 'behaviours for learning' and the Training and Development Agency (TDA) sponsored an Initial Teacher Education Professional Resource Network (IPRN) entitled *Behaviour4Learning*.

An internet search using the term 'learning behaviour' or 'behaviour for learning' will quickly reveal many schools using these terms within their policies on behaviour and learning. Some readers may be in schools, such as the one described by Elkin (2004), where the approach employed is entitled *Behaviour for Learning* but there is no direct link with the conceptual framework that underpins this book. It is important to note that the juxtaposition of the terms 'learning' and 'behaviour' does not necessarily imply some agreed meaning or carry the same implications for practice. This chapter focuses on the concept of learning behaviour as described in Powell and Tod's (2004) publication *A Systematic Review of how Theories Explain Learning Behaviour in School Contexts* and in Chapter 2 of this book.

What do we mean by learning behaviours?

The EPPI-Centre review (Powell and Tod 2004) identified a set of learning behaviours drawn from Qualified Teacher Status (QTS) standards (DfES/TTA 2002) that could help teachers identify a set of purposes and/or activities relevant to all pupils and curriculum areas. These were:

- engagement;
- collaboration;
- participation;
- communication;
- motivation;
- independent activity;
- responsiveness;
- self-regard;
- self-esteem;
- responsibility.

The purpose of this list was to provide examples of learning behaviour relevant to the teacher standards (DfES/TTA 2002) at the time, rather than to attempt to prescribe or establish a definitive set. These are broad terms; they can be considered as higher level learning behaviours in the sense that they transcend curriculum areas, age and stages of development and are likely to be of lifelong relevance to the learner. These, like others we might add such as 'resilience', 'resourcefulness' and 'confidence', are too broad for operational purposes as they do not readily support monitoring and evaluation. For example, if we were seeking to improve 'collaboration' we would need to have a clear idea of specific learning behaviours that would indicate progress. These might include:

- takes turns using equipment;
- volunteers own ideas in a small group;
- waits to speak while others are talking;
- self-monitors his/her contribution and adjusts if necessary (e.g. recognises if s/he is dominating a discussion or talking too much);
- accepts ideas offered by others, even when different to his/her own.

It should be evident that the learning behaviours in this list vary in their level of sophistication. For example, sharing equipment might be a learning behaviour we would aim to develop in a young child whereas self-monitoring one's own contribution is a more advanced skill. Target learning behaviours need to be identified that are appropriate for the pupil's age and stage of development.

Ultimately, it is for the teacher to define the particular learning behaviours that it is appropriate to develop in the pupils they are working with. Behaviour management has often encouraged a language that is focused on defining and reducing unwanted behaviours. Some teachers, therefore, may have had limited practice and experience in thinking about what learning behaviours are needed across contexts to improve their pupils' learning and behaviour. Reflective Exercise 3.1 provides the opportunity to rehearse the identification of target learning behaviours.

An illustrative resource list of learning behaviours is also included in Appendix 1.

Reflective Exercise 3.1

For each scenario below consider the learning behaviour you would want to promote:
- Aisha is very vocal and disruptive in class which frequently leads to her being sent out.
- Ryan is regularly involved in playground incidents for which he blames other pupils.
- Reece presents as moody and unpredictable.
- Molly reacts negatively to praise.
- Aiden rips up his work and throws it away.
- Scott makes negative self-reference statements – frequently starting by saying 'I can't do this' when presented with an unfamiliar activity.
- Mohammed seeks frequent, non-specific support and reassurance.
- Paige avoids failure and is very sensitive to any perceived criticism.

1 Would it have been easier to identify the learning behaviours if you knew the pupil?
2 If so, why do you think this is?
3 If you knew the pupil, what sorts of factors would you have taken into account that these brief scenarios cannot provide?

In identifying learning behaviours it is helpful to consider the following points:

- The learning behaviour should be positively expressed.
- It may simply be the opposite of the unwanted behaviour.
- It may be a behaviour that is incompatible with the problem behaviour (i.e. if the pupil exhibited this behaviour then, by definition, they would not be exhibiting the problem behaviour).
- It should be possible to identify assessable indicators based on the pupil's progress in learning.
- If you have selected a disposition (e.g. confidence, resilience) you should be able to identify some behaviours that would indicate its development.

You might like to go back to Reflective Exercise 3.1 and review your suggested learning behaviours against these points.

Other possible sources of learning behaviours

A number of current and past policy and guidance documents produced by central government provide, implicitly or explicitly, an indication of the types of learning behaviours viewed by policy makers as important to develop. In addition to considering these, this section of the chapter also explores two examples of independent authors who have offered a perspective on the sorts of behaviours it is desirable to develop in pupils.

The Qualifications and Curriculum Authority document *Supporting School Improvement: Emotional and Behavioural Development* (QCA 2001) emerged from QCA-commissioned research carried out by the University of Birmingham School of Education Assessment Research Unit. The project was aimed at developing criteria that schools might use for measuring pupils' emotional and behavioural development. Drawing on a range of existing criteria used throughout local authorities in England, the criteria developed by the Birmingham team addressed three distinct aspects of behaviour:

Table 3.1 Criteria for measuring emotional and behavioural development

Learning behaviour	Conduct behaviour	Emotional behaviour
1 Is attentive and has an interest in schoolwork.	1 Behaves respectfully towards staff.	1 Has empathy.
2 Has good learning organisation.	2 Shows respect to other pupils.	2 Is socially aware.
3 Is an effective communicator.	3 Only interrupts and seeks attention appropriately.	3 Is happy.
4 Works efficiently in a group.	4 Is physically peaceable.	4 Is confident.
5 Seeks help where necessary.	5 Respects property.	5 Is emotionally stable and shows good self-control.

Source: QCA 2001.

- learning behaviour;
- conduct behaviour;
- emotional behaviour.

The QCA (2001) guidance outlined five criteria (Table 3.1) for each aspect supported by descriptors and a record sheet.

The QCA's (2001) descriptors for the three aspects are shown below:

Learning behaviour
- *Is attentive and has an interest in schoolwork* e.g. is not easily distracted, completes work, keeps on task and concentrates, has good motivation, shows interest, enjoys schoolwork.
- *Good learning organisation* e.g. works systematically, at a reasonable pace, knows when to move on to the next activity or stage, can make choices, is organised.
- *Is an effective communicator* e.g. speech is coherent, thinks before answering.
- *Works efficiently in a group* e.g. takes part in discussions, contributes readily to group tasks, listens well in groups, and works collaboratively.
- *Seeks help where necessary* e.g. can work independently until there is a problem that cannot be solved without the teacher's intervention.

Conduct behaviour
- *Behaves respectfully towards staff* e.g. respects staff and answers them politely, does not interrupt or deliberately annoy, does not show verbal aggression.
- *Shows respect to other pupils* e.g. interacts with other pupils politely and thoughtfully, does not tease, call names, swear, use psychological intimidation.
- *Only interrupts and seeks attention appropriately* e.g. behaves in ways warranted by the classroom activity, does not disrupt unnecessarily, or distract or interfere with others, does not pass notes, talk when others are talking, does not seek unwarranted attention.
- *Is physically peaceable* e.g. is not physically aggressive, avoids fights, is pleasant to other pupils, is not cruel or spiteful, does not strike out in temper.
- *Respects property* e.g. values and looks after property, does not damage or destroy property, does not steal.

Emotional behaviour
- *Has empathy* e.g. is tolerant of others, shows understanding and sympathy, is considerate.
- *Is socially aware* e.g. interacts appropriately with others, is not a loner or isolated, reads social situations well.
- *Is happy* e.g. has fun when appropriate, smiles, laughs, is cheerful, is not tearful or depressed.
- *Is confident* e.g. is not anxious, has high self-esteem, is relaxed, does not fear failure, is not shy, is not afraid of new things, is robust.
- *Is emotionally stable and shows self-control* e.g. moods remain relatively stable, does not have frequent mood swings, is patient, is not easily flustered, is not touchy.

(QCA 2001: 10–11)

This allocation of behaviour into three areas is interesting in that it resonates with our Behaviour for Learning conceptual framework that seeks to address the development of social, cognitive and emotional learning behaviours. If we scrutinise the QCA lists closely it is apparent that they include both *skills* (e.g. 'good learning organisation') and *dispositions* (e.g. 'is confident'). This is an important distinction and one that we explore later in this chapter.

The Key Stage 3 National Strategy Behaviour and Attendance Core Day 1 (DfES 2003b) materials suggest a range of 'behaviours for learning'. These are shown in Table 3.2.

Table 3.2 Suggested behaviours for learning

Positive interaction staff/pupil	Listening to each other. Responding to requests. Speaking politely. Asking questions. Showing concern and understanding. Following instructions and requests.
Sensible use of resources	Bringing correct material to class. Sharing equipment. Looking after own/others property. Keeping desk/classroom tidy.
Appropriate use of language	Speaking politely. Using proper names. Waiting turn to speak. Listening to ideas of others without negative comment. Giving way in an argument. Accepting ideas and suggestions of others and acting upon them. Tone of voice congruent with body language. Appropriate tone of voice for task.
Acceptance of new challenges	Setting appropriate goals. Taking risks. Trying new things. Asking for help. Using peer support. Making mistakes and moving on. Self-aware – knowing how and when to get help.

continued

Table 3.2 Continued

Able to work independently	Correct equipment for tasks. Good time-keeping. Attention focused on task. Ignoring distractions. Persistent. Monitoring own progress.

Source: © Crown copyright [2003] Department for Education and Skills (DfES 2003b).

Effective Lessons and Behaviour for Learning (DfES 2004c) also used the terms 'learning behaviour' and 'behaviour for learning', stating: 'Specific learning behaviours need to be taught, reinforced and reviewed in the same way as any other skill we expect children to master' (DfES 2004c: 5). However, the document did not dwell on what these learning behaviours might be, only providing an indication through some examples in a staff development activity. These were:

- sharing space;
- hands up;
- listening to each other;
- cooperating in a group;
- waiting turn.

(DfES 2004c: 10)

In addition to the examples from government documents outlined above that have explicitly used the terminology 'behaviour for learning' and 'learning behaviour', a number of others have referred to skills and dispositions that it is thought desirable to develop in individuals in order to achieve more holistic outcomes from learning across a range of contexts. These descriptors have not been referred to as learning behaviours but suggest directions and purposes that could support teachers in identifying which particular learning behaviours they need to promote. For example, in DoH/DfES (2004) guidance intended to raise pupil attainment, promote social inclusion and reduce health inequalities it was suggested that the following behaviours contribute to the development of health and wellbeing:

- being an effective and successful learner;
- making and sustaining friendships;
- dealing with and resolving conflict effectively and fairly;
- being able to solve problems with others and alone;
- managing strong feelings such as frustration, anger and anxiety;
- recovering from setbacks and persisting in the face of difficulties;
- working and playing cooperatively;
- competing fairly and losing with dignity and respect for competitors;
- recognising and standing up for your rights and the rights of others;
- understanding and valuing the differences between people and respecting the right of others to have beliefs and values different from your own.

(DoH/DfES 2004: 7)

In contrast to these more social and emotionally relevant behaviours, the DfES White Paper *14–19 Education and Skills* (DfES 2005e), in considering learning for 14–19-year-olds, included a list that seems very much linked to cognitive activity and traditional 'attainment', albeit within the context of proposals for a curriculum that included an applied vocational focus. The White Paper (DfES 2005e: 41) identified the following key thinking and learning skills that can readily be reframed as learning behaviours:

- Enquiry, includes: asking relevant questions, planning and testing conclusions.
- Creative thinking, includes: suggesting hypotheses, imaginatively challenging ideas.
- Information processing, includes: locating and classifying information.
- Reasoning, includes: explaining opinions, actions and decisions, using deduction.
- Evaluation, includes: assessing evidence, judging against criteria and values.

A feature of much of the educational policy developed during the Labour government's period in office (1997–2010) was a more explicit focus on the skills and dispositions necessary for learning. This is illustrated in the publications considered above, but also in the explicit recognition through the SEAL materials (DfES 2005c, 2007b) that there were social, emotional and behavioural skills involved in learning, and the incorporation of a list of what were termed 'thinking skills' in the 1999 version of the National Curriculum (DfEE/QCA 1999a, 1999b). More recently there has been a shift in emphasis, with the most recent incarnation of the National Curriculum (DfE 2014a) reinforcing a more traditional perspective on school learning, based on curriculum subjects and associated bodies of knowledge. It is a shift reflected in the first stated aim of providing pupils 'with an introduction to the essential knowledge that they need to be educated citizens' (DfE 2014a: 6). Yet, despite this overt interest in the knowledge aspect of school-based learning, careful scrutiny of the National Curriculum (DfE 2014a) reveals that there is still some implicit recognition of the social and emotional aspects of learning. For example, it refers to 'engagement with and motivation to study science' (DfE 2014a: 169) and it is also possible to find words such as 'participate' and 'confidently' in the text. In relation to writing (DfE 2014a: 32) and reading (DfE 2014a: 36), pupils are required to 'develop positive attitudes'. The statutory requirements for spoken language also contain a number of points that could be viewed as learning behaviours.

In moving in the direction of a curriculum based on the acquisition of key knowledge, underpinned by a belief in the value of cultural literacy (Hirsch 1987, 2006), it is important to recognise that curricular learning requires the development of a range of cognitive, social, and emotional learning behaviours.

Resilience is referred to in a number of current and recent government documents. As its title suggests, in *Teaching Approaches that Help to Build Resilience to Extremism among Young People* the development of resilience is seen as necessary to protect against extremism (Bonnell *et al.* 2011). Though not presented as a single list in way that it is below, the suggestion from this document (Bonnell *et al.* 2011) is that to build young people's resilience to extremism teachers need to provide opportunities for pupils to:

- explore, understand and celebrate their personal identity;
- use critical thinking skills to appreciate different perspectives;
- foster a positive sense of self;
- develop confidence and a sense of self-worth;
- think critically and independently;

- develop awareness that views and experiences other than their own exist in the world;
- communicate clearly without causing offence to others;
- work collaboratively;
- develop skills for team working and positive interaction, including:
  - the ability to listen to others;
  - the ability to communicate clearly without causing offence to others;
  - the ability to work collaboratively to achieve a shared goal;
  - the ability to negotiate with others;
  - patience when working with others who may have a different level of ability.

Many of these skills and dispositions would seem to be important learning behaviours to develop in all pupils, regardless of whether this would also protect against extremism.

The Education White Paper *Educational Excellence Everywhere* talks of supporting schools 'to develop pupils into well-rounded, confident, happy and resilient individuals to boost their academic attainment, employability and ability to engage in society as active citizens' (DfE 2016b: 124). It provides some insight into the specific learning behaviours that a resilient individual might exhibit, referring to knowing how to persevere, how to bounce back if faced with failure, and how to collaborate with others at work and in their private lives.

Guidance on mental health in schools (DfE 2016c) aims to 'help schools promote positive mental health in their pupils and identify and address those with less severe problems at an early stage and build their resilience' (DfE 2016c: 4). The strengthening of resilience is seen as a key factor in preventing the development of mental health difficulties. Drawing on Rutter (1985), the DfE (2016c) suggests resilience involves these related elements:

- a sense of self-esteem and confidence;
- a belief in one's own self-efficacy and ability to deal with change and adaptation;
- a repertoire of social problem-solving approaches.

The DfE (2016c: 34) suggests that children who are mentally healthy have the ability to:

- develop psychologically, emotionally, intellectually and spiritually;
- initiate, develop and sustain mutually satisfying personal relationships;
- use and enjoy solitude;
- become aware of others and empathise with them;
- play and learn;
- develop a sense of right and wrong; and
- resolve (face) problems and setbacks and learn from them.

The consideration of policy and guidance in this section illustrates that there has been recognition by policy makers over many years that learning behaviours have a relevance to academic learning, as well as social and emotional development. This resonates with the principles underpinning the Behaviour for Learning conceptual framework presented in Chapter 2 of this book. The relatively recent interest (e.g. Bonnell *et al.* 2011; DfE 2016b, 2016c) in promoting resilience is interesting and provides an example of an issue that can sometimes exist with the learning behaviours that are presented in national policy and guidance documents. In seeking to address ongoing and emergent government and societal concerns through such documents, some of the identified learning behaviours are often somewhat aspirational and may not be easily achievable for certain pupils – including some of those who policy makers most hoped to positively influence. The need, when thinking about defining learning behaviours, is to balance what are predominantly the behaviours necessary for the smooth running of the organisation and beneficial to wider social contexts and the behaviours necessary for learning that are intrinsically valuable to the learner. This can be understood through a simple example. A teacher may identify a learning behaviour of 'bringing the right equipment to the lesson'. In itself, this is context specific and relates to the teacher's need. The smooth running of the lesson would be interrupted if multiple pupils did not have the necessary equipment. However, it should be recognised as serving the dual purpose of ensuring class organisation and readiness whilst promoting the development of responsibility and/or independence. Evidence of developing responsibility or independence then becomes the evaluation criteria.

Pre-dating the use of the term by the QCA (2001) and Powell and Tod (2004), White and Mitchell (1994) referred to the following as 'learning behaviours':

- pupil rarely makes contributions of own ideas to lessons;
- pupil expects to be told what to do – not prepared to try and work it out;
- pupil accepts what they hear or read without question;
- pupil repeats the same mistakes time and time again;
- pupil fails to make links with other lessons;
- pupil tells the teacher when they do not understand;
- pupil asks the teacher why they went wrong;
- pupil refers to previous work before asking the teacher for help;
- pupil thinks through their ideas before offering an opinion – and is able to justify what they have said;
- pupil looks for link with other subjects.

White and Mitchell's work was focused on science teaching but the learning behaviours are likely to be relevant to any lesson. An interesting feature of their list, and our reason for highlighting it, is that it introduces the possibility of what we might term 'negative' learning behaviours. Teachers therefore need to be aware that, through both their teaching methods and their behaviour management strategies, they could be promoting unhelpful or unwanted learning behaviours. A salient point too is that, looked at in terms of the success criteria of securing compliance, the first five bullet points on the list are not problematic. Rarely contributing in lessons, for example, does not present a behaviour management problem. It is only when it is evaluated in terms of learning that this behaviour presents as a significant issue to be addressed.

Within his book *Building Learning Power*, Guy Claxton (2002) does not use the term learning behaviour, but he provides a useful language for talking about the skills and dispositions involved in learning, emphasising the importance of the development of 'reciprocity', 'reflectiveness', 'resilience' and 'resourcefulness'. Each of these four broad areas are broken down into individual attributes. His list below (Table 3.3) provides a useful and often insightful view that has resonance with teachers' experiences.

It can be seen from Table 3.3 below that there is an opportunity to replace an emphasis on behaviour management that may emanate from 'off task' behaviour or a pupil's comment of 'It's boring Miss', with a focus on developing 'tolerance of the

Table 3.3 Attributes that underpin 'learning power'

Resilience	*Being ready, willing and able to lock on to learning*
Absorption	Flow – the pleasure of being rapt in learning.
Managing distractions	Recognising and reducing interruptions.
Noticing	Really sensing what is out there.
Perseverance	Stickability, tolerating the feelings of learning.
Resourcefulness	*Being ready, willing and able to learn in different ways*
Questioning	Getting below the surface, playing with situations.
Making links	Seeking coherence, relevance and meaning.
Imagining	Using the mind's eye as a learning theatre.
Reasoning	Thinking rigorously and methodologically.
Capitalising	Making good use of resources.
Reflectiveness	*Being ready, willing and able to become more strategic about learning*
Planning	Working learning out in advance.
Revising	Monitoring and adapting along the way.
Distilling	Drawing out from experience.
Meta-learning	Understanding learning, and yourself as a learner.
Reciprocity	*Being ready, willing and able to learn alone and with others*
Interdependence	Balancing self-reliance and sociability.
Collaboration	The skills of learning with others.
Empathy and Listening	Getting inside others' minds.
Imitation	Picking up others' habits and values.

Source: Claxton 2002.

feeling of learning' (Claxton 2002: 17). It does take self-control and responsibility to stick at something that is perceived as hard and/or boring and individual learners need to be prepared for this particularly as they progress through their schooling. This is of particular significance for improving the educational outcomes for pupils with SEN who, by definition, experience 'a significantly greater difficulty in learning than the majority of others of the same age' (DfE/DoH 2015: 16). For them, a lot of school-based learning may be experienced as difficult and so, arguably, they may actually need more self-control and responsibility than their peers without SEN.

As they go through the education system, pupils will need to learn to sustain effort that is uncomfortable and which clashes with other competing social and personal agendas. No teacher, parent or carer underestimates the challenge of how to foster the kind of effort that is needed for exam preparation and assignment completion. What is apparent however is that such behaviour does not just appear once a pupil has reached the age of 16 and is reminded 'if you do not improve your attitude to work you will not pass your exams'. It needs to be developed over time and with support. It is influenced by the individual's beliefs about the place of effort in success and the differing values placed by their peers and others on 'being clever' and 'trying hard' – as if the two were somehow mutually exclusive. Clearly influences of home, community and culture also have an effect on the individual's disposition towards tolerating the uncomfortableness of sustained effort. Recognition that this is the case and that some pupils will need support to 'tolerate the feelings of learning' does however provide a more productive stance associated with the development of responsibility and self-discipline (Duckworth and Seligman 2006) than viewing lack of effort as purely a behaviour management issue.

Understanding learning behaviours as skills and dispositions

We noted in preceding sections that learning behaviours may take the form of skills and/or dispositions. Claxton (2006) succinctly captures the distinction stating:

> Put crudely, when you have learned a skill, you are able to do something you couldn't do before. But you may not spontaneously make use of that ability when it is relevant in the future, if you do not realise its relevance; or if you still need a degree of support or encouragement that is not available. In common parlance, it is not much use being *able* if you are not also *ready* and *willing*.
>
> (Claxton 2006: 7)

This is a distinction we can illustrate through an example. If you have a pupil in your class who presents as a detached and rather passive learner you might appropriately plan to foster the learning behaviour of asking for help when needed. In order to choose the appropriate strategies you would need to explore whether the pupil's reluctance to ask questions is related to their language and communication skills and/or the willingness to ask the teacher a question. An apparent lack of willingness may reflect, among other things, a lack of confidence or limited interest in the subject.

Words such as 'disposition' or 'attitude', when used by teachers, tend to function as explanatory constructs to describe individual differences in behaviour, such as, 'He's got a bad attitude to school'. Although, as explanations, they are understood and rarely questioned, their definition is often imprecise. However, in the literature definitions vary, as explored by Carr and Caxton (2002). Definitions they cite confirm the difficulty of securing a precise definition, though an agreed understanding about the nature of dispositions is conveyed. Katz (1988: 30, cited in Carr and Claxton 2002: 10) suggests that: 'Dispositions are a very different type of learning from skills and knowledge. They can be thought of as habits of mind, tendencies to respond to situations in certain ways'. Perkins (1995: 275, cited in Carr and Claxton 2002: 10), however, states that 'dispositions … are proclivities that lead us in one direction rather than another, within the freedom of action that we have'.

In his research Claxton (1999) noted that 'learning power' consisted of two interrelated facets: capabilities and dispositions. Capabilities are the skills, strategies and abilities which learning requires or, as Claxton (1999) puts it, the 'toolkit' of learning. These capabilities are necessary but not sufficient to be a good learner. As we know from looking at the differences in classroom behaviour, pupils have to be disposed to learn. That is, they need to be ready and willing to take learning opportunities, as well as able to do so. To return to an earlier point, the National Curriculum requires pupils to 'develop positive attitudes' in relation to reading (DfE 2014a: 36). Carr and Claxton (2002: 10), drawing on Katz (1993), make the point that 'there is a big difference between being able to read and having the disposition to be a reader'. A positive attitude is a disposition and so is different from the ability to read. Similarly, we might make a distinction between having the ability to listen and being disposed to listen. It is a distinction we need to consider when attempting to understand the behaviours pupils currently exhibit and the learning behaviours we are seeking to promote.

A disposition is likely to be more entrenched within the individual's make-up and characteristics as a consequence of their ongoing response to, and attempts to 'make sense' of, their own personal life experiences. In contrast, capability may be more easily influenced through appropriate teaching. It is important and indeed encouraging that the capability and disposition components of learning behaviours interact (Mruk 1999; Miller and Daniel 2007; Marsh and Martin 2011). This provides opportunities for each of these components to influence the other positively and for teachers to decide between strategies.

The challenge for teachers is to promote positive or 'good' learning behaviours. To do this they need to know more about them. One construct thought to be influential in the development of learning dispositions is relationship with self. Terms associated with this relationship include self-concept, self-esteem, self-efficacy and self-confidence. For example, if a pupil is interrupting others in the class we would need to know whether they have not yet developed the *skills* to ignore distractions and/or relate appropriately in a class setting, or whether the behaviour has the purpose of affirming their own thinking about themselves, which might be: 'I don't think I can do this work so I will distract others and neither the teacher nor peers will find out that I cannot do it'. For this reason we need to find out more about the relative contribution of 'skill' and 'will' in the incident so that we can identify the best strategies to use and decide upon how we will evaluate the efficacy of that strategy use.

Within the context of the Behaviour for Learning approach teachers are encouraged to ask themselves:

- Does the learning behaviour I have chosen to develop primarily focus on a skill or disposition?
- What evaluation criteria will I use in evaluating the efficacy of this strategy?

In some cases there may be additional concerns relating to the interdependence of dispositions and capabilities. For example, a teacher may seek to improve a pupil's capability in phonics through intensive practice but in so doing adversely affect the pupil's disposition towards reading for pleasure. The teacher therefore needs to be alert to the possibility that the promotion of one (e.g. capability) may compromise or have a negative impact upon the other (e.g. disposition).

The description of desired traits and behaviours in the above sections have highlighted the need for teachers to promote and develop both the 'skill' and 'will' components of their pupils' learning behaviours. One of the issues arising from this for teachers is how to measure progress in the development of a pupil's learning behaviour in order to provide evidence about the efficacy of their strategy choice. The next section addresses this issue.

Identification of the target learning behaviours

This chapter has considered a range of sources that provide an indication of what some of the behaviours necessary for learning might be, even if these are not specifically described as learning behaviours. The sources were selected for illustrative purposes only to contribute to an understanding of what we might mean when we refer to a 'learning behaviour' within the context of the Behaviour for Learning approach. It is not therefore a case of deciding whether our preference is for Claxton's (2002) list or the QCA (2001) interpretation or any of the others. Rather the priority, and significant shift in thinking, is defining the behaviour(s) that we want to promote. This is, however, in itself, only part of the process. The message that it is important to focus on the behaviour we *do* want is not a new one in the field of behaviour management. We might, for example, want the pupil to remain in their seat, put their hand up rather than call out, or use language appropriate to the classroom. Though it is a desired behaviour that is defined, the focus is still on achieving 'compliance behaviour' rather than developing 'learning behaviour'. The link, therefore, is not always made with learning. Ofsted (2004) identified the problem that while many schools were able to point to improvements in the behaviour of pupils identified as having social, emotional and behavioural difficulties – in terms, for example, of a reduction in referrals to the Senior Leadership Team or in the use of sanctions – few analysed the progress such pupils made in their learning. This, Ofsted (2004) suggested, meant the schools were unable to evaluate the impact of their provision for these pupils.

The Behaviour for Learning approach endorses the importance of focusing on behaviours that the teacher wants to promote, but it encourages reflection on a *purpose* beyond simply stopping unwanted behaviour or promoting behaviours required by policy makers, institutions and practitioners. The purpose is the development of learning behaviour relevant to the individual. It is this purpose that influences the selection of strategies and approaches and evaluation criteria.

Table 3.4 includes examples of real comments that we have either heard from secondary aged pupils during our classroom observations or had reported to us by teachers as concerns. Some, such as homophobic and other discriminatory comments, are likely to warrant a particular school response in line with its relevant policy. Our purpose in presenting them here is to consider the clues the use of these types of comment give the teacher about the possible learning behaviours to target. The teacher may then choose to promote these learning behaviours through relationship with the curriculum, relationship with others and relationship with self, depending on which area they feel will be most appropriate and in which they feel most confident.

Within Table 3.4 there is no attempt to explore the underlying purpose of this behaviour for the pupil concerned or view the behaviour in context. Usually the class and/or subject teacher will know the individual pupil well enough to decide if their comment was a 'one off' immediate reaction or a comment more frequently heard from them. The teacher would have more information at their disposal to form a judgement on which learning behaviour needed to be prioritised for action. Once this decision has been made, strategies can be identified and criteria determined for assessing progress in developing the learning behaviour.

Assessing progress in the development of learning behaviours

Within the Behaviour for Learning approach, the impact of standard practice and any adaptations to standard practice, targeted interventions and/or support is based on the emergence of identified target learning behaviour(s). Even when working at the level of extended use (see Chapter 2) we would be assessing the impact of interventions based on the emergence of learning behaviour(s) that are associated with the relationship area(s) we are seeking to strengthen.

In many cases, the learning behaviours identified from a range of sources in this chapter lack the precision of the measurable competencies that often characterise assessment in

Table 3.4 Linking pupil comments to learning behaviour

Relationship area	What a pupil might say	Learning behaviour to work on?
Self	'Can't do it.'	Self-belief. Self-efficacy. Independence.
	'It's not worth the effort, I'm going to go on reality TV anyway.' 'I don't really understand this bit.'	Planning and prediction. Choices and consequences. Resourcefulness.
	'It wasn't just me doing it.' 'I can't be bothered.'	Perseverance/persistence. Responsibility: ability to admit fault/accept consequences. Motivation.
Others	'He's rubbish at this.'	Use of appropriate language. Respect and empathy.
	'He's gay. I'm not working with him.'	Acceptance and understanding of difference. Self-evaluation of personal prejudice.
	'He doesn't care what I think so there's no point.'	Self-efficacy. Resilience.
	'I don't understand **any** of it.'	Metacognition. Resourcefulness.
	'We're doing it this way.' 'He's special [needs]. Why is he in my group?'	Collaborative working/compromise. Respect and empathy. Self-evaluation of personal prejudice.
Curriculum	'I hate Maths because the teacher's rubbish.'	Express and justify opinions appropriately. Respect and empathy. Attribution style.
	'I haven't done it before so I'm not doing it.'	Flexibility. Openness to change. Take risks in own learning.
	'GCSEs are stupid. I don't need to know any of this.'	Responsibility. Responsiveness to school systems. Predict consequences.

educational contexts. This is understandable if learning behaviours are viewed as unique individual responses to the experiences and opportunities provided in the group settings of the school and the classroom. For example, if we have a pupil in the class who we feel has 'low self-esteem' we may seek to improve this situation. Although we can identify self-esteem as a focus for effort we may not be able to explicitly describe what learning behaviour we expect to see for any one individual. This is simply because how an individual demonstrates their self-esteem will depend on the context and their individual characteristics. One pupil, for example, may express low self-esteem by being loud and disruptive, whereas another may be quiet and reticent. For this reason, we do not seek to pre-define learning behaviours in any rigid way, but we do need to identify and share with the pupil the aspects of their learning they need to develop. We return to the issue of learning behaviours associated with self-esteem in Chapter 6.

Though our rationale for a lack of prescription may be clear, it does raise some issues as educational assessment of behaviour, particularly in the field of SEN, has tended to place emphasis on SMART (specific, manageable, achievable, relevant and timed) (Lloyd and Berthelot 1992) targets. For example, though acknowledging outcomes do not 'always have to be formal or accredited', the current SEND Code of Practice (DfE/DoH 2015: 163) stresses that they 'should be specific, measurable, achievable, realistic and time bound (SMART)'. We are accustomed therefore to embracing the readily measurable and shunning that which is seemingly amorphous or less well defined.

In the case of learning behaviours, we would adopt a view expressed by Muncey and McGinty (1998: 173), who noted that we need 'to measure what is valuable rather than merely value what is easily measurable'. Few would argue that most of the desired learning behaviours described so far in this chapter are valuable, but a possible criticism is that some are difficult to measure. They are not always readily observable behaviours in the same way as behaviours such as 'waiting your turn to speak' or 'bringing the correct equipment to a lesson' are.

If we are to work successfully with the concept of learning behaviours it is necessary to address the need for measurability without reducing them to a checklist of behaviours to be achieved by certain ages. The problem of measuring learning dispositions has been more fully addressed by Carr and Claxton (2002). We have found that mapping the behaviours that you might want to promote in an individual around a more generic learning behaviour such as, for example, 'collaboration' or 'responsibility' is useful for identifying and measuring progress. Such planning allows for personalisation and acknowledges that individuals vary in the way they demonstrate their development and progress towards any particular learning behaviour. An example of such planning is given in Figure 3.1. It extends the reference earlier in this chapter to learning behaviours associated with collaboration.

In looking at Figure 3.1 it can be seen that it only describes a few of the many behaviours that could be identified as contributing to the successful completion of a collaborative task. These behaviours involve a subtle interplay of relationship with curriculum, relationship with others and relationship with self. Conceivably, for example, a pupil approaching a collaborative activity may feel motivated about working with other peers but also motivated to avoid compromising his/her relationship with self. Therefore, if we have a pupil who displays a difficulty working in a group, targeting their social skills may not suffice. It is likely that we will also need to look at the cognitive (e.g. task requirements) and emotional (e.g. pupil's perception of self) components that are contributing to the difficulties experienced in working with others.

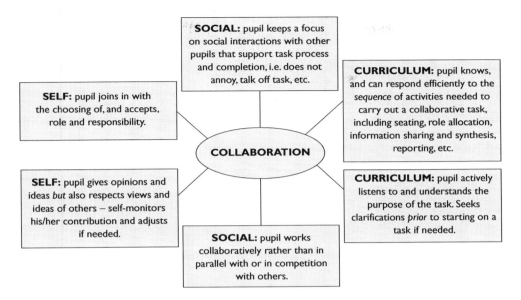

SOCIAL: pupil keeps a focus on social interactions with other pupils that support task process and completion, i.e. does not annoy, talk off task, etc.

CURRICULUM: pupil knows, and can respond efficiently to the *sequence* of activities needed to carry out a collaborative task, including seating, role allocation, information sharing and synthesis, reporting, etc.

SELF: pupil joins in with the choosing of, and accepts, role and responsibility.

COLLABORATION

SELF: pupil gives opinions and ideas *but* also respects views and ideas of others – self-monitors his/her contribution and adjusts if needed.

CURRICULUM: pupil actively listens to and understands the purpose of the task. Seeks clarifications *prior* to starting on a task if needed.

SOCIAL: pupil works collaboratively rather than in parallel with or in competition with others.

Figure 3.1 Identifying learning behaviours.

The range of behaviours shown in Figure 3.1 may be specific to the individual or apply to others in the class. Unlike generic, higher level learning behaviours, such as collaboration, that transcend curriculum areas, age and stages of development, these 'sub' learning behaviours may be different depending on the age and stage of development of the learner and the curriculum area being taught.

In looking at the reciprocal and interacting relationships that characterise 'collaboration' in school settings, it is not surprising that collaborative activities often trigger disruptive behaviour. The main issue is that we cannot assume that pupils of a certain age have developed the necessary learning behaviours needed for learning in small group settings. We can however observe how pupils are responding, identify what behaviours we would like to promote and then seek to operate an appropriate strategy. For a pupil who knows how to behave but has chosen not to, such a strategy might be a standard rule reminder; for example, 'David, remember our class rule, please listen and wait your turn, thanks'. However, in the case of a pupil (or group) who has not yet developed the desired learning behaviour, it may be necessary to directly teach it or provide other learning opportunities for its development.

We would not support a view that seeks to define and prescribe which learning behaviours pupils should achieve at certain ages (e.g. 7, 11 and 14 years) in the form of prescribed competencies. This would lead to yet another norm-referenced, age-related set of targets that socially constructs an underachieving group, with all the connotations of such a group requiring targeted interventions and 'specialist' input. This is at odds with the Behaviour for Learning perspective which sees the class or subject teacher as having the responsibility for developing learning behaviour through all aspects of their teaching.

Though we have purposely set out not to prescribe a specific approach to assessment, it is easy to see how a simple Likert scale could be used if desired to provide baseline and post-intervention data. The example in Table 3.5 uses the same

Table 3.5 An example of a simple recording format for capturing baseline and post-intervention data

Learning behaviour	Frequency currently exhibited					
	Not at all	Rarely	Sometimes	Fairly often	Often	Always
Pupil joins in with the choosing of, and accepts, role allocation and responsibility.						
Pupil gives opinions and ideas *but* also respects views and ideas of others – self monitors his/her contribution and adjusts if needed.						
Additional notes						

headings as the QCA (2001) in *Supporting School Improvement: Emotional and Behavioural Development*.

Alternative headings might be *not present, emerging, developing* and *secure*. This set of headings avoids the problem with a frequency scale (such as the one used in Table 3.5) when focusing on learning behaviours that a pupil does not have to demonstrate often, but are very important in those particular situations where they are required. Unlike the scale now used by many schools in response to the removal of levels from the National Curriculum, we have not included a *Mastery* category as this is difficult to interpret in relation to many learning behaviours. We do, though, think it is useful to have a category that reflects the possibility that the learning behaviour is not currently present within the pupil's repertoire.

In relation to any recording sheet based solely on a predefined list, we would reiterate the point that when assessing the development of learning behaviour it is important to be open to the possibility of other unanticipated indicators of a positive change. If using a recording method such as this, it should not prevent us noticing equally valuable but unpredicted related learning behaviours that are emerging. This is particularly true where the target learning behaviour is a disposition or we are working at the level of extended use (see Chapter 2) and so are using emerging learning behaviours as indicators of positive change in one of the three Behaviour for Learning relationships. Leaving some rows blank and a space at the bottom of the record sheet for additional comments (see Table 3.5) helps to address the issue.

Though the checklist approach may have a practical appeal, the 'look, listen and note' method of assessment that was advocated within the 2007 version of Early Years Foundation Stage guidance (DfES 2007c) offers the advantage of being a very immediate and continuous type of formative assessment. Used within the context of the Behaviour for Learning approach, it would involve the teacher or other adult noting on a sticky note or similar any learning behaviours exhibited by the pupil at any time, in any context, and transferring these to a more permanent record later. For example, the collected notes could be used to inform completion of a table like the one shown in Table 3.5. Though it is usually associated with the Foundation Stage, the 'look, listen and note' approach is likely to have utility across all age ranges in the assessment and promotion of learning behaviour.

Conclusion

This chapter has sought to clarify the origins, purpose and thinking that has underpinned the development and usage of the term 'learning behaviour' within the context of the Behaviour for Learning approach presented in this book.

Many pupils will develop appropriate learning behaviours without any targeted intervention as they travel through phases of their schooling. For these pupils, the teacher's priority will be to provide opportunities through all aspects of their teaching for the development of these learning behaviours. Knowledge of the class as a whole and groups within it will inform judgements about the learning behaviours to develop. Though in-depth information on the nature of learning behaviour is available in this chapter if required, it is likely to be sufficient for the teacher to conceptualise a learning behaviour simply as a skill or disposition it is necessary for a pupil to develop in order to be an effective learner. The lists in this chapter from a variety of sources, as well as the resource list in Appendix 1, are intended to provide the stimulus for thinking about what some of these skills and dispositions might be. Focusing on the development of learning behaviour has implications when considering behaviour management strategies. When we adopt this focus there is a clear rationale for using the positive descriptive feedback and language of positive correction described in Chapters 9 and 10 respectively as, in both cases, the pupil is provided with information on the kinds of behaviours required.

For some pupils a more systematic approach to the development of learning behaviours may be necessary. As we covered in Chapter 2, for some pupils focusing on developing some specific learning behaviours will be sufficient to bring about positive behavioural change. For others it will be necessary to target one or more of the Behaviour for Learning relationships. Particular learning behaviours would be identified to develop that would contribute to a positive change in the relationship. When working at either of these two levels a rigorous approach to observation and assessment is required in order to determine the specific learning behaviours to develop.

The more detailed consideration of the nature of learning behaviour and the methods of evaluating progress discussed in this chapter will be of particular relevance. For example, recognising whether the current behaviour relates to a disposition or undeveloped skills will be important in both identifying the target learning behaviour(s) and determining adaptations to standard practice, targeted interventions and/or support that is necessary. A recording format based on the one presented in Table 3.5 or the 'look, listen and note' approach might be employed as the method of assessing progress in the development of the target learning behaviour and evaluating the impact of adaptations to standard practice, targeted interventions and/or support.

A focus on the development of learning behaviours and the use of them as evaluation criteria is central to the Behaviour for Learning approach and allows teachers to support the development of skills and dispositions that impact on educational and longer term social and personal outcomes. Intrinsic to the Behaviour for Learning approach is recognition of the interdependence of social, emotional and cognitive aspects of learning. When choosing strategies to promote learning behaviours it is necessary for the teacher to recognise and use this interdependence. Within the Behaviour for Learning conceptual framework the term 'relationship' is used to reflect the reciprocity inherent between the pupil and their environment. In the next chapter we explore in depth what we understand by a relationship within the context of the Behaviour for Learning approach. In Chapters 5, 6 and 7 we then look specifically at what we mean by relationship with curriculum, relationship with self and relationship with others.

Chapter 4

Relationships for learning

Introduction

In the previous chapter we explored the concept of 'learning behaviour' and its utility when defining behavioural targets and monitoring and evaluating progress in relation to these. The Behaviour for Learning approach is predicated on the view that the development of learning behaviour is influenced by a set of relationships – relationship with the curriculum and/or task, relationship with others and relationship with self. Respectively, these reflect the cognitive, social and emotional components of learning. In preceding chapters we have tacitly invited acceptance of our application of the term 'relationship' in relation to these. Few teachers, or others working with children and young people, would argue with the view that 'positive relationships with significant others are cornerstones of young people's capacity to function effectively in the social, affective and academic domains' (Martin and Dowson 2009: 351). In this chapter we set out our particular reasons for applying the term 'relationship' and examine what needs to be understood by it when putting the Behaviour for Learning approach into practice. The chapter acts as an introduction to the three following chapters that consider each of the Behaviour for Learning relationships in turn.

Recognition of the importance of relationships

Most schools and their teachers would probably agree with the view that good teacher–pupil relationships are crucial to the development of an effective learning environment. This has been endorsed by research (Hattie 2009). Good teacher–pupil relationships at age 14 are positively associated with progress between Key Stage 3 and Key Stage 4 and consistently negatively associated with engagement in risky behaviours at the ages of 14 and 16 (Chowdry *et al.* 2009). It is also recognised that the quality of peer relationships experienced by pupils in school affects their academic performance, wellbeing and engagement, absenteeism, vulnerability to bullying, behavioural difficulties, drug usage, social difficulties and mental health (McGrath and Noble 2010).

The importance of the teacher–pupil relationship has been acknowledged in sets of professional standards for teachers (TTA 1998; DfES/TTA 2002; TDA 2007; DfE 2011b) produced over the years. The different sets of standards have used slightly different wording. The 1998 set referred to 'positive and productive relationships' (TTA 1998: 7), the 2002 set required 'successful relationships, centred on teaching and learning' (DfES/TTA 2002: 12) and the 2007 set expected teachers to establish 'fair, respectful, trusting, supportive and constructive relationships' with their pupils (TDA 2007:

15). The current set refers to the need for teachers to 'maintain good relationships with pupils' (DfE 2011b: 12). In addition, government guidance on the knowledge, skills and understanding needed by trainees in order to be able to manage pupils' behaviour has stated that: 'Trainees should understand that good relationships are at the heart of good behaviour management. They should be able to form positive, appropriate, professional relationships with their pupils' (TA 2012: 2).

Despite this emphasis on the teacher–pupil relationship, *The Good Childhood Report* (Children's Society 2015) indicates that children in England ranked in the bottom third of countries for liking going to school and 14 out of 15 for their relationships with teachers.

Although the reliability of these findings may be questioned as they were based on pupils' perception of their relationships with their teachers, it is important to note that it is the experience of a relationship for the individual concerned that is likely to influence their behaviour. This prompts the interesting question of whether a relationship can be judged to be 'good' or 'positive' without the perspective of both parties in that relationship. Assessment of a teacher's ability to form 'good' (DfE 2011b: 12) or 'positive, appropriate, professional relationships' (TA 2012: 2) with their pupils would require not only some objective criteria but also reference to pupils' subjective experiences of their relationships with their teachers. In the case of most other human relationships, responsibility for maintaining the relationship rests with both parties, but its quality would only be judged to be positive if both parties experienced it as such.

The focus on the teacher's side of the relationship in documents such as the Teachers' Standards (DfE 2011b) and the guidance on teacher training in relation to behaviour (TA 2012) is understandable given their purpose. Their aim is to support the development of competent practitioners and so they must carry the expectation that teachers relate to pupils in a way that the profession and the public would consider appropriate and professional. It is also reasonable to argue that we might be able to make a fair prediction of what most pupils would experience as a good relationship. However, at the level of the individual pupil experience, notions of 'positive' or 'good' are problematic. Within a relationship 'positive' and 'good' need to be evaluated against both the teacher's criteria and the pupil's experience.

The emergence of national guidance for schools (DfE 2016c) to address concerns (e.g. Children's Society 2015) about children and young people's mental health has encouraged a stronger focus on underlying factors that impact on a pupil's relationship with peers and adults and their ability and willingness to engage with the learning opportunities available to them. The DfE document *Mental Health and Behaviour in Schools* (DfE 2016c) sought to outline for schools 'what they can do and how to support a child or young person whose behaviour – whether it is disruptive, withdrawn, anxious, depressed or otherwise – may be related to an unmet mental health need' (DfE 2016c: 4). The stronger focus on mental health in national guidance places further requirements on teachers to understand how pupil behaviour and wellbeing can be positively influenced through improving the quality of relationships that they build in their classrooms. There are two main strands to the development of a focus on relationships in schools (Roffey 2010). One concerns the influence of a school culture and climate that values, models and fosters positive relationships. The other is the use of curricular opportunities (e.g. DfES 2005c, 2007b) to directly or indirectly teach social, emotional and behavioural skills. Teachers also have a professional responsibility, embedded within past and professional standards (e.g. TDA 2007; DfE 2011b), to build relationships with pupils that support progress and learning. The school has a role in providing the contexts, the curriculum and the conditions that allow pupils to learn how to develop and improve their skills in forming relationships with others.

As the preceding paragraphs have outlined, there is awareness of the role of relationships in school learning. Research (e.g. McGrath and Noble 2010) has highlighted the importance of both pupil teacher–relationships (Chowdry et al. 2009) and peer relationships (McGrath and Noble 2010), linking these to both immediate and longer term outcomes. The direct reference to the teacher–pupil relationship in present and past sets of professional standards (TTA 1998; DfES/TTA 2002; TDA 2007; DfE 2011b) demonstrates that competence in forming and maintaining relationships with pupils is viewed as important by policy makers. Though we understand the reasons for their use in documents of this type, terms such as 'good relationships' (DfE 2011b: 12) or 'positive, appropriate, professional relationships' (TA 2012: 2) place emphasis on the teacher's input and assume a predictable resulting experience of the relationship for the pupil. Government guidance on mental health and behaviour (DfE 2016c) recognises that there may be psychological factors influencing a pupil's relationship with peers and adults and their ability and willingness to engage with the learning opportunities available to them. This is coupled with optimism that actions at a variety of levels by the school can exert a positive influence that improves these relationships and reduces barriers to learning. There is implied recognition that, by the school or individual staff doing something different or additional, the pupil's relationship with adults, peers and curricular learning can be improved.

What is distinctive about 'relationships for learning'?

The policy links between behaviour, mental health and wellbeing, along with emphasis on building positive relationships in school explored in the previous section of the chapter endorse the thinking behind the Behaviour for Learning conceptual framework. However, the Behaviour for Learning approach is unusual in both its identification of three relationships for learning and the way in which these are conceptualised.

As Chapter 2 outlined, the Behaviour for Learning approach seeks to develop learning behaviour through an emphasis on building positive relationships in the following three areas:

- relationship with self;
- relationship with the curriculum;
- relationship with others.

The focus on these three relationships allows teachers to plan for, and address, the social, emotional and cognitive aspects of learning that impact on pupil behaviour in the classroom. The use of the term 'relationship' may initially seem odd, particularly when applied to the 'curriculum' and 'self'. Its use is intended to draw parallels with other relationships with which teachers and others will be familiar and capitalise on a general understanding of what is meant by a relationship. For example, we tend to think of a relationship as being created between two people. Whether the relationship is experienced as positive or not will be influenced by what both people contribute. Importantly, actions by one person can change how the relationship is experienced by the other – this may be for better or worse. If instead of thinking of a relationship between two people, we think of a pupil having a relationship with the curriculum we can apply a similar line of thinking. The pupil is contributing something to the relationship in terms of skills and dispositions. The teacher's curricular and pedagogic knowledge means they can work via the curriculum to develop the skills and dispositions in the pupil that will positively influence the relationship.

The personal knowledge we all have of building, sustaining and ending relationships in our everyday life is helpful in developing a working understanding of why we use the term relationship within the Behaviour for Learning approach. However, we need to recognise that the school setting offers a different environment for relationship building. In school, individual pupils are required to 'do'/learn what is required of them, within a group setting along with their peers. Individual pupils need to adapt to the group setting but also retain their sense of identity and self-worth. It is important for them to develop and sustain the personal resilience needed to cope with their academic and social learning. Within our own personal relationships the purposes and contexts are varied and we tend to act and judge them very differently. Within school settings the purpose for the teacher is judged against the extent to which the relationships support pupil learning.

When thinking about the implications for practice of a focus on relationships for learning there are number of key points to recognise:

- As with all other relationships, interactions are *reciprocal* and *dynamic* – you do something, the pupil responds, you react to that response and so on.
- Each person in the relationship *experiences* and *interprets* what the other is saying/doing. As the professional in the relationship, you have to try to understand how pupils are experiencing and interpreting your behaviour.
- Relationships, like all communication, have *cognitive*, *emotional* and *social* components. What another person says to us influences how we feel and what we do next. This interdependence of social, emotional and cognitive factors allows us to build and repair relationships in a variety of ways. This might be through reasoning, showing empathy and understanding or sharing interests and activities.
- Your professional role in developing relationships in the classroom differs from your personal relationships in that you have to keep the focus on relationships that support *learning* in the group setting of the classroom.
- You are aiming, within the relationships, to develop *learning behaviours* and reduce/eliminate behaviours that prevent the class or individuals from taking part in, and benefitting from, the learning opportunities of the school/class.
- Relationship building takes place in the *public arena* and as such you are expected to remain calm and model appropriate relationship behaviour.
- Individual pupils are conscious of the public nature of the classroom and their behaviour may communicate to you that they seek to *preserve their individuality* (e.g. through non-compliance) or to gain the attention and *approval of their peers* (e.g. by chatting, messing about).
- We cannot know what another individual is thinking and so we tend to use their *behaviour* as a guide to how the relationship is progressing.
- Within the classroom the speed and interdependence of cognitive, emotional and social interactions make for an ever-changing situation. Timely action is needed if situations are to be de-escalated.
- Teachers need to develop an awareness of how their *personal style* of communicating impacts on their professional responsibility for 'building relationships for learning'.

The role of schools and their teachers in developing relationships for learning

Teacher involvement in the building of positive relationships with pupils is of paramount importance given that the behavioural difficulties exhibited by some pupils can be attributed to factors outside the school context. Some pupils may bring to school a view that much of school learning is boring and irrelevant to their lives. They may also have developed a perception of themselves that leads us to attribute their behavioural problems to low self-esteem or a lack of self-efficacy. Some have developed relationship styles with others that are characterised by being very loud, aggressive, demanding of attention or withdrawn. Such behaviours can become habitual if they have developed over time and are reinforced by others influential in a pupil's life. These descriptions reflect, respectively, what the pupil is contributing to their relationship with the curriculum, to their relationship with self and to their relationship with others.

The school offers a very different environment from that experienced by some pupils outside it. For example:

- The school offers structure, stability, purpose, behavioural expectations, rewards and sanctions that apply to *all* pupils.
- Teachers are expected to model communications that convey respect, fairness, interest and concern for their pupils.
- Teachers are trained to promote learning, achievement and appropriate social behaviour in their pupils.

Within this setting pupils will be actively forming relationships. The pupil brings with them a whole range of skills and dispositions that contribute to the quality of their relationship with the curriculum, with self and with others, but actions on the part of individual teachers and the school, through its systems, processes and culture, also make a powerful contribution. This is a perspective that reflects Rutter et al.'s (1979) seminal research in the school effectiveness field that found that differences in the behaviour and attainment of pupils in the schools studied could not be explained by different intakes or levels of social disadvantage but were attributable to factors within the school.

Our use of a conceptual framework based on three relationships is not intended to deny the complexity of classroom interactions (Hayles 1991). It merely aims to provide a workable model that allows teachers to plan for, and address, the social, emotional and cognitive aspects of learning that impact on pupil behaviour in the classroom. Teachers and their pupils all have personal needs against which they can judge 'how things are going in the classroom'. Although within the Behaviour for Learning conceptual framework (Chapter 2, Figure 2.1) relationships with self, the curriculum and others are presented separately, in reality, of course, the they are not experienced by the pupil in a compartmentalised way. The aim for the teacher is to maintain a *balance* between these three relationships so that an understandable emphasis on subject teaching and academic attainment does not damage the pupil's belief about themselves or their relationships with their peers and teacher. For example, an overly competitive culture and a lack of consideration for how individual pupils are experiencing this in the classroom can lead to an imbalance between the three learning relationships.

For teachers and schools seeking to determine how best to improve relationship building in school there remain inherent difficulties in securing an evidence base that can be used to guide and develop practice. Personal qualities identified as desirable for relationship building are often referred to as 'soft skills' that include competences in areas such as communication, empathy, conflict resolution, active listening and creative problem solving. As we have stressed previously in this chapter, the effectiveness of any relationship cannot be unilaterally judged but is dependent on the *subjective* experiences and interpretations of the individual participants. A relationship style that is effective for most of a class might still be perceived and experienced as negative by an individual member of that class. For example, Hayes (2012: 108) suggests pupils like teachers who are firm but fair but 'are ill at ease with teachers who hector, complain, agitate or fulminate'. This may not be true for the pupil who is regularly, or perceives themselves to be, on the receiving end of firmness. The pupil may even interpret and experience this as hectoring, complaining, agitation or fulmination. The pupil may be wrong in their appraisal and the firmness may be a justifiable response to their behaviour but if we focus on the relationship we would have to conclude that it is not experienced as positive by at least one of the two parties involved.

How might you as a teacher experience the three Behaviour for Learning relationships?

The moment you walk into your classroom or greet the pupils waiting outside, you are actively involved in building *'relationships for learning'*. You will always need to be mindful of how what you are saying and doing is being received and interpreted by your pupils.

Although in this book our use of the Behaviour for Learning conceptual framework is primarily focused on children and young people in educational settings, our understanding of the nature and influence of the three relationships can be enhanced by first reflecting upon how such a model relates to the teacher. Consider the following scenario:

Scenario 4.1

You have had a difficult day. Year 7B has constantly interrupted your teaching and you feel you have not got through the lesson content. As a beginning teacher, you are worried that this may reflect badly on your progress when your tutor or school-based mentor is observing. Jason refused to do any work and publicly announced to the class, 'It's boring, Miss'. You are worried that he is winning the 'battle' by reducing your authority and showing no respect to you as a teacher.

As the teacher you may have a number of responses to this. You might respond to this experience by saying to your colleagues, 'I have just had 7B … they are impossible … I've done my best with them but it is hopeless … how are we supposed to raise standards with pupils like that?' However, on reflection (see Table 4.1) you may start thinking about the relationships that underpin *your* learning in this context as a way of helping you to plan for your next session with Year 7B.

When thinking in this way you will be able to see how the three relationships that underpin your own learning behaviour in the classroom are interlinked and how these

Table 4.1 Reflection on relationships and your learning behaviour

	What am I thinking?	How am I feeling?	What the class might be experiencing and learning
Relationship with self	I must not let the class see that I am worried; I must not fail – I want them to like and respect me.	A bit fearful, anxious at times; but more confident when things are going well.	Some hesitancy in delivery of lesson content; lack of clarity of expectation regarding outcomes to be achieved; signs of anxiety and vulnerability, e.g. changes in pitch and tone, irritation, over-reaction to minor interruptions.
Relationship with others	I must keep the pupils on task – I mustn't lose control. I wish my mentor/tutor could have seen things when they were going well.	Excited at putting my lesson plan into action with the class; but worried that it may go wrong and they will be noisy.	Your positive behaviour management statements; your emphasis on control; your concern with how other adults see you – with possibly less emphasis on pupil learning needs; your worry and vulnerability.
Relationship with curriculum	I must 'get through' these topics during this lesson; I want them (the class) to be interested and enjoy the lesson.	Panicky because time is moving on and not all the objectives for the lesson have been met.	A well-prepared lesson with emphasis on what must be learned; lack of flexibility; hurrying up of responses and questions; irritation with diversions; requirement for conformity seems more important than whether pupils are interested and involved.

are seen or experienced by individuals in your class. It follows that when you left the classroom saying, 'Class 7B are impossible', the class may have been thinking, on the basis of what they experienced, that 'Miss/Sir is not really interested in us unless we give her/him the answers s/he wants and let her/him get on with what s/he wants to teach us.'

In reality, of course, you *are* interested in your pupils' learning and many of the class members are interested in the subject you are teaching. There is a risk that these very positive features are being affected by your own relationships: with yourself, with your class and other staff, and with your subject.

Consider, for example, the message you give to individuals in your class when you start the lesson by asking them to write down the learning objectives. Are you doing this because it is deemed to be 'good practice' and because you are expected to do this by Ofsted and others, or are you seeking to build a reciprocal relationship with the pupil and give them clear information about what you expect their contribution to be to this relationship? Recognition of the need for a reciprocal relationship based on clear expectations is reflected in Sir Alan Steer's (quoted in Wilby 2008: 2) question from a 2008 interview:

> how often (in your schooling) did anybody sit you down and say: 'this is why we are doing this topic and this is what you have to do to be successful.' And when you got your work back did anyone say: 'if you'd done it this way you'd have got an A not a D.'

Exploring issues of reciprocity and interdependence

Table 4.1 sought to focus your attention on the impact that your own relationship with self, the curriculum and others has on pupil learning through the column 'what the class might be experiencing and learning'. Whatever else changes in your think- ing and teaching as you progress through your training and career, impact on pupil learning is, after all, your main area of concern. By keeping a focus on the two-way aspect of the relationships you are building with your class, you will become more skilled at anticipating and evaluating what they are experiencing and learning from your behaviour. Just as with the pupils, what you as the teacher bring to each of the three relationships is likely to be unique. However, for the purposes of an example, it is possible to suggest some generic components applicable to most teachers (see Figure 4.1).

The links between the three relationships should be evident. If the lesson is not going to plan and behaviour is deteriorating then one option might be to change the activity or teaching approach. The teacher's possession of knowledge of altern- ative activities or ways of teaching the topic will determine whether they can do this, but factors related to their relationship with self may influence their readiness to take this course of action. However, we should also recognise that the teacher's awareness that they possess good knowledge of alternative activities or ways of teaching the topic may positively impact, for example, on their confidence as they know that if things are not going well they have an alternative course of action available. Reflective Exercise 4.1 requires you to think about these sorts of points, inviting you to think about what you bring to each of the Behaviour for Learning relationships.

Relationship with self
Examples:

- Confidence
- Resilience
- Self-efficacy
- Self worth
- Attribution style and locus of control

Relationship with others
Examples:

- Willingness and ability to form and maintain appropriate relationships with children and young people;
- Willingness and ability to form and maintain appropriate relationships with colleagues and other adults.

Effectiveness of teaching

Relationship with the curriculum
Examples:

- Knowledge of curriculum and pedagogy;
- Repertoire of teaching approaches;
- Enthusiasm for subject;
- Knowledge of classroom and group management approaches.

Figure 4.1 The teacher's Behaviour for Learning triangle.

Reflective Exercise 4.1

Think about two lessons you have taught recently, one of which you thought went well and one with which you were not so happy. In both cases think about:

- How were your relationships with yourself, with others, and with the curriculum 'experienced' by individuals in your class(es)? What learning behaviours do you think were being fostered in your pupils?
- Which of the three relationships (with self, with others and with the curriculum) had the greatest influence, positive and negative, on *your* behaviour?
- Which of the three relationships do you feel it would be easiest to improve in order to achieve better learning behaviour in your classroom?

You will notice from Table 4.1 and your self-reflection, that two key messages from this chapter are reinforced:

- learning relationships are *reciprocal*;
- they are influenced by context and can be *changed* and *improved*.

These points are of considerable importance and we can explore them by reflecting on the nature of a typical conversation between two people. When we engage in conversation we are aware of the two-way nature of the activity and consequently keep a focus on the *purpose* of our activity which is to 'communicate' with the other person. During the process of conversation we constantly monitor the other person's response to check their engagement and understanding and adjust our responses accordingly. As a teacher, the underlying need to build a relationship and promote communication with individual pupils is paramount but in the context of the classroom the 'conversation' is typically from one person (i.e. the teacher) to a group. The close monitoring and instant adjustment that characterise one-to-one conversations and ongoing relationships are not possible and so it is important to keep in mind the question: 'What do I want the individual pupil to learn and what information can I use to monitor his/her response?'.

This may appear obvious but under pressure and within constraints of time it is often more feasible to just prioritise the monitoring of: 'How well am I doing in terms of class control and getting through what I planned to get through?'.

There are of course also reciprocal influences involved within and between the relationships outlined in the Behaviour for Learning conceptual framework. In looking at the planning diagram (Figure 4.2), it can be seen that any intervention made to improve pupils' learning behaviour through an emphasis on *one* of the three areas (curriculum, self and others) is likely to have an effect on the other *two*. Thus, if we choose to focus on the cognitive areas of development through an emphasis on adjustment to curriculum

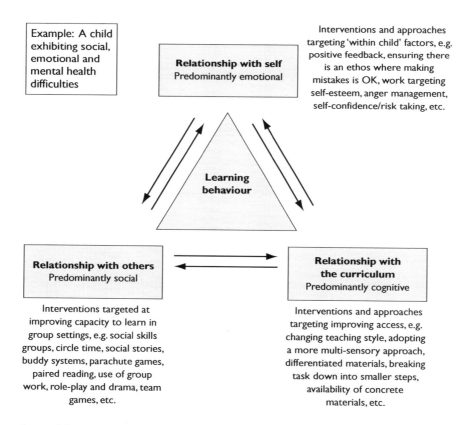

Figure 4.2 How commonly used classroom strategies link both learning and behaviour through the Behaviour for Learning conceptual framework.

delivery and assessment and, as a consequence, the pupil achieves greater understanding of the lesson, then his/her relationship with self is likely to improve – at least for the short term. This could additionally lead to improved social behaviour with others in the classroom in the form of, for example, less 'messing about' and reduced irritation to peers and the teacher.

The importance of the *interdependence* of the three relationships within the Behaviour for Learning approach is that:

1   It acknowledges that the promotion of effective learning behaviours in school contexts involves attention to the social, emotional and cognitive factors that influence relationships.
2   It affords teachers *flexibility* in allowing them to select a particular relationship to strengthen that best matches their current level of confidence and competence. As an example, a beginning teacher may feel more comfortable concentrating on curriculum planning and delivery as a way of improving individual learning behaviour, whereas a more experienced teacher, who feels at ease with curriculum content and requirements and is familiar with the pupils in their class, is likely to feel confident in tackling some of the more challenging social and emotional relationships involved in classroom learning. In selecting strategies for teaching, the notions of *choice* and *feasibility* allow for ongoing professional development and address the guilt that teachers may experience in an era in which prescriptions for 'good practice' through paper and electronic formats are in abundance (Ellis *et al.* 2008).
3   It reflects the dynamic and changing nature of pupil responses to teaching across contexts and conditions and acknowledges that the teacher is involved in the process of responding to the often complex needs of individual pupils and therefore has to make multiple decisions in non-routine situations (Haggarty 2002). Conceived of in this way, teaching is viewed as an intellectually challenging task in which teachers continually examine and refine their practice.

Conclusion

The importance of positive teacher–pupil and peer relationships is well recognised; recent guidance (DfE 2016c), focused on children's mental health, reflects awareness that pupils' curricular learning and the relationships they are able to form and maintain with peers and adults is affected by their emotional health and wellbeing. Through this chapter we hope to have encouraged readers to move beyond acceptance that fostering positive relationships is important, to consider the way in which relationships are conceptualised within the Behaviour for Learning approach.

The language of relationships can be helpful in reflecting the reciprocal and dynamic interactions that underpin teaching and learning in classrooms. It reinforces that idea that pupils are not passive recipients of *either* the behaviour management *or* the learning strategies used in their classroom. For example, praising pupils is an effective strategy for many but for some pupils they may interpret the praise they are given as patronising or publicly embarrassing. The pupil who receives and interprets the teacher's praise as possibly inappropriate, patronising or sarcastic will react differently to the pupil who perceives it to be appropriate, rewarding and genuine. How a pupil experiences and interprets a strategy has important implications for improving *both* pupil behaviour and learning. For one pupil their behaviour and learning is likely to be influenced positively;

for the other pupil the teacher has to rethink their choice of strategy. By using the term 'relationship' the Behaviour for Learning approach explicitly acknowledges that simply to tackle behaviour problems by continually focussing on *either* the teacher's behaviour and strategy use *or* the pupil's repertoire of behaviours will not always bring about the desired change in behaviour. It is the dynamic and reciprocal *relationships* that the pupil develops with themselves (relationship with self), their teachers and peers (relationship with others) and the curriculum (relationship with the curriculum) that need to be understood and improved as a route for effecting changes in behaviour.

In terms of supporting national priorities related to mental health, wellbeing and resilience, a focus on the three relationships enables schools to recognise both individual sources of influence and how these can be used in combination. Schools can offer individuals experiences and opportunities that have the potential to impact positively on their mental health, wellbeing and resilience through:

- a relationship with the curriculum that allows individuals to attain, achieve and experience feelings of success and a sense of competence;
- a group setting that affords individuals opportunities to model, form and experience positive social relationships and associated feelings of belonging and being valued;
- a safe and controlled setting in which the individual can experience but make positive use of failure, develop independence and experience an increasing sense of autonomy.

The three chapters that follow consider each of the three Behaviour for Learning relationships in more detail.

Chapter 5

Relationship with the curriculum

Introduction

In the previous chapter we outlined that a core feature of the Behaviour for Learning conceptual framework is that it places emphasis on three interdependent relationships that underpin learning and behaviour in school contexts. This endorses the view that learning and behaviour are influenced by the quality of relationships that characterise classroom interactions. This chapter explores the Behaviour for Learning approach to building and maintaining a positive relationship with the curriculum. It discusses how focusing on improving a pupil's relationship with the curriculum will simultaneously improve their behaviour and achievement.

As we noted in the previous chapter, although the Behaviour for Learning conceptual framework (Chapter 2, Figure 2.1) presents relationship with self, with the curriculum and with others as three distinct elements, in reality the pupil does not experience these separately. Ongoing research linked to learning, wellbeing and behaviour in schools (e.g. Roffey et al. 2017) and research into how neuroscience can inform practice in the classroom (e.g. Hohnen and Murphy 2016) is consistent with the Behaviour for Learning approach's explicit recognition that cognitive, social and emotional factors are interdependent and have to be considered when planning to improve classroom learning and behaviour.

Teacher training and professional development is mainly focused towards the development of expertise in promoting subject attainment and achievement. This is undertaken within a national context of political agendas, curriculum requirements, professional standards and inspections. The next section takes a brief look at the current National Curriculum and professional standards for teachers.

Relationship with the curriculum: The national context

The school curriculum comprises all learning and other experiences that each school plans for its pupils. The National Curriculum forms one part of the school curriculum. Teachers in state maintained schools in England are required to follow the National Curriculum.

It is noteworthy, given more recent emphasis in policy on mental health and preparation for future employability, that Section 78 of the 2002 Education Act requires maintained schools[1] to offer:

a balanced and broadly based curriculum which –
(a) promotes the spiritual, moral, cultural, mental and physical development of pupils at the school and of society, and

(b) prepares pupils at the school for the opportunities, responsibilities and experiences of later life.

(Education Act 2002: 53)

Government guidance on the National Curriculum states:

3.1 The national curriculum provides pupils with an introduction to the essential knowledge they need to be educated citizens. It introduces pupils to the best that has been thought and said; and helps engender an appreciation of human creativity and achievement.
3.2 The national curriculum is just one element in the education of every child. There is time and space in the school day and in each week, term and year to range beyond the national curriculum specifications.

(DfE 2014a: 6)

It is important to recognise in point 3.1 that what constitutes the 'essential knowledge they need to be educated citizens' is interpretable. It can be judged against what the government has decided to assess or what educators feel represents essential knowledge in their subject area. Point 3.2 affords the option for time to be allocated to what might be perceived as perhaps broader and more engaging topics for pupils.

A good knowledge of the subject curriculum and associated assessment approaches will allow teachers to offer subject choices and clusters of subjects best suited to individual pupils' strengths and preferences.

Point 3.2 above affords schools a degree of flexibility in the overall curriculum that they offer. However, because schools and their pupils are judged against national age-related expectations, there may be a limit on how feasible it is for schools to take advantage of this flexibility, particularly those that are struggling to reach floor standards (DfE 2017c, 2017d). This might limit the extent to which schools can 'afford time and space' to move 'beyond the national curriculum specifications' (DfE 2014a: 6) and provide wider learning opportunities. This could restrict professional creativity in addressing motivational issues for some pupils, in particular those with learning or behavioural difficulties.

Given the history of the National Curriculum (see Roberts 2017), it is likely that it will change during a pupil's time at school. Although teachers will be required to comply to national curriculum guidance, there is currently optimism that in terms of teaching methods there is a move away from professional prescription towards professional freedom (Fordham 2017).

Teachers' Standards

Teachers' Standards 'define the minimum level of practice expected of trainees and teachers from the point of being awarded qualified teacher status (QTS)' (DfE 2011b: 3). The main requirements from the published standards that provide the context for this chapter are in the Preamble and Part One ('Teaching'). The Preamble states: 'Teachers make the education of their pupils *their first* concern, and are accountable for achieving the highest possible standards in work and conduct …' (DfE 2011b: 10, emphasis added). Part One stipulates that teachers must: 'Set high expectations which *inspire, motivate* and challenge pupils' (DfE 2011b: 10, emphasis added) and 'Manage behaviour effectively to ensure a *good* and safe *learning* environment' (DfE 2011b: 12, emphasis added).

The National Curriculum (DfE 2014b), Teachers' Standards (DfE 2011b) and national accountability and assessment procedures provide a context that influences the nature and purpose of a relationship with the curriculum. It can be helpful to consider that both teachers' and pupils' relationship with the curriculum is brokered within this context. It is important for teachers, seeking to improve their pupils' behaviour, to consider how their own relationship with the curriculum is being experienced by individuals in the class group.

The next section explores the Behaviour for Learning approach to building and maintaining a positive relationship with the curriculum for pupils in the group setting of the classroom.

Relationship with the curriculum

Behaviour for Learning definition

The dynamic interactions that make up the reciprocal activity between the learner and the school curriculum/subject. This involves being able and willing to access, process and respond to the information available through the curriculum.

Is it valid for pupils to have a 'relationship' with the curriculum?

The rationale for viewing pupils as having a 'relationship' with the curriculum (brokered mainly by teachers) is that the pupil is not a passive recipient of what the teacher delivers. The teacher does something, the pupil responds, the teacher reacts to that response and so on. In this way, the interaction is reciprocal and dynamic – a key characteristic of a relationship.

What are the advantages of the relationship approach?

Policy aimed at improving both 'educational outputs' and pupil behaviour tend to focus on what *the teacher* needs to do in order to improve pupil learning. The problem with this teacher–led approach is that learning requires a dynamic interaction between the teacher and the pupil.

The notion of reciprocity engenders a way of thinking by teachers about what an individual's behaviour is communicating. Thinking in this way can lead to a more effective response from the teacher. For example, when approaching behaviour from the perspective that it is influenced by the pupil's relationship with the curriculum it is important to identify when and why pupils have 'disengaged' from the curriculum and use strategies which work on building the relationship.

Characteristics of a relationship with the curriculum

Before trying to work on developing and improving a pupil's relationship with the curriculum, it is helpful to look at that relationship in a little more detail and consider its key characteristics. It is also important to consider how a pupil's experience of their relationship with the curriculum differs from that of their teachers. Table 5.1 seeks to inform these differing perspectives.

Table 5.1 Teacher and pupil judgement of a good relationship with the curriculum

	Teacher's view	Pupil's view
Purpose of relationship with the curriculum	Teachers have a professional responsibility to improve attainment and foster motivation for curriculum learning. Pupils and teachers are assessed by both ongoing progress and prescribed age-related learning outcomes. The teacher's relationship with the curriculum is necessarily influenced by this.	This will vary between pupils. For some it has no clear purpose that they have thought about – school attendance is compulsory and being in school involves curriculum learning; it is just accepted. Within this group some pupils might be primarily motivated by social relationships and/or engaging in play/sporting activities in school breaks. For some pupils it may have a clear purpose, e.g. to be recognised for their achievement and/or gain qualifications that are required for higher education or employment. Some pupils have a genuine interest in certain subject areas and engage in curriculum learning to pursue these interests further.
Does it vary between individuals?	For the majority of teachers, their relationship with the curriculum is likely to be strongly influenced by their professional responsibility to improve National Curriculum attainment. There are likely to be some variations in the extent to which individual teachers value and relate to the curriculum they are prescribed to teach. For some, motivation derives from their own enjoyment of the subject and their desire to engender the same interest and enjoyment in their pupils. For others, motivation stems from their interest in the social and interpersonal development of pupils through the curriculum.	It is personal and consequently varies depending on the individual and their family, cultural influences, the school environment and community demographics.

Does it change over time?	A teacher's relationship with their subject area is likely to be relatively stable; their relationship with teaching may be enhanced or damaged by experience of teaching and demands of the profession.	It can change with context – younger children experience very different approaches to learning (e.g. more child initiated) that subsequently change as they progress through schooling. For older pupils, the purpose of the relationship may be experienced as increasingly focused towards summative outcomes. Although the majority of pupils adapt to these changes, some develop a negative relationship with the curriculum.
What is expected from the relationship?	The teacher may judge the relationship to be 'good' because the pupil achieves the learning objective.	While success is a very important factor in the pupil's judgement, they may also judge their relationship with the curriculum against social and emotional criteria. For example, some pupils might perceive they have a 'good' relationship with areas of the curriculum because they like the teacher or the group they are with. Others might enjoy the structure and security inherent in engaging in some prescribed curriculum tasks within the safe setting of their classroom.
How might the relationship be judged?	The teacher may seek to judge the relationship against: • time-framed, predetermined indicators, such as end of Key Stage assessments; and/or • formative assessment criteria that may identify changes in pupil attitude and rate of progress.	The pupil may be judging the relationship on a more day-to-day basis against the extent to which it has been beneficial to them in a variety of ways such as personal success, peer involvement, the attraction of positive teacher attention or avoidance of negative teacher attention.

Table 5.1 illustrates that there are likely to be differing perceptions about the nature and purpose of the relationship with the curriculum from the teacher's and from pupils' viewpoints. Generally, if pupils' perspectives are aligned with those of their teachers, the pupils will find it much easier to develop a successful relationship (as is the case in relationships between individuals). Pupils whose views on the curriculum significantly differ from those of their teachers are more likely to struggle to develop a positive relationship with the curriculum.

It is useful for us to try to understand the relationship from the pupil's point of view. If, for example, a pupil's main reason for coming to school is social (see Chapter 7) they are more likely to prioritise peer approval and collaborative learning activities over publicly given teacher acknowledgements for curricular achievements and endeavours. For some individual pupils, the purpose of getting sent out of class for misbehaviour (i.e. sanctioned) could be that they experience both peer approval (for 'mucking about') and also get to spend some time with a member of the pastoral team who gives individual attention, listens to their perspective and works with them to plan personalised 'solutions'.

While teachers may be able to judge a pupil's attitudes to the curriculum through observations, actively seeking the pupil's views not only allows teachers to understand their attitudes, but has the added benefit that it supports the pupil's need to have some involvement and sense of control over their day-to-day experience of learning. This is consistent with Murphy *et al.*'s (2010: 4) view in their report for the Wellcome Trust that: 'Children should be consulted about decisions that are being made about their learning and assessment. They provide a legitimate, important perspective which can serve to improve policy and practice.' A similar theme is reflected in Pavlou and Kambouri's (2007: 283) view that: 'An important element in the process of facilitating and supporting pupils' learning is adults' willingness to really listen to pupils and understand them.' They clarify that in using the term 'understanding pupils', they 'do not simply refer to acquiring knowledge about their developmental level, abilities and learning strategies but more importantly to responding to their motivations, prior conceptions and attitudes towards the subject they are learning' (Pavlou and Kambouri 2007: 283, citing Cochran *et al.* 1993).

What are the differences between a relationship with the curriculum and a relationship with individuals?

As with all models, it is important to understand their limitations in order to use them effectively. There are clear differences between a relationship with the curriculum and other types of relationships experienced in our everyday lives, which teachers need to bear in mind.

These differences include:

- The pupil does not typically choose which subject areas they are required to relate to.
- Within school contexts pupils are not permitted to end the relationship even if it is experienced negatively by them.
- The teacher brokers the relationship with a number of individuals in a group setting.
- The relationship typically has a predefined purpose (usually curriculum learning) with assessed outcomes.

When considering the construct of a 'relationship' we will now look at how we might further understand, from the literature, what it might mean in practice to have a positive relationship with the curriculum. In extrapolating relevant information, we have focused on the following three questions to address whole-class, individual and teacher perspectives:

1   How do we tend to monitor pupils' relationship with the curriculum?
2   How can learning behaviours or a cluster of learning behaviours be used as indicators of the pupils' relationship with the curriculum?
3   How might teachers improve their pupils' relationship with the curriculum through their teaching?

The next three sections of this chapter address these questions.

Monitoring relationships with the curriculum

When we adopt the approach of thinking in terms of a *relationship* with the curriculum it becomes necessary to consider how to assess the nature and quality of the relationship currently and determine ways of monitoring any changes. This section looks at how we tend to judge pupils' relationships with the curriculum using 'time on task'.

Time on task

The EPPI-Centre review of research (Powell and Tod 2004) noted that the majority of studies linked to behaviour in school contexts were concerned with pupils both starting and staying on task. Swinson (2017) also identified a number of studies from the 1990s that used on task behaviour as a measure to evaluate Canter and Canter's (1992) Assertive Discipline approach.

It is important to grasp how we might judge a relationship with a construct such as the 'curriculum'. Using 'time on task' as a measure is understandable given that 'on task' is easily observable behaviour that can be used by teachers and their assessors to scan the response of the whole class. It clearly has some validity as a measure in that securing some form of 'joint attention to task' between the teacher and the pupil is frequently a necessary requirement for learning to take place.

Almost inevitably, a focus on 'on task' behaviour generates a concern to identify and reduce 'off task' behaviour. This has a number of limitations both in terms of assessing learning and classroom behaviour:

*   There is an assumption that being off task is negatively correlated with learning. This may not necessarily be the case. For example, a pupil who might be observed to be off task may be thinking about the task, looking away from the task to generate a question or looking around for non-verbal cues from the teacher or peers that s/he is 'responding as intended', etc.
*   The pupil may have developed a range of strategies in the form of general 'busyness' that create the *impression* of being on task. However, they are not engaged in the intended learning.
*   The pupil is prepared to persist with the activity in order to secure an external reward (e.g. a good grade, approval). This does not necessarily lead to feeling

positive about the subject and could lead to the development of a negative relationship with the curriculum.

- Constructing 'off task' behaviour as a behavioural difficulty denies the fact that most children, like most adults, will go off task from time to time and re-focus their attention if necessary.
- The identification that a pupil is off task gives little indication of the reason; neither does it inform strategy selection. Table 5.2 gives some examples of the many reasons for off task behaviour and illustrates the many different strategies that may need to be employed.

Table 5.2 Off task behaviour: possible explanations, theoretical underpinning and strategy use

Reason for off task behaviour	Theory	Possible strategy to address
Child is getting more attention by being off task.	Behavioural	Reward on task behaviour.
Child thinks he is unable to do the task.	Cognitive	Encourage child to reappraise the task, identify what parts of the task he can do, etc.
Child fears failure.	Affective	Strategies to build 'self-esteem' – offer increased adult or peer support. Depersonalise failure.
'He has a brother who is just the same.'	Social/environmental	Possibly nurture group and/or work with parents/guardians/carers.
Perhaps the child has a biologically influenced difficulty (e.g. dyslexia, autism, ADHD, SLCN)	Biological	Assess behaviour over a range of contexts. Consult with SENCO and parents/guardians with view to medical referral or multi-agency assessment.
Child not ready to work independently.	Developmental	Set more suitable learning challenges – if feasible allocate additional teaching assistant/learning support assistant support.

Source: adapted from Powell and Tod 2004.

The utility of using 'time on task' to monitor relationships with the curriculum

Due to the limitations mentioned above, on task behaviour cannot in itself suffice as a measure of how well pupils are *learning*. A possible exception might be individual pupils whose behaviour is of particular concern. It can be useful to observe/collate information on 'on and off task' behaviours across a range of conditions (e.g. one to one, in a small group, undertaking self-initiated activities in different subjects) in order to find out more about the possible reasons for an individual's behavioural differences in class. However, in general, if we want to make a judgement about the quality and efficacy of pupils' relationship with the curriculum then we need to move towards observing their learning behaviours.

How can learning behaviours or a cluster of learning behaviours be used as indicators of the pupil's relationship with the curriculum?

As discussed above, it is clear that using solely 'time on task' as the means of assessing behaviour and learning is not satisfactory. The Behaviour for Learning approach offers an alternative method. Outcomes are judged against clear criteria, which is normally the extent to which the targeted learning behaviours have improved and/or developed.

In Chapter 3 we identified a range of learning behaviours from the literature and policy documents which have been considered necessary in order to improve attainment in schools. The behaviours we have selected are also compatible with current thinking about the need to recognise the cognitive, social and emotional aspects of learning (e.g. DfES 2005c, 2007b; Weare 2015; DfE 2016c; Roffey *et al.* 2017). Curriculum learning behaviours reflect a *disposition*, or personal willingness, to take part in the lesson and the organisational and planning *skills* needed to access the necessary information within a group setting.

In using these descriptions of learning behaviours from the literature and policy documents for illustrative purposes, we do not necessarily endorse them as either definitive or essential. They are not intended to be prescriptive or exhaustive and teachers are unlikely to be considering all of these all the time. A long list of learning behaviours is also provided in Appendix 1 to support teachers in choosing those most relevant to their subject and setting. The key point is that teachers can consider their own practice and choose what learning behaviours they would like to develop in their pupils rather than what behaviours they would like to reduce or eliminate. These behaviours can be used by teachers to assess the strength of the relationship between a pupil and the curriculum, as an alternative to 'time on task'. Reflective Exercise 5.1 provides an opportunity to practise selecting learning behaviours using the list contained in Table 5.3.

Reflective Exercise 5.1

Think about a pupil in your class who is presenting behaviour that is having a negative impact on his/her learning. Circle or highlight those behaviours in Table 5.3 that you consider it would be necessary to develop and/or strengthen.

Looking at the overall pattern of learning behaviours that you have selected for development do you consider that the pupil's behaviour in class can be attributed to:

1   Mainly cognitive aspects of learning?
2   Mainly social aspects of learning?
3   Mainly emotional aspects of learning?

Reflective Exercise 5.1 illustrates that by looking at the overall pattern and/or cluster of learning behaviours it is possible to find out more about how the pupil is relating to the curriculum.

In summary, the Behaviour for Learning approach asks teachers to judge relationships on what learning behaviours are seen, rather than simply focusing on the time on task as a measure of pupil engagement.

It is a helpful idea to remember that in human relationships the strength of that relationship is not judged on the amount of time spent together, but rather on the *quality* of

Table 5.3 Examples from literature and policy documents of learning behaviours associated with curriculum learning in classrooms

Cognitive	Social	Emotional
Brings necessary equipment to class.	Can convey to teacher that help or clarification is needed.	Willing to relate to and respond to teacher.
Has strategies for focusing and refocusing attention.	Can work productively with others.	Willing to focus attention.
Has the language and working memory space to process information.	Is able to control need for peer attention.	Can persist and tolerate difficult feelings associated with learning new things.
Has grasped what is required for task completion.	Willing and able to share equipment.	Is willing to recognise what parts of the task can be done independently.
Monitors own understanding of the task	Actively listens to teacher instructions	Has an interest in school work; has positive attitudes towards the subject
Knows time frame involved for task and plans accordingly.	Knows when it is appropriate to speak.	Has awareness of what s/he can do and where help is needed.
Plans and works out learning in advance.	Knows and responds to class rules for asking questions.	Has positive beliefs about self-efficacy.
Able to plan sequence of actions needed within the task.	Can wait for teacher attention	Is willing to respond to feedback
Has strategies for reminding self of task instructions	Willing and able to follow class rules relating to behaviours that direct attention away from curriculum learning such as using mobile phones, interrupting others, getting out of seat, etc.	Is willing to work independently.
Can select where to apply attention.	Uses respectful language to teacher and peers.	Is able to tolerate and use critical feedback.
Actively seeks coherence, relevance and meaning within the given task.	Can time and ask questions appropriately.	Is willing to refer to previous work before asking the teacher for help.
Actively looks for links with other subjects or similar activity.	Can work with peers to review own and others' work.	Is willing to consider a change of strategy.
Can plan and prioritise actions that meet task requirements.	Can identify and communicate positive aspects of peers' work.	Is willing to take some responsibility for own learning.
Is able to check own work against teacher's expectations.	Takes appropriate responsibility for part in any group activity – positive or negative.	Is able to complete work without destroying it.

the interaction between people. The next section looks at how these learning behaviours can be developed to improve pupils' relationship with the curriculum.

How might teachers improve their pupils' relationship with the curriculum through their teaching?

We now move on to look at teaching strategies for the development of learning behaviours that will bring about an improvement in pupils' relationship with the curriculum and thus their behavioural and academic outcomes. These strategies might be focused towards mainly cognitive, mainly social or mainly emotional factors depending on the nature of the pupil's observed learning behaviours (or lack of) and their teacher's understanding of the purpose the existing behaviours are serving for the pupil.

Instead of the teacher thinking about how best to reduce and/or stop an individual pupil's disruptive behaviour so that everyone can get on with their learning, they would work through the three questions below:

1   What learning behaviours would I expect to see from the class for this curriculum activity? How will my lesson support the development of these behaviours?
2   Why are some individuals not exhibiting these behaviours? What purpose is the pupil's current behaviour serving for them?
3   Based on the answers above, what strategies do I feel able to employ in order to bring about an improvement in behaviours that support curriculum learning?

The thinking behind this approach is that, rather than simply demanding that pupils exhibit the required learning behaviours (i.e. repeatedly telling pupils to do x or y), the teacher should reflect on 'why' they are not exhibiting these and use that knowledge to consider the best strategy to use. To understand why a pupil is not exhibiting a certain learning behaviour the teacher needs to consider what is negative about the pupil's relationship with the curriculum as that will be driving the behavioural response to it.

We now move on to consider how we might bring about a positive change in the pupil's relationship with the curriculum, particularly for those pupils who might be described as being 'poorly motivated'.

Motivation

The importance of motivating pupils is covered in the Teachers' Standards (DfE 2011b). As we noted previously, the teacher is required to: 'Set high expectations which inspire, motivate and challenge pupils' (DfE 2011b: 10). The Standards also specify the need to 'manage classes effectively, using approaches which are appropriate to pupils' needs in order to involve and motivate them' (DfE 2011b: 12)

Motivation is a core driver for any relationship and is particularly important for developing and maintaining pupils' relationship with the curriculum. We tend to think of motivation as a force or energy, internal to the individual, that we can influence through judicious combinations of extrinsic tangible reward and positive feedback (see Chapter 9). The overall trajectory within and between school phases is to reduce pupils' reliance on external motivators (extrinsic) and encourage the development of internal motivation (intrinsic) so that individuals become self-initiated, self-controlled independent learners.

Lack of motivation to form a relationship with the curriculum

It is important to note that teachers need to develop motivation specifically for developing a relationship with the curriculum, not simply increase motivation in general. Pupils with behavioural difficulties do not necessarily lack motivation; they just do not have the motivation to do the things that are asked of them in the classroom. Some pupils have plenty of motivation for developing strategies to avoid work, annoy their teachers and chatter to friends. Outside of a school context most pupils will be motivated by something. Some of these activities may be viewed as positive, such as hobbies and pastimes; others, such as vandalism and other forms of socially unacceptable activity, may not be seen as positive.

Motivational drivers

In looking at motivation for learning in school, McLean (2009) proposed a model based on needs that all humans share. Although different models and descriptors are used, there is consensus that as humans we all strive to achieve, to belong and be valued and to have a sense of autonomy. Table 5.4 depicts how this model of motivation can help us to understand what is driving pupils to behave in the way they do in the classroom.

Table 5.4 How a needs-led approach can support an understanding of pupils' behaviour in the classroom

Needs that drive pupil responses	Resulting positive classroom behaviour	Resulting 'defensive/negative' classroom behaviour
To achieve and succeed	Will be motivated by experiencing success and achievement. Will be responsive to curriculum requirements and be willing to develop and maintain appropriate learning behaviours.	Will put energy into behaviours that s/he decides are personal achievements, i.e. successfully avoids his/her lack of competence being made public by refusing to start work.
To belong and be valued by others	Works within the group setting so as not to annoy peers or teacher and may secure recognition and praise from others.	Seeks to be recognised within the group by 'being a laugh', 'playing up', 'winding up the teacher', etc. (Would this pupil have an identity if s/he was not known as a behaviour problem?)
To have some control and independence	Accepts some responsibility for own learning and progress. Monitors own work and reflects against given criteria for success, asks questions, suggests different/better ways of doing the task, offers suggestions and ideas.	Motivation for control and independence directed towards non-compliance/refusal ('No one tells *me* what to do', 'I'm *not* doing it, it's boring', etc.). Seeks to control pace and content of lesson through his/her own behaviour.

Source: adapted from Ellis and Tod 2015: 59.

Through reference to McLean's (2009) model teachers can try to see which human need is not being met by the pupil's relationship with the curriculum and use that information to plan what to do to bring about change. Case Study 5.1 and the discussion that follows looks at how the 'needs-led' model might work in practice.

Case Study 5.1

Zoe, a Year 4 pupil, regularly disrupts lessons. She often calls out when instructions are being given by the teacher. When required to work independently or as part of a group she will often call across the room to peers or to the teacher. She also tries to engage others on her table in conversation and if they ignore her she persists, becoming louder or reaching over and tapping them to gain their attention. Sometimes she shuffles on her chair, gradually moving it further away from the desk until one of her peers notices and remarks or an adult intervenes. When the teacher verbally directs Zoe back to the task she usually initially complies but then disrupts again with a different behaviour.

The teacher needs to find out why Zoe is misbehaving. This requires the teacher to draw on their knowledge of Zoe and the pattern and type of her behaviour to decide which basic need is driving the behaviour. Key questions might be:

• Is it to meet a social need?
• Is it because she cannot succeed at the curriculum task and seeks success by doing something she experiences that she is 'good at' such as 'messing around'?
• Is she seeking some control by irritating the teacher, interrupting others' learning and refusing to be controlled by the school's behaviour management strategies in the classroom?

It is reasonable to conclude that Zoe has motivation to achieve all three of the human needs described in Table 5.4. From Zoe's perspective, her behaviour is rational even if it is difficult for her teachers to see why she risks getting into trouble and incurring sanctions. Zoe's behaviours reflect those that we associate with being motivated. For example, Coles and Werquin (2005, cited in Lord and O'Donnell 2005: 4) describe learner motivation as: 'a range of an individual's behaviours in terms of the way they personally initiate things, determine the way things are done, do something with intensity and show perseverance to see something through to an end.' Zoe does have those motivational behaviours. The issue for Zoe (and her teacher) is that the direction for her motivational behaviour is primarily outwards towards others.

The aim for Zoe in developing increased motivation for curriculum learning is to increase her competence in curriculum learning so that she can experience more success. This will involve *both* adjustments to the curriculum and the use of strategies that redirect her motivational behaviours towards curriculum learning. This will involve using the existing range of curriculum teaching strategies employed in class but, if feasible and appropriate for the task, building in more cooperative and/or collaborative learning opportunities. Table 5.5 sets out some learning behaviours that the teacher might select from as the focus for development when attempting to build Zoe's motivation for curriculum learning. These are divided into those which are skills and those related to the pupil's disposition.

Table 5.5 Learning behaviour related to motivation

Skills	Will/disposition
• Can self-direct attention in order to locate any personal interest in task or subject.	• Is willing to search for interest in task or subject.
• Clarifies the purpose, process and outcome criteria of the task.	• Is willing to initiate.
• Retains a focus on the purpose and outcome criteria.	• Is willing to persevere.
• Pursues coherence, relevance and meaning.	• Is willing to direct attention to the task in hand.
• Responsive to teacher's motivational strategies, e.g. asks questions, volunteers information.	• Is responsive and will ask questions and volunteer information.
• Is able to get started on tasks without delay.	• Is willing to get started without complaining or moaning about having to get on with learning.
• Can plan steps in task needed for successful completion.	• Gets started without using delaying tactics.
• Is able to persist and tolerate the uncomfortableness of effort.	• Is willing to imagine what it feels like to succeed.
• Has strategies for sustaining attention and effort.	
• Can sustain a focus on positive outcomes.	

The learning behaviours in Table 5.5 have been selected as they are the behaviours that would be expected from a pupil we would describe as being motivated. The development of these learning behaviours for all pupils, particularly those who are described as poorly motivated, supports them to make a purposeful and active contribution to their relationship with the curriculum. A range of strategies for developing motivation are included in Appendix 2.

Another important contribution to research and practice that aims to address motivational issues of learning is growth mindset.

Growth mindset

'Growth mindset' is a term used by American psychologist Carol Dweck (2006) to describe an individual's belief that intelligence can develop, and that effort leads to success. Dweck contrasts this with a fixed mindset where pupils believe their basic abilities and their intelligence are just fixed traits. Dweck's research in this area has influenced educational practice the US and increasingly in the UK. An internet search reveals many schools that refer to growth mindset on their websites. For teachers, the implication of Dweck's (2006) work is that they need to promote a growth mindset in their pupils through all aspects of their teaching but particularly through different forms of feedback. In adopting this approach, the teacher would seek to reinforce a belief that performance at school and in life can be changed by our attitude, and particularly by how we cope with setbacks.

Dweck has produced a range of compelling evidence (e.g. Mueller and Dweck 1998) to support her claims regarding the benefits of a growth mindset. Some debate continues in online opinion pieces (e.g. Kohn 2015; Alexander 2017; Chivers 2017; Young

2017) regarding these claims and some attempts (e.g. Li and Bates 2017) to replicate the findings of Dweck's previous growth mindset studies have been unsuccessful. In research published by the Education Endowment Foundation, Rienzo et al. (2015) found that pupils who had been involved in the growth mindset workshops run as part of their research made an average of two additional months' progress in English and Maths but concluded that 'these findings were not statistically significant, meaning that we cannot be confident that they did not occur by chance' (Rienzo et al. 2015: 3). They went no further than suggesting that 'the finding for English was close to statistical significance, and this suggests evidence of promise' (Rienzo et al. 2015: 3). More recently Sisk et al. (2018: 569), based on two meta-analyses, concluded that 'the "mindset revolution" might not be the best avenue to reshape our education system' but that disadvantaged students who are academically at risk might benefit from mindset interventions. As Dweck's (2006) concept of growth mindset gains traction in UK schools it is likely that more research will emerge in relation to both its interpretation and impact on underachievement in UK classrooms.

From a Behaviour for Learning perspective, in order to have a dynamic *relationship* with the curriculum pupils need to actively contribute to their curriculum learning. Dweck's (2006) work places emphasis on specific aspects of this contribution, focusing attention on the set of self-beliefs pupils hold regarding the progress and success they can experience in their learning.

The importance attached by Dweck to a growth mindset links with a point we develop in the next chapter regarding the way in which pupils attribute setbacks and difficulties in their learning and progress. As an example, if a pupil is asked why they have done badly in a Science test they may say, '*I can't do Science, I'm not clever enough*'. For this pupil the causal attribution they have made relates to something that they believe is fixed, permanent and not in their control. In this case the pupil is unlikely to try to bring about change by increasing the effort they are making or developing any resilience to the setbacks experienced during the learning process. If, however, the pupil had said, '*I didn't do that well this time but I know that I do better when I spend more time on things and put more effort in*', their causal attribution relates to internal, temporary, specific and controllable factors. In this case the pupil believes that they have some control over their learning and they can use this to make more effort and progress in their Science.

Dweck (2006) highlights that this is also true in relation to our successes. This has particular implications for how we feed back to pupils regarding their learning. Mueller and Dweck (1998: 50) suggested that 'when students succeed, attention and approbation should be directed at their efforts or work strategies'. They recommend that 'children should be praised for the process of their work (e.g. focusing on the task, using effective strategies, or persisting on challenging problems) rather than for the end product and the ability that produced it' (Mueller and Dweck 1998: 50). To illustrate this through a simple example, it is the difference between saying 'well done, that looks like it took a lot of effort' and 'well done, you're so clever'. The former attributes the success to the effort made. Effort is presented as changeable and controllable; confronted with a more difficult task success might be achieved by putting in more effort. In contrast, the latter form of praise ('you're so clever') implies that a fixed or stable trait (i.e. cleverness/intelligence) has determined the success. In Mueller and Dweck's (1998) experiments, children with a fixed mindset who had been praised for their intelligence were less persistent after failure and their performances deteriorated (Ziegler and Stoeger

2010). An important phrase in the Mueller and Dweck (1998: 50) quote above is 'when students succeed'. In an interview reported in an article (Gross-Loh 2016) in *The Atlantic* magazine, Dweck expressed concern that some teachers had grasped the central idea regarding the need to focus on the effort when providing feedback but not the importance of showing 'how effort created learning progress or success'. It is important that the feedback takes the form of 'process praise', focusing on the learning process and conveying how effort, good strategies and effective use of resources lead to better learning.

Focusing on the development of a growth mindset potentially allows individual pupils to experience success in relation to the progress they make and to have some control over their own learning outcomes. This is important for the development of self-efficacy (see Chapter 6).

The preceding section on motivation sought to engender a way of thinking about what a pupil's behaviour is communicating to us about their motivation for relating to the curriculum. We now move on briefly to two enduring, but more recently highlighted, areas crucial for improving learning outcomes, particularly for pupils who are considered to be underachieving. These are working memory, and communication that supports the development of metacognition.

Working memory: Issues of cognitive load

We have included coverage of cognitive load because of the crucial role memory plays in learning. Increased awareness of this role can help us to understand why some pupils experience behaviour and learning difficulties in the classroom. Recent recommendations (DfE 2016d) for the core content of initial teacher training (ITT) identified cognitive load as an important factor affecting pupils' education that trainees should be introduced to.

Working memory can be defined as the memory system where small amounts of information are stored for a very short period of time (Peterson and Peterson 1959). Due to this limited capacity it is important to transfer relevant material to long term memory. This is the memory system where large amounts of information are stored. There is no known limit to how much stored information can be processed at one time (CESE 2017). In long term storage, elements of information are organised according to how they will be used. This allows information to become more meaningful for the individual and to be retrieved and linked to other information. In seeking to discuss issues of capacity, the term 'cognitive load' is used to refer to 'the total amount of mental energy imposed on working memory at an instance in time' (Cooper 1998).

In relation to school learning, it is important that attention is given to issues of working memory capacity. If pupils are overloaded with information in their working memory and cannot efficiently transfer relevant elements to long term storage their learning is adversely affected. For some the overload of information will be experienced emotionally through anxiety and frustration. These emotions may be expressed in a variety of ways ranging from withdrawn behaviour through to verbal or physical aggression.

A recently published Australian report (CESE 2017) provides relevant guidance on ways in which teachers can seek to manage cognitive load through a range of approaches. We have drawn on this to provide the recommendations below.

- *Provide worked examples*
  A 'worked example' is a problem that has already been solved for the learner, with every step fully explained and clearly shown. This reduces the burden on working memory and provides the pupil with an external, more permanent reference point. As pupils progress with their learning and become more proficient in the subject, teachers would seek to reduce reliance on worked examples. Increasingly pupils would be exposed to problem-solving tasks that require greater independence.
- *Reduce unnecessary or redundant information*
  Pupils do not learn effectively when their limited working memory is directed to unnecessary or redundant information (e.g. if the task is explained and then they are given unnecessary examples or additional unnecessary verbal guidance). It is important to remember this when pupils are learning new information or if cognitive overload appears to be contributing to difficulties in learning and behaviour. This does not preclude the teacher from using additional information to support learning, providing the pupil experiences this as supportive rather than as overload. For example, for some pupils a diagram and print conveying the *same* information may contribute to cognitive overload as they try to process the two forms separately; for others it could provide externalised support that facilitates the processing of new information from working memory to long term storage.
- *Reduce the need for 'split attention'*
  When pupils are confronted with multiple sources of visual information, such as diagrams, labels and explanatory text, this potentially adds to the cognitive load. This is because the pupil is required to hold *multiple* sources of information in their working memory at the same time and to mentally integrate them. This split attention effect can be reduced by integrating the different sources of information. For example, a teacher could incorporate labels into diagrams rather than placing them in the text below or to one side.
- *Use visual and auditory modes of communication*
  Using visual and auditory modes of communication can decrease extraneous load on working memory. There is evidence to suggest that working memory can be subdivided into auditory and visual streams (Baddeley and Hitch 1974; Baddeley 1983, 2002). The implication of this is that presenting information using both auditory and visual working memory can increase working memory capacity (Penney 1989). For example, when using a diagram and text to explain a concept, it may be beneficial to pupils if the written text is communicated verbally.

While acknowledging that cognitive load is a factor affecting pupils' learning, it is important to recognise that much of the research has focussed on mathematics, science and technology. Considerably less research has been carried out to investigate 'whether cognitive load theory is effective for teaching in less technical, or more creative subject areas – such as literature, history, art and other humanities subjects' (CESE 2017: 8). Research on cognitive load has offered support to the view that guided direct instruction represents a more efficient form of teaching than discovery learning (i.e. problem solving, authentic learning tasks, etc.). Both guided instruction and forms of 'discovery' learning have been endorsed at times within educational policy and guidance. Whether guided instruction or 'discovery' learning is endorsed by national policy, the relative merits of these teaching approaches are likely to remain a subject of debate among different subject teachers and teachers who work in different school phases. However, cognitive load theory has enduring implications for teachers in terms of how learning can be improved and intended learning outcomes reliably assessed.

The original development and application of cognitive load theory outlined above was in a context of teaching specific subject knowledge that required new information to be processed effectively and transferred to long term memory. Our experience from talking with teachers would suggest that the term 'cognitive load' is being applied more widely in schools as a general explanation for pupils experiencing a feeling of overload resulting from the amount of information they are holding in their heads. Although this represents an interpretation from the original theory (e.g. Sweller 1988, 2010), it clearly has utility in focusing teachers' attention on the amount of information they are expecting the pupil to process and the extent to which this information is 'new' to the individual concerned. Consider, for example, the following instruction: 'Thomas, put that away in your tray now. You need to move quietly to the mat, sit on the floor, face the front and listen to the story.' This contains a lot of individual elements that need to be understood and acted upon in a relatively short timeframe. The cognitive load experienced by Thomas will depend on the extent to which he has automated these behaviours as this determines the amount of conscious attention he needs to devote to these within the timeframe given. We can also speculate that Thomas's difficulties may be exacerbated if, as well as processing this information, he is also dealing with intrusive thoughts relating to ongoing social and emotional issues.

Communication

Assuming pupils are motivated to develop a relationship with the curriculum, it is crucial that they are guided towards what they are required to do in order to experience the benefit of success from engaging in this relationship. Personal relationships characteristically rely on this type of brokering through language. If we apply this principle to a relationship with the curriculum it requires the pupil to both understand communication *from* the curriculum (via the teacher) and be able to express their feelings, thoughts and responses in return.

Language development and competence, both oral and written, play a significant role in pupils' relationship with the curriculum. Teachers will be aware that for some of their pupils this may be a specific barrier, limiting the extent to which they can respond to some of the language-based strategies for relating effectively to the curriculum.

Improving communication through effective teacher–pupil dialogue

In this section we are concerned particularly with developing the *reciprocal* communication necessary for engagement with, and response to, the curriculum. Table 5.6 illustrates some of the effective strategies teachers use when brokering pupils' reciprocal relationship with the curriculum.

Many of the strategies and terms included in Table 5.6 are likely to be familiar to teachers. The strategies seek to identify and respond to features of an effective relationship by offering pupils the opportunity to:

- experience reciprocity through connecting with the subject knowledge and the teacher's thinking;
- make mistakes and learn from them;

- have their contribution acknowledged and valued;
- be able to say what they could contribute and be supported to contribute further;
- become actively engaged and involved;
- have some control over their contribution to, and experience of, the relationship.

Table 5.6 Characteristics of effective teacher-initiated dialogue

Characteristic	*Description (adapted from Kyriacou and Issitt 2008)*
Transformative listening	This relies on teachers listening to pupils' contributions in a manner that conveys that there is a genuine 'meeting of minds' and that the teacher is willing to change their own thinking in the light of what the pupil has said. Teachers may be able to do this through asking a question they do not know the answer to, responding to pupils' suggestions, asking for feedback from the whole class or asking a pupil to explain their ideas to the class.
Encouraging high-quality pupil dialogue	There is a need for teachers to be accepting towards pupils' contributions, to encourage pupils to develop their contributions further and, indeed, to allow the direction of a lesson to follow the pupils' contributions. Being accepting towards pupils' contributions may enhance the quality of the discourse, but may also create a tension for the teacher in wanting to direct pupils' attention towards acceptable strategies within the particular curriculum area.
Inclusive teaching	Teachers can convey to *all* pupils, regardless of ability, that their contribution is equally valued and that all pupils in the class are engaged and have their answers taken seriously. More able pupils are more likely to engage in productive exchanges. Their answers may be taken more seriously by the teacher and consequently they may be 'given the floor' more frequently and, cumulatively over the lesson, for longer periods of time than their peers. Inclusive teaching involves strategies to make sure less able pupils also feel able to contribute and have their ideas taken seriously, so that they do not develop a self-identity as non-participants.
Scaffolding	Scaffolding is when the teacher provides support (or scaffolds) to help pupils' learning. This enables pupils to build on prior knowledge. Different types of scaffolding can be used by teachers. For example, the teacher may focus pupils' attention during a class discussion on key features and merits of particular strategies suggested by other class members for solving a challenging problem. Another example is to discuss with pupils a deliberate mistake in order to identify and clarify the nature of the mistake, thereby focusing pupil attention on the key features of investigating the particular problem at hand.

Improving communication through modelling

When seeking to address behavioural issues that are adversely affecting a pupil's relationship with the curriculum it is worth thinking about the following questions: 'Do they understand *what* I am telling them to do?' and 'Do they know *how* to do that?'. For some pupils it can be helpful to model any new learning behaviours that the teacher is trying to develop. This chapter has been consistent in acknowledging that, as building a relationship with the curriculum involves communication between the learner and the teacher, it is important that the pupil has clear information about what the teacher is expecting them to learn and how that learning will be evaluated.

The Education Endowment Foundation (EEF) provides an example of how a Maths teacher might model what is expected from the pupil at the start of a problem-solving task. Although the example is within the context of a Maths lesson, these steps could also usefully be applied to the development of curriculum related learning behaviours (e.g. getting started on a task, planning steps to completion, persisting, making an effort, setting targets) as part of any class teaching. The EEF (2017) suggests that while demonstrating the solving of a problem, a teacher could model to pupils how to plan, monitor and evaluate their thinking by reflecting aloud on a series of questions. These could include:

- What is this problem asking?
- Have I ever seen a mathematical problem like this before? What approaches to solving it did I try and were they successful?
- Could I represent the problem with a diagram or graph?
- Does my answer make sense when I re-read the problem?
- Do I need help or more information to solve this problem? Where could I find this?

(EEF 2017: 21)

The example taken from EEF (2017) was located within a section on metacognition. We have used their example here, in our section on communication, as it supports pupils to develop increased awareness of what their approach to learning needs to involve.

It takes time for pupils to imitate, internalise and independently apply strategies that improve their self-directed and independent learning. It would seem important that teachers model core curriculum learning behaviours across subjects and phases as a way of communicating to pupils what specifically is required, and allow them to practise this.

The preceding sections have sought to promote an enhanced understanding of the reciprocal nature of the relationship between the pupil and the curriculum. Our selection of material from the plethora available on teaching and learning has sought to encourage teachers to think more explicitly about how their pupils are experiencing curricular learning in the classroom. We are conscious that we have not included many other effective teaching strategies that teachers use in their day-to-day teaching and in which they have developed expertise. These will undoubtedly improve their pupils' relationship with the curriculum. Table 5.7 illustrates how a number of recognised effective approaches to teaching can be located within the relationship model that underpins the Behaviour for Learning approach.

Higgins *et al.* (2007) also identify a number of necessary conditions for the approaches in Table 5.7. These conditions, taken directly from Higgins *et al.*'s (2017: 17) report, are listed in Table 5.8 together with a Behaviour for Learning comment.

The Behaviour for Learning comments in Tables 5.7 and 5.8 emphasise how whole-class teaching approaches can be personalised by explicitly focusing on how some

Table 5.7 Effective approaches to develop pupils' learning capabilities

Effective approach (Higgins et al. 2007: 2)	Behaviour for Learning comment
Structured tasks that focus on specific metacognitive strategies in the context of the lesson/subject.	Personal relationships break down because individuals do not know what they are required to do. Skills and strategies have to be learned and – in the case of the curriculum – taught.
Capacity in lessons for more explicit transactions between the learner and the teacher concerning the purpose of the activity.	The relationship needs to be explicitly and openly monitored so that both sides know the other's perspective. Personal relationships sometimes break down on the basis of one partner saying, 'How am I expected to know what you wanted me to do?'.
Small group interactions promoting the articulation of the use of strategies during teaching.	Pupils need safe places with peers to identify and practise strategies appropriate for their age group – and at times to learn about peers' successful strategies.
Mechanisms built into the task to promote the checking of mutual understanding of the goals by peers and with the teacher.	This allows the pupil a role in the relationship and opportunity to check what is wanted and what they can give, etc. – e.g. 'Am I doing OK? … you could help by …'.
Enhanced opportunities for the learner to receive diagnostic feedback linked directly to the task.	The pupil needs information on *how* to make things better and not just to be told that what they had done was not good enough.

individual pupils may be experiencing these approaches. By adjusting the approach and/ or the supportive conditions the teacher can positively influence the pupil's relationship with the curriculum.

Conclusion

In this chapter we have explored the nature and purpose of a relationship with the curriculum. The importance of a relationship model is encapsulated by Sarah Lawrence-Lightfoot, a professor of education at Harvard's Graduate School of Education. She considers that 'one thing all good teachers have in common is they regard themselves as thinkers, as existing in the world of ideas' and suggests that for teachers 'the currency is ideas – but ideas as conveyed through relationships' (Moyers 1989: 159).

The Behaviour for Learning approach builds on the recognition that teachers' area of expertise is in promoting curriculum learning. Teachers are trained to develop their expertise in improving academic achievement and reducing discrepancy within and between schools in terms of educational outcomes. Consequently, in addressing behavioural issues the first consideration for teachers should be the potential to bring about positive change by improving their pupils' relationship with the curriculum. The teacher has a number of variables within their control related to the curriculum that can

Table 5.8 Supportive conditions for effective approaches

Conditions (Higgins et al. 2007: 17)	Behaviour for Learning comment
The teacher needs to have an alignment of a good understanding of learning, in terms of the subject and the context (what European educationalists would call 'didactics').	The teacher needs to understand where the difficult subject parts are for pupils and identify which of these can be learned through more 'fun' activities and collaborative work, and which parts have to be taught more formally.
There is also the need for the teacher to have access to concrete tools and strategies to guide the learner and enhance opportunities for feedback.	The teacher needs to know that for some pupils 'more of the same' will not suffice. Pupils may need to develop their repertoire of strategies so that they do not persist with those that have proven unsuccessful. This can be achieved through development of metacognition and the provision of opportunities to explicitly learn about effective strategies used by other pupils.
Both teachers and learners should have an orientation towards learning characterised by a willingness to engage in dialogue and negotiation regarding the intent and purpose of a particular teaching and learning episode.	In any personal relationship it is often not easy to guess what is expected by the other person. Open and clear negotiations about intent and purpose are essential to avoid misunderstanding and breakdown; the relationship is necessarily reciprocal and involves a willingness on both sides.
The focus should be on how to succeed in terms of the selection of appropriate strategies and making the right effort, rather than on ability.	Relationships for everyone require commitment and effort – it is not going to be lovely and fun all the time but both sides should see the benefit from actively pursuing the relationship. No one is born 'good at relationships' so there is a need for teachers to convey a view that values pupil progress in relation to being 'good at being in the relationship' rather than 'good at the product of that relationship'.

be positively manipulated to improve the quality of this relationship. Recognising teachers' existing expertise, this chapter has purposely not sought to explain how to teach. Its aim, instead, has been to encourage further thought about those variables that may either impact negatively on behaviour or represent routes for changing behaviour.

Through the notion of a *relationship* with the curriculum we have directed attention to both what the pupil and the teacher contribute. The pupil is not viewed as a passive recipient of the curriculum on offer. An increased awareness of how the pupil experiences their relationship with the curriculum, and how they communicate that experience through their behaviour, can support teachers in identifying the changes they can make to their practice and to those learning behaviours that the pupil needs to develop.

A pupil's relationship with the curriculum is a high stakes relationship that develops during their years of schooling. It can be costly for the individual personally and for society in general if that relationship breaks down. Some pupils may not realise the importance of this relationship or how it can be developed and improved until it is too late to effect a change. This chapter has emphasised the need for teachers to explicitly communicate what is required from the relationship and how improvement can be achieved. The next chapter explores how the pupil's relationship with self affects behaviour and learning in school.

Note

1 Academies are also required to offer a broad and balanced curriculum in accordance with Section 1 of the 2010 Academies Act.

Chapter 6

Relationship with self

Introduction

In the previous chapter we covered the topic 'relationship with the curriculum', exploring the central importance of this relationship within school-based learning. In that chapter we noted that as well as addressing cognitive aspects of learning it was also necessary for teachers to recognise the importance of social and emotional aspects of learning. It is important to recognise that 'although most pupils have access to the emotional and social resources that facilitate their learning and development, significant numbers of children and young people in the UK do not' (Roffey 2016: 30). Such pupils are more likely to exhibit behaviours such as defiance, disengagement and disruption that interfere with their own and with others' academic learning.

This chapter seeks to address some of the emotional issues that influence pupils' behaviour and learning through examining their relationship with self. Most teachers are fully aware that no *one* set of strategies or approaches to promote learning or manage behaviour works for every pupil. It is important therefore to develop an understanding of why some pupils respond in a way that adversely affects their own, and sometimes others', progress in learning.

It is well documented, and stressed throughout this book, that a number of interacting factors can influence individual differences in behaviour. In this chapter the focus is on 'within child' emotional factors, often conceptualised as how the individual is feeling and perceiving their experiences. These areas of individual difference are often signposted with the prefix 'self'. For example, we might refer to self-esteem, self-belief, self-concept or self-worth. We use the term 'relationship with self' to reflect the dynamic interaction between the *internal* mental state and emotional feelings of the individual and *external* factors within their environment. This perspective allows schools and their teachers to positively influence a pupil's relationship with self through the contexts they create and the manner in which they teach and manage their classrooms.

Although we refer to three separate relationships (i.e. curriculum, self and others) that reflect the cognitive, emotional and social aspects of learning, our conceptual model is based on an understanding of the dynamic interdependence between these. It follows that in seeking to positively influence a pupil's relationship with self we can use either or both of the other two relationships to support this endeavour.

National recognition of the importance of relationship with self

A concern about the negative impact of some pupils' social and emotional behaviours in school settings is not new with published interventions being evident for the last two decades (Weare and Nind 2011). Many terms are used to signpost these interventions and initiatives including, 'social and emotional learning' (SEL), 'emotional literacy', 'emotional intelligence', 'resilience', 'life skills' and 'character education' (Weare 2010). More recently, UK guidance documents and national reports have tended to focus on the terms 'mental health' (e.g. DfE 2016c), 'resilience' (e.g. Bonnell *et al.* 2011) and 'wellbeing' (e.g. Weare 2015).

In their systematic review of previous reviews of mental health work in schools, Weare and Nind (2011: 29) 'identified evidence-based interventions and programmes and extracted the general principles from evidence-based work'. Several studies identified by Weare and Nind's (2011) review reported on interventions that showed generally positive impacts on aspects of children's learning, behaviour and attitudes towards school. Recognising competing priorities for schools, Weare and Nind (2011: 64) recommended that it was important that those involved in leading mental health work 'demonstrate how work to improve the mental health of students can benefit what schools see as their core business: academic learning and achievement, school attendance and behaviour for learning'.

This suggestion has resonance with the rationale behind the Behaviour for Learning approach. It is an approach rooted in schools' key role of promoting learning and achievement through the development of appropriate learning behaviours. The pupil's relationship with self is intrinsic to the Behaviour for Learning approach both through the role it plays in influencing the pupil's relationship with the curriculum and how it helps us to understand and address behaviour problems in school contexts.

In looking at the relevance of relationship with self for teachers it is relevant to consider both the Teachers' Standards (DfE 2011b) and policy initiatives that relate to wider societal aims such as building resilience, wellbeing and mental health. The Teachers' Standards (DfE 2011b) include a number that make reference to skills and dispositions we would view as directly relating to the pupil's relationship with self (emphasis added):

- set goals that stretch and challenge pupils of all backgrounds, abilities and *dispositions*;
- demonstrate consistently the *positive attitudes*, values and behaviour which are expected of pupils;
- encourage pupils to take a *responsible and conscientious attitude* to their own work and study;
- promote a *love of learning* and children's *intellectual curiosity*;
- guide pupils to *reflect on* the progress they have made and their emerging needs;
- manage classes effectively, using approaches which are appropriate to pupils' needs in order to involve and *motivate* them.

If these aspirations for improved learning, behaviour and 'wellbeing' outcomes are to be realised it follows that any prescribed changes to factors in the school environment will need to be accompanied by strategies to bring about changes within the individual.

National reports and policy and guidance for schools give credence to the view that there is a need to give more focused attention to the psychological and emotional dimensions of pupil learning and behaviour. Within the Behaviour for Learning approach we explore and address these dimensions through 'relationship with self'. This term is likely to be unfamiliar to most schools and their teachers, although widely used terms in educational policy and practice, such as self-esteem, serve to highlight the importance of a pupil's subjective experiences and responses to their existing school contexts and practices. The next section examines what we mean by the term 'relationship with self.'

Relationship with self

The term 'relationship with self' is rarely used except within the context of the Behaviour for Learning approach. The meaning conveyed within the term is, however, likely to be understood by most people. When you reflect upon the meaning of the term you will recognise that you bring to your teaching the view you have constructed of yourself from the unique and personal experiences you have had to date. This view shapes your own personal perception and interpretation of events and situations. So, for example, if you communicate any problems you are having with behaviour management to a person who has responsibility for supporting your professional development (e.g. a tutor or mentor) they might encourage you to look at the issue or incident from another point of view or perspective as a way of enabling you to move from your subjective, emotionally influenced view to a more objective, cognitive and social appraisal of the situation.

You are probably not consciously aware of all the aspects of self you have constructed and would have to think about your responses to questions such as 'How would you describe your ideal self?', 'Do you feel valued?' or 'Would you say you had high or low self-esteem?'. Nevertheless, you have formed a view of yourself and this continues to develop in response to your experiences. These views and perceptions will have a pervasive influence on how you think, feel and behave.

In seeking to use relationship with self as a focus for improving learning and behaviour in the classroom, it follows that teachers need to consider the question 'What is the pupil's behaviour communicating about what they are experiencing, thinking and feeling?'.

Although teachers do not use the term 'relationship with self' they typically acknowledge that behaviour is influenced by how a pupil thinks and feels about themselves. Some teachers may, for example, explain a pupil's off task behaviour by saying:

- 'I think he is messing about because he believes he is not as clever as he would like to be' (i.e. a self-esteem issue).
- 'He knows how to do the work but he doesn't think he can sustain the effort to succeed' (i.e. a self-efficacy issue).
- 'He isn't going to change because he thinks that it is someone else's fault that he is the way he is. He thinks it's up to the school or his teachers to make things better for him' (i.e. a locus of control issue).

(Ellis and Tod 2015: 33)

These explanations for a pupil's behaviour serve to illustrate the different aspects of a pupil's relationship with self. We have included in brackets the names of the constructs that have been applied in the literature to explain these different aspects of 'self'. These are explored later in this chapter. The important point to make is that, when seeking to stop or reduce unwanted behaviour, our strategy choice is likely to be influenced by the explanations we make regarding the reasons behind that behaviour. These explanations largely reflect the reciprocal and interdependent relationship between the social, emotional and cognitive components of classroom learning and behaviour.

Defining relationship with self

Definition of relationship with self

The dynamic and reciprocal interaction between the individual's existing thoughts, perceptions and feelings that serve to make sense of their previous and ongoing experiences.

Within the Behaviour for Learning approach we refer to a *relationship* with self in order to:

- reflect the dynamic interdependence between the individual's 'inner' thinking, perceptions and feelings; schools offer opportunities to influence how an individual is thinking and in so doing can positively impact on pupils' existing perceptions and feelings;
- emphasise that an individual's relationship with self develops from the dynamic and reciprocal interaction between the *internal* mental state of the individual and the *external* factors within their environment.

Our definition affords teachers the opportunity to use a two-way or combined approach and therefore offers a choice a strategies. For example, in considering the first bullet point above, if a pupil *believes* they are 'useless' at school, and behaves accordingly, their teacher and others could encourage them to adopt a way of thinking such that a *relative* rather than *absolute* judgement is made about their competence (e.g. '*I am not the only one who finds this subject difficult*', '*I can do some of it*', '*I am able to succeed at other things*', etc.). The teacher has the option to use the peer group, formative feedback and aspects of their subject curriculum, to enable the pupil to adjust their *thinking* and subsequent perceptions and feelings about themselves.

In the case of the second bullet point above, if a pupil perceives that they are *unable* to achieve in school, based on previous experience of failure, and behaves accordingly, their teacher has the option, based on their expertise in teaching and learning, to make appropriate adjustments to their teaching. This use of *external* factors to influence the *inner* mental state of the individual is likely to be the strategy of choice for teachers because it fits in with their everyday role of meeting the learning needs of *all* their pupils.

This two-way approach that seeks to change factors in the individual's environment *and* within the child is consistent with resilience-based approaches to mental health. For example, Miller and Daniel (2007: 606) note that 'a resilience-based approach concentrates on building a protective and supportive network around the child – but also identifying and nurturing areas of strength within the individual'.

Strengthening an individual's resilience has been widely advocated across the caring professions with recent emphasis on schools' role in this endeavour for reasons of mental health, behaviour and extremism (e.g. Bonnell *et al.* 2011; DfE 2016c).

Relationship with self can seem to be the most daunting of the three Behaviour for Learning relationships to change. The reasons for this include:

- For all pupils this relationship has developed over time and therefore some aspects are likely to be relatively resistant to change. Its development is subject to a number of factors which may be outside the teacher's sphere of influence.
- This relationship is strongly linked to emotion and affect which are known to be powerful determinants of behaviour.
- The teacher cannot easily access or assess the pupil's relationship with self and has to hypothesise or infer what it might be the from pupil's verbal and non-verbal behaviours.
- The pupil may not be conscious of how this relationship can influence, and is influencing, their behaviour. They may not have the language and communication skills to convey to others how they are thinking and feeling. The individual's particular relationship with self may not appear rational to others. Often a pupil responds positively to an intervention for a period of time only to revert back to their old behavioural patterns for no apparent reason, and to the frustration of their teachers.

The emotional aspect of learning and behaviour is intrinsic to both the pupil's relationship with the curriculum and their relationship with others and, as such, it contributes to the development of both positive and negative learning behaviours. In referring to relationship with self and emotional aspects of learning in schools we are aware that we are touching upon areas with which Ecclestone and Hayes (2009) and Ecclestone (2015) take issue (see Chapter 1, Reflective Exercise 1.2). Our stance is very clear: we do not seek to pathologise the normal human feelings experienced during learning in educational settings. As humans, we can and do at times feel:

- disappointed or cross when we fail;
- ill at ease when we compare our performance with some others;
- the discomfort of effort and persistence;
- resentful of the time 'work' takes away from more pleasant activities;
- anger towards those whose judgement of our work does not match our own;
- irritated and annoyed when working with some others;
- resentful if our 'work in progress' or our answers to questions are put up for peer group scrutiny;
- dissatisfied with our finished work;
- pressured if too much is asked of us;
- anxious about change;
- upset when friendships are not working.

All these feelings are part of learning and, as they will be lifelong learners, we need to prepare pupils for this reality. Such feelings may become problematic if they become the *dominant* and *persistent* experience for the pupil. Our purpose in considering relationship with self is to improve pupils' learning behaviours so that we can harness their potential for learning, develop their tolerance and resilience and, most of all, develop their autonomy. Arguably, successful learners do not learn without effort but, unlike those we might consider less successful learners, their effort more frequently results in a positive outcome. When successful learners seek to 'make sense' of their learning experiences they are dealing with a different ratio of positive to negative feelings and are able to make a more balanced judgement such as, '*This is difficult for me but I've worked at this kind of problem before and succeeded eventually with effort, so I can do it again*'. This way of thinking leads to persistence and is a style that teachers would want to develop in all their pupils. A pupil who has not experienced much success might think: '*I can't do this – others can do it easily, no one has told me how to do it – I don't want to do it anyway.*' This type of thinking makes this pupil vulnerable as they have not acknow-ledged effort as a variable in their own or others' learning. The pupil has chosen to attribute blame outside herself/himself, in this case to the teacher. Having 'made sense' of their experiences to herself/himself in this way the pupil is unlikely to take any responsibility for their own learning because they do not perceive that they have any control over it.

We cannot escape from the fact that, however good our intentions for our teaching, individual pupils will seek to 'make sense' of their experiences from their personal per-spectives. For a few pupils this may lead to emotionally influenced dispositions and behaviours that are either transient or entrenched and which significantly interfere with their academic learning and social behaviour in the classroom.

In order to support these pupils who may well have, and continue to experience, damaging life experiences, there is a need for schools and their teachers to secure a better balance between the positive and negative feelings associated with their school learning. Teachers can make a positive contribution through their influence on pupils' dispositions towards learning and achievement.

In identifying difficulties linked to the pupil's relationship with self our main clues come from their presenting behaviour. Examples of behaviour that is influenced by relationship with self include:

*   reluctance to try new things;
*   being easily frustrated from lack of immediate success or understanding;
*   attitudes that are hypercritical, negative, sarcastic and cynical;
*   withdrawal, depression and unwillingness to communicate;
*   blaming behaviour outside themselves;
*   dependency on others to tell them what to do, what is good, what is acceptable;
*   lying;
*   non-compliance with authority.

The potential of these behaviours to impact negatively on the pupil's relationship with the curriculum and relationship with others is immediately apparent. It is, of course, the case that the behavioural expressions of relationship with self vary within and between individuals. The 'making sense' aspect of relationship with self is unique to the indi-vidual and this process is influenced by ongoing changes to the pupil's environment. The above list of behaviours is essentially 'problematic' in the classroom. Some pupils who experience significant levels of anxiety and stress may develop less disruptive behaviours. These may include withdrawn behaviours that an observer might interpret as the pupil being quiet and compliant. These behaviours are not troublesome for the class, but in seeking to remain unnoticed individuals are at risk of not being identified and/or not having their needs addressed. In the longer term such behaviours can result in disaffection and depression with consequent adverse effects on the individual's life chances and wellbeing.

Although we refer to relationship with self rather than other widely used constructs that relate to 'self', it is necessary to understand how these constructs and their underlying processes have developed to both explain and address individual differences in behaviour. The next section gives a brief overview.

Constructs and theoretical perspectives related to relationship with self

There is a vast range of literature and many different constructs and theoretical perspectives associated with 'self'. This overview briefly covers both historical definitions that have lasted over time and recent developments that are relevant for classroom practice.

It is important to note when reading this section that there is a significant lack of consensus in the literature about the definition, meanings and mechanisms of constructs such as self-esteem and self-efficacy (e.g. Tafarodi and Milne 2002; Miller and Daniel 2007). Differing definitions need to be considered as they lead to alternative practical consequences for the way in which these constructs are measured and used in both research and practice.

Self-esteem

The term 'self-esteem' is widely used in schools, and also appears in policy and guidance documents as a focus for intervention (Kilbride 2014). As Emler (2002) points out, there is also a popular view that low self-esteem is the source of all manner of personal and social ills.

Research on 'self-esteem' has a long history dating back to William James' book *The Principles of Psychology* in 1890 (Miller and Moran 2012; Kilbride 2014). Since then various writers and researchers have sought to define not only what is meant by self-esteem but also the effects of putative high or low self-esteem. Self-esteem is a construct and one that is made particularly complicated by the variability in definitions. There is a vast range of literature on self-esteem and it is located in many academic disciplines (Miller and Moran 2012). Various researchers (e.g. Mruk 1999; Lawrence 2006) have also synthesised ideas from the earlier works of others and developed their own definitions and conceptual models of self-esteem.

We have approached this section by considering contributions from different writers and researchers to current perspectives on self-esteem. We have been selective and identified perspectives that we consider to be most helpful in relation to school-based practice. Our discussion is based on three broad perspectives identified by Mruk (1999) through his analysis of the most important studies in the area of self-esteem (Miller and Moran 2012). These are *self-esteem as competence*, *self-esteem as self-worth* and *self-esteem as competence and worthiness*.

Self-esteem as competence

James (1890/2007) introduced the idea that self-esteem relates to competence. He offered the following, now frequently quoted, definition of self-esteem:

Our self-feeling in this world depends entirely on what we back ourselves to be and do. It is determined by the ratio of our actualities to our supposed potentialities: a fraction of which our pretentions are the denominator and the numerator our success: thus,

$$\text{Self-esteem} = \frac{\text{Success}}{\text{Pretensions}}$$

Such a fraction may be increased as well by diminishing the denominator as by increasing the numerator.

(James 1890/2007: 310–11)

The ratio within James' (1890/2007) definition was of particular importance as it presented self-esteem as something that we could attempt to measure using mathematical principles. Essentially, for James, an individual's self-esteem was determined by whether what they could actually do matched what they aspired to do. He gave the example of a rower who aspired to be number one in the world but whose competence did not allow them to be more than second best. As James (1890/2007: 310) explains, the fact 'that he is able to beat the whole population of the globe minus one is nothing; he has "pitted" himself to beat that one; and as long as he doesn't do that nothing else counts.' James' definition and analogy present self-esteem not only as competence-orientated but also dynamic in the sense that it is open to change. Either improving the rower's competence to the point where they could achieve the first place or encouraging them to readjust their aspirations could improve their self-esteem. In a school context we might apply a similar principle; we can potentially work on either 'side' of the discrepancy to bring about positive change to an individual's self-esteem.

The influence of James' (1890/2007) work can be seen in subsequent models of self-esteem that focus on the discrepancy between what an individual aspires to do and what they have managed to achieve.

The important point to note when considering James (1890/2007) work and other competence-based theories of self-esteem is that 'success' is defined and judged by the individual. It follows that a pupil can be judged to be successful in school by reference to externally prescribed criteria such as exam grades but not judge themselves to be successful against the internal subjective criteria they have set for themselves. There is a need to consider a pupil's personal experience of success when seeking to judge their self-esteem.

Self-esteem as self-worth

Both Rosenberg (1965) and Coopersmith (1967) adopted a different perspective to James (1890/2007) and viewed self-esteem in terms of worthiness. This perspective addresses the concern that competency models of self-esteem that focus on success alone do not take into account broader factors such as the overall opinion the individual has of herself/himself. The self-esteem as worthiness perspective is reflected in Coopersmith's (1967: 5) well known definition of self-esteem as: 'the evaluation which an individual makes and customarily maintains with regard to himself: it expresses an attitude of approval or disapproval, and indicates the extent to which the individual believes himself to be capable, significant, successful, and worthy.'

Fundamental to an individual's sense of self-worth is the belief that they are liked, valued and respected. Questions from Rosenberg's (1965) widely used self-assessment questionnaire provide an insight into how those who approach self-esteem from the self-worth perspective seek to understand how an individual views herself/himself. The questionnaire contains ten statements and respondents are asked to indicate their level of agreement on a four point scale ranging from strongly agree to strongly disagree. The statements are:

1   On the whole, I am satisfied with myself.
2   At times, I think I am no good at all.
3   I feel that I have a number of good qualities.
4   I am able to do things as well as most other people.
5   I feel I do not have much to be proud of.
6   I certainly feel useless at times.
7   I feel that I'm a person of worth, at least on an equal plane with others.
8   I wish I could have more respect for myself.
9   All in all, I am inclined to feel that I am a failure.
10   I take a positive attitude toward myself.

(Rosenberg 1965: 17–18)

It should be clear from this set of questions how the self-esteem as self-worth perspective differs in its concerns and priorities from the self-esteem as competence perspective. The questions are entirely focused on the individual's general feelings about themselves, reflecting Rosenberg's (1965: 30) view that self-esteem is 'a positive or negative attitude toward a particular object, namely, the self'.

In looking at the trajectory of development of self-worth some theorists (e.g. Bowlby 1953, 1969) place emphasis on the first nurturing experiences for the child with their primary care giver. The resultant Attachment Theory has been influential in explaining individual differences in children's behaviours and informing practice and therapeutic approaches across health, education and social work settings. There is also evidence that '[s]ecure attachment is … associated with greater emotional regulation, social competence, and willingness to take on challenges' (Bergin and Bergin 2009: 141) and is, in turn, associated with higher achievement. Secure attachments develop from nurturing relationships, and there can be negative implications if a child cannot rely on an adult to respond to their needs in times of stress (Sroufe and Siegel 2011).

Self-worth is the *perception* the individual has of herself/himself that has been formed and continues to be influenced by a range of feedback and experiences. For example, in school the pupil learns through a range of experiences whether they are the type of person who is popular and/or valued by peers and teachers 'because of who they are'. At home a different set of feedback and experiences will contribute to the development of this aspect of self. Of relevance to teachers is that individuals interpret their experiences in the way that makes sense to them. For example, a pupil who is reprimanded by a teacher could interpret this experience in a variety of ways, such as:

•   I am a badly behaved or disruptive person.
•   That's fair; I deserved to be told off. I know the rules and I chose to ignore them.
•   The teacher is having a bad day. Sometimes adults have bad days.
•   This teacher doesn't like me, but that's OK because I can't expect to like everyone or everyone to like me.
•   I am not the kind of person that teachers like.

- I don't really care because teacher disapproval or approval doesn't matter to me.
- This was unfair on this occasion, but sometimes adults are like that.
- This is unfair and a confirmation that I am a person who teachers treat unfairly.

However, it is impossible to separate this interpretation from the nature of the feedback received. If, for example, the teacher frequently labels the pupil rather than the behaviour (e.g. 'you are unkind' rather than 'that was an unkind thing to do'), it is more likely that over a period of time the behaviour will form part of the pupil's view of themselves (e.g. 'I am an unkind person'). Past experience will also affect the interpretation of events. If a pupil has been used to frequent criticism from parents/carers, perhaps based on developmentally unrealistic expectations in relation to behaviour, perceived criticism by the teacher may have a confirming quality that contributes to the pupil's image of themselves as 'badly behaved'.

It is important to recognise, of course, that how the individual views herself/himself may be different to how others view her/him. The child's self-worth may be built on a view of herself/himself as witty, entertaining and generally a bit of a joker. Depending on how these qualities manifest themselves in the classroom, the teacher might view the same child as disrespectful or disruptive. Working with this view we can see that in the social and academic context of the classroom there are considerable opportunities to enable the individual to either confirm or reject the judgements they are making of themselves.

Lawrence's (2006) discrepancy model

Though we would not position Lawrence (2006) alongside seminal writers such as James (1890/2007), Rosenberg (1965) and Coopersmith (1967), his perspective on self-esteem is worthy of consideration in its own right. Lawrence's *Enhancing Self-Esteem in the Classroom* (2006), currently in its third edition, has provided much helpful guidance for teachers over the years (Miller and Moran 2012). Lawrence views self-esteem as resulting from a discrepancy between an individual's self-image and their ideal self. The idea of some form of discrepancy determining an individual's self-esteem had been established by James (1890/2007), and the specific idea of a discrepancy between self-image and ideal self is identifiable in a range of literature (e.g. Silber and Tippet 1965; Coopersmith 1967). However, Lawrence's contribution was the use of this idea to develop a model of self-esteem that teachers could readily understand conceptually and relate to practice.

Lawrence (2006) views an individual's self-esteem as resulting from the combined elements of the size of the discrepancy between self-image and ideal self and the extent to which any discrepancy is a source of concern to the individual. Like James (1890/2007), Lawrence (2006) presents self-esteem as dynamic; in order to raise a pupil's self-esteem, we could aim to reduce the gap between who they think they are (self-image) and who they aspire to be (ideal self).

An individual's self-image is the perception they have of themselves and so reflects the self-worth perspective of self-esteem. A person's self-image may be accurate, in the sense that it matches how others view them, or inaccurate. Though an individual's self-image is, as its name suggests, a view the individual holds of herself/himself, this is informed by a variety of sources. The various influences we considered previously when discussing self-worth are equally applicable when we consider how an individual's self-image is shaped.

Though an individual has a degree of free choice in constructing their ideal self, feedback from a range of sources exerts a major influence on what they aspire to do and to be. These sources implicitly and explicitly convey messages to the individual regarding the traits and competences considered desirable by others. Commonly cited sources include the media (e.g. celebrity status, talents and lifestyle), parents (e.g. academic success, sporting prowess) and peers (e.g. popular, entertaining).

The child quickly learns that certain skills and behaviours are valued in certain contexts. As the child gets older peers exert an influence that can be more powerful than that of either teachers or parents. During transition a pupil who exhibited behaviour in primary school that is consistent with 'normal to high' self-esteem may exhibit problematic behaviour in secondary contexts. This can be understood as a consequence of the dominance of an ideal self that is increasingly influenced by a peer group that values being popular more highly than being 'clever and well behaved' – which are traits that are likely to be prioritised by the child's parents and teachers. Increasing access to social media provides pupils with opportunities to not only receive constant information about trends in beliefs, values, appearance and so on but to *select* and *pursue* those that confirm their own view and status of self.

The significant issue for teachers to consider is the status and influence of ideal self within the mind of the individual. In school contexts it is not problematic if it serves to motivate curriculum learning by providing 'achievable but challenging' targets or to support social and sporting relationships. However if facets of ideal self, informed from different environmental experiences, are incompatible (e.g. home versus school) then the pupil's own perception of success will be variable and self-esteem may become fragile.

Hierarchical models of self-esteem

A number of writers (e.g. Shavelson *et al.* 1976; Shavelson and Bolus 1982; Lawrence 2006) have presented models that recognise the existence of multiple 'self-esteems' (see Figure 6.1), with overall self-esteem (i.e. global self-esteem) being influenced by self-esteems over a range of academic and non-academic areas. This denotes that self-esteem

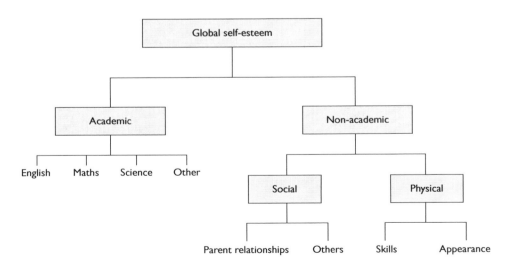

Figure 6.1 The self-esteem hierarchy.
Source: Lawrence 2006: 12.

is multifaceted and hierarchically organised. It is, of course, good practice in schools to influence global self-esteem by recognising and reinforcing individuals' achievements and attributes in all areas. However, a simple conceptual additive model cannot be applied because self-esteem is a subjective judgement with some domain specific self-esteems having more value to the individual than others. A pupil who is successful academically may place less value on this aspect of self than on experiencing 'failure' in non-academic areas such as popularity with peers (Social) and being judged as physically skilled and/or attractive (Physical). This can become a dominant self-esteem that has a negative and pervasive effect on the pupil's overall self-esteem through the high value placed on it by the individual.

Self-esteem as competence and worthiness

In his comprehensive review of research studies, Mruk (1999) identified that many approaches to the study of self-esteem fall into two major camps (Miller and Moran 2012). There are those that concentrate on judgements of competence (e.g. James 1890/2007) and those which focus primarily on self-worth (e.g. Rosenberg 1965; Coopersmith 1967). In addition, Mruk (1999) noted the work of Nathaniel Branden (1969) who considered competence and worthiness to be equally important components of self-esteem. This was reflected in Branden's definition of self-esteem:

> Self-esteem has two interrelated aspects: it entails a sense of personal efficacy and sense of personal worth. It is the integrated sum of self-confidence and self-respect. It is the conviction that one is *competent* to live and *worthy* of living.
>
> (Branden 1969: 110)

As Miller and Moran (2012: 43) suggest, this means

> that for individuals to have high self-esteem they must feel confident *both* about their sense of self-worth ('I am a good person, entitled to care and respect from others') and their sense of self-competence ('I am able to meet the challenges I face in life').

Individuals who are low in both self-competence and self-worth are likely to present as having what Miller and Moran (2007: 45) term 'classic low self-esteem'. Those who have a more positive sense of worth and competence are likely to present with higher self-esteem. Table 6.1 presents some examples of behaviours we might typically associate with low and high self-esteem.

The two-dimensional model also allows for other combinations than those depicted in Table 6.1. It is also possible to have low self-worth and high self-competence or vice versa. Mruk (1999) viewed these two categories as representing two different forms of defensive self-esteem. The key point to recognise is that 'when one component is missing or deficient, self-esteem must suffer too' (Mruk 1999: 160). The problem for teachers is that the way the pupil presents may not suggest a self-esteem issue. Behaviours associated with the presence of either positive competence or positive worthiness may mask this. For example, a pupil with high competence and low self-worth may appear quite successful and excel in some areas whereas a pupil with low competence and high self-worth may give the impression of being very confident.

Table 6.1 Behaviours typically associated with low and high self-esteem

	Characteristic behaviour	*Self-worth*	*Self-competence*
Low self-esteem	Negativistic in outlook.	Low	Low
	Reluctant to contribute to class activities.	Low	Low
	Have negative perceptions of their own abilities.	Low	Low
	Low expectations of favourable outcomes.	Low	Low
High self-esteem	Positive in outlook.	Medium–High	Medium–High
	Contribute to class activities.	Medium–High	Medium–High
	Belief in their own abilities.	Medium–High	Medium–High
	Normal/high expectations of favourable outcomes.	Medium–High	Medium–High

Source: based on Miller and Moran 2012.

The salient point to take from these two additional categories is that how pupils express their self-esteem (i.e. their self-worth and self-competence) through their behaviour varies between individuals. Some children may express their self-esteem by being quiet and withdrawn, by making negative self-referent statements and through a range of other behaviours we might intuitively associate with low self-esteem. Others might exhibit behaviours that are loud or appear confident, even boastful, that do not necessarily match with our assumptions regarding the way an individual with low self-esteem will present. We cannot, therefore, rely on attributing a pupil's behaviour to 'high' or 'low' self-esteem based on our own views on how we think pupils with high self-esteem or those with low self-esteem might behave. This is a view supported by Miller and Moran (2005) who identified a mismatch between teachers' judgements of their pupils' self-esteem and the pupils' own self-reports.

The utility of a two-dimensional model of self-esteem based on both competence and self-worth is that it offers choices of strategy for improving self-esteem. Figure 6.2 illustrates how we might synchronise this model of self-esteem with the Behaviour for Learning conceptual framework (see Chapter 2). It relates to an individual pupil who is considered by teachers, and other staff, to have significant emotional problems that they have attributed to 'low self-esteem'. This is having a pervasive effect on the pupil's curriculum learning and behaviour with others. The pupil is likely to have 'raise self-esteem' as one of their targets. Based on the principles of the Behaviour for Learning approach the teacher would identify the learning behaviours they want to promote to bring about positive changes. Figure 6.2 identifies some possible behaviours but teachers would identify those pertinent to the individual pupil. The learning behaviours have been categorised into:

- those that support the development of the pupil's relationship with the curriculum, with others and with self, reflecting the Behaviour for Learning conceptual framework;
- those that support the development of self-worth and self-competence – as suggested by Mruk's (1999) two-dimensional model of self-esteem.

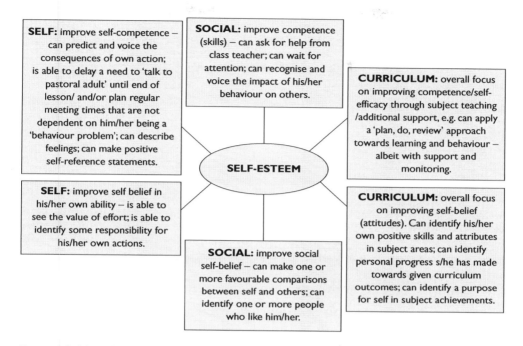

Figure 6.2 Identifying example learning behaviours associated with self-esteem.

This level of planning would only be needed for a few pupils who are likely to need more support than other members of the class. The planning diagram could be used to ensure that all those involved with the individual pupil were fully aware of the focus for intervention and the evaluation criteria (i.e. development of targeted learning behaviour).

Reciprocal Effects Models (REMs)

The emergence and application of two-dimensional theories such as the one above depicting self-esteem as being made up of constructs relating to *both* self-worth and self-competence are particularly important for teachers who seek to bring about positive changes to a pupil's self-esteem. To do so would require raising both elements of self-esteem, with self-worth being more elusive in terms of identification and intervention in school contexts than self-competence which can be directly strengthened through curricular activities. Research into the relationship between these components supports Reciprocal Effects Models (REMs) which offer the potential to focus on the *reciprocal relationship* between components as a route to impacting positively on both components. These REMs also offer the potential to harness the power of one strong component to improve the other. The role that teachers have in developing the self-competence aspects of self-esteem through their focus on academic achievement can have a positive effect on self-worth aspects (Marsh and Martin 2011).

Self-efficacy

In the previous section we referred to self-competence but the term 'self-efficacy' is sometimes used as an alternative as, 'a generalised sense of efficacy is synonymous with self-competence' (Miller and Daniel 2007: 609). Self-efficacy is a term that may be used more frequently in schools.

Self-efficacy can be defined as an individual's judgement of their ability to execute successfully a behaviour required to produce certain outcomes (Gibson and Dembo 1984; Bandura 1986). Self-efficacy involves both efficacy expectations and outcome expectancy (Gibson and Dembo 1984). Bandura (1977) defined outcome expectancy as a person's estimate that a given behaviour will lead to certain outcomes, and efficacy expectation as their conviction that they can successfully execute the behaviour required to produce those outcomes. Self-efficacy is not primarily concerned with the skills that an individual has, but with their judgements about these skills and their capacity to execute them. These two elements lead the individual to have certain *beliefs* about themselves. If, for example, a pupil is told '*Come on, you can do it if you try*', they may agree with the teacher's judgment but judge themselves to be incapable of making and sustaining the effort required.

The importance of understanding the construct of self-efficacy is that if a pupil *believes* that they cannot successfully complete a task, they develop behaviours in support of that belief. This in effect results in them being rooted in a vicious circle of experiencing a lack of success that serves to fuel their beliefs surrounding self-efficacy. Based on this assumption it follows that the most effective way to break a pupil's 'low self-efficacy – low successful task completion – low self-efficacy' cycle is to adopt teaching strategies that serve to enable the pupil to experience an increase in successful task completion.

Tasks and feedback that give the pupil objective information that they are developing increasing competence can have a positive effect on their subjective view of self. The construct of self-efficacy links to the broader idea that an individual has the ability to influence what happens to them through the actions that they take. The extent to which a person believes their own actions influence what happens to them relates to their locus of control and attributional style. This has relevance for practice as it allows teachers to explore the pupil's inner thoughts through paying close attention to their causal attributions.

Attributions and locus of control

The construct of 'locus of control' (Rotter 1954) can be thought of as a continuum that stretches from a belief, at one end, that whatever happens to us is entirely within our control ('internal locus of control') to a belief at the other that whatever happens to us is entirely beyond our control ('external locus of control') (Lawrence 2006). To be located at either extreme poses problems for the individual. If we believe everything is entirely determined by us then every unfortunate, chance event is constructed as a personal failing. If we believe everything is entirely determined by others, then we become passive victims of circumstance with no personal agency. From this description, the links between self-efficacy and locus of control are immediately evident.

Attribution theory shares a number of common ideas with the constructs of locus of control and self-efficacy. When we experience an event in which we succeed or fail, we will generate explanations (or 'attributions') about the cause (Porter 2007). Some of these attributions will be internal, relating to the behaviour of the individual, others will be external factors such as luck, other people's behaviour or factors in the environment. People have causal explanations for their own behaviour (intrapersonal attributions) and for other people's behaviour (interpersonal attributions) (Chaplain 2003a, 2003b). These attributions may be faulty (Porter 2007) and have subsequent effects on behaviour.

Drawing on the work of Weiner (2000), Porter (2007: 80) provides a useful analysis of the four properties our attributions have:

- Where we *locate* the cause of events – whether we believe them to be due to internal versus external forces.
- Whether we see these forces as *durable* (e.g. personal traits such as ability) or *temporary* events (e.g. lack of effort).
- Whether the causes are *pervasive* (e.g. inability at Maths) or *specific* (e.g. not understanding fractions).
- How *controllable* we believe events to be.

If a pupil attributes a difficulty experienced to internal, temporary, specific and controllable factors, then this encourages them to engage and persist. However, if the pupil blames external sources that are permanent, pervasive and uncontrollable, then they are unlikely to try to change their behaviour because they feel powerless to affect what happens to them. In its extreme form this pattern could be regarded as 'learned helplessness' (Seligman 1975). Some pupils display learned helplessness in terms of giving up when faced with a situation they perceive to be difficult because they believe any change or progress towards any favourable outcome is beyond their control.

Listening to the words pupils use when talking about incidents in which they have been involved can provide valuable clues about their locus of control and attributional style. The explanations may allow us to identify where they have placed blame and whether they feel they could personally do anything that would help to avoid such incidents. If it is evident that they have largely an external locus of control or are attributing externally then this might be addressed through work that encourages a reframing of events through a reappraisal of beliefs about why these occurred.

Implications for practice

Self-esteem is a construct used to explain individual differences in the way a person is thinking, feeling and being. We do not have access to the mind of the individual and therefore it is helpful to have theories and models that have developed from research that have utility in practice. In extracting implications for practice from the three models outlined (i.e. self-esteem as competence, self-esteem as self-worth and self-esteem as self-worth *and* competence) it is important to note that models have been developed to make what is a complex area easier to understand. They are only models and as such do not represent the reality of what is going on in a pupil's head as they seek to make sense of their world. Given that caveat we have extracted the following implications for practice:

- Use a simple discrepancy model in the classroom, i.e. self-esteem as the gap between self-image and ideal self; teachers can aim to reduce the gap by:

- improving self-image and self-efficacy by enabling pupils to experience more success, particularly through improved achievement;
- using peer group views and discussions and curriculum sources to adjust the pupil's ideal self.

- Try to look at behaviour from the pupil's perspective in order to think of the purposes it is serving for them.
- Create classroom atmospheres that support the use of praise and positive feedback for *all* pupils such that their success to failure ratio is positive.
- Be vigilant about making sure the individual pupil knows and personally values what the praise has been given for. It is important to be honest and proportionate in this feedback.
- Foster a classroom climate where errors and mistakes are accepted as part of the learning processes (Miller and Daniel 2007).
- Monitor the pupil's style of attribution and locus of control. Use peers and the curriculum to bring about any necessary changes that will positively effect development of *some* personal responsibility and belief that they have some control over their own behaviour and learning;
- Aim to depersonalise information about behaviours and attitudes that have been identified as problematic for the pupil. This allows for personal behaviour and learning issues to be dealt with objectively as it reduces the emotional dimension. It is possible to use real life events, stories from history and fictional accounts focusing, for example, on how a person has recovered from or made positive use of a setback or failure.
- Aim to develop and foster teacher–pupil and peer relationships in the classroom that impact positively on the development of pupils' self-worth.

Limitations

In noting the utility of theories and research surrounding self-esteem there are some limitations, particularly when considering why and how we should seek to 'raise the self-esteem' of individuals as a route to improving attainment and wellbeing and fostering mental health. It is important to note that:

- Caution is needed in collating and interpreting studies of self-esteem due to the fact that self-esteem has been defined and assessed differently in many of these.
- Many studies concerned with 'self' look at the degree of association between variables (e.g. self-esteem and disruptive behaviour). These studies therefore need to be recognised as correlational in design. When such studies are used to inform practice it would be inappropriate to assume a *causal* link in such a way that, for example, the construct of self-esteem is used both as a diagnosis ('*the pupil has low self-esteem*') and a prescription for treatment ('*we need to raise their self-esteem*') (O'Brien and Guiney 2001; Emler 2002).
- Emphasis on practice to raise self-esteem is based on a view that low self-esteem necessarily has a negative effect on behaviour. Although high self-esteem has been positively correlated with confidence and activity levels that can have a positive effect on learning and behaviour, there is also evidence (Emler 2002) that high self-esteem could be a risk to society in terms of individuals valuing themselves too much and presenting behaviours that have a negative effect on others. Emler's

(2002) review of literature on self-esteem supported Baumeister *et al.*'s (2003) finding that low self-esteem was not a risk factor for educational problems such as violence, bullying, delinquency, racism, drug taking or alcohol abuse.

The Behaviour for Learning approach seeks to harness the utility of the existing knowledge base on 'self' but to address the critiques outlined above. The next section outlines the key principles of this approach.

Key principles of Behaviour for Learning approach

The Behaviour for Learning perspective on self-esteem and the associated constructs covered in this chapter is underpinned by a number of key principles:

- The term 'relationship with self' is used in contrast to constructs such as self-esteem. Using the term 'relationship' emphasises the reciprocal, dynamic and interdependent relationship between the individual and their environment. This places emphasis on an ongoing process and explicitly acknowledges that this relationship develops and changes over time. It is subject to the influences from both long-term and shorter-term experiences. To this end, the *quality* of the relationships that underpin classroom teaching (e.g. relationship with curriculum, relationship with others) are paramount in informing the development of strategies for positively influencing the pupil's relationship with self.
- The Behaviour for Learning approach seeks to harness the extensive knowledge base surrounding 'self' to promote relationships in school settings (see Chapter 4) that support *all* individuals to experience success from their own achievements, feelings of belonging and self-worth and a sense of autonomy (McLean 2009).
- Self-esteem is not something we can see or measure but only infer from the behaviours we observe. In practice teachers need to identify what learning behaviours they need to promote in order to impact positively on pupils' relationship with self. This identification of learning behaviours to replace 'identification of low self-esteem' allows for both disruptive *and* detached behaviour to be addressed.
- Learning behaviours (see Appendix 1) cover both the skill and will (disposition) aspects of behaviour and as such are compatible with models of self-esteem that use either competence, or worthiness or both as defining features. This compatibility allows teachers to both benefit from, and critically appraise, the enduring knowledge base that surrounds self-esteem and any emergent developments.
- The emphasis is on practice that seeks to develop learning behaviours that are characteristic of individuals who are able to benefit from the achievement and belonging aspects of the school environment. These learning behaviours serve to support the development of resilience to some of the ongoing experiences involved in school-based curriculum and social learning such as sharing adult attention, effort, persistence, failure, the boredom of everyday routine, the break-up of friendships, negative comments and the need to develop increasing responsibility and independence.
- Importantly, the emphasis on learning behaviours allows teachers to use progress in the development of these behaviours as evaluation criteria against which to judge the efficacy of their strategy use.

Improving relationship with self through the Behaviour for Learning approach

Earlier on in this chapter we listed examples of behaviour that is influenced by relationship with self. Table 6.2 uses those same behaviours to describe the processes involved in the Behaviour for Learning approach to improving a pupil's relationship with self. The process involves the following stages:

1   identify the problem behaviour(s);
2   think about and seek to assess what purpose the behaviour(s) is serving for the individual;
3   define the positive learning behaviour(s) you want to promote;
4   decide whether your preferred focus for action is the curriculum or peers/social;
5   evaluate progress against the emergence of the desired learning behaviour.

Table 6.2 is not prescriptive but used to illustrate processes involved in positively influencing a pupil's relationship with self. The behaviour the individual shows serves a purpose from their perspective and then can become a habitual way of behaving. The aim is to seek to influence a change in their behaviour that they experience as being beneficial to them. This positive learning behaviour can be developed by using curriculum sources and information from peers.

It is important to note that a person's relationship with self develops over time and has a pervasive lifelong effect on significant aspects of their life such as their experience of success, relationship with others and sense of value and autonomy. It is important that schools harness their expertise in promoting learning and managing behaviour within group settings to foster the development of a positive relationship with self for all pupils.

Conclusion

There is an ongoing and increasing national agenda for improving wellbeing and mental health. Schools have been identified as places that can make a significant contribution to this agenda. This is not surprising given that schools offer unique opportunities to promote achievement, and controlled and safe social contexts in which individuals can experience and benefit from positive relationships with others. Pupils bring to school perceptions and judgments of themselves that have a pervasive effect on how they respond to their experience of schooling. The most extreme negative outcome of many years of schooling would be that individuals perceive that they have not achieved anything, have no friends, no value and scant self-belief that they can improve their wellbeing or life chances.

Policy and guidance for schools makes reference to the need to 'raise self-esteem' as a route to improving individuals' wellbeing and mental health. The vast range of literature on self-esteem is useful in helping us to understand what might be going on in a pupil's mind and directs our attention towards classroom experiences from the pupil's perspective. However, self-esteem is a construct that aims to explain how individuals develop subjective perceptions and judgements that influence their attitudes and behaviour in the classroom. Knowing the explanation does not necessarily result in a solution in the way that, within a medical model, pursuing cause and effect leads to

Table 6.2 Addressing behavioural problems often associated with relationship with self

Presenting behaviours	Purpose for the individual	Learning behaviour for development	Focus of Strategy section
Reluctance to try new things	Avoids/delays the experience of failure.	Can see some benefit in making mistakes.	*Curriculum:* e.g. explore through examples in literature/sport etc. *Social:* use examples from peers.
Being easily frustrated from lack of immediate success or understanding	Dependent on external immediate rewards.	Can tolerate delay of reward in favour of reward for effort and 'progress towards success'.	*Curriculum:* increase self-efficacy through rewarding steps taken towards overall task completion. *Social:* discuss strategies for promoting persistence and effort.
Blaming behaviour outside themselves	Delays punishments or sanctions; protects self from admitting fault.	Can identify some responsibility for the incident.	*Curriculum:* locus of control and attribution: whole class plus using subject material where appropriate.
Falling out with peers	Although not beneficial as the pupil probably wants friends, it might be to reaffirm the self-image that 'no one likes me' or to get control in a situation where the pupil lacks competence.	Can accept that falling out is not that unusual, and able to identify strategies and responsibility for repair and reconciliation	*Social:* work on social competences; work on relative rather than absolute judgements, e.g. 'some people like me'; use strategies that offer the pupil some choice over who they work with.
Lying	Delays 'uncomfortableness' and 'sanctions': reinforces their self-perception and judgement of the situation.	Can recognise consequences to self and others of lying.	*Curriculum:* examples of the pitfalls of lying through examples in the media, literature or history; use these examples to debate with class alternatives to lying.

prescriptions for treatment. The term 'mental health' tends to refer to mental ill-health and risks being located within a medical model with 'raising self-esteem' viewed as a treatment option.

Within the Behaviour for Learning approach we use the term 'relationship with self' to describe a model for addressing emotional aspects of learning and behaviour. It is a model that allows for emphasis on the reciprocal interaction between the external factors within the classroom environment and the pupil's subjective interpretation of these factors. Changes can then be brought about to the way the individual is thinking and feeling through personalising learning and social opportunities in the classroom.

It is unlikely that teachers currently think about 'relationship with self' and may be more familiar with the term 'self-esteem'. However, their concern is about changing pupil responses from negative to positive in terms of supporting pupil achievement. Approached from the Behaviour for Learning perspective, this involves identifying what emotionally influenced learning behaviours need to be promoted and developed in all pupils, with some pupils requiring increased emphasis on this aspect of learning. In this chapter we have sought to harness the existing and emerging knowledge base to inform strategy choice for this endeavour. Individuals cannot escape from their relationship with self and its pervasive effect on achievement and wellbeing. It is crucial that at all stages of an individual's schooling, a positive and proactive approach is adopted in fostering this aspect of children and young people's development.

Chapter 7

Relationship with others

Introduction

The Behaviour for Learning conceptual framework seeks to support teachers in understanding the complexity of the classroom relationships that impact on pupils' behaviour and learning. In the two preceding chapters we have discussed pupils' relationship with the curriculum and relationship with self. In this chapter we discuss relationship with others. This is the more 'traditional' relationship within the Behaviour for Learning approach. Readers are likely to have personal experience of a variety of social relationships and to recognise the impact of these on their own learning experiences and educational outcomes.

In schools the main focus is necessarily on promoting curriculum learning and achievement. Schools and their teachers have a professional responsibility to create contexts and conditions in which learning is promoted for *individuals* within the *group* setting of their school and classrooms. The heterogeneous nature of the school population is such that pupils vary in the extent to which they adapt to the social context of school. Such a context has to have in place policies and procedures for the development and management of social learning behaviours. In seeking to develop these social learning behaviours teachers have to accept that as their pupils progress through their schooling they increasingly access wider social groups that are not so easily monitored and managed by adults who have been allocated responsibility for the care, wellbeing and safety of children and young people. Both these out-of-school social relationships and, of course, in-school peer relationships, are increasingly conducted through electronic methods of communication, meaning pupils can function socially while they are physically alone.

Within a school, pupils are required to take part in learning that involves others. Teachers have a key role in both harnessing the opportunities and managing the risks inherent within the social context of the classroom.

Relationship with others in school contexts

Definition of relationship with others

Being willing and able to interact socially and take part in learning that involves others, and join in aspects of school life as a member of the school community.

The individual needs to be both willing and able to interact socially with others in order to benefit from the learning opportunities on offer in the school. As noted throughout this book, two characteristics of relationships are that:

- they are reciprocal; and
- they are influenced by context and can be changed and improved.

In seeking to foster the individual's relationship with others teachers need to combine these two aspects of relationships. The teacher needs to:

1   Recognise that pupils bring to school with them social behaviours that have developed in their previous and present family and community environments. These social behaviours may positively or negatively influence their response to the group learning setting of the classroom.
2   Understand that the repertoire of social behaviours that the pupil brings to school has a reciprocal effect on their learning and emotional experiences. In other words, the social learning behaviours the pupil brings affect their learning and emotional experiences which in turn affect their social learning behaviours.
3   Harness the opportunities offered by the school and classroom environment to model and foster the development of positive social relationships that support the pupil's learning, self-worth and need for friendship.

Importance of relationship with others in school contexts

Most schools and their teachers would agree with the view that good pupil–teacher and peer–peer relationships are crucial to the development of an effective school learning environment. This has been endorsed by research (Hattie 2009). The quality of peer relationships experienced by pupils in school affects their academic performance, wellbeing and engagement, absenteeism, vulnerability to bullying, behavioural difficulties, drug usage, social difficulties and mental health (McGrath and Noble 2010). Good teacher–pupil relationships at age 14 are positively associated with progress between Key Stage 3 and Key Stage 4 and consistently negatively associated with engagement in risky behaviours at age 14 and 16 years (Chowdry et al. 2009).

A number of the Teacher Standards' (DfE 2011b) either make reference directly or indirectly to relationships or place responsibility on teachers to promote appropriate social behaviour. Within the context of the overall requirement that teachers must 'make the education of their pupils their first concern ... forge positive professional relationships ... and work with parents in the best interests of their pupils' (DfE 2011b: 10), teachers are required to:

- 'take responsibility for promoting good and courteous behaviour both in classrooms and around the school' (DfE 2011b: 12).
- 'maintain good relationships with pupils, exercise appropriate authority, and act decisively when necessary' (DfE 2011b: 12).
- '[treat] pupils with dignity, building relationships rooted in mutual respect, and at all times [observe] proper boundaries appropriate to a teacher's professional position ... showing tolerance of and respect for the rights of others' (DfE 2011b: 14).

Government policy and guidance has also consistently required schools to promote emotional health and wellbeing (e.g. DoH/DfES 2004) with a more recent emphasis on addressing increasing concerns about mental health (e.g. DfE 2016c). The guidance document *Mental Health and Behaviour in Schools* (DfE 2016c) includes a table containing an extensive list of risk factors and protective factors for mental health and wellbeing. A number of risk factors related to the pupil's relationship with others are listed, including a breakdown in or lack of positive friendships, peer pressure and deviant peer influences and poor pupil–teacher relationships. Good communication skills, sociability and positive peer influences are considered to be protective factors. The overall theme within the guidance is the need for schools to be aware of, and where possible reduce, risk factors and also to foster protective factors in order to develop the pupil's resilience.

As the preceding points illustrate, within government documents there is an expectation that teachers will foster, develop and improve pupils' social relationships with others. The length of statutory schooling is such that both the phases of school learning and the developmental age of the pupils involve a trajectory of changes to the nature and purpose of a pupil's relationship with others. Teachers have a role in brokering their pupils' relationship with others within their own school. However, as is the case with curriculum learning, teachers need to know how to work effectively within their own school phase, to be aware of the social aspects of learning that have not developed in the previous phase and prepare pupils for their next phase.

Changes to relationship with others during the school years

In this section we consider how a child's relationship with others changes as they progress through their education from their earliest learning experiences through to the end of Key Stage 4. This is important for teachers as, although they may teach a particular age range, an understanding of how pupils' social relationships develop at earlier and later stages can contribute to more realistic behavioural expectations when receiving a new class at the start of the year and inform priorities in preparing pupils for the next phase of their education.

In Table 7.1 we proffer a sequence of stages of development. For each of these, consideration is given to the role of the adult and peers in supporting the development of the pupil's relationship with others. It should be noted that the age ranges we have allocated to each stage are a guide based on a child following a typical developmental trajectory. As with any staged approach related to development, the suggestion is not that there is a rigid division between stages. There will be a gradual transition as the child increasingly demonstrates the behaviours and characteristics associated with the next stage.

A salient point to note from Table 7.1 is that the individual's learning and behaviour is initially *dependent* on the adult and then progresses to the pupil being *responsive* to adults before reaching a stage where they can be encouraged to become more self-directed and *responsible*.

Social relationships with adults and peers play an important role in facilitating learning as children progress through the Early Years Foundation Stage and begin Year 1. In order to facilitate this, teachers need to provide opportunities for their pupils to develop competence in relating to others. Alongside this they also need to offer supportive relationships that allow their pupils to increasingly manage any stresses or tensions they may experience when learning in group situations.

Table 7.1 Changes to a child's relationship with others as they progress through different phases of learning

Stages of development	Role of adult	Role of peers
Stage 1: Birth to 11 months The child is reliant on the adult and needs to feel safe and outsource stress.	The adult (usually a parent or carer) provides a climate of acceptance and care. When the child experiences stress (e.g. hunger, sleep, cold, etc) the adult's response is timely and appropriate. In this way the child learns to outsource their stress and experience feelings of safety and comfort. This experience is typically associated with the development of secure attachments.	Relationship with peers/siblings could reduce or increase stress.
Stage 2: 12–36 months The child is reliant on the adult. The aim is to secure some shared attention with the child so that the adult can support the development of attention, add commentary and positively reinforce any achievements.	The adult works from the child's interest using child-initiated learning and forming personalised relationships that support the development of joint attention. They may involve siblings or peers to encourage social relationships in preparation for learning in larger groups. The task needs to be within the child's achievable level but offer some challenge.	Peer involvement is often spontaneous and unplanned. Such involvement may be experienced by the child as positive or negative.
Stage 3: 36 months–end of Foundation Stage With Stage 2 in place the aim is for the adult to support the child to engage in learning which brings success, and allows them to become excited and motivated by learning.	The adult needs to be consistent and nurturing. Child-initiated learning continues to be important but there is increasing use of adult directed activities. The adult provides contexts for learning and interesting tasks that are realistic but challenging so that the child is neither bored nor overwhelmed. The adult is nurturing in the way that stress is managed for the child and learning is facilitated. The child is exposed to routines and rules that offer predictability and security as they progress from Early Years to Year 1. Appropriate social behaviour is recognised and positively reinforced. The child needs to increasingly attribute success to their own actions. This will motivate them to achieve more success.	The presence of peers provides opportunities for the child to increase their competence (e.g. developing social vocabulary) in social situations. Any stress experienced by peer involvement is largely managed by the adult.

Stage 4: Key Stages 1 and 2

The child is required to become less dependent on the adult for their own learning. They need to develop beliefs about themselves as learners and begin to recognise how their learning 'mindset' impacts on their learning behaviour. The aim is for the child to develop positive beliefs so that they will not be put off by setbacks and demonstrate hard work and resilience.

The adult brokers a relationship with the child that is supportive, encouraging and makes them feel valued and that they belong. It is a less protected and protective relationship. Classroom relationships become more of an influence on learning. The teacher provides opportunities for pupils to learn and practise working productively with others. The pupil is encouraged to become less dependent on the adult to start and persist with their learning. Effort with work and being able to work with others is positively reinforced.

Peers can positively impact on pupil learning by allowing individuals to get on with their work and exhibiting prosocial behaviour. They can negatively influence the child's progress by exhibiting irritating, distracting or bullying behaviour.

Stage 5: Key Stages 3 and 4

Research by Blakemore (2008) on changes that occur in the adolescent brain suggests there is heightened sensitivity to peer and other personal relationships. Acceptance becomes fundamental to the experience of social relationships and self-worth (Somerville 2013).

Adults need to be sensitive to the impact of social rejection and social shaming on adolescent pupils in the classroom. The pupil needs to feel safe and experience positive relationships with teachers and others in order to help with stress levels. Teachers need to be mindful that adolescents are very sensitive to put downs and criticism.

Opportunities for collaboration and cooperation can support pupils to develop team working and develop increased awareness of others' social behaviour. Use curricular opportunities (e.g. Personal, Social, Health and Economic education) to give pupils the space and time to explore in an objective way issues and concerns about relationships with peers and others.

Peers can positively impact on pupil learning by providing friendships. These friendships can provide the opportunity to share and discuss feelings. Peers can also use heightened sensitivities to rejection or break-ups to exclude or bully others.

Teacher–pupil relationship

As we noted previously, the importance of the teacher–pupil relationship is highlighted through the Teachers' Standards (DfE 2011b) and in guidance documents (e.g. DfE 2016c) that seek to improve pupil behaviour and mental health in schools. Its importance is also recognised in research. Within her review of evidence from empirical studies that explored pupils' perspectives on aspects of their primary schooling, Robinson (2014: 6) reported that: 'Findings from research studies clearly indicate that the formation of positive relationships amongst and between adults and pupils, together with the absence of bullying, are significant contributory factors in primary pupils' enjoyment of school.'

The teacher–pupil relationship needs to be considered from the perspective and experience of the individuals involved. The teacher–pupil relationship has to bridge the gap between:

1   developing a professional relationship with a group of individuals in order to promote learning and achievement; and
2   trying to ensure that individuals within the group experience a personalised element within that professional relationship, particularly those who are considered to be vulnerable.

Teachers are placed in a vulnerable position within the group setting of the classroom. Any mistakes they make are public and are likely to be remembered by the class. Where the teacher already has an established relationship with the class or has a range of successful previous experiences to draw upon, any mistake can often be easily addressed, being perceived by both teacher and pupils as temporary, atypical and repairable. However, for trainees and newly qualified teachers (NQTs) in particular, the relationship with others can be experienced as an unusual one in that, although as a teacher they are in a position of designated authority, they are also acutely aware of the potential for any mistakes to influence pupil perceptions of their competence and authority. With no previous terms of reference within the relationship any mistake may be seen by pupils, and potentially the teacher, as permanent, typical and irreparable. For the teacher this initial relationship with their class may be based on an avoidance of mistakes, perceived as carrying a high-risk and underpinned by an assumption of a lack of empathy from the other party. It is little wonder therefore that a key concern for many teachers at this early stage of their career is losing control of the class.

When pupils are asked to think about what makes a good teacher they tend to think about interpersonal skills rather than just issues of pedagogy or other technicalities of teaching. For example, Robinson (2014), drawing on Hopkins' (2008) earlier work, suggests that:

> In primary pupils' eyes, a 'good' teacher is one who is strict and fair, who has good organisational skills, and has enthusiasm, commitment and excitement for the work in hand; a good teacher is also one who is not seen to have 'favourites' and one who makes pupils feel that 'everyone is special'.
>
> (Robinson 2014: 12)

Reflective Exercise 7.1

Teachers on our courses have noted the following breakdown points in their relationship with their classes:

- when the class is 'out of control';
- when pupil(s) are blasé and just don't care;
- when pupil(s) accuse you of being unfair when you were not;
- when they manipulate the behaviour system;
- when they are simply not interested in you and ignore you;
- when they repeatedly do something when you have asked them not to;
- when they deny doing something when you have seen (or can see) them do it;
- when they make personal criticism of your teaching or compare you unfavourably with another teacher.

  1 How might a view that *teaching is all about relationships* help you to analyse what has gone wrong in these instances?
  2 What do you think are the underpinning issues in relation to your planning and thinking to avoid each of these breakdowns?

Robinson (2014: 12), again drawing on Hopkins (2008), also suggests that: 'Pupils had less regard for, and reported not liking, teachers who shout, especially those who shout at whole classes when the shouting is aimed at a minority of pupils, and "moody teachers who did not like the work".'

These views suggest that the pupils reported on both the professional and personalised aspects of their teachers' behaviours. Pupils' liking of teachers who make them feel that 'everyone is special' suggests that pupils value a relationship that allows their individuality to be recognised within the group setting of the classroom. It is an unusual relationship; although, as just one human being relating to another, the teacher may have many different ways they could 'get on' with a child or young person, they are in a 'professional position' (DfE 2011b: 14) and need to 'exercise appropriate authority' (DfE 2011b: 12). It is also a relationship with a primary purpose of promoting learning, which makes it very different to most, if not all, other relationships in which either the teacher or the pupil are involved. Table 7.2 provides an opportunity to consider the nature of the teacher–pupil relationship. It is useful for teachers, particularly those who may be only a few years older than their pupils, to reflect upon the way they approach their teaching. Table 7.2 can support them in this process.

The four categories in Table 7.2 are, of course, stereotypes and do not reflect the fact that teachers can exhibit a mixture of these characteristics and that there may be some variation depending, for example, on pressures on the teacher at a given time. When reviewing your scores you ideally want the higher ratings to fall within the 'friendly' section and your lower ratings to fall in the other three sections.

The characteristics of the teacher in each of these categories will affect the development of learning behaviour. The behaviour of the 'aggressive' teacher may lead to pupil compliance and may even lead colleagues to view this individual as a 'good' behaviour manager if evaluated against this criterion. However, the methods of gaining compliance may stifle risk taking in learning as pupils do just enough to avoid drawing attention to themselves. Their learning is only at the level of behaving appropriately to

Table 7.2 Teacher characteristics and the pupil–teacher relationship

Relationship	Teacher characteristics	Not at all like me				A lot like me
Friend	Colludes with pupils' expectations rather than setting own.	1	2	3	4	5
	Behaves in a way they believe will appeal to pupils.	1	2	3	4	5
	Has no control over the learning behaviours promoted. Without this leadership many learning behaviours that develop may be negative, such as task avoidance.	1	2	3	4	5
	Knows pupils as individuals but climate leads to a lack of boundaries in what personal information pupils share with the teacher and how they share it.	1	2	3	4	5
	Openly shares own personal information.	1	2	3	4	5
	Adopts pupil terminology and style of language when correcting misbehaviour.	1	2	3	4	5
	Has to use higher level sanctions before pupils take notice.	1	2	3	4	5
	Reacts to pupils' responses and attempts to please.	1	2	3	4	5
	Experiences pupil misbehaviour as personal hurt.	1	2	3	4	5
Friendly	States expectations, both academic and behavioural.	1	2	3	4	5
	Models appropriate behaviour (e.g. is polite).	1	2	3	4	5
	Knows pupils as individuals and is clear about his/her pastoral role.	1	2	3	4	5
	Plans lessons that make use of and gently extend pupils' learning behaviours.	1	2	3	4	5
	Only shares personal information they are comfortable to share and that is appropriate to a teacher–pupil relationship.	1	2	3	4	5
	Positively corrects misbehaviour.	1	2	3	4	5
	Respects pupils' feelings when correcting work or behaviour.	1	2	3	4	5
	Uses respectful language.	1	2	3	4	5
	Knows when to adopt a flexible approach rather than rigorously pursuing consistency.	1	2	3	4	5
	Uses a staged response when correcting behaviour starting with the least intrusive strategy (see Chapter 10)	1	2	3	4	5
	Decides when to adapt teaching and own behaviour based on pupils' responses.	1	2	3	4	5
	Misbehaviour is seen as something that needs to be dealt with calmly and efficiently in order to cause least disruption to teaching and learning and maintain positive relationships.	1	2	3	4	5

	1	2	3	4	5
Distant					
Assumes pupils know expectations, both behavioural and academic.	1	2	3	4	5
Doesn't know pupils as individuals.	1	2	3	4	5
Plans 'safely', based on learning behaviours pupils already have.	1	2	3	4	5
Rigidly adheres to the concept of consistency.	1	2	3	4	5
Very mechanistic in responses to behaviour – if the pupil does X then I do Y.	1	2	3	4	5
Highly task oriented and unwilling to deviate from plans.	1	2	3	4	5
Doesn't view pastoral issues as part of his/her remit.	1	2	3	4	5
The notion that pupils' feelings may be affected by their style of correction of work or behaviour does not feature in their thinking.	1	2	3	4	5
Misbehaviour is seen as an irritation that gets in the way of plans and is a threat to completion of the task.	1	2	3	4	5
Aggressive					
Assumes pupils know expectations, both behavioural and academic, but that many wilfully disregard these.	1	2	3	4	5
Knows the 'trouble makers'.	1	2	3	4	5
Responds aggressively to pupils.	1	2	3	4	5
Confrontational.	1	2	3	4	5
Regularly makes 'examples' of pupils.	1	2	3	4	5
Disproportionate responses to minor misbehaviour.	1	2	3	4	5
Uses personal 'put downs' and sarcasm.	1	2	3	4	5
Little regard for pupils' feelings when correcting work or behaviour.	1	2	3	4	5
Misbehaviour is seen as a personal challenge and a threat to status.	1	2	3	4	5
Judges success in terms of compliance behaviours rather than learning behaviour.	1	2	3	4	5
Fear and coercion are seen as legitimate methods of achieving good order and discipline.	1	2	3	4	5

avoid negative comments, reprimand and sanctions. As such behaviour can become highly context dependent, with pupils behaving in this class for fear of the adult response but not internalising any notions of how human beings should behave towards one another. Instead, they are presented with a model of a person in a position of authority, who may be bigger and stronger, having the right to coerce those who are in the position of subordinates and who may be smaller and weaker.

The 'distant' teacher denies the importance of the social and emotional aspects of learning. Teaching becomes problematic for this teacher when pupils do not already have the necessary learning behaviours to tackle the type of learning that is required. When planning the teacher does not take these learning behaviours into account and instead focuses primarily on content. This teacher is likely to place their faith entirely in systems; pupils who do not respond to standard strategies may quickly be viewed as having a behavioural difficulty. Typically, the teacher will plan well within the capabilities of pupils' learning behaviour and so lessons may be unadventurous and perceived by many of the class as boring.

The teacher who attempts to be a 'friend' to the class relinquishes their social leadership role and effectively hands the agenda to the pupils. The risk is that this teacher may be popular with the class for a time, but the pupils may then feel betrayed as soon as an attempt is made to set any boundaries or correct behaviour. The learning behaviours that develop in this class tend to develop in a rather ad hoc manner and in some cases may be negative (such as task avoidance).

The 'friendly' teacher effectively takes account of and balances the social, emotional and cognitive components of learning. The teacher does not shy away from a leadership role but recognises that the purpose of this is to promote learning behaviour, not simply to achieve compliance.

Having reflected on the type of relationship teachers are brokering with their pupils it is important to consider how this might be experienced by some individual pupils in the class group. For some it may be a critical relationship in terms of their learning and development. As Roffey (2016: 34) points out: 'For children to thrive they need at least one person who they can trust, thinks they are worthwhile and lets them know that they are lovable and capable.' Such relationships are usually formed with family members. In the absence of a nurturing home environment children still need to experience this type of relationship.

In Werner and Smith's (1992, cited in Roffey 2016) longitudinal study, the person most often encountered as a positive role model outside the family was a favourite teacher. Marzano *et al.* (2003, cited in Roffey 2016) also found that higher quality teacher–student relationships led to 31 per cent fewer discipline and related problems.

While it is neither feasible nor appropriate to build a personal relationship with all individual pupils it is, as we have suggested, possible to personalise individual pupils' experience of their relationship with their teacher, giving additional emphasis to those pupils considered to be vulnerable. Suggestions for relationship building with individuals in the class include:

- showing interest in the pupil as a person, e.g. ask them about their interests, views, etc.;
- giving them some time and attention;
- listening to their viewpoint and taking it on board;
- asking their opinion;

- referring to them by name;
- conveying that the behaviour is the problem, not the person;
- providing positive feedback – explicitly noting good behaviours and positive characteristics;
- protecting them from failure, rejection and humiliation;
- empathising, showing concern about their progress and wellbeing;
- being fair;
- where necessary, explaining the reasons for giving a reward or sanction;
- being straight, honest and clear with them;
- being trustworthy and reliable;
- being positive – give them hope; avoid phrases such as 'You never know how to behave' or 'It's always you, isn't it?' that convey little faith in their ability to change.

Teachers are required to relate to the class group in a way that prioritises academic learning. Most individual pupils within the group strive to experience personal friendships and also a sense of belonging. Both the individual teacher and the individual pupil need to retain their sense of identity and experience some autonomy within the classroom setting.

Having considered aspects of the teacher–pupil relationship we now move on to look at the pupil's perspective.

Pupils' relationship with teachers

Earlier in the chapter we noted that pupils' relationship with their teachers changes as they move through the stages of schooling towards further education, higher education and employment. For the child, the adult–child relationship in an early years setting or Reception class is likely to be very different from that experienced in the subsequent phases of their education. Usually in the former:

- the child initiates;
- the child has chosen to direct their attention to the activity;
- adult intervention is through shared and not directed attention;
- the child monitors their own pace and direction;
- the involvement of other children is unintentional but valued;
- there is not necessarily a prescribed end point;
- the reward is intrinsic to the activity.

In an early years setting or Reception class the adult frequently uses the child's interests or next steps to develop learning through offering a breadth of opportunities or resources for the child to use in a variety of ways. The adult is led by the child's interest and involvement and gives them space and time to explore and test out their ideas. The adult focuses on providing the child with a safe environment that will enable them to develop confidence and control over their own learning. Through their non-intrusive, non-judgemental presence, the adult builds a relationship that enables them to find out about the child's interests, personal preferences and approaches to learning. Interaction with peers can support the individual child to relate to others through a shared interest in the play activity s/he has chosen. The presence of the adult protects the child from any antisocial behaviour and so positive peer relationships are experienced alongside the child's pursuit of their chosen interest. The adult is establishing a supportive personalised relationship with the child in order to enable them to benefit from current learning opportunities and the future learning opportunities that school will offer. Routines within the early years setting or Reception class afford the child experience of the structure involved, and social behaviours expected, in subsequent stages of their education. Within their early years setting or Reception class, individuals retain their identity by having the opportunity to report personal news items to the group. This also allows the group to know more about the individual child. This can support the individual in choosing friends through shared interests and experiences, leaving them less reliant on peer relationships that have happened incidentally through the social relationships of their family and their friendship and interest groups.

Once the child makes the transition from the Foundation Stage to Key Stage 1 they may increasingly be required to:

- adapt to sharing adult attention with others;
- make an effort with work that they are not necessarily interested in;
- tolerate being compared to others, sometimes openly;
- work alongside and sometimes collaboratively with peers they may not know or like;
- conform to rules and other expectations they may not see the point of in order that the rest of the class can get on with learning.

From the individual's perspective of being in the school classroom, they have to maintain a balance between 'fitting in with the group' and retaining their individuality. Those who over-prioritise 'fitting in' can become passive recipients of the learning opportunities available in the classroom. Although not displaying behavioural problems they are at risk of not drawing attention to themselves or any difficulties they are experiencing with their learning. Those who seek to impose their individuality within the group can become loud, argumentative, bossy, demanding of attention and so on.

The potential gap between the relationship with others expected by teachers in the classroom and that demanded by pupils can lead to the classification of particular social behaviours as behavioural problems. Pupils may, for example, see it as normal and necessary to socialise whilst they are learning whereas teachers may regard too much talking as a behavioural issue.

In her review of previous research, Robinson (2014) refers to John–Akinola et al.'s (2014) study of 248 primary school pupils. The pupils reported that positive interpersonal relationships, feeling a sense of belonging, having friends and playing sports all contributed to their enjoyment of school (Robinson 2014). In a number of studies reported by Robinson (2014) there was the common theme that pupils placed high value on both the social aspects of school and being actively involved in hands–on activities that required participation with others.

While teachers are aware that most pupils have a preference for the social aspects of school learning that are experienced through active participation and collaborative activities, they also know that they are required to improve their pupils' academic outcomes which are largely measured through ongoing assessments, national test scores and exam grades. Consequently, teachers need to develop in their pupils appropriate social behaviours that will allow them to learn and achieve within the group setting of the classroom. Teachers have opportunities to broker effective social relationships through their curriculum teaching. Examples include:

- choosing tasks and grouping strategies that place emphasis on the social learning behaviours needed to achieve academically and provide experiences of success;
- illustrating successful/unsuccessful social relationships, e.g. through stories or text analysis, etc.;
- role-playing different social scenarios (when appropriate for subject learning);
- teaching social skills explicitly to the class and through targeted group work;
- regularly reminding pupils what social learning behaviours are required so that those who do not know how to behave are provided with information to guide them;
- using the resource of the whole class group to model, reward and debate socially appropriate behaviour.

While it is clear that building relationships for learning must take advantage of the potential of the class peer group for improving behaviour, it is crucial that close attention is paid to how this potential can be maximised (Roseth *et al.* 2008). It is the grouping of pupils – in other words, the 'relationship mix' – that may require more thought than a simple instruction to 'get into groups' if the intended learning outcomes are to be met.

The strength of using the curriculum and, for example, group assemblies and tutor group meetings to foster awareness of effective social relationships is that the target pupil(s) can reflect upon the information without being overly emotionally involved. If the pupil's own behaviour is used as a basis for analysis (as might be the case following an altercation with a peer) the pupil is often too emotionally involved in defending their position to listen to reason. 'Depersonalisation' through the curriculum is a means of modelling and developing appropriate relationship behaviour. The curriculum is a resource that is unique to schools and can be used in their quest to foster appropriate relationships with others.

Pupils' relationship with peers

Many pupils show a preference for teaching that includes activity and engagement with peers (Smith *et al.* 2005; Robinson 2014). However, unless this is what the teacher has prescribed for the particular task being undertaken, they may be annoyed by the low level chatter that results from this pursuit of social interaction. Increased engagement in social activity outside the classroom through social networking sites, mobile phones, e-mails and other forms of electronic communication has contributed to the level of social interaction expected by pupils. For some pupils arriving home from school opens up a whole world of communication which is not 'face-to-face' and allows them to practise making relationships in which they have more perceived control. This is not to argue for a restriction on such activities but to acknowledge that children and young people now have numerous means of communicating with peers and forming social relationships that were not open to previous generations.

Robinson and Fielding's (2014) review of published research on pupils' views about primary schooling provides an insight into peer relationships within the classroom. Pupils said that in the classroom they learned from working with peers by giving help and exchanging ideas but also recognised that 'working with friends can hinder learning if friends talk rather than work' (Robinson and Fielding 2014: 2). Primary pupils also looked forward to extending their friendship groups in secondary school but were anxious about being bullied. From the review of research it was found that:

> Pupils tend to be unhappy with pupil groupings in situations where they are separated from friends; when they have to work with children they find uncongenial and uncooperative; or when the grouping results in too much or too little being demanded of them.
>
> (Robinson and Fielding 2014: 1)

The nature of peer relationships assumes a level of importance when it impacts negatively on relationships for learning. This happens when it is more important to the pupil to relate to their peers and so they prioritise this over their relationship with their teacher and the curriculum. Some pupils find it difficult to prioritise long-term gain (e.g. getting good grades) over the short-term gains experienced from the pleasure of other activities (e.g. mucking about, banter with peers, etc.).

Even if, through behaviour management approaches, the teacher is able to control unnecessary chatter, some pupils may not have developed the social learning behaviours needed to learn in the group setting of the classroom. The next section looks at the nature and development of these behaviours.

Social learning behaviours

Teachers have an important role in promoting and developing social learning behaviours. These are needed in order that pupils can communicate with teachers and others to support their learning, and engage effectively in group work. As already suggested, pupils can, of course, communicate with peers outside the classroom and beyond the school gate. However, electronic means of communication do not involve the same demands as traditional face-to-face interaction or require children and young people to develop the same skills in order to effectively communicate. They allow individuals to communicate without being interrupted, and without monitoring responses to their input using cues such as facial expression. Communication can be ended by, for example, switching off the mobile device or deleting friends. The DfE (2016c) guidance, *Mental Health and Behaviour in Schools*, noted that having a 'repertoire of social problem solving approaches' (DfE 2016c: 8) is an important protective factor that enables children to be resilient when they encounter problems and challenges. Schools are places that can support the development of these within a relatively safe and controlled setting.

In seeking to promote social learning behaviours for classroom learning it is important to note that from a Behaviour for Learning perspective a pupil's relationship with others cannot be viewed in isolation from their relationship with self and with the curriculum. There is an interdependence between the three relationships during learning in classroom settings. As Claxton (2002: 43) suggests,

> Good learners balance their relationships with other people, being willing to be interdependent, without becoming either too dependent on others for support or feedback, or too aloof and unwilling to take criticism or to work as part of a team.

Table 7.3 lists a number of learning behaviours that relate to learning with others. These have been taken from the literature and some are phrased negatively. It should be noted that this is in contrast to our view that learning behaviours should be positively phrased. We have sought to place these learning behaviours into categories that may help you decide whether they should be primarily addressed through working with others (social), may require additional teaching of skills to individuals (cognitive) or have a strong emotional or dispositional component (emotional). Given the interdependence between these categories, it is likely that readers will have differing views as to which column the identified learning behaviours should be placed in. We have also allocated the learning behaviours to the category of either communication or collaboration. In effect, the 'social' column suggests that the learning behaviours can be applied to a range of settings involving peers and the teacher; the 'cognitive' column looks at the skills that the pupil has or needs to develop; and the 'emotional' column looks at how the pupil might be thinking or feeling. For example, the pupil may have the skill to 'listen to others' but choose not to do so because they need to seek the attention of others at that point in time.

In seeking to examine how the pupil's relationship with others influences their relationship with the curriculum and relationship with self it is useful to consider the following questions:

1   *How best can the pupil learn as an individual while being taught in the classroom?*
    An appropriate relationship with others in this case may be considered by schools and teachers as one in which the pupil learns to avoid distractions, other pupils remain controlled and the teacher maintains discipline in order to allow individuals to get on with learning. The purpose of the relationship with the curriculum is mainly evaluated against individual progress in relation to defined curricular objectives. Pupils who persistently have difficulty ignoring distractions from others, or who contribute to those distractions or who fail to relate effectively to their teacher are often considered to have behavioural difficulties.

2   *What does the pupil learn about their relationship with self and relationship with others while they are building a relationship with the curriculum in school-based curriculum contexts?*
    In this case it is accepted that the pupil needs to be placed with others in order to learn and practise the social conventions of behaviour. The pupil also needs to be placed with others as it is through comparisons that the individual establishes their own identity and makes judgements about their own worth. In this case 'others' are a necessary resource.

3   *What can a pupil learn from others that they could not learn as well on their own?*
    In this case others are a resource, contributing to a construction of knowledge that the individual could not achieve on their own.

4   *What is it necessary for groups to learn in school contexts that are relevant to groups and to those individuals who make up those groups?*
    This refers to learning as a collective activity and is likely to have a group goal for the organisation or group itself. An example within a school context might be the school football team. Though individuals within the team may be coached, the primary purpose of the coaching is to enhance the individual's contribution to the development needs of the team. Learning is situated, intended to be applied in a particular context – in this case a football match. While there may be some monitoring and evaluation of individual performance, success is ultimately judged against performance of the group.

Table 7.3 Learning behaviours necessary for collaborative working

	Social	Cognitive	Emotional
Communication	Is an effective communicator.	Seeks attention appropriately.	Respects the teacher and is cooperative and compliant, responding positively to instruction.
	Speaks politely.	Appropriate tone of voice for task.	
	Uses proper names.	Tone of voice is congruent with body language.	Behaves respectfully towards staff.
	Waits turn to speak.		Shows concern and understanding.
	Interacts politely with the teacher.		Does not talk back to the teacher or aim verbal aggression at the teacher.
			Does not show physical aggression towards adults or other pupils.
			Does not physically pick on others.
			Is not cruel or spiteful to others.
			Avoids getting into fights with others.
			Does not strike out in anger, have temper tantrums or aggressive outbursts.
Collaboration	Works efficiently in a group.	Works efficiently in a group, e.g. takes part in discussions.	Respects other pupils and uses appropriate language, e.g. not swearing or calling them names.
	Has the skill of learning with others.	Contributes readily to group tasks.	
	Listens to what others have to say and consequently adds positively to group discussions.	Listens well in groups. Works collaboratively. Only interrupts and seeks attention appropriately.	Treats other pupils as equals and does not dominate them by intimidation or abuse.
		Does not disrupt unnecessarily, or distract or interfere with others.	Respects the views or rights of other pupils and avoids bullying or intimidation.
			Does not pass notes, talk when others are talking, does not seek unwarranted attention.
			Is physically peaceable. Respects property.

Reflective Exercise 7.2

In looking at questions 1–4 above:

- Which purpose or purposes do you tend to prioritise in your classroom?
- How does that purpose impact on your strategies for building relationships with others in your classroom?
- Can you identify some learning behaviours you think it would be necessary to develop in relation to each of the four questions above?

The choice between an approach based on *controlling* peer social interaction and an approach based on *using* peer social interaction is more often based on personal preference and experience than it is on evidence. It also cannot be expected that if a teacher is good at one approach they will necessarily be good at the other. Both require different planning, different objectives, different assessments, different evaluations and different preparation of pupils. Traditionally, when we use the term 'behaviour management' we are thinking about how to manage the group so that the individual can get on with their learning. However, some researchers have studied how best we can prepare individuals to work in groups and this activity is discussed under the broad umbrella of collaborative learning.

The next section critically reflects on different priorities for collaborative learning that arise from questions 1–4 above. It needs to be noted that although we have used these questions to depict different relationships with others they are not mutually exclusive and so do not appear in classrooms in such a distinct form. We are mindful too of inherent methodological challenges for classroom-based research in this area given Johnson *et al.*'s (2000) view that no other pedagogical practice simultaneously generates such diverse intended and unintended outcomes as collaborative learning.

Critical reflection on different priorities for collaborative learning

Priority 1: Building relationships with others that seek to allow the individual to learn individually in the classroom

Within classroom contexts the kinds of learning behaviour identified in the literature is, not surprisingly, concerned with pupils being able to work together but in an essentially controlled manner. In order for pupils to be perceived to be working effectively in groups they are often expected to work within non-confrontational boundaries in which 'argument' or 'disagreement' with others is not seen as being supportive to academic learning. Table 7.3 includes learning behaviours from the literature considered to be relevant to both communication and collaborative learning. We can see that in these examples the pupil's relationship with others is expected to be one in which emotions and feelings are kept under control in order to minimise discord and disruption.

This contrasts with expectations surrounding pupils' relationship with the curriculum which, as we noted in Chapter 5, is considered to be effective if there is a close interplay between emotional and cognitive aspects of learning. This results in pupils being motivated and involved such that they initiate learning, persist, apply and sustain effort, are creative and welcome cognitive challenge and dissonance.

Clearly most pupils in schools can, and do, adopt a socially active (e.g. by asking for clarification or help when needed and working collaboratively with peers without 'mucking about') and cognitively active (e.g. thinking and problem solving) approach to learning, while at the same time being controlled and responsive to class rules and disciplinary frameworks. Any mismatch between social and cognitive requirements does not then cause a problem for the pupil and their teachers. However, some pupils may find it more difficult to adapt to the demands for active cognitive processing within a class context based on social peace and compliance and this can lead to behavioural difficulties. Either the pupil does not have the maturity or self-control to switch from noisy but slightly controlled social interaction (low-level chatter) to quiet but internally active learning, or they find it very difficult to achieve active cognitive processing unless they can manipulate and manage the information 'outside their head' through, for example, discussion, hands on activity and information and communication technology (ICT). In particular, pupils who have low levels of working memory, including many with SEN, struggle to meet the demands of complex tasks that require them to process, maintain and store information simultaneously. It is suggested that this difficulty may underpin their failure to make 'normal' educational progress (Alloway *et al.* 2005). It follows that those pupils who experience difficulty in retaining and processing the information contained in task related or disciplinary instructions may also be wrongly seen at times to be non-compliant.

Schools seek to improve attainment through managing social behaviour in the classroom so that individual pupils can 'get on and learn' and also by providing opportunities for pupils to learn from each other. Schools and their staff will normally reflect a preference towards one or the other approach, as will individual pupils. Closer alignment of teacher and pupil preferences can be achieved through grouping strategies and by adjustments to task requirements and learning objectives.

There is limited evidence that working in a team achieves cognitive outcomes that cannot be matched or exceeded by the most capable group member (Slavin 2004). Slavin (2004: 275) writes that:

> learning is completely different from 'group' outcomes. It may well be that working in a group under certain circumstances does increase the learning of the individuals in that group more than would working under other arrangements, but a measure of group productivity provides no evidence one way or another on this; only an individual learning measure that cannot be influenced by group member help can indicate which incentive or task structure is best … learning takes place only between the ears of the learner.

The view that the most capable learner in the group can do just as well on their own masks the view that the other members of the group may learn better than they would individually simply by interacting with this 'capable' learner and acquiring strategies and approaches to learning that they did not previously have in their repertoire. Although such individual learning could not be assessed from the group task outcome it still could have taken place 'between the ears of the learner'.

Within schools there is a need to retain a core emphasis on building a positive relationship with the curriculum so that attainment in subject areas can be improved and gaps between high and lower attainment groups can be reduced. However, global and national initiatives for social inclusion, alongside a need to prepare young people for teamwork in the workplace and to promote social cohesion and citizenship, indicates that collaborative learning is likely to remain an area of importance and one for further development within school contexts.

Priority 2: Learning social behaviour from others

Improved social and emotional outcomes such as increased motivation, higher self-esteem and improved communication are consistently reported as outcomes from collaborative learning. Indeed Kreidler (1984) saw his main educational goal for teaching his primary school class as developing the skills of cooperation through the employment of six principles: cooperation; caring; responsible decision making and conflict resolution; communication; the appreciation of diversity; and the appropriate expression of feelings. He reported that by using these principles children's work and the classroom atmosphere improved drastically (Powell 1993). Such a view on the strength of social learning comes from the work of Bandura who states that:

> Learning would be exceedingly laborious, not to mention hazardous, if people had to rely solely on the effects of their own actions to inform them what to do. Fortunately, most human behavior is learned observationally through modelling: from observing others one forms an idea of how new behaviors are performed, and on later occasions this coded information serves as a guide for action.
>
> (Bandura 1977: 22)

Bandura's Social Learning Theory explains human behaviour in terms of continuous reciprocal interaction between cognitive, behavioural and environmental influences and as such reflects the underpinning principles of the Behaviour for Learning approach.

Priority 3: Improving individual academic learning through relationship with others

Damon (1984: 335, reported in Slavin 2004) integrated theoretical perspectives, including Piagetian and Vygotskian, to outline a conceptual foundation for peer-based education, suggesting that:

- Through mutual feedback and debate, peers motivate one another to abandon misconceptions and search for better solutions.
- The experience of peer communication can help a child master social processes such as participation and argumentation, and cognitive processes, such as verification and criticism.
- Collaboration between peers can provide a forum for discovery learning and can encourage creative thinking.
- Peer interaction can introduce children to the process of generating ideas.

(Damon 1984: 335, cited in Slavin 2004: 284)

The use of the word 'can' in Damon's conceptual framework is important. It conveys the potential of peer-based education but acknowledges that although research studies have secured the necessary conditions to test out the realisation of these aims, evidence from classroom settings has yet to be secured.

It is likely that peer-based education, not only because of improvements in academic learning but also to address concerns about a range of antisocial behaviours, will continue to be on the educational agenda. Parsons *et al.* (2008: 20) reported that schools sought to impact on a number of areas through the use of peer-based strategies. In order of priority these include:

1   improved academic performance/attainment;
2   reduction in bullying;
3   improved attendance;
4   fewer exclusions.

As Parsons *et al.* (2008) acknowledge, findings from such studies are positive and rich in anecdotal and qualitative evidence relating to the 'experience' of both mentor and mentee. However, there is less rigorous data on whether academic attainment, attendance and behaviour had improved as a consequence of peer- based interventions.

Priority 4: Learning about groups from groups

Because collaborative learning involves 'team work', a much valued activity in the workplace, there has been interest in work that seeks to harness school and business perspectives to promote more effective learning. In her study on decision making in small groups in primary Science, Maloney (2007) required the group to:

a   discuss most or all of the evidence made available;
b   test alternative choices and consider both positive and negative issues of the possible outcomes;
c   provide claims supported by evidence;
d   engage in sustained dialogue by making claims, reviewing evidence and discussing arguments as an iterative process.

(Maloney 2007: 378)

Maloney then used Belbin's (1981) framework for 'useful people to have in teams' to analyse the pupils' roles and responsibilities to see if there was any potential from practices in business management to make pupils' learning in groups more effective. Belbin noted that 'what is needed is not well balanced individuals but individuals who balance well with each other' (Belbin 1981: 75). Although a literal interpretation of this comment is not advocated, the sentiment behind it is clear.

Some of the positive and negative roles outlined were chair, discussion manager, information manager, promoter of ideas, distracter, contributor and non-responsive contributor.

Maloney (2007) reported from the research that pupils can be clear about the contribution they make to the team and can be aware of other people's contributions and how these can be coordinated. This has implications for how teachers make decisions about which pupils are placed in what groups depending on the purpose of the task. This resonates with work in multi-agency settings that refers to the 'skill mix' of the partners involved.

Having looked at the different perspectives and reasons for building positive relationships with others, there are clearly issues for preparing pupils to engage in collaborative activity through the promotion of relevant learning behaviours. These will depend on the purpose for the collaboration, the tasks set and the evaluation criteria used. Grouping of pupils is likely to be different depending on the teacher's perceived need for building relationships with others in the classroom. Given the aspirations for collaborative working in addressing cognitive, social and emotional aspects of learning it is noteworthy that Pollard *et al.* (2000: 171) found that teachers typically 'applied criteria related to attainment (usually referred to as "ability") and behaviour or social relationships to decide which children should work together'. In her review of research and practice in cooperative learning, Gillies (2016) noted that there was overwhelming support for cooperative learning as a pedagogical practice that promotes both socialisation and learning. Teachers play a key role in structuring groups so that key components likely to facilitate cooperative learning are evident. They also have a role in promoting appropriate interactions so that pupils engage in problem solving, reasoning and learning that they are unlikely to do on their own.

Bullying in schools

It is not within the scope of this chapter to cover bullying in any depth. However, it is important to recognise that bullying represents a particular form of relationship with others based on a perceived imbalance of power between the victim(s) and perpetrator(s). The DfE (2017e: 8) defines bullying as 'behaviour by an individual or group, repeated over time, that intentionally hurts another individual or group either physically or emotionally'.

As previous government guidance (DCSF 2007a) indicated, bullying can take many forms including:

- name–calling, taunting and mocking;
- making offensive comments;
- kicking, hitting and pushing;
- taking belongings;
- inappropriate text messaging and emailing;
- sending offensive or degrading images by phone or via the internet;
- excluding people from groups;
- gossiping, spreading hurtful and untruthful rumours.

DfE (2017e: 8) guidance notes that bullying 'is often motivated by prejudice against particular groups, for example on grounds of race, religion, gender, sexual orientation, special educational needs or disabilities, or because a child is adopted, in care or has caring responsibilities'. Stereotyping can also be a factor as bullying may be 'motivated by actual differences between children, or perceived differences' (DfE (2017e: 8).

Although schools typically adopt a zero tolerance approach to bullying, individuals still report experiencing bullying and the long-term and pervasive effects it has on their lives. Minton (2017) reports that there has been little change in this since a large-scale study was undertaken in the UK nearly 30 years ago. The implication is that schools need proactive measures to create the context and conditions so that bullying is less likely to occur but also to ensure there are robust reactive strategies in place for those occasions when it does.

Reactive strategies range from more punitive or sanction-based approaches, through restorative practices, to more indirect and non-punitive approaches. Research conducted by Thompson and Smith (2011) suggests that the vast majority of schools rely on the use of direct sanctions as their reactive strategy for dealing with bullying. Around two-thirds of schools in Thompson and Smith's (2011) research used restorative approaches.

Although we need to know how to respond when bullying occurs, as with behaviour generally it is preferable to focus on prevention and early intervention. Kyriakides and Creemers (2013) suggest that teacher–pupil relationships, policies for behaviour outside the classroom (e.g. fighting in the playground) and the quality of the school learning environment are significantly related to lower levels of bullying. Classroom teachers have an important role to play in tackling bullying in that they are in a position to know which pupils in their class are likely to be vulnerable to bullying and they can observe classroom relationships and subtle changes in an individual's behaviour on a day-to-day basis. They are also aware of the level of development of their pupils' 'relationship with others' and are able to detect the difference between pupils who 'can't' and pupils who 'won't' behave in a prosocial way with their peers. Table 7.4 provides a more detailed list of behaviours that could either represent bullying or give an indication that a pupil is being bullied. This can help teachers with early identification of bullying. In the case of behaviours that could represent bullying, pupils, teachers and parents need to distinguish between isolated unpleasant behaviours that need to be dealt with appropriately in line with the school's behaviour policy and those that represent bullying because they are 'repeated over time' (DfE 2017e: 8).

Table 7.4 Examples of behaviours that might be associated with perpetrators and victims of bullying

Examples of behaviours of perpetrators

- Making nasty comments (including by message, graffiti or notice).
- Imitating a pupil or mocking their behaviour or anything else about them.
- Laughing at or dismissing a pupil's contributions in the classroom or elsewhere.
- Making gestures towards someone which are designed to belittle or ridicule them.
- Teasing someone (for example) by calling them names or being sarcastic.
- Preventing someone from moving freely, blocking their way.
- Making gestures that could be perceived as threatening.
- Interfering with or knocking over another pupil's equipment.
- Deliberately and persistently not choosing certain individuals to work with or physically moving away from other individuals.

- Posting rumours, lies or inaccurate information with the intention of intimidating someone.
- Sending anonymous, unsolicited messages or making silent calls.
- Deliberately attempting to isolate or exclude someone, or separate them from others (e.g. sending messages warning others not to mix with someone).
- Attempting to force someone to do or say something by threatening to reveal something about them (blackmail).
- Threatening to reveal someone's (supposed) sexual orientation without their knowledge, understanding or permission ('outing').
- Making or sharing images or films which ridicule or undermine someone so as to isolate or exclude them socially.

continued

Table 7.4 Continued

Examples of behaviours that might be indicative of experiencing bullying

- Reluctance to sit with peers in the canteen or other occasions where there is a choice of where to sit.
- Unwilling to go to school or return to school after a period of absence.
- Becoming withdrawn, anxious, or less confident.
- Decline in the standard of school work.
- Possessions (e.g. clothes, books) are damaged or 'go missing'.
- Becomes aggressive, disruptive or unreasonable, and perhaps starts to bully others.
- Gives unlikely excuses for damaged or lost equipment, physical injury or the need for money.
- Asks/pleads with peers, staff or parents not to say anything about what they have seen or been told.
- Becomes unwilling to use the internet or mobile phone.
- Parents/carers report a change in the pupil's behaviour at home (e.g. difficulty in sleeping, eating habits, stops talking about school or friends).
- Changes in emotional response (e.g. crying, heightened emotional sensitivity, increased 'neediness').
- Drops or loses interest in hobbies or other activities.
- Reluctance to go out with school friends or to evening events.
- Reluctance to let others (e.g. friends, parents) see their phone or email account.

Minton (2017) is of the view that it is not enough to rely on strategies of awareness raising and behaviour management and suggests that anti-bullying programmes in schools need to be strategically revised with attention being given to the role of prejudice as an underlying factor in bullying and in other forms of aggressive marginalisation. Strategies available to teachers which contribute to the development of a relationship with others that improves learning and social behaviour and support school policies for tackling bullying, prejudice and discrimination include:

- choosing tasks and grouping strategies that place emphasis on the social learning behaviours needed to achieve success;
- regularly reminding all pupils what social learning behaviours are required;
- using the resource of the whole-class group to model, positively reinforce and discuss socially appropriate behaviour;
- expecting and enforcing certain standards of social behaviour in the classroom (e.g. challenging if others laugh at another pupil's response in class);
- teaching social skills and developing cooperative and collaborative learning behaviours through targeted group work;
- discussing the nature of friendship and exploring the difference between judging popularity by the quality of friendships and by the numbers of contacts on social media sites;
- discussing what it means to be popular and whether being popular is a stable attribute;
- illustrating successful/unsuccessful social relationships through depersonalised activities, e.g. through stories, literature, historical events, examples from reality TV or current affairs, etc.;

- ensuring pupils are exposed to positive images of disability and difference;
- critically exploring negative portrayal of disability and difference in children's literature, other literature and films;
- discussing through examples from the curriculum outcomes from discriminating against particular groups on the grounds of religion, race, disability, gender, sexuality, etc.;
- challenging the use of language by pupils that is based on discrimination or stereotyping (e.g. pejorative use of terms related to disability or difference);
- working on developing empathy from an early age – this can be through depersonalised activities (e.g. stories, role-play) but also through the approach used when dealing with behaviour linked to falling out with peers;
- seeking to develop the skills and dispositions that build resilience to bullying from an early age (e.g. sense of self-worth, self-confidence, assertiveness, social problem-solving ability);
- role-playing different bullying scenarios so, for example, perpetrators can role-play victims so that they experience the two sides; pause the action at intervals to highlight points where different behavioural choices could be made and discuss the possible alternative responses;
- exploring the roles and responsibilities of bystanders who are aware of bullying, witness it and possibly even find it entertaining;
- providing opportunities to learn and rehearse stock responses to behaviour experienced as bullying;
- ensuring there are easily accessible systems for reporting bullying of self or others.

Bullying is likely to continue to be a problem in schools. Anti-bullying policies and strategies in schools should be known to all teachers and rigorously applied. There will always be individuals whose relationship with others is weighted more towards their own need for attention and control than on the feelings and wellbeing of others. Schools offer a unique opportunity to develop and foster a relationship with others that pays due regard to individuals' personal needs but balances this with their responsibility to also pay due regard to the social and emotional needs of others.

Conclusion

The school itself, and classrooms within it, provide a social context for learning that requires individuals to build relationships with their peers and teachers. Relationship with others is accepted as an integral part of school learning both for teachers and their pupils. Teachers are typically placed on their own in classrooms to build relationships with individuals in their class whilst pupils are required to learn in groups and relate to one influential, but potentially vulnerable, adult. The balance of power and dynamics involved ensure that pupil behaviour and teacher competence and confidence in managing this behaviour remains on the educational agenda, with a current focus on low-level disruption (e.g. Ofsted 2014a)

This chapter has highlighted competing aims associated with relationship with others. The pupil is often required to ignore distractions and work independently in pursuit of experiencing success and achievement that will offer more choices for further education, higher education and employment and in so doing impact positively on their wellbeing. However, many pupils, particularly younger pupils and those who lack motivation for academic learning, report a strong preference for teaching that involves active participation with peers. Additionally, risk factors for mental health include poor or harmful social relationships with both adults and peers. Having friends and experiencing positive relationships with others improves resilience to the experience of the naturally occurring ups and downs in school learning and in life.

School provides long-term exposure to a variety of social relationships within a relatively safe and controlled setting. Staff are trained to harness the benefits of promoting learning and positive social behaviour in groups and managing the risk to individuals of negative social behaviours.

In seeking to balance requirements to focus on curriculum attainment and the preference for many pupils to work actively and in groups, teachers aim to include learning opportunities that involve cooperative and collaborative learning. The benefit of these approaches in promoting socialisation and learning is well documented. However, such approaches involve careful planning and grouping with clear objectives for the social and learning outcomes. They do not provide a quick fix to concerns about behavioural problems in schools, pupil wellbeing and developing self-motivated, social responsible, employable citizens.

Relationship with others has to be considered as crucial to pupils' wellbeing and achievement throughout their school lives and beyond. In this chapter, and throughout this book, social, emotional and cognitive relationships for learning are viewed as interdependent. Social learning behaviours need to be developed and promoted within all phases and subject areas so that the group context of the school supports rather than harms the development of pupil's learning and emotional wellbeing.

Chapter 8

Whole-school approaches and the school behaviour policy

Introduction

As outlined in Chapter 1, government policy and guidance (e.g. DES 1989; DfES 2003a; DCSF 2009; DfE 2016a) has consistently emphasised the importance of a whole-school approach to managing pupil behaviour. A school's behaviour policy is a key document defining this approach. The requirement for schools to have a behaviour policy is firmly established in legislation (e.g. Education Act 1997; School Standards and Framework Act 1998; Education and Inspections Act 2006). The overriding purpose of a whole-school approach is to secure an environment in which every pupil can benefit from the learning opportunities on offer. An effective whole-school approach will provide a stable, safe and predictable environment for staff and pupils. When adopting the Behaviour for Learning approach, it is necessary to develop whole-school practices and processes based on their compatibility with the basic principles of promoting learning behaviour and protecting and enhancing the three relationships – with self, with others and with the curriculum – that underpin its development. Emphasis is also placed on how the whole-school approach and the behaviour policy are experienced and interpreted by individuals.

This chapter initially considers some of the implications for the development of a whole-school approach to behaviour if a Behaviour for Learning perspective is adopted. Whole-school behaviour policies are then critically examined in relation to their capacity to promote learning behaviour and maintain and develop the three relationships that underpin its development. It is recognised that for most classroom teachers, rules, rewards and sanctions are the aspects of policy with which they will be engaged on a daily basis in order to 'manage behaviour effectively to ensure a good and safe learning environment' (DfE 2011b: 12). A substantial proportion of the chapter is devoted to reviewing rules, rewards and sanctions in relation to their purpose and compatibility with the principles of the Behaviour for Learning approach. The final part examines some specific, popular overarching frameworks for managing behaviour.

A whole-school approach

The Behaviour for Learning conceptual framework presented in Chapter 2 (Figure 2.1) has a circle surrounding the triangle of influence, bearing the title 'school ethos'. The Elton Report (DES 1989) used the phrase 'school atmosphere' and recently Bennett (2017) has referred to 'school culture'. Though it is possible to make distinctions, essentially these terms all capture the idea that there is a 'feel' to the school. Bennett (2017:

6) uses the phrase 'the way we do things around here' in relation to 'school culture'; this is a description that could also be applied to 'school ethos' but we would suggest the latter term reflects that there is also a more experiential dimension that we could summarise as 'what it feels like to be here for staff and pupils'. All of the school's policies, practices and processes shape this experience. They also convey explicit and tacit assumptions about the school's underlying principles and values, the skills and dispositions that are valued and its purposes as an organisation.

While it is common to talk about the desirability of a positive ethos, it is important to recognise that ethos is something experienced by individuals. What is generally experienced as positive by many may not be for some. For example, a strong academic ethos may positively influence the aspirations of some but be experienced as relentless pressure by others. Though establishing a positive ethos is something schools do in order to benefit groups, the responses of individuals need to be monitored in terms of what these reveal about the learning behaviours being developed and the impact on each of the three Behaviour for Learning relationships.

A complicating dimension for school leaders when considering ethos and attempting to bring about change is that practice influences ethos and ethos influences practice in a reciprocal, dynamic relationship. For example, if a school operates a punitive regime based on identifying and punishing wrongdoing and rule infringement, this creates an ethos where identifying and punishing wrongdoing and rule infringement is expected. It becomes very difficult for existing staff to break out of this cycle and new members of staff may find it very difficult to resist the ethos. Similarly, for pupils the ethos may be one in which being sanctioned (or 'getting done') is the norm and where minor 'victories' over the system bring esteem among peers. It is equally difficult for existing pupils to break out of this cycle and new pupils may find it very difficult to resist the ethos.

Though a school's ethos is influenced by many factors, in the context of this book it is the contribution of the whole-school approach to behaviour and the behaviour policy that it is most relevant to consider. Figure 8.1 includes a range of processes that contribute to a whole-school approach to behaviour. It distinguishes between universal processes experienced by all pupils and the proactive and reactive processes experienced by some pupils. In defining some processes as reactive the suggestion is not that these are unnecessary or inappropriate. The important element in the diagram is the central arrow. Most schools collect a range of qualitative and quantitative data on pupils' behaviour, for example, logging incidents or sanctions issued. It is important not just to collect data but to use it. The fact that a pupil is beginning to encounter higher level sanctions or their behaviour has led to physical intervention by staff (see Chapter 11) should trigger further investigation and the implementation of supportive interventions. For a school adopting the Behaviour for Learning approach, the priority would always be to move back to the proactive side of Figure 8.1. using the conceptual framework (Chapter 2, Figure 2.1) as a problem- solving and planning tool (see Chapters 2 and 12).

The willingness to adopt the type of approach represented in Figure 8.1 depends on recognition of a fundamental distinction between a focus on a 'problem pupil' and a focus on 'problem behaviour'. Drawing on the work of Fogell and Long (1997), Table 8.1 provides an opportunity to explore this issue.

It should be clear from Table 8.1 that the ethos would be very different for both staff and pupils in a school that adopts a predominantly 'problem pupil' focus compared to one that focuses on the behaviour as the problem rather than the individual.

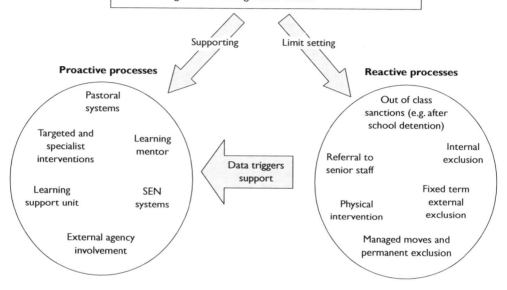

Figure 8.1 Processes contributing to a whole-school approach to behaviour.

It is also evident that much of the language in the 'problem behaviour' column is that of relationships, using terms such as 'collaborative' and 'shared aims' and emphasising the importance of the active involvement of all stakeholders. It should be recognised that the 'problem behaviour' perspective is not suggesting that misbehaviour should be ignored or that staff should be left feeling unsupported. The key difference is in the purpose and priorities. This reflects a distinction drawn by Evans (2011) between authoritarian and authoritative schools. In her report for Barnardo's, Evans (2011) cites Pellerin's (2005) research in US schools which demonstrated that disengagement was worse in schools with authoritarian approaches to discipline. She also reports Gregory *et al.*'s (2010) finding 'that a "tough love" combination of both structure and support that characterised authoritative schools resulted in less bullying and victimisation than in schools which simply adopted a '"get tough" or authoritarian approach' (Gregory *et al.* 2010, cited in Evans 2011: 4). The focus on 'problem behaviour' reflects the principle of unconditional positive regard, which involves accepting the individual as a person of worth without seeking to approve of his/her behaviour (Gatongi 2007). Such a perspective requires us to recognise that behaviour represents a form of communication and has a purpose for the individual. This is not the same

Table 8.1 Differences between a 'problem pupil' and a 'problem behaviour' perspective on behaviour

Use the table below to rank your school or a school that you know well against these statements:

Problem pupil	1	2	3	4	5	Problem behaviour
Reactive Deals with crisis situations; finds culprit when trouble occurs.	1	2	3	4	5	**Proactive** Plans strategies to pre-empt problem behaviour.
Confrontational Depends on sanctions to control undesired behaviour – emphasis on labelling, reprimand and punishment.	1	2	3	4	5	**Positive** Catches spontaneous positive behaviour and rewards it; emphasis on identifying good models of behaviour.
Fault finding Believes that the pupils are at fault or must change first.	1	2	3	4	5	**Initiating** Involves all staff, pupils, parents to achieve shared aims.
Individualist Each teacher depends on their own resources.	1	2	3	4	5	**Collaborative** Whole-school polices developed.
Authoritarian Minimal involvement of pupils, parents or staff team in decision making.	1	2	3	4	5	**Democratic** All staff, pupils and parents actively involved.
Status focused Concern is with behaviour that challenges staff and authority.	1	2	3	4	5	**Welfare focused** Concern is on relationships between staff and pupils.

Source: Fogell and Long 1997: 14.

as condoning it; understanding what the individual is communicating through their behaviour and the purpose it currently serves is the first step towards changing it.

Approaching behaviour policies from a Behaviour for Learning perspective

In adopting a Behaviour for Learning perspective when considering school behaviour policies, emphasis is placed on clarity about purpose and priorities, awareness of what is implicitly and explicitly promoted, the contribution to the development of learning behaviour and the influence of any practices specified within policy on the three core relationships within the conceptual framework.

Clarity about purpose and priorities

In unreservedly acknowledging the necessity and utility of behaviour policies, it is also necessary to be realistic about their purpose, priority and what they can hope to achieve. The elements of a behaviour policy that inform day-to-day classroom practice are typically rules, rewards and sanctions and often some advice on general behaviour management strategies. The primary purpose is to promote good behaviour and discourage poor behaviour among the majority in order to secure certain standards of behaviour from *groups* (i.e. the school population as a whole and individual classes). Evaluation of a school's behaviour policy needs to be made against the purpose for which it was designed. The difficulty occurs when policy makers and individual schools attempt to evaluate whole-school policies predominantly in terms of the impact on a minority who fall outside the influence of the rules, rewards and sanctions that typically characterise such policies. Typically, these pupils define themselves through the frequency and intensity of their behaviour (DfE 1994b) and the very fact that this is not ameliorated by the behaviour management techniques usually employed by the school (DfES 2001). While we are not suggesting that these pupils should be seen as exempt from, standing outside of – or beyond – the influence of policy, to evaluate the school's behaviour policy against these pupils' behaviour is likely to lead to a frustrating quest for a set of systems that will work for all pupils. The best a school can aim for is a policy that leads to fewer pupils falling outside it, coupled with clear systems of pupil support for those who, within a system designed for groups, inevitably do fall outside the policy. Undoubtedly, some discipline systems, such as those that either allow minimal scope for professional judgement in responding to pupils as individuals or contain numerous 'obscure, arbitrary or petty rules' (DES 1989: 100) that have to be enforced, are likely to lead to more pupils falling outside day-to-day policy.

From a Behaviour for Learning perspective it is necessary to accept that a behaviour policy is designed for groups but will be experienced and interpreted by individuals. This means that though the policy may achieve its primary aim of securing the behaviour of groups and could be evaluated as successful against this purpose, individuals may experience it less positively.

In aligning behaviour policies more closely with the Behaviour for Learning approach, greater emphasis is placed on how individuals might experience and interpret the practices and approaches employed. However, we need to acknowledge that even when adopting a Behaviour for Learning perspective, decisions about practices and approaches to be encouraged through policy can only be based on a prediction about how a 'typical' pupil might experience these. As a basic principle, any practice or approach should not be to the detriment of one of the three relationships. For example, a sanction that contained an element that a pupil may find humiliating or embarrassing would risk impacting on relationship with self. Similarly, using copying out of a reading book as a sanction risks undermining relationship with curriculum as the pupil may come to associate both reading and writing with punishment. As we shall explore in more depth in Chapter 10, punishing all pupils for the behaviour of some may be to the detriment of relationship with others if it leads to resentment between peers and towards the teacher. In terms of actively promoting learning behaviour, it would be difficult to claim that every sanction can achieve this. However, attention needs to be given to whether positive learning behaviours are being discouraged or negative behaviours promoted by any aspect of policy. For example, if the regime is such that pupils perceive that making a mistake in a curriculum area will be attributed to a lack of concentration, poor motivation or lack of effort and result in a reprimand or sanction then this may undermine risk taking, creativity and the recognition that effective learning involves making errors and learning from these.

Rules, rewards and sanctions

Reflecting national guidance (e.g. DES 1989; DfE 1994a, 2016a; DCSF 2009) produced over many years, rules, rewards and sanctions tend to form the operational core of most schools' behaviour policies. The use of rewards and sanctions is rooted within a behaviourist tradition. The underlying assumption is that if pupils are demonstrating the required behaviour, as defined by the rules, and something rewarding happens as a result it will increase the likelihood of them behaving in this way in the future. Similarly, if pupils misbehave and something they dislike happens they will be less likely to behave in this way in the future. The origins of the behaviourist approach can be traced back to the work of Skinner, Watson and Pavlov. Skinner's experiments in this field were initially laboratory based and involved rats and pigeons being trained to carry out simple tasks such as pressing buttons to release food. The behaviour pattern of pressing a button became associated with a reward, in this case food, and hence the desired behaviour pattern was repeated again and again. Skinner subsequently generalised his discoveries about animal behaviour to humans. Though the behaviourist approach is often associated with the use of rewards and punishment, Skinner himself did not favour the use of punishment, believing it to be ineffective (Wheldall and Glynn 1989; Pound 2005).

There a number of important considerations to take into account when we attempt to draw on behaviourist principles to design behaviour policies. These include:

- What, as adults, we consider to be aversive may not be for the pupil. Some pupils might, for example, like being out of class and therefore a time-out room that is intended to reduce a particular behaviour may be reinforcing it.
- What, as adults, we consider to be rewarding may not be for the pupil. Being singled out for praise, for example, may be embarrassing for some pupils and consequently they may exhibit less of the behaviour that gains praise.
- Unlike pigeons or rats, the majority of pupils can interact verbally with us. Others can interact through alternative and augmentative communication. This provides plenty of other ways to promote positive behaviour and develop higher level problem-solving skills.
- Pupils will have a view of the person providing the reward or sanction. A reward or sanction may mean more or less to the individual depending on whether they

like or respect this person. Pupils may also have a perception of the rewarder or sanctioner's view of them. Relationships are therefore important.

- The pupil can reflect upon the experience of being disciplined and render it 'unfair' in their minds.
- There may be many other rewarding or punishing factors present besides the ones the teacher is controlling. For example, while the teacher may use ignoring as a response to attention seeking behaviour, it may be the attention of peers that is more important to the pupil.
- For those pupils who *do* respond to the approach there is a need to consider why they do and whether what they are learning from this is helpful. If, for example, the reason that the pupil behaves is to avoid sanctions or to gain reward we might question whether this is sufficient learning. It may be that they *only* demonstrate these behaviours when these rewards or sanctions are available. In other words, there may be little intrinsic motivation to behave in a particular way and so the behaviour is unlikely to transfer to occasions and situations when the reward is not available. For example, the pupil may behave in the classroom but not in the playground.

These considerations raise a number of issues for practice:

- It is necessary to recognise that a set of rewards and sanctions devised for a group will impact differently on individuals.
- Because we are dealing with people rather than rats or pigeons we have other tools at our disposal – such as talking to them!
- Relationships are important. For example, a reward from someone who is liked and respected is likely to be more powerful in influencing behaviour.

It should also be remembered that neither rewards nor sanctions can compensate if the pupil is either not developmentally ready or has not yet acquired the underlying skills to demonstrate the required behaviour. Rewards and sanctions are only likely to make an impact in cases where:

- The pupil knows what is expected of them.
- The pupil has the necessary skills to do what is expected of them.
- The pupil is developmentally ready to do what is expected of them.
- The pupil is not meeting other more important needs by *not* demonstrating the required behaviour – for example, the pupil may value the sense of belonging they feel when their peers laugh at their disruptive behaviour more than they value any reward on offer or fear any sanction.

With these preliminary thoughts in mind we will consider rules, rewards and sanctions individually and in more depth.

Formulating rules

Rules should be few in number and restricted to those that protect the rights of all members of the class, including the teacher and other adults. According to Hook and Vass (2002) and Rogers (2011) rules might therefore relate to:

- the right to emotional safety;
- the right to physical safety;
- the right to be treated with dignity and respect;
- pupils' right to learn;
- teachers' right to teach.

Reflective Exercise 8.1

Allocate your school rules to each of these five rights:

- the right to emotional safety;
- the right to physical safety;
- the right to be treated with dignity and respect;
- pupils' right to learn;
- teachers' right to teach.

Are there any rules that did not connect with one or more of these rights?
Is this still an important rule to have? Why?
How would you explain the rationale for it to your pupils?

As the Elton Report (DES 1989) noted, it is advisable to frame rules positively. There are three main reasons for doing this:

1   A positively expressed rule provides information on the expected behaviour.
2   If we tell someone *not* to think of something, they will probably, at least momentarily, think of that thing. If pupils are going to momentarily think of something, then it would be better that it was the required behaviour. The rule might therefore be, 'We use respectful language', rather than 'Do not swear'.
3   A positively expressed rule helps a teacher to frame their correction positively (see Chapter 10) because they only need to formulate a sentence around the wording of the rule.

From a Behaviour for Learning perspective, positively phrased rules reflect the principle of keeping a focus on those behaviours that are necessary for learning in a school environment.

In formulating the rules, it is necessary to distinguish between behavioural requirements that relate to the protection of rights and those that are simply concerned with the smooth running of the school. The latter represent routines. Routines are important and can be thought of as 'regular practices that we should proactively teach students (rather than tell then assume they know) to make events run smoothly' (Hook and Vass 2002: 49). Chaplain (2003b: 152) offers another definition, suggesting routines are 'procedural supports, used to manage everyday social behaviour around school and in class, as well as supporting teaching and learning'. At whole-school level there may be routines related to moving around the school, coming into the building at the start of the day or after break or lunchtime, late arrival, entering and exiting classrooms, wet break times, the dining hall, bus queues and the storage of coats and other personal belongings. Together the school's rules and routines contribute to an environment in which pupils know what to expect and what is expected of them.

The use of rewards

A school behaviour policy will typically set out the school-wide systems for rewards. Some systems are based on teachers and others giving a reward that has value in its own right to the individual. Other schools will operate systems where a reward given to an individual or group contributes towards an individual, class or house total that will eventually lead to a higher reward.

Examples of rewards include:

* verbal or non-verbal indication of approval of the behaviour;
* positive referral (usually) to senior staff;
* stickers and stars;
* raffle tickets;
* merits and house points;
* certificates;
* celebration assemblies;
* special privileges;
* 'Congratulations' and 'Good news' postcards home;
* personalised letters to parents;
* positive phone calls home.

Rewards that engage support from parents can act as a powerful incentive but it does need to be remembered that, for a variety of reasons, not all parents will provide this support. For some pupils, the receipt of the reward from their teacher may still have value even though they do not get the added value of parental approval that the approach is intended to trigger. For others, the presumption of parental approval being available may provoke negative feelings about the reward, about their relationship with their parents and possibly about their teacher for not recognising their circumstances.

The use of raffle tickets typically involves these being given to pupils as a reward with a draw being conducted, perhaps at the end of the week, and prizes awarded. Pupils need to have a basic grasp of probability at the level of recognising that gaining more tickets increases the chance of winning. The frustrating element for some pupils may be that they receive a lot of raffle tickets but win nothing, whereas a pupil who gained just one was drawn as the winner. Older pupils may simply accept that this is an inevitable characteristic of a raffle, but younger children may feel that it is unfair.

The approach of referring pupils who have behaved well to a senior member of staff is helpful in overcoming the general perception that this is where they are sent for misbehaviour. It helps to send a message that members of the senior leadership team are interested in hearing about good behaviour and so fits with the general principle of placing the emphasis on the positive. At the level of individual experience, it is important to remember that, for some younger pupils in particular, referral to the head teacher or other member of the senior leadership team, even for a positive reason, may be daunting. If the teacher can predict that this will be how the pupil experiences the reward, then it would be better to use an alternative method of reinforcement.

Rewards need not just be for the individual pupil, they can be for the whole class or groups. It is important, particularly with individual reward schemes, to ensure that motivation to achieve the reward does not lead to a level of competition between pupils that undermines the desirable learning behaviours of cooperation and collaboration. Individual rewards that contribute to a class reward can help to overcome this issue and readers may wish to consider this option.

The use of sanctions

A sanction can be considered as a formal action taken by the school in response to misbehaviour that has not been ameliorated by a range of strategies. A challenging question to consider is the purpose of a sanction. Government guidance produced in 2009 suggested that it was to:

- impress on the perpetrator that what he or she has done is unacceptable;
- deter the pupil from repeating that behaviour;
- signal to other pupils that the behaviour is unacceptable and deter them from doing it.

(DCSF 2009: 29)

Learning does not feature highly within this agenda, but this does not mean learning does not take place. The individual pupil's interpretation will determine the resulting learning and this may not reflect any of these purposes. The three stated purposes do not have strong connotations of learning from your mistakes or learning better ways of behaving or relating to others, except in the sense possibly of learning not to commit the same offence again because something unpleasant will befall you *if* you are caught.

Sanctions, in the traditional form of responding to misbehaviour by doing something to the pupil that we believe they will dislike, offer little potential to promote positive learning behaviours. They also carry an inherent risk of impacting negatively on the three relationships that underpin the development of learning behaviour. Particular problems associated with sanctions include:

- They form an inappropriate model for human relationships (Kyriacou 1998).
- They may foster anxiety among some pupils. Typically, those pupils who are most worried by sanctions are those who would respond to skilful use of other strategies – such as talking to them about their behaviour.
- The pupils who most frequently encounter the sanctions are likely to be those with little regard for authority or the values of the school and are therefore the least likely to respond by behaving better in the future (Kyriacou 1998). Behavioural change in these pupils is more likely to be achieved through cognitive-behavioural interventions that tackle underlying beliefs, attitudes and attributions.
- They run the risk that any remorse the perpetrator may feel is replaced by concern for what will happen to them. Effectively, this allows the perpetrator to transform themselves into the victim (Galvin 1999).
- They lead to resentment of the person enforcing the sanction; resentment is not a good basis for a positive relationship.
- They tend not to motivate pupils to improve and may instead encourage pupils to develop strategies to avoid being caught.

- They focus on the misbehaviour (Kyriacou 1998) rather than alternative ways of behaving in the future.
- They do not promote good behaviour directly but simply serve to suppress misbehaviour (Kyriacou 1998).

Within the context of the Behaviour for Learning approach, sanctions need to be seen for what they are: a means by which the school can demonstrate its disapproval that *may* have a deterrent effect on the individual and on others. This is not intended as a pejorative comment; pragmatically sanctions are necessary to allow staff to feel supported, for pupils to recognise that there are consequences and to maintain parental confidence. Though sanctions primarily have a role in limiting behaviour (Hook and Vass 2002), by considering the nature of the sanction and the manner in which it is applied we can seek opportunities to develop learning behaviour or the three relationships that underpin its development. At the very least, we need to ensure that the sanction and the manner in which it is applied does not carry a predictable risk of undermining the development of positive learning behaviours or impacting negatively on the three Behaviour for Learning relationships.

Common sanctions used by schools include:

- verbal or non-verbal indication of disapproval of the behaviour;
- removal from the group (in class);
- withdrawal from a particular lesson or peer group (e.g. by sending to another class or another location specifically intended for this purpose);
- withholding participation in an activity or event that is not an essential part of the curriculum;
- referral (usually) to senior staff;
- withdrawal of specific privileges;
- carrying out a useful task in the school;
- a variety of forms of detention;
- a fixed period of internal exclusion;
- a fixed period of external exclusion;
- permanent exclusion.

Some writers (e.g. Canter and Canter 1992; Dreikurs *et al.* 1998; Hook and Vass 2002) and some schools use the term 'consequence' as an alternative to 'sanction' with the intention of conveying the idea that the pupil, through their behaviour, is making a choice and so determining what happens. The term has less punitive connotations than the word 'sanction' and from a Behaviour for Learning perspective we would endorse the idea that, potentially, the language of consequences encourages pupils to recognise that through their actions they determine what happens to them. This can contribute to the development of self-efficacy and responsibility. However, different writers, like different schools, attach different meanings to the term 'consequences'. Canter and Canter (1992), for example, refer to consequences such as being last in line, working away from peers for a period of time in the classroom, staying behind after class, missing free time and having their parents called. To us this does not sound significantly different to the traditional idea of a sanction, particularly in view of Canter and Canter's (1992) suggestion that to be effective a consequence must be an action the pupil does not want or like. Hook and Vass (2002) attach a different meaning to the term 'consequence', drawing parallels with the natural consequences people experience in life as a result of the actions they take. For Hook and Vass (2002) consequences, whether positive or negative, result directly from the choice the pupil makes. They suggest that in constructing consequences it is important to consider five key questions:

1 Are they fair?
2 Are they reasonable, i.e. matched to the event?
3 Are they in the person's best interests in terms of helping them to make more useful choices?
4 Are they related as far as possible to the event so the connection is obvious?
5 Are they largely known or predictable so people can make informed choices?

(Hook and Vass 2002: 47)

Hook and Vass's (2002) use of the term consequences draws on neo-Adlerian theory (Porter 2007), which advocates the use of both natural and logical consequences. A natural consequence is the natural outcome of an individual's actions that occurs without adult intervention, such as getting wet when you stand outside in the rain (Harrison 2004, cited in Porter 2007). Simply letting events take their course poses considerable problems in school contexts as we cannot legitimately allow pupils to put themselves or others in dangerous situations. Porter (2007) also makes the point that pupils deserve protection from events which, though not physically harmful, may be psychologically harmful. Therefore, although, for example, a natural consequence of antisocial behaviour may be rejection by one's peer group, the detrimental effect on the pupil's relationship with self and relationship with others is too high a price to pay in order to teach that there is a consequence of the behaviour (Porter 2007).

Logical consequences attempt to retain the cause-and-effect quality of natural consequences but are defined by the teacher. Unlike Canter and Canter's (1992) concern with the pupil's dislike of the consequence, a logical consequence should be helpful rather than hurtful (Nelsen et al. 2000). For example, completing work missed through misbehaviour makes up for the missed learning; apologising privately to a peer helps the aggrieved party to feel better; and cleaning graffiti off the wall restores the area to its original condition. Logical consequences typically have a reparative, 'offence-related' quality. Drawing on the work of Albert (1996) and Nelsen et al. (2000), Hardin (2008) put forward the '5Rs of logical consequences' set out in Table 8.2.

We are in a policy context where the terms 'punishment' and 'sanction' tend to be used (e.g. DfE 2016a) rather than 'consequence' but the principles in Table 8.2 can still be usefully applied. From a Behaviour for Learning perspective the key points to note about these principles are that:

- There is an emphasis on self-efficacy. The pupil is encouraged to recognise that what they choose is instrumental in determining the outcomes for them.
- The focus is on the choice made rather than the individual. The consequence and the implied disapproval are of the act, not the person. Though we cannot *guarantee* how every individual will interpret and experience the consequence, this affords a *degree* of protection to the individual's relationship with self.
- A degree of protection is afforded to the teacher–pupil relationship. The consequence is the result of a choice made within a known framework. It is not the result of animosity, frustration or simply the teacher having an off day.

Table 8.2 The 5Rs of logical consequences

Related	A consequence should be logically connected to the behaviour. The more closely related to the consequence, the more valuable it is to the student.
Reasonable	A consequence should be equal in proportion and intensity to the misbehaviour. The purpose is for the students to see the connection between the behaviour and the consequences, not to make them suffer.
Respectful	A consequence should be stated and carried out in a way that preserves a student's self-esteem. It addresses the behaviour, not the character of the student.
Reliably enforced	A consequence should follow misbehaviour. Threats without action are ineffective. Consistency is the key.
Revealed	A consequence should be revealed (known) in advance for predictable behaviour such as breaking class rules. When misbehaviour occurs that was not predicted, logical consequences connected to the misbehaviour should be established.

Source: Hardin 2008.

The emphasis on choice and consequences is not without critics. Kohn (2001), criticising the work of writers such as Canter and Canter (1992) and Dreikurs *et al.* (1998), suggests that the choice offered is little more than a pseudo–choice amounting to doing exactly what is expected by the teacher or facing the consequences; he argues that the distinctions made between punishment and consequences are little more than semantics.

Arguably, whether we define what we do when pupils infringe the rules as a sanction, a punishment or a consequence, it is the individual's experience and interpretation that matters. For example, what the school considers to be a logical consequence designed to develop responsibility may be perceived by the pupil as an arbitrary punishment. With any sanction it is important that we consider carefully what we are promoting and the learning, helpful and unhelpful, that might occur as a result.

Some specific frameworks for managing behaviour

Many schools will formulate their own frameworks for managing behaviour, drawing on advice contained in national guidance documents (e.g. DfE 2016a). Others will adopt a recognised approach or package. In this section we consider three such approaches: Assertive Discipline and other tariff-based systems, zone boards and 'golden time'.

Assertive Discipline and other tariff-based systems

We have used the term 'tariff systems' to reflect a particular type of behaviour policy that prescribes in quite a rigid way the expected teacher response to pupil behaviour. A well-known example is Canter and Canter's (1992) Assertive Discipline approach. In *Excellence for All Children*, the DfEE (1997) endorsed the Assertive Discipline approach, suggesting it could help schools to establish settings where pupils were encouraged to behave well and where there were clear guidelines for behaviour (Hallam and Rogers 2008). As Swinson (2017) notes, a number of evaluations (Nichols and Houghton 1995; Swinson and Melling 1995; Woods *et al.* 1996; Swinson and Cording 2002) have reported positively on the effects of Assertive Discipline. According to Swinson (2017: 18) these evaluations showed 'an improvement in pupil behaviour in terms of on-task behaviour and a marked reduction in disruptive incidents'. In addition, there were some social and emotional benefits as 'both teachers and pupils reported more enjoyable lessons and hence an improvement in teacher–pupil relationships' (Swinson 2017: 18).

Assertive Discipline is based on establishing clear, unambiguous rules of conduct, together with continuous positive feedback when the rules are followed and a hierarchy of sanctions for rule-breaking (Fletcher-Campbell and Wilkin 2003). Canter and Canter (1992: 88) suggested some example 'discipline hierarchies'; their proposed sequence for secondary age pupils is shown in Table 8.3.

In the examples provided for Key Stage 1 and Key Stage 2 the suggestion from Canter and Canter (1992) was that on the second and third occasions the consequence was a period of time working away from the group. In our experience, many UK schools adopting Assertive Discipline used loss of parts of break time as the consequence. Canter and Canter (1992) acknowledge that in earlier versions of their work they had suggested that the teacher should record the names of pupils on the board with ticks added for the additional steps. By 1992, they had moved away from this idea for the reason that 'some individuals have misinterpreted the use of names and checks on the board as a way of humiliating students' (Canter and Canter 1992: 90). They instead suggested the teacher should 'write the disruptive student's name on a clipboard or in a record book and calmly say, for example, "Janet, you talked out. That's a warning"' (Canter and Canter 1992: 90). Despite this change in view by Canter and Canter (1992), the use of names on the board is often thought of as a characteristic of assertive discipline.

The well-known class reward system of collecting marbles in a jar was also popularised through Canter and Canter's (1992) Assertive Discipline programme. When the teacher, or other adult, spots an individual or group demonstrating positive behaviour they award a marble which is placed in a jar. When a certain level is reached, the class receives a treat such as watching a DVD. We are sceptical about the operation of this system when the class's marble-linked reward always seems to conveniently coincide with the end of term; for such a system to be credible pupils need to have a sense that

Table 8.3 Canter and Canter's suggested sequence of consequences for secondary age pupils

First time a student breaks a rule:	Warning.
Second time:	Stay in class 1 minute after the bell.
Third time:	Stay in class 2 minutes after the bell plus write in behaviour journal.
Fourth time:	Call parents.
Fifth time:	Send to principal.
Severe clause:	Send to principal.

Source: Canter and Canter (1992: 88).

the reward can be gained either more or less quickly and that this is influenced by their behaviour, not by the calendar.

If we use class rewards they should be framed in such a way that a strong emphasis is placed on the positive effects of working together, rather than on highlighting those individuals who hinder progress towards the goal. There should also be a balance between rewards for individuals, for groups and for the whole class. If, for example, marbles are only ever given for the whole or the vast majority of the class behaving well, on the occasions when the teacher does not consider that a marble is deserved it can send a message to individuals that their personal decision to behave in the required manner is neither recognised nor rewarded. Whole-class rewards used in this way may begin to share some of the disadvantages of whole-class sanctions that we explore in Chapter 10.

We would suggest that marbles, like any reward given for a specific instance of behaviour, should not be taken away. Our argument is that any reward given is for the instance of positive behaviour that has occurred and any subsequent misbehaviour does not change that fact. To remove the reward effectively sends the message that the earlier positive behaviour counted for nothing. An exception is where the reward is in the form of ongoing higher levels of independence or responsibility and is contingent on the behaviour continuing. An example might be a pupil who, after a history of absconding from school, has sustained a period without incident and is now allowed to take the register to the school office accompanied by a peer. If this pupil leaves the premises whilst on this errand it would be reasonable to withdraw this level of responsibility. The purpose here is not to remove responsibility as a sanction but to protect the pupil.

As a long established package (e.g. Canter and Canter 1976), Assertive Discipline (Canter and Canter 1992) has spawned a number of derivatives and behaviour policies devised by schools which sometimes display its elements, such as names on the board or marbles in a jar, or reflect its principles.

A more recent package that employs a similar tariff-based approach to Assertive Discipline is Behaviour For Learning (BFL). Though bearing the same name, this approach should not be confused with the Behaviour for Learning model advocated by Powell and Tod (2004) or presented in this book. This system, which was originally developed in a Birmingham secondary school, has found favour with politicians and been adopted by a range of schools across the country (Smithers 2005). The BFL approach (Elkin 2004: 6) sets out four levels of consequence (abbreviated to C):

C1 Verbal warning.
C2 Second verbal warning.
C3 Detention for one hour, usually the next day.
C4 Isolation from peers in the school's isolation unit for one, two or three days; or exclusion.

Under this system, if a pupil is rude, shouts out or behaves inappropriately in class they could be issued with a C1 by the teacher. If the pupil persists, the teacher might then issue a C2. The verbal warnings are not centrally recorded but the advice is that the teacher makes a note of them by, for example, writing them on the board during the course of the lesson, based on the rationale that pupils can see exactly where they are within the sequence. The approach keeps dialogue to a minimum. If a pupil misbehaves, the teacher would simply say, for example, 'Kelly – C1'. Teachers are trained to be decisive and clear, but calm and not angry, in communicating a warning (Elkin 2004).

Tariff-based systems raise a number of issues when considered from *our* Behaviour for Learning perspective. They can be used in quite a mechanistic manner, based on an almost formulaic principle of 'if the pupil does X, then the teacher does Y', that discourages teachers from using professional judgement about the best approach with a particular pupil at a particular time. Watkins and Wagner (2000: 49) go as far as to suggest that through tariff systems such as Assertive Discipline teachers 'are invited to become automata rather than professionals or even humans'. This can lead to some pupils being escalated rapidly through to exclusion as class teachers rigidly adhere to the predefined sequence of consequences without recognising when an alternative approach might be more appropriate.

Rigid use of tariff systems does not encourage discussion or problem solving on the part of the teacher or the pupil. Although such approaches often refer to the notion of choice and responsibility, critics suggest that realistically the only choice offered by a package such as Assertive Discipline is 'Behave or else!' (Curwin and Mendler 1989; Porter 2007). In effect, responsible behaviour is defined as little more than doing what you are told, with 'good choices' being those that the teacher approves of (Porter 2007). Porter (2007) argues that within communication theory, the right to be assertive is mutual: one person's right to assert his/her needs guarantees the other's equal right to the same. It is this reciprocity, Porter (2007) continues, that distinguishes assertiveness from aggression. In this sense, the title Assertive Discipline, is something of a misnomer as the approach does not adhere to this principle; it is based entirely on what the teacher will do to the pupil with very little opportunity for the pupil to assert their view. Indeed, attempting to assert their view should, if the system is followed, result in another consequence.

These types of approaches minimise dialogue between teachers and pupils when misbehaviour occurs. This can be beneficial in schools where teachers regularly get involved in long-drawn-out disciplinary interactions (Watkins and Wagner 2000) but ultimately it is not based upon relationships. This seems evident in approaches such as 'Kelly, that's a C1' or 'Kyle, that's a warning'. These have the feel of cold transactions rather than proper human interactions necessary for the development of relationships.

Zone boards

Since the first edition of this book was published, we have become very aware of the increase in the use of zone boards in schools. Our own attempts to trace the origins of this approach have proved fruitless, though the similarity in approaches used by schools who employ this method would suggest that zone boards are attributable to a specific source. The fact that, through internet searches, we could readily identify many schools using the approach but have so far been unable to find any clues as to its origins is interesting in itself, in terms of the extent to which strategies for behaviour are selected based on awareness of their provenance and systematic evaluation of evidence of effectiveness. Zone boards can be seen as representing an evolution of the three zone systems used by schools based on a happy face, a neutral face and a sad face (or a sun, a sun partially obscured by a cloud and a cloud). There are also some parallels with Kuypers' (2011) zones of regulation, though an essential and defining difference is that in this cognitive-behavioural intervention the four coloured zones represent different states of emotional arousal. The pupil is taught to recognise when they in a particular zone and to use self-regulation strategies. This is very different to zone boards where the teacher allocates the pupil to a coloured zone based on whether they are following the class rules.

The zone board should be displayed in a prominent position in the classroom, ideally in close proximity to a positively expressed set of class rules. The board is divided into several coloured sections or 'zones'. Though the three zones of green, amber and red are arguably sufficient, from our experiences we are aware that many schools have added silver and gold.

Each pupil's name is written on a moveable marker. Some schools use the pupil's photograph as well as their name. The distinctive feature of the zone board system is that all pupils start in the green section. This position indicates that the pupil is behaving and approaching their learning in line with the school's rules and general expectations. Where silver and gold zones are used, pupils can move into these if their behaviour or approach to learning is considered by the teacher to be over and above the school's rules and general expectations. Individual schools will have their own ideas about the type of behaviours that warrant a move to the silver or gold zones and how sparingly these should be used. It is also for individual schools to decide whether and how rewards are linked to the green, silver and gold zones. If silver and gold zones are used, the teacher needs to ensure that the green zone does not lose value in pupils' eyes and come to represent nothing more than being average.

Amber is a warning zone. The pupil's name would be moved into this section if they failed to keep to one of the class rules or refused to follow an instruction. In most schools this would be preceded by a warning. The amber zone represents an opportunity for the pupil to think about their behaviour and make a choice to behave differently in order to return to the green zone again. There is no sanction for being in the amber zone. The key to the success of the zone board system is that the teacher is focused on positive behaviour and so looks for opportunities to move pupils back from amber to green. The red zone is for pupils who continue to break the rules after being placed in the amber zone or for specific, serious misdemeanours. There would usually be a sanction attached to landing on this area of the board. There will be variations in how schools use this system, but it should be possible to move back to the green section from the red, even though this would not remove the sanction. For this reason, the teacher would need another method of recording when the pupil had received a deferred sanction rather than relying on their position on the zone board at the end of the lesson.

From a Behaviour for Learning perspective, zone boards can be viewed as reinforcing the idea that certain behaviours are necessary for learning within a classroom setting. Pupils who exhibit these remain in the green section. There is scope for the teacher to teach directly, as well as indirectly, the kind of behaviours necessary to remain in the green zone. Zone boards are also often described by the schools that use them as promoting learning and behaviour. We would see this as a positive quality, although the challenge for teachers is to ensure that the zone board is genuinely used to acknowledge effort and positive attitudes to learning, not just academic success and rule-keeping behaviour. Learning behaviours related to reflection and choice are encouraged by the use of the amber zone. This links to self-efficacy; there are actions that are within the pupil's power to take that can affect outcomes for them. The public nature of the zone board raises some concerns regarding the possible effect on the pupil's relationship with self. Though many pupils will see it as a fair and transparent system, for some individuals being placed in the red zone may be experienced as embarrassing or a form of public shaming. This can trigger quite strong emotions, including resentment towards the teacher. For other pupils, being placed in the red zone may reinforce their identity as a pupil who behaves badly. It is for this reason that the teacher needs to be constantly monitoring changes in behaviour in order to look for opportunities to move the pupil back to the green zone. If the zone board system is used effectively, pupils should not be left languishing in the red and amber zones for extended periods of time.

Golden time

Jenny Mosley advocates the use of 'golden time' (Mosley 1996; Mosley and Sonnet 2005). This can be viewed as a strategy in its own right for 'rewarding and celebrating behavioural success' (Mosley and Sonnet 2005: 19). However, it is important to acknowledge that Mosley (Mosley 1996; Mosley and Sonnet 2005) has presented it as part of a broader whole-school approach to behaviour.

The use of 'golden time' involves establishing with classes that there is a period of time, usually part of a Friday afternoon, when pupils are able to engage in an activity of their choice from the range that is offered. Where this is used school-wide, it can even be organised with different activities offered in different classes, with the pupils choosing which room to go to. At the start of the week every pupil starts off with the same amount of 'golden time'. If an individual pupil misbehaves they lose some minutes of 'golden time'. Misbehaviour is any behaviour that infringes the 'golden rules'. Although, therefore, 'golden time' is presented primarily as an approach for rewarding behaviour, the sanctions are inextricably linked. The appeal of 'golden time' for many teachers is that it addresses the concern that some pupils who behave well all the time can get overlooked in reward systems. Using the 'golden time' approach, every pupil gets the reward unless they do something that causes the teacher to deduct minutes.

Mosley and Sonnet (2005) suggest a visual warning, in the form of a laminated card, is used before minutes are deducted, based on the principle that the pupil is then able to make a choice about whether to continue with the behaviour that will lead to the loss of minutes. At the end of the week pupils who have lost minutes have to sit and wait for this period of time before being allowed to start their 'golden time' activity. The use of a sand-timer is advocated so that the pupil can see this time passing. The suggestion is also that the waiting pupils should be able to see the others who are engaging in the golden activities. Mosley and Sonnet (2005: 45) state that

> It is essential for the child to have their metaphorical nose pressed against the window of opportunity they chose to kick in! The sound of laughter, the chinking of dice and flourishing of dressing up clothes are all reminders of what they are missing.

Arguably, the implicit message this gives is 'See, if you'd behaved yourself, you could be having fun now'. Rogers (2011) advises against saying this sort of thing verbally when, for example, keeping a pupil behind at break time; we would suggest that it is also questionable whether we should be taking an action that conveys this implicitly. Mosley and Sonnet, however, defend the system stating:

When they have lost five minutes, or one minute, and are looking at a sand-timer, they will be very clear – if the visual warnings are properly carried out – that they chose that consequence. They are reflecting on their behaviour – they are reflecting on the fact that they have lost a part of their privilege – and that this was their choice. So, I believe that sanctions uphold the self-esteem of children because they give them safe boundaries and show them that adults care enough about them to put the consequences into action.

(Mosley and Sonnet 2005: 116)

Ultimately, whether the pupil experiences loss of 'golden time' in the positive manner suggested by Mosley and Sonnet (2005) depends on the individual pupil's interpretation and attributions. Some may well view it as a just consequence for their actions, while others may see this as their teacher trying to hurt or embarrass them. Individual interpretation and experience is always the challenge to whole-school systems.

Conclusion

A school's behaviour policy is an important document in supporting an overall whole-school approach to managing behaviour. From a Behaviour for Learning perspective, the key consideration is the compatibility of any practices advocated in the policy with the principle of at least protecting and, when possible, enhancing the three relationships (with self, with others and with the curriculum) and fostering the development of positive learning behaviours. Essentially, in identifying practices and approaches schools always need to have regard for:

- the effect on the three Behaviour for Learning relationships; and
- the effect on the development of learning behaviour.

It is important to be open to the possibility that there are some practices that may be counterproductive when evaluated against these criteria, despite apparent effectiveness in maintaining good order and discipline.

For most pupils, a framework of rules, rewards and sanctions that reflect these general principles will suffice for most of the time – indeed we would go as far as to suggest that there are many pupils who would actually behave well regardless of whether there were rewards and sanctions on offer. Ultimately, however, behaviour policies cannot realistically be expected to work for all pupils because they are designed for groups but experienced and interpreted by individuals. Continuously changing policy in an attempt to capture those who fall outside it is likely to prove disappointing. A policy that is necessarily designed on the basis of the best fit for the majority cannot take account of every individual's personal interpretation and experience of it. An effective whole-school approach will offer overall consistency but respond flexibly and supportively to those pupils whose behaviour is 'not ameliorated by the behaviour management techniques usually employed in the school' (DfES 2001: 53).

Chapter 9

Promoting learning behaviour in the classroom

Introduction

For the majority of pupils, for the majority of the time, the teacher will be seeking to maintain and develop their relationship with the curriculum and the range of learning behaviours associated with this. It will not be necessary to specifically target relationship with self or relationship with others, only to have regard for these. Rather, in seeking to foster a positive relationship with the curriculum, the teacher will:

- seek to recognise any opportunities to strengthen relationship with self and/or relationship with others in order to support the pupil's relationship with the curriculum;
- keep a watchful eye on any practices and approaches employed to develop relationship with the curriculum in order to identify any risks these may pose to relationship with self and/or relationship with others.

Such a remit encompasses all aspects of learning and teaching and clearly full coverage of such a broad topic is beyond the scope of this book. There are numerous texts that will support the reader in engaging with these wider issues. Our priority is to equip readers with a way of thinking, based upon the Behaviour for Learning conceptual framework, that enables them to relate any activity undertaken as part of learning and teaching to the development of learning behaviour and the promotion of the under-lying relationships. This chapter therefore seeks to explore a number of generic issues that are relevant to consider across curriculum subjects and age ranges.

Lesson management: Core teacher skills

How the teacher manages the lesson sets the parameters in which learning behaviours and relationships develop. Though now almost 50 years old, a number of ideas from Jacob Kounin's (1970) seminal text on discipline and classroom management are still referred to explicitly or indirectly in many texts on behaviour and classroom management. Kounin (1970) studied the practice of a range of teachers, initially with the expectation of finding out more about the nature and effect of what he termed 'desists'. Kounin used the term desist 'to designate a teacher's doing something to stop a misbehavior' (Kounin 1970: 2). Examining videotapes of classroom practice, Kounin (1970) drew the conclusion that the quality of the desists used by teachers he observed bore no relationship to the pupils' reaction. He went further, suggesting that

The finding of no relationship between teachers' desist techniques and the behaviour of children held for the immediate reaction of children to specific desists, as well as for the overall amount of deviancy and deviancy-contagion present in a classroom.

(Kounin 1970: 143)

Kounin's (1970) findings support the view expressed in this book that while behaviour management techniques are necessary they are not, by themselves, sufficient in securing better classroom behaviour. In the light of these findings, Kounin (1970) reappraised his initial premise and shifted the focus from disciplinary techniques to questions about classroom management in general, identifying a set of key teacher behaviours, including:

- withitness;
- overlapping;
- smoothness;
- momentum;
- group alerting.

Our observations in classrooms and discussions with trainees, initial teacher education tutors and practicing teachers would suggest that, despite the age of the original research, Kounin's categorisations are helpful in identifying what it is that effective teachers do that secures better behaviour. In Behaviour for Learning terms these categories reflect important teacher behaviours in maintaining multiple relationships within the classroom.

Withitness

Kounin used the term 'withitness' to describe the teacher's ability to be aware, and to convey to the class that they are aware, of what is going on in all parts of the classroom. In Behaviour for Learning terms withitness represents the teacher's active awareness and monitoring of the multiple relationships that exist within the classroom.

Overlapping

The multiple events that occur in a classroom do not occur in a step-by-step fashion; lots of things happen at the same time. Teachers learn to monitor, or at least to appear to monitor, simultaneous events, and some pupils learn to avoid this monitoring (Watkins 2016). Kounin (1970) described 'overlapping' as the ability to attend to two or more events simultaneously. This ability directly contributes to the teacher's degree of withitness.

Smoothness

Kounin (1970: 74) defined 'smoothness' as 'the absence of dangles, flip-flops, and thrusts'. He used these somewhat unusual terms to describe certain teacher behaviours that could impact on smoothness:

- 'Dangles': Kounin defined a 'dangle' in terms of a teacher starting an activity or instruction and then turning attention to something else before resuming.

- 'Flip-flops': Kounin defined a 'flip-flop' in terms of the teacher appearing to terminate one activity, starting another, and then, for no apparent reason, returning to the first (Froyen 1993).
- 'Thrusts': Kounin defined 'thrusts' in terms of a teacher suddenly 'bursting in' on pupils' activities with an order, statement or question, with little attempt to gauge the readiness of the group to receive the message.

The time when these behaviours often occur is when the teacher is managing the transition between lessons or parts of a lesson.

Momentum

Kounin (1970) used the term 'momentum' to describe the teacher's ability to keep lessons and the activities within them moving forward at an appropriate pace. Kounin used the contrasting concept of 'slowdowns' to illustrate the meaning of momentum. One of the 'slowdowns' that is worthy of closer examination is 'overdwelling' (see Table 9.1).

An important point to note in relation to overdwelling is that it is the *unnecessary* emphasis that is problematic. There may be times when, for example, a Year 1 teacher needs to remind the class about how s/he expects them to sit or the correct way to hold a pencil. Being aware of the potential detrimental effects of overdwelling on momentum allows the teacher to use professional judgement to decide whether to focus on these sub-parts of the main task.

Kounin (1970) identified fragmentation as a particular form of 'slowdown' produced by the teacher breaking down an activity into sub-parts when the activity could have been performed in a single unit. Fragmentation can take a number of forms. A teacher might require individual members of a group to do something singly and separately that

Table 9.1 Four main types of overdwelling

Type of overdwelling	Description
Behaviour overdwelling	Spending longer than necessary on addressing behaviour, e.g. lecturing the child at length about the misdemeanour.
Actone overdwelling	Over-focusing on a sub-part of a task to the degree that it distracts from the task itself, e.g. over-focusing on how to hold the pencil, how to sit, how and where to stand, which way to face, etc.
Prop overdwelling	Over-emphasising the equipment used in the lesson and losing focus on the activity, e.g. taking too long explaining what equipment is necessary, or how to use it or slow methods of providing it for pupils.
Task overdwelling	Over-elaboration of explanations and directions beyond what would be required for most children to understand how to get on with the task, e.g. explaining a task and then giving unnecessary examples or adding unnecessary verbal guidance to a group already working.

Source: based on Kounin 1970.

the whole group could be doing as a unit at the same time. Such an approach inevitably leads to some pupils having to wait for extended periods of time. An example would be calling pupils to come and collect a piece of equipment one by one. Another form of fragmentation is when a teacher breaks a meaningful instance of behaviour into smaller components and focuses on these separate sub-parts when the behaviour could have been performed as a single, uninterrupted sequence. The problem is compounded when the sequence is so obvious that some pupils move ahead of the instructions and are left waiting while others catch up.

Group alerting

There will be occasions, which Kounin (1970) categorised as 'recitation', when the teacher is addressing the class and requires individual pupils to ask or answer questions or feedback on an activity they have undertaken. A challenge in some classes is to maintain the attentiveness and involvement of others whilst another pupil is speaking. 'Group alerting' refers to the degree to which the teacher attempts to involve *non-reciting* pupils in the 'recitation' task, maintain their attention and keep them 'on their toes' or *alerted* (Kounin 1970). Questioning technique is therefore particularly relevant in a consideration of more effective group alerting. There needs to be a high expectation among pupils that they could be asked to contribute. The traditional approach of inviting pupils to put up their hands and then choosing someone, often the first with their hand up, to answer is problematic. Pupils are effectively choosing whether to be involved or not. If they choose not to put their hand up, then there is minimal risk of being asked.

Evaluating the significance of Kounin's work

The significance of Kounin's (1970) work is that it involved comparison of video-taped behaviour of teachers who were regarded as having few discipline problems with teachers who had frequent problems (Kyriacou 1998). Kounin was not, therefore, attempting to promote a packaged method of managing behaviour but to understand what it was these two types of teachers did that could explain the differences. The fact that he discovered that the action which teachers took in response to a discipline problem had no consistent relationship with their managerial success in the classroom (Watkins and Wagner 2000) has important implications for the focus of efforts to secure more positive patterns of behaviour in classrooms. The findings challenge the assumption that the answer to the problem of unwanted behaviour is to find more strategies for dealing with it. As Charles (2002) points out in his commentary on Kounin's work, teachers still need to know what to do when, despite demonstrating the qualities highlighted in the research, problematic behaviour occurs. While this is a valid point, it is important to recognise that this was not Kounin's priority; his emphasis was on developing a better understanding of what happens in classrooms. The enduring significance of Kounin's work is that it provides guidance on behaviours teachers need to develop in themselves in order to manage and promote learning in group settings.

Our exploration of Kounin's (1970) work has only served to highlight some general good practice principles for group management that will help to maintain positive behaviour in the classroom. However, if we accept that promoting learning and managing behaviour are intrinsically linked, then it is necessary to recognise that pupil behaviour will be influenced by a far broader range of teacher attributes that contribute to effective teaching. Coe *et al.* (2014), for example, suggest six categories into which these attributes might fall: (pedagogical) content knowledge, quality of instruction, classroom climate, classroom management, teacher beliefs and professional behaviours. It is not our intention, nor is there the space available, to produce a detailed account of the behaviours of effective teachers. Readers interested in a broader perspective on what makes an effective teacher may wish to consult Coe et *al.* (2014) *What Makes Great Teaching?* or Lemov (2015) *Teach Like a Champion 2.0.* The former is a review of the existing research evidence on the core elements of effective teaching; the latter is a more practical text that sets out 62 specific techniques that the author suggests will contribute to effective teaching.

Rules and routines

As Chapter 8 suggested, there is likely to be an overarching set of rules for the school and a number of school level routines. Schools will vary in the extent to which teachers are expected to develop their own classroom rules and routines. In some cases, the school's whole-school approach to behaviour will be based on a common set of rules and routines that apply across all classes. This section will have less relevance to readers in such settings.

Classroom rules, while guided by the school rules, can be adapted to suit the class. For example, the language used to express the rule in a Year 1 class may be different to that used in a Year 6 class. Just as with the whole-school rules covered in Chapter 8, classroom rules should be positively expressed and few in number. In thinking about the areas the class rules might cover it is useful to draw on the five broad themes identified by Hargreaves *et al.* (1975) to categorise the rules used by teachers:

- the talk theme, e.g. rules covering different noise levels expected at various times;
- the movement theme, e.g. rules covering pupils leaving their seats, moving around the classroom and entering and leaving the room;
- the time theme, e.g. rules covering being punctual, starting tasks promptly and using time appropriately to tackle the task set;
- the teacher–pupil relationship theme, e.g. rules covering the ways pupils are expected to speak to the teacher or seek teacher attention;
- the pupil–pupil relationship theme, e.g. rules covering how pupils are expected to treat each other

For younger pupils in particular, a visual reminder of a rule, such as a cartoon drawing or a photograph, can be helpful in supporting the written version. If a visual reminder is used, we would suggest this should depict the rule being followed rather than broken, because the purpose is to provide guidance on the *required* behaviour. This is particularly true if the reason for the visual reminder is to support pupils who may have difficulty in reading the written rule.

From a Behaviour for Learning perspective, the concern is the extent to which the classroom rules promote learning behaviour or protect the three relationships that underpin its development. Table 9.2 provides an opportunity to explore this issue. Review your classroom rules using the table below.

Table 9.2 Reviewing school rules from a Behaviour for Learning perspective

School Rule	What learning behaviours does this rule seek to promote?	Which of the three Behaviour for Learning relationships does it seek to protect or enhance?

Now consider the following questions in relation to Table 9.2:

- Were there any rules where you could not identify a positively expressed learning behaviour that the rule was seeking to promote?
- Were there any rules where you could not identify at least one of the three behaviour for learning relationships that it was seeking to protect?
- If you could not identify either a learning behaviour or a relationship for a particular rule, do you think it is still necessary? Why?

Reflective Exercise 9.1

Think about a rule (or a stated or well-known expectation) you have broken recently (e.g. taking food or drink into a computer suite, not wiping down equipment at your local gym after use, copying a music CD for a friend, cycling on the pavement, exceeding the speed limit).

Consider these questions:

- Why did you do it?
- How did you justify it to yourself?
- What was the *possible* consequence (for you or others) of doing it?
- What was the consequence (for you or others) of doing it on this particular occasion?
- What would have made you more likely to adhere to the rule or expectation?
- Are there some rules or expectations you would not consider breaking? What is different about these?

What can we learn from this personal reflection in relation to:

- The types of rules we set in schools?
- How we present and discuss these rules with pupils?
- The judgements and assumptions we make about pupils who break rules?

As we noted in Chapter 8, routines differ from rules as they are ways of doing things that, once taught to pupils, help make daily events and processes run smoothly. For example, a teacher might establish routines for gaining class attention, entering and exiting the classroom, the distribution and collection of materials and equipment, asking for help or answering questions, transitions between activities or the problem-solving process to be followed when pupils are stuck with an aspect of a task. The distinction between rules and routines is not rigid but thinking in these terms will be helpful in keeping the list of rules reasonably short. There is no reason why a teacher should not display reminders of the routines separate from the rules, or even develop a 'sub-set' of rules that apply to a particular area of the classroom (e.g. the book corner) or particular activities (e.g. group work) if this is felt to be helpful. The main point, however, is that, whatever else exists, pupils are aware of an overarching concise set of class rules that protects rights. Rogers (2011) reports encountering classrooms with 20 or more rules on the wall. It is unlikely pupils would remember all of these.

Planning for predictable occurrences

Watkins (2016) suggests that classroom events are unpredictable and to a large extent this is true. With approximately 30 individuals in a classroom it is impossible to predict with any certainty how each will respond to a given situation. However, within the overall unpredictability there are some predictable occurrences that we can plan for. Examples of predictable events include:

- pupils who arrive late;
- pupils who do not have the right equipment;
- uniform infringements;
- pupils who bring 'banned' items into lessons;
- pupils who have missed important prior learning (e.g. absence through illness or exclusion);
- problematic behaviours related to the subject being taught;
- pupils who call out;
- pupils who complain about seating plans;
- pupils who refuse to comply with instructions or argue back.

Some of these occurrences relate to the individual's behaviour (e.g. arguing back). Chapter 10 provides some guidance on forms of teacher language that may be useful in addressing these issues. Other predictable occurrences on the above list are organisational issues (e.g. forgetting equipment) that can lead to delays and loss of lesson pace and impact on behaviour. It is also important to recognise problematic behaviours that relate to the subject being taught. Examples include lessons such as Science, ICT, Music or PE where equipment is available that pupils may either use when they should not or use inappropriately. The key point about predictable behaviours is that we can be fairly sure we will encounter them at some point and we can therefore plan preventative approaches and responses. In Behaviour for Learning terms, the teacher, in identifying predictable occurrences, is attempting to avoid events that could put the three relationships (with self, with others, with the curriculum) under unnecessary stress. If we take, for example, a Year 8 pupil who arrives late to a lesson there is potential for difficulty with regard to each of the three relationships:

- relationship with self: 'I'll feel embarrassed walking in after everybody else has started';
- relationship with others: 'What should I say to the teacher? What will my teacher say to me? Will my teacher be cross? How should I act in front of my peers? Can I balance looking nonchalant in front of my peers whilst appearing sufficiently contrite for my teacher?';
- relationship with the curriculum: 'Now I've missed the start I might not know what to do'.

Of course, not all pupils who arrive late will experience this. The point we are making is that some might and this can be planned for by identifying the predictable occurrence and developing some strategies. Table 9.3 provides some examples.

In addition to these types of predictable behaviour-related occurrences there are a number of predictable occurrences in learning that may impact on behaviour. An inevitable occurrence is, for example, that pupils will, from time to time, encounter a problem with their work and find it difficult to continue. This is a classroom management issue as the teacher needs to be able to share attention between perhaps 30 pupils, and at times it can feel like an impossible task to give attention to those who need it at the time they need it. Long queues at the teacher's desk lead to a significant loss of learning time. They can lead to problematic behaviour if the teacher's view is obscured or low-level behaviour occurs in the queue or between those in the queue and those sitting down. While moving around the class and going to those indicating that they are stuck offers a better alternative, it potentially places the teacher in a reactive position and, unless they are able to deal with individual difficulties quite quickly, leaves other pupils waiting passively for assistance. There is therefore a need to develop in pupils strategies to use rather than waiting for adult intervention. When pupils are stuck it is an opportunity to develop resourcefulness and encourage them to take responsibility for finding a solution rather than being dependent on adult intervention. This development can be supported by the teacher establishing an explicit, stepped process that they expect pupils to work through when they are stuck before asking for adult help. This should be displayed and if appropriate visually supported by cartoons or photographs.

Planning with learning behaviour in mind

In planning a lesson it is possible to predict points within it that will require pupils to demonstrate particular learning behaviours. This is illustrated in Figure 9.1.

Thinking about a lesson in this way allows the teacher to make choices where individuals, groups or the class as a whole will be required to demonstrate undeveloped or emerging learning behaviours. The teacher might, for example, decide to:

- provide additional support at the key points;
- provide 'scaffolds' or more structure;
- plan to meet the learning objectives of the lesson through different activities that reduce demands on as yet underdeveloped learning behaviours.

The risk, if the teacher does not identify points within the lesson that require pupils to demonstrate undeveloped or emerging learning behaviours, is that these become behaviour 'hot spots' that require the use of reactive behaviour management strategies.

Table 9.3 Planning for predictable occurrences

Example of predictable occurrences	Possible strategies
Forgetting equipment	• Have equipment available to loan. If it is functional, but basic, there is less incentive for pupils to keep it. • Have systems for monitoring the loan and return of equipment. • Accept you will have some losses of loaned equipment. • Be aware of developmental issues – how much responsibility can pupils be expected to take? • Support pupils in improving personal organisation by providing checklists. • Enlist parental support if possible and appropriate. • Implement programmes to teach personal organisation skills.
Calling out	• Ensure class rules positively specify the required method of asking for help or making a contribution to discussion. • If expectations apply in a particular lesson that are different to the standard class rules make this explicit verbally and if necessary with visual back up (e.g. a symbol). • Rehearse in advance a range of positive corrections that you will use if pupils call out, including the use of non-verbal cues such as 'blocking' gestures while taking answers from pupils who have put their hands up (see Chapter 10).
Touching or generally fiddling with subject specific equipment when they should be listening to the teacher's introduction	• Consider whether equipment needs to be out on desks at this stage. • Consider whether the amount of equipment available can be reduced to bare essentials and the rest given out or collected by pupils when they need it. • Make expectations and timescales clear, letting the class know that you will be talking for a specified period of time and then they will have the opportunity to use the equipment. • Rehearse in advance a range of positive corrections that you will use if pupils touch or fiddle with equipment, including non-verbal cues such as 'looks' and tactical pauses. • With younger classes consider a 'good listening' posture such as hands in laps or arms folded. We would recommend teaching 'natural' listening postures such as those that might be used in adult life rather than unnatural positions such as 'finger on lips' or 'hands on heads'. It is important to remember teaching a listening position does not ensure good listening *is* taking place, only that equipment is less likely to be touched.
Arriving late to lessons	• At the start of the academic year establish an expectation that pupils who arrive late to lessons *briefly* apologise for this and go straight to their seat. • Follow up on the reasons for lateness later if necessary. • Ensure accessible seating is available for latecomers, preferably in groups that can absorb the new arrival with minimal fuss. • Have time filling activities available to occupy those whose lateness causes them to miss the instructions necessary to start the planned task. Once others are working independently you can then go to the latecomer and explain the task to them.

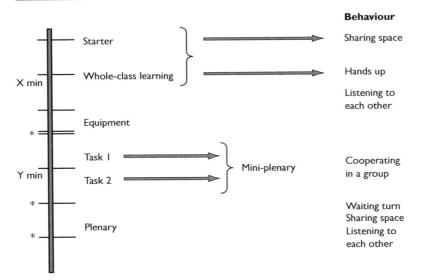

Figure 9.1 Identifying required learning behaviours.

Source: © Crown copyright [2004] Department for Education and Skills (from DfES 2004c).

If these points can be identified in advance the teacher can use proactive strategies drawing on their expertise in promoting learning.

Using the language of learning behaviour

An important way in which we can promote learning behaviour is by explicitly focus-ing upon it in the lesson. This simply involves the teacher looking for opportunities where they can comment on the learning behaviours that pupils have either already demonstrated or that will need to be employed in tackling a task. In many ways this does not involve teachers in adopting a new practice. It would not be unusual, for example, for a teacher to say: 'I'd like you to work together to find as many different circuits as you can that will light the bulb.' However, often the 'working together' element remains just a necessary part of the instruction. Other learning behaviours such as 'resourcefulness' (i.e. the pupils need to find *different* ways, not just one right answer) and 'resilience' (i.e. some ways will not work and pupils will need to accept this and continue trying to find ways that do) also remain at an implicit level. Approached from a Behaviour for Learning perspective the teacher might:

- Place more emphasis on the learning behaviours in the introduction to the activity. For example, the teacher might say something like, 'For this activity you are going to need to collaborate. Can anybody tell me what *collaborate* means?'. Or, 'For this activity, you're going to need to be resourceful. You'll need to come up with lots of different ways to light the bulb. Not all of the ways you think of will work, but that's OK because even when things don't go right we can learn from it.'
- Acknowledge the learning behaviours while monitoring pupils' involvement in the activity. For example, the teacher might say something like, 'I can see you're taking

time to listen to everyone's suggestions', to pick up on a specific aspect of collaboration. Alternatively, targeting resilience, the teacher might say, 'It can be frustrating when things don't work out first time, but you stuck at it. How did those first unsuccessful attempts help you to find the circuits that did work?'.

- Draw attention to the learning behaviours used in the plenary. Typically, the plenary will focus on eliciting from pupils what have they learned about circuits. This, of course, remains an important element, but in addition the teacher might ask, 'What do you think helped your group to collaborate successfully?'.

Increased emphasis is placed on encouraging pupils to think not just about *what* they are learning but also about *how* they are learning. Some readers may have encountered the work of Wallace (2000, 2001) or Claxton (2002). Both authors offer approaches intended to develop pupils' capacity to think strategically about the skills they use when learning.

Managing feedback

The Assessment Reform Group (2002) advised that teachers should be aware of the impact that comments, marks and grades can have on pupils' confidence and enthusiasm and that they should be as constructive as possible in the feedback they give. They advised that comments that focus on the task rather than the person are more constructive for both learning and motivation. We would endorse this; as we shall discuss later, the more feedback relates to an evaluation of the person the greater the potential for problems, even when that evaluation is positive. However, we would add that comments should also focus on the learning behaviours exhibited by the individual.

It is common in texts on behaviour management for the message to be that we must praise pupils. The DfES (2004d) even attempted to define a ratio for this, suggesting eight positive comments for every negative comment. Other sources (e.g. DCSF 2009) refer to a 5:1 ratio of rewards to sanctions. While we recognise that the intention is to reinforce the message that teachers should attempt to create a positive ethos that would be easily eroded by the dominance of negative comments, defining a ratio neglects the point that factors such as whether the opinion of the praiser is valued by the praisee will have an impact.

From a Behaviour for Learning perspective that seeks to maintain strong links between learning and behaviour, we do not make a distinction between *praise* and other forms of teacher feedback. If a pupil has completed a learning task suitable to their level of ability the teacher is likely to have few qualms about providing some positive feedback, together with some constructive, developmental comments if there are errors. Positive feedback in relation to behaviour should be little different.

Unlike praise, positive feedback places less emphasis on the *evaluative* element (e.g. 'good', 'well done', 'brilliant', 'fantastic', etc.) and more on the *descriptive* element. For example, we might say to a group of pupils: 'This group's worked well together. I liked the way you took turns using the equipment. That's good cooperation.'

We can analyse each component:

- '*This group's worked well together*'
  This includes some evaluation through use of the word 'well' and serves to signal to the group that the positive comment is directed at all of them.

- '*I liked the way you took turns using the equipment*'
  This is a specific statement describing the behaviour and is the key element in the message.
- '*That's good cooperation*'
  In this case the teacher takes the opportunity to relate the specific behaviour (turn-taking) to a broader learning behaviour.

It will not always be possible to capture all these elements, but wherever possible there should be a descriptive element present. For example, a secondary teacher might say to a Year 9 pupil who frequently forgets their planner but has brought it on this occasion: 'Glad to see you've remembered your planner. Well done'.

Again, we can analyse each component:

- '*Glad to see you've remembered your planner*'
  This contains a brief evaluative comment ('glad') but the major focus is on description. The learning behaviour is not explicitly acknowledged, but the particular case of behaviour identified ('remembering your planner') links to *responsibility* and *independence*.
- '*Well done*'
  This is an evaluative comment, but the assumption here is that the teacher is just making a pleasant remark, accompanied by a smile. It would be less appropriate if delivered in a highly effusive manner as both teacher and pupil know that bringing a planner is a basic expectation.

The important feature of the descriptive element is that it is factual. In a sense, even the accompanying evaluative component, 'I liked the way you …', in the first example is also factual as it is a statement of the teacher's opinion, which can still exist as true even if the pupil has a different view. In contrast, more full blown evaluative praise is easier for the pupil to reject on the grounds that:

- It does not fit with their image of themselves either as a learner or as a person. For example, a pupil with low self-esteem might find it difficult to accept a judgement such as, 'Well done, what an artist you are!', as it does not fit with how they view themselves. The pupil may attempt to resolve any dissonance between their own view and the positive evaluative comment by attributing externally (e.g. the teacher is just saying it but doesn't really mean it) or by taking some action (e.g. destroying their work or misbehaving) that attracts peer and adult reactions more consistent with their own view of themselves. A descriptive comment such as, 'I like your choice of colours and the way you've blended the reds and oranges together for the sunset', might be easier to accept. It is couched in terms that make it explicit that this is the teacher's opinion and it may not necessarily be the same as the pupil's. The descriptive comment can still exist as true even if the pupil dislikes their piece of work or subsequently destroys it.
- Many evaluative terms such as 'fantastic', 'great' and 'well done' are cultural and generational. Children and young people may have a different vocabulary for expressing approval. However, this should not lead us to assume that 'borrowing' their language of approval will address this issue. Older pupils, in particular, may

resent it simply because the language is *theirs*. It is also often difficult for the adult to use it credibly.

- They do not believe the praise. They may think the teacher is just praising them because it is their job. They may even construe it as simply an attempt to manipulate and modify their behaviour. Age and stage of development are factors, of course, but when teachers engage in gushing praise over, for example, remembering to bring a pen or a ruler it is understandable that some pupils may be a little cynical.

The third bullet point above raises the issue that positive feedback and any rewards should provide feedback on performance and provide some encouragement. The feedback or rewards given should not feel manipulative or controlling or encourage the individual to depend solely on someone else's approval (Kohn 1999). The aspiration for any reward, including positive feedback, is the development of intrinsic motivation. Ultimately our use of positive feedback is part of a learning process that allows pupils to develop their own aspirations, set themselves standards and goals and make honest appraisals of their performance in relation to these. This is not achieved if we adopt approaches that foster and sustain dependence on adult evaluations and decisions about what is 'good' or 'bad', rather than helping them to form their own judgements (Kohn 1999).

Depersonalising positive feedback

For some pupils even descriptive feedback may be difficult to accept. In such cases, teachers may find it beneficial to depersonalise feedback. The teacher might, for example, say: 'I'm pleased with how everyone collaborated on this activity today.' In this situation the teacher is recognising the learning behaviour ('collaboration') explicitly but is leaving the individual pupil to recognise that they, through the use of the word 'everyone', are included in this comment. Essentially, the teacher is recognising what the pupil is bringing to the situation in terms of their relationship with self and making a judgement about a strategy that allows reinforcement of the learning.

Use of public or private positive feedback

Some pupils prefer public acknowledgement while others prefer low-key and one-to-one feedback. If we are adhering to the principle that a major purpose of providing positive feedback is to encourage more of this behaviour in the future, then it makes sense to attempt to deliver any positive comment in the form that the pupil prefers. To return to a familiar theme, it is a question of evaluating the efficacy of a strategy based on how the individual experiences it. If the individual finds coming to the front to hold up their good piece of work embarrassing or an ordeal, their interpretation may be that this is not positively reinforcing at all. They may conclude that to produce only adequate work is the safer option in order to avoid this experience in the future.

With all of these thoughts in mind, consider how you would respond to each of the brief scenarios in Reflective Exercise 9.2.

Reflective Exercise 9.2

In each of these short scenarios there could be a justification for providing some positive feedback. Consider:

1   What, if anything, would you say or do?
2   What were the factors you took into account in making your judgement?
3   What learning behaviour(s) were you attempting to promote or reinforce?

- You notice that a group of six Year 4 pupils, supported by a teaching assistant, is engaged in the lesson. They always get on quietly and behave well (based on DfES 2004a).
- Kyle, Year R, has been at primary school for four weeks. He has often been resistant to written activities during teacher directed learning time. You notice today that he has chosen to do a writing activity during child initiated learning time for the first time.
- Stacey and Naomi, both Year 7, hardly ever volunteer to give answers, they are quiet, always complete work to a good standard and rarely ask for help. Today is no different (based on DfES 2004a).
- Sunil is a shy Year 1 pupil. You notice him contributing verbally to a group activity (based on DfES 2004a).
- Staff believe Krishtina, Year 9, seeks attention through confrontation. Today you see her standing calmly in the lunch queue (based on DfES 2004a).
- Chris, Year 5, frequently calls out in lessons. You have had to give him a couple of reminders so far this lesson to put his hand up. During the independent working phase of the lesson you notice that he has put his hand up and is waiting.
- This morning you had to ask the deputy head to collect Robbie from your lesson because he was being so disruptive. This afternoon Robbie has settled well to his work.
- Despite his protestations of innocence, you have given Emir, Year 8, a lunchtime detention for flicking a pen top across the room. At the start of break Ryan comes to you and admits that he flicked it and feels that Emir shouldn't take the blame. (As well as considering how you would respond to Ryan, what are you going to say to Emir?)

Mediating the interpretation and experience of feedback

If a teacher says to a pupil, 'I know you are having difficulty with this. Don't worry – I'm going to help you' (DfES 2004e: 58), a number of interpretations are possible. The pupil might simply conclude, 'I've made some mistakes. The teacher understands that it's causing me some problems and is going to go through it with me.' However, they may make less positive interpretations such as, 'difficulty is just another word for failure' or 'Why am I being told not to worry? Does this mean there is something I should be worrying about?'. Even the notion of 'help' may carry connotations of neediness and dependency. As an alternative, we might reframe this comment in a manner that conveys that learning is sometimes challenging and involves making mistakes. Alternatives include:

- 'It's making you think because you are learning something you didn't know before and I am here to help.'

- 'When you find something challenging, it is an opportunity to learn something new.'
- 'Now you'll learn something that you didn't know before. Then it won't be hard the next time you meet it.'
- 'This is how we learn. If everything is easy, it means you already knew how to do it, so there's no new learning.'

(DfES 2004e: 58)

Though these statements target the maintenance of a positive relationship with the curriculum, they are also framed in such a way that the pupil's relationship with self is not compromised. The implicit message is, 'It's not you that is at fault, this is what learning is sometimes like.' However, having said that, if this is what learning is *always* like for an individual it requires considerable resilience to remain engaged. We should also recognise that, however appropriate, positive and well-intentioned the comments, the pupil will experience and interpret them as an individual. For example, the pupil who regularly hears, 'If everything is easy, it means you already knew how to do it, so there's no new learning', may well glance around and make some negative appraisals about self from the fact that the teacher is seemingly not needing to have this interaction with most of the other pupils.

For some pupils we need to go further in attempts to protect the three relationships and adopt a form of language that focuses any sense of blame away from the pupil. Examples include:

- 'What do we need to remember here?' (DfES 2004f, 2004g).
  This has a less negative connotation than 'What have you forgotten?' and puts the emphasis on something positive the pupil can do (i.e. remember) rather than a failing (i.e. forgetting).
- 'Lots of people get mixed up on this bit' (DfES 2004g).
  This depersonalises the error and encourages the pupil to recognise that others also make mistakes. We should be aware that this may not be effective with all pupils as they may only be concerned that *they* are experiencing this difficulty currently – whether anybody else has may be of little consequence or comfort. Think of anything that you have failed at, such as a driving test or an interview for a job you really wanted. Would it have helped if someone had told you at the time that it happens to lots of people?
- 'I'm sorry, I should have made it clearer' (DfES 2004f, 2004g).
- 'Which part didn't I explain well enough?' (DfES 2004f, 2004g).
  The last two examples are effectively saying, 'It's not you, it's me'. The teacher is tactically taking the blame for the difficulty the pupil is experiencing in order to avoid damage to an already fragile relationship with the curriculum and relationship with self.
- 'OK, so you haven't quite mastered it yet' (DfES 2004f, 2004g).
  The use of 'yet' demonstrates an expectation that the pupil is capable of mastery. The statement also recognises that there are necessary stages in learning on the way to mastery.
- 'Up to now this bit has proved a little tricky' (DfES 2004f, 2004g).
  This is a deliberate attempt to diminish the significance of the difficulty. The teacher is attempting to limit the possibility of the pupil seeing this as a global

failing. The use of the word 'bit' conveys that this piece of learning is only one element; by implication there are other 'bits' that the pupil may be able to do. The assessment that this activity is 'a little tricky' conveys that the difficulty is not insurmountable. Coupling this with 'up to now' encourages optimism that this difficulty will not always be present.

Positive feedback and behaviour for learning: A summary

Well-timed, targeted and well-formulated positive feedback can be very important in terms of its potential to reinforce a learning behaviour and positively affect the three behaviour for learning relationships. As the preceding examples have shown, feedback can be phrased to explicitly or implicitly reinforce a learning behaviour. By positively commenting on pupil performance the teacher can also seek to develop each of the three relationships. For example, if a pupil has a poor relationship with a particular curriculum area then the teacher could combine the setting of a task where there are regular opportunities for success with a heightened level of positive feedback. Likewise, a teacher may seek to build their relationship with the pupil by making a point of recognising and remarking positively on the pupil's efforts. For example, while the teacher may not view a Year 9 pupil remembering to bring a planner to a lesson as praiseworthy in itself, they may recognise that to pleasantly acknowledge this behaviour is an implicit way of saying to the pupil, 'I *do* notice when you get things right too; this relationship isn't about me giving you a hard time when you get things wrong'. Positive feedback also has the potential to contribute to the development of a positive relationship with self. However, we make this point with some caution. As we considered in Chapter 6, feedback from a variety of sources is important in developing a positive relationship with self. Many pupils probably like and benefit from some positive comments on their efforts. This should not lead us to assume that apparent difficulties in the area of relationship with self can be resolved by providing *more* positive comments. As we have considered in the discussion of more descriptive approaches to positive feedback, pupils who present as experiencing difficulties with relationship with self may reject positive comment. In such cases the use of positive feedback needs to be handled carefully and would necessitate close monitoring of the pupil's response to judge how this is being experienced and interpreted.

The use of extrinsic rewards

In Chapter 8 we discussed the use of rewards and the expectation in national guidance (e.g. DfE 2016a) that schools include rewards as part of their behaviour policy. Used well, different forms of extrinsic rewards can be effective in promoting positive patterns of behaviour in the classroom. However, a number of writers have expressed concerns regarding their use.

Clarke (2001) has argued that external rewards such as stickers, smiley faces, team points, gold cards and various other schemes encourage pupils to strive for reward rather than achievement. She also claims that a negative by-product is that pupils focus on ego-involved attributions and comparisons with peers. In this second observation, Clarke (2001) is highlighting a potentially detrimental effect on the pupil's relationship with others. Pupils are effectively encouraged to develop a relationship with others that is based on competition rather than collaboration.

Kohn (1999) has also produced compelling arguments against the use of extrinsic rewards, suggesting that individuals' interest in what they are doing typically declines when they are rewarded for it. For example, Kohn (1999) reports work carried out by Lepper *et al.* (1973). In this American study 51 pre-school children were given the chance to draw with Magic Markers. Some of them were told that if they drew pictures they would receive a special personalised certificate, decorated with a red ribbon and a gold star. Between a week and two weeks later the children were observed again. Those who had been told in advance that they would receive a certificate seemed to be less interested in drawing with the Magic Markers than the other children. Not only that, they were less interested in using the Magic Markers than they had been before the reward was offered. Kohn (1999) makes the point that, 'If you have been promised a reward, you come to see the task as something that stands between you and it' (Kohn 1999: 65).

If Kohn (1999) is correct, then the potential for damage to the individual's relationship with the curriculum is clear: individuals are discouraged from taking risks, thinking creatively and challenging themselves. Instead the focus may be on doing what is sufficient to secure the reward. Arguably, whether the use of rewards has this effect or not is likely to be determined by how they are used. If a teacher regularly says directly to a pupil, 'If you do this page of questions you will get a sticker', then the risk is likely to be increased that the pupil will focus on the reward and see the task as an obstacle in its way rather than something intrinsically valuable.

The arguments presented by Kohn (1999) and Clark (2001) serve to illustrate that we need to continually monitor the effect of our strategies on the pupil in terms of the learning behaviour encouraged and the effect on the three Behaviour for Learning relationships.

Extrinsic motivators such as stickers and house points can make a useful contribution in positively reinforcing learning behaviours and can also be used to maintain and develop the three Behaviour for Learning relationships. However, as a class-wide strategy they need to be used to spontaneously reinforce the positive learning behaviours exhibited, rather than in the context of 'if you do X then you will get Y'. This is not to dismiss the utility of a more structured behaviourist approach of this sort in changing the presenting behaviour of particular individuals by explicitly linking the demonstration of required behaviour to a particular reward. Rather, we recognise that at a class level this type of approach is neither desirable nor necessary.

Extrinsic rewards should always, if at all possible, be accompanied by feedback that lets the pupil know what the reward is for. The long-term purpose should be to develop in the pupil learning behaviours that are sustainable without reliance on external reward. The emphasis is on moving the pupil on, eventually, to the point where the reward is no more than an appreciative gesture that says to the pupil, 'you're doing OK and I've noticed'.

Managing the physical environment to promote learning behaviour

The seating arrangements within the classroom convey a powerful message about the type of learning that will take place and the learning behaviours that the teacher wants to promote. The arrangement in Figure 9.2 suggests that much of the learning will be teacher-led with the teacher imparting knowledge from the front, in quite a didactic way, that learners are expected to absorb. For the teacher the question is whether this

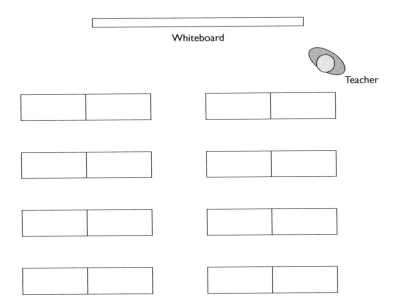

Figure 9.2 Seating in rows.

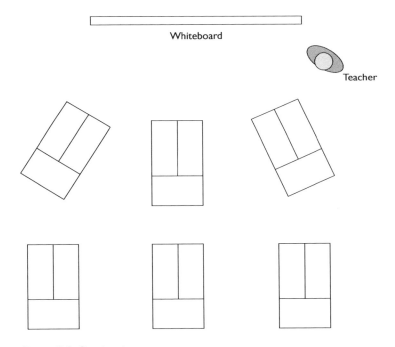

Figure 9.3 Seating in groups.

arrangement, though good for teacher control, promotes learning behaviour. The teacher will need to give particular consideration to the promotion of learning behaviours such as collaboration and cooperation and the opportunities to develop pupils' relationship with others as these are not naturally encouraged by the seating arrangement in Figure 9.2. In supporting pupils in whom the teacher wants to promote learning behaviours related to 'independent activity' this seating arrangement may assist by reducing distractions. Simply getting pupils to move chairs around to form small groups in certain lessons where collaborative learning is necessary may be all that is required.

The seating arrangement in Figure 9.3 sends a strong message that collaboration and cooperation are desired in this classroom. Pupils are arranged so that they can make easy eye contact with others and look over shared materials. There is a potentially problematic mismatch if the nature of the lesson requires individual, quiet working and desks are arranged in groups like this, which encourage discussion and collaboration. Teachers therefore need to either move furniture to reflect the nature of the learning or at least be very clear in setting out their expectations when a different way of working is required to the one that the seating arrangement appears to encourage.

Positioning of furniture alone does not dictate whether learning behaviour will be developed and there is no one arrangement that is ideal for its promotion. What is important is that the teacher uses furniture layout consciously as a resource to promote learning behaviour, capitalising on strengths and compensating for the limitations of each design.

Seating arrangements in the foundation stage

Due to the unique nature of teaching and learning in the Early Years Foundation Stage (DfE 2017g), seating arrangements in the classroom are likely to be very different to those found in Key Stage 1 and Key Stage 2 and secondary schools. The Foundation Stage teacher is starting from the priority of establishing a classroom (and outdoor) environment that represents the seven areas of learning from the Foundation Stage curriculum – though it is generally accepted that Personal, Social and Emotional Development spans across the other six areas and does not need to be represented by a separate physical area. A significant proportion of learning is child initiated and involves children moving to different areas to take advantage of the learning opportunities that the teacher has set up. The learning behaviours the Foundation Stage teacher aims to promote do not necessitate a seated place for each child and indeed this might be counterproductive, discouraging them from experiencing activities located in other areas. Instead, with a class of 30 the Reception teacher might, for example, make provision for two groups of children to be seated around tables at a time. A 'group' might consist of six children. There may also be another group of tables without chairs where craft or construction activities take place. Thought would also need to be given to the location of these different areas and the atmosphere that it is desirable to achieve within them. For example, it would be sensible to locate the reading area (needing calm and quiet) away from the construction or music area where noisier activities take place. There will be times during the day when the teacher needs to group all of the children together and, to achieve this, a large carpeted area in the room is necessary. A teacher's desk is unnecessary, apart from perhaps as a flat storage surface, as the nature of Foundation Stage teaching and learning is such that there would be few, if any, occasions when the teacher should be seated at it.

Conclusion

This chapter has focused on a range of factors that influence the development of learning behaviour and the promotion of the three relationships within the Behaviour for Learning conceptual framework. There are many more besides those we have covered.

Kounin's (1970) work provides a powerful example of the need to maintain a focus on the teacher behaviours that *keep* the classroom running smoothly rather than placing undue faith in what he termed 'desists' (but we might term 'behaviour management strategies') as a means of promoting learning behaviour.

The rules and routines contribute to the maintenance of a physical and emotionally safe, predictable classroom environment in which pupils are able to take advantage of the learning opportunities on offer. They can also be evaluated in terms of their potential contribution to the development of learning behaviour and the protection and enhancement of the three Behaviour for Learning relationships. Predictability is not just important for pupils. This chapter has also encouraged the teacher to be proactive by attempting to identify predictable occurrences and plan for these.

As discussed in previous chapters, learning behaviours associated with motivation are perhaps the most important to promote. The language used by teachers when providing feedback on both learning and behaviour has an important role to play in promoting and maintaining motivation. As this chapter has illustrated, it is possible to develop this language by considering it from the perspective of the pupil's possible experience and interpretation as the recipient.

In the final part of the chapter the physical environment was considered. Inevitably there will be a degree of compromise as different types of learning may be required at different times, but it is important to be conscious of the implicit message the usual furniture arrangement conveys regarding the learning behaviours required. The difficulty for pupils can be when there is an apparent contradiction between the implicit message from the physical layout and the teacher's expectations.

Chapter 10

The use of positive correction

Introduction

The term 'positive correction' relates to what Kounin (1970) referred to as 'desists'. These are behaviour management techniques used when a pupil behaves in a manner considered by the teacher to be unacceptable in the classroom context. As we explained in Chapter 9, Kounin's (1970) research found that desist techniques for dealing with misbehaviour 'are not significant determinants of managerial success in classrooms' (Kounin 1970: 71). The implication is that, while teachers need to be competent and confident in the use of a range of strategies for responding to individuals, becoming better at desist techniques alone – where *better* is interpreted as simply meaning knowing *more* strategies – is ultimately unlikely to make a significant impact on how the class behaves as a group.

The strategies outlined in this chapter need therefore to be afforded their proper status. They are not a substitute for a well-planned lesson that sets suitable learning challenges, recognises and responds to pupils' diverse needs and identifies and seeks to overcome potential barriers to learning and assessment for individuals and groups (DfE 2014a). As lists from a number of government documents (DES 1989; DfE 1994a, 2011c; TA 2012) presented in Chapter 1 illustrated, there are also many other factors that influence pupils' behaviour within the classroom besides what the teacher does when misbehaviour occurs. However, it would be professionally naïve to assume that there will not be occasions when pupils behave in a manner that requires the teacher to intervene in some way. While teachers cannot realistically anticipate and prepare for the entire range of pupil responses they will experience in the classroom (Powell and Tod 2004), there are certain behaviours, such as those identified by Ofsted (2014a), that they are likely to encounter. Thinking in advance about the possible strategies that might be employed can contribute to the teacher's feelings of confidence and competence.

In this chapter we provide an example set of strategies that we believe represent good practice in those situations where it is necessary to correct or direct a pupil's behaviour. Our selection has been made based on the potential of the strategies to be delivered in a manner that retains a focus on promoting learning behaviour and protects the three Behaviour for Learning relationships.

Why positive correction?

The phrase 'positive correction' was used within National Strategy documents (e.g. DfES 2003b, 2004a) to capture the idea that teachers should seek to frame their correction and direction positively when misbehaviour occurs.

A positive correction might, for example, be:

'Stacey, facing this way, thanks.'

We could contrast this with what could be termed a negative correction, such as:

'Stacey, stop turning round.'

The message that it is better for teachers to frame corrections in terms of the behaviours they want to see is frequently stated. Such an approach keeps the atmosphere of the classroom more positive than frequent use of statements beginning or containing 'don't', 'no' or 'stop'. If we accept the Elton Report finding that 'schools with a negative atmosphere will suffer more from bad behaviour than those with a positive one' (DES 1989: 89), then there is an obvious rationale to this approach. There is also an argument that stating the required behaviour encourages the pupil to bring an image of this to mind rather than the unwanted behaviour (Hook and Vass 2002). Comedian, actor and broadcaster Russell Brand illustrates this point when recounting a childhood incident:

> But in the sentence, 'Don't stamp on those flowers', the word 'don't' is feeble, impotent and easy to ignore, whereas 'STAMP ON THOSE FLOWERS' has a real linguistic verve; 'stamp on those flowers' could be a slogan, a catchphrase, a banner under which nations could unite. So the moment he shuffled out of view, all old and friendly, I stamped on them flowers.
>
> (Brand 2007: 30–1)

Reflective Exercise 10.1

Framing corrections positively requires thought and practice because it may not be intuitive. The following suggestions are based on examples offered by Rogers (2011) as possible alternatives to a negatively framed response of 'Don't call out':

- 'Hands up without calling out, thanks.'
- 'Remember our class rule for asking questions.'
- 'Hands up so I can see your voice.'
- 'I can hear questions; I can't see hands up.'
- 'I get concerned when several of you call out. We end up not able to hear anyone. I'd like you to remember to put your hands up.'

Consider each of these responses, imagining yourself saying them and the pupils you work with hearing them:

- Which of these suggested responses do you think you could deliver credibly and with confidence?
- Is the response consistent with your personal style (TA 2012)?
- How do you think pupils in the year group you teach would experience and interpret your use of this response?
- Do you think any of the responses pose specific problems for particular pupils in terms of recognising the intended message?

The key message from Reflective Exercise 10.1 is that positive correction, like other aspects of behaviour management, can never be reduced to the level of a script or recipe to be followed. Strategies need to be selected based on purpose, compatibility with the teacher's personal style and awareness of how they are likely to be experienced and interpreted by the pupil(s) they are directed towards.

As a general approach, the use of positive correction minimises the risk of undermining the pupil's relationship with self and their relationship with others, particularly with the adult who is doing the correcting or directing. A poor relationship with a particular teacher at secondary school can also lead to a poor relationship with the curriculum subject they teach, even to the extent of influencing a pupil's choice of GCSE options. This notion of damage to the three relationships is illustrated through the examples in Table 10.1.

Table 10.1 Examples of teacher comments that can negatively impact on the three relationships

Statement	Potential negative impact on
'Connor, are you completely stupid?'	Relationship with self Relationship with others (i.e. with the teacher)
'I've just about had it up to here with you.'	Relationship with self Relationship with others (i.e. with the teacher)
'If you carry on like that you'll have no friends.'	Relationship with self Relationship with others
'This is the kind of writing I'd expect from a Reception child' (said to a Year 4 pupil).	Relationship with self Relationship with the curriculum

Hopefully these represent extreme examples that are seldom heard in classrooms, but they are nevertheless illustrative of how the language we use can be very powerful in its negative impact on the three relationships.

When thinking about positive correction and a form of language that maintains the three Behaviour for Learning relationships there are a number of general principles that we can adhere to. These are outlined in Table 10.2.

Though positive correction should be the focus, the suggestion is not that adults should never say 'no'. For young children in particular, it may be appropriate to respond to more serious behaviours with a clear, brief message such as 'No, we don't throw the toys' or 'No, we don't hit people'. On the occasions when this is necessary it will be more effective in an environment where positive correction is generally used and it is not just one of the many 'No' messages the child hears.

Rogers (e.g. 2011) and Hook and Vass (2002) have comprehensively described the language teachers can use in the management of behaviour, particularly in the area of positive correction, and we would commend these sources to readers. A number of Rogers' (1990, 1997, 2002) techniques have been advocated in Key Stage 3 National Strategy Behaviour and Attendance materials (DfES 2003b, 2004a). The risk, however, is that teachers become attracted to techniques and place their faith in the magic of the method. In other words, it would be possible to arm ourselves with a stock of lines acquired from Rogers (2011), Hook and Vass (2002) and National Strategy documents (e.g. DfES 2003b, 2004a) without fully grasping that:

- Though the adoption of these forms of language can contribute to more positive relationships, they are always delivered within the context of an existing relationship, which may be good, bad or indifferent, and this will influence how they are received.
- We need to be able to deliver the line credibly, in a way that fits with our personality and values.
- We need to be able to select and adapt the line for different pupils.
- The pupil will have a reaction to the line and we need to be responsive to this – we cannot expect any interaction to follow a rigid script.
- These lines will not work every time with every pupil; we are simply increasing the likelihood of a more positive outcome because they are respectful and rooted in relationships.

With these cautionary thoughts in mind, we can consider a number of key strategies that the reader may find useful in maintaining relationships at times when these are potentially under pressure.

Table 10.2 General principles for positive correction

General principle	Reasons
Language used is respectful. Keep the focus on the behaviour. Avoid 'put downs' and devaluing terms.	• Maintaining the pupil's relationship with self by showing that, whatever their behaviour, they are still worthy of being spoken to respectfully.

Avoid strategies aimed at embarrassing a pupil in front of peers.	• Maintaining the pupil's relationship with others:
	  – it is difficult to maintain a relationship with someone who places you in this position;
	  – peers may form a negative image of the pupil and be less willing to form and maintain relationships;
	  – peers may use the pupil as a scapegoat;
	  – if the pupil has been embarrassed in front of peers this may adversely affect his/her relationship with them.

Model appropriate behaviour.	• The pupil will learn from what you model. If you respond to misbehaviour with verbal aggression, disproportionate anger or sarcasm, you are modelling many of the behaviours that we would not wish pupils to exhibit.
Encourage reflection, emphasise choice.	• Your responses to misbehaviour can encourage the use of learning behaviour (e.g. reflection, taking responsibility).
Any strategy or approach used should contribute to the pupil learning more than just not to do it again in order to avoid reprimand/punishment	• Some approaches that may be effective at stopping behaviour are not necessarily effective at promoting learning behaviours.

Some key strategies for positive correction

Physical proximity

By moving into the pupil's area of the room, perhaps while continuing to address the class, and just pausing by the pupil momentarily, the teacher can convey the message that the behaviour has been noticed. This strategy is mainly suitable for minor off task behaviour.

Tactical ignoring

Tactical ignoring is a technique referred to by Rogers in a number of publications (e.g. Rogers 1997, 2011; Rogers and McPherson 2008). It involves consciously deciding not to directly address a particular behaviour. This strategy is useful for minor off task behaviour where the teacher is confident that the pupil will re-direct themselves to the task in hand without adult intervention. Once the pupil has re-directed themselves to the task the teacher might choose to make a positive comment on this on task behaviour.

Proximity praise

Proximity praise can be used in conjunction with tactical ignoring. Again, mainly useful for low level misbehaviour, this involves tactically ignoring the pupil's misbehaviour whilst giving positive feedback to a pupil nearby who is demonstrating the required behaviour. For example, if Kerry in Year 4 is turning around and talking the teacher might say to another pupil near to her, 'Naomi, I can see you're facing the front ready to listen'. The premise is that Kerry will hear what the required behaviour is and adjust her behaviour accordingly. The technique is made more powerful if, as soon as Kerry demonstrates the required behaviour, the teacher directs some positive feedback to her. Overall, this is probably a strategy that has less utility in a secondary school environment. It is only likely to be effective if it is *teacher* approval that matters to the pupil concerned. As pupils get older it is likely that peer-group approval will matter more.

Non-verbal signals

Most teachers already use a range of non-verbal signals. The 'teacher look' is one common example. This typically involves slightly prolonged eye contact, often coupled with a pause in speech, to indicate disapproval. There are numerous other examples:

- Raised eyebrows or pointing at the clock or at written expectations on the walls all have the capacity to prompt pupils to address their behaviour, while representing a low level of intrusion on the part of the teacher (Galvin 1999).
- Perhaps more commonly in primary classes, a teacher might put their finger to their lips to convey the need for quiet.
- If a pupil is frequently turning around, the teacher might catch their eye and make a rotating movement with their hand to indicate the need to face the right way.
- The teacher raising their own hand can act as reminder to a pupil who calls out that they need to put their hand up.

• The teacher extending their arm horizontally with fingers pointing upwards and palm facing the pupil can be used to block a pupil's verbal interruption or as a signal to wait.

Many of these techniques are intuitive. Most pupils would understand their meaning without being told in advance. In highlighting the use of non-verbal signals as a specific strategy, Rogers (1997) also suggests that teachers can develop what he terms *privately understood signals* to be used with individuals or the class. These are signals where the meaning would not necessarily be clear without some prior explanation. Rogers (2007) gives the example of four fingers extended downwards to represent the four legs of a chair. This 'four on the floor' gesture offers a more positive alternative to repeated requests to pupils to sit properly.

Depersonalised comment

Rogers (2011) uses the term 'incidental language' to describe a technique involving the teacher making a casual observation with the implied meaning that the pupil or pupils need to address the issue. An example would be the teacher who, walking past a group, comments, 'It's a little noisy over here', or 'One or two people are talking a little too loudly.' The strength of this technique is that it depersonalises the correction. However, it needs to be used with some thought as some pupils, such as those on the autism spectrum, may apply a literal interpretation and not pick up on the implied need for action.

There are other forms of depersonalised comment. For example, the teacher might say, 'I can still hear one or two people talking', or 'I'm just waiting for everybody to be facing this way.' Essentially, the teacher's purpose is that individuals privately recognise that they are required to adjust their behaviour and take responsibility for this. It is important to note that the strengths of depersonalisation are undermined if, for example, a teacher, having noticed a particular pupil has not joined in an activity, says, 'Next time I expect everyone to join in, even Jessie'. If we have judged depersonalisation to be the correct strategy then it is important that we understand and stick to the principles. Adapting it by adding the pupil's name in this way makes it very personalised. This is likely to change the way in which the strategy is experienced and interpreted by the pupil.

Simple direction

A simple direction (Rogers 1990, 1997, 2011), as its name suggests, involves telling the pupil what you require. An example would be, 'John, getting on quietly, thanks.' Using the pupil's name helps to alert them to the fact that there is an incoming message. This is important as pupils can sometimes find themselves in trouble simply because they have not heard the first part of the instruction and have consequently not done as asked. Rogers (2007) advocates the 'pause … direct' (or 'tactical pause') technique, which involves saying the pupil's name, more than once if necessary, pausing and then delivering the message. The example would therefore become, 'John … John … getting on quietly, thanks.' Tone of voice is important; the teacher should not signal growing irritation through the way in which they repeat the pupil's name.

Rule reminders

We suggested in Chapter 9 that there should be a clear, positively expressed set of rules displayed in the classroom. This opens up a range of positive, correctional language for the teacher. Rule reminders (Hook and Vass 2002; Rogers 2007, 2011, 2012) can take a number of forms. It is possible to say, for example, 'John, remember our rule for asking for help', or 'John, we put our hands up to ask for help.' In both cases the purpose is to minimise any dialogue so that the teacher is not distracted from other priorities such as taking questions from other pupils who have put their hands up. When the teacher wants the pupil to verbally rehearse the rule, they might phrase the rule reminder as a question such as, 'John, what's our rule for asking for help?'. A teacher would only pose the question if they judged that at this point in the lesson they could afford to open up dialogue. If, for example, the interruption came part way through an explanation to a focus group, then a straightforward ruler reminder expressed as a statement may be better.

Use of questions

Hook and Vass (2002) refer to the use of casual questions as a strategy for managing behaviour. Examples include:

- 'How's it going here?'
- 'OK, so you're clear about what you're doing?'
- 'Have I explained that well enough for you?'
- 'Do you know what you need to do next?'

The strength of the examples given here is that they encourage a learning rather than a disciplinary focus to the interaction. In terms of strategy selection, the teacher needs to bear in mind that by asking a question it invites an answer. Often the priority is to maintain the pace of the lesson and so the teacher would not want to open up dialogue.

Rogers (1997, 2011, 2012) and Rogers and McPherson (2008) describe a more structured use of questions. This is a more complex technique than Hook and Vass's (2002) casual questions, as the teacher enters into the dialogue with a particular sequence of questions and responses in mind. Again, this approach would only be used if the teacher wanted to open up dialogue. The 'question and feedback' technique involves the teacher asking an open question such as, 'What are you doing?'. Even this first question needs careful consideration. Tone of voice will be a major factor in determining how the pupil experiences and interprets this question. The aim is to deliver it as a neutral, quite casual enquiry. It would be possible, however, to deliver it accusingly or inquisitorially and so caution needs to be exercised.

Readers are probably already able to predict the range of answers to the question above which might include, 'Nothing', or 'My work'. As with all techniques, the teacher's personality is a factor. Both of these pupil responses may be experienced by some teachers as irritating. Effective use of this technique depends on the ability both to ask the initial question in a neutral manner and to react calmly to the pupil response in order to steer the focus back to learning. If, as an individual, a teacher feels that they cannot do this, then this technique is not for them. With this caveat in mind, the two examples in Table 10.3 illustrate how this technique can be very effective.

Table 10.3 Two examples of the use of questions

Example 1	
Teacher:	'What are you doing?'
Pupil:	'Nothing.'
Teacher:	'What should you be doing?'
Pupil:	'My work.'
Teacher:	'OK, so what's the next thing you need to do?'
Example 2	
Teacher:	'What are you doing?'
Pupil:	'My work.'
Teacher:	'OK, so what's the next thing you need to do?'

In both examples there is the possibility that the pupil may respond to the teacher's last question by saying that they do not know. In this case the teacher is able to return to a learning focus and explain. If, however, the pupil gives a response that indicates that they do know what to do then the teacher can simply say something like, 'OK, so if you make a start now and I'll come back in a few minutes and see how you're getting on'. Again, the dialogue and the teacher–pupil relationship have returned to a learning focus.

In most cases pupils will recognise the implication within the 'What are you doing?' question that the teacher has noticed exactly what they are doing and will reply 'Nothing' or 'My work'. However, as we have indicated, we are not working to a script. Some pupils may reply with a description such as, 'I was only talking to Terry', or 'I needed to get something from my bag', or even the very honest, 'I was just messing about.' The teacher is still able to follow this with the question, 'What should you be doing?', and then use the sequence outlined in examples 1 and 2 (Table 10.3). Alternatively, the teacher might decide that partial agreement, covered later in this chapter, is the more appropriate strategy to use.

Choice and consequence

A common message in relation to behaviour management is that pupils make choices about their behaviour (e.g. Canter and Canter 1992; Hook and Vass 2002; Dix 2007; Rogers 2011). They may, for example, choose not to treat another pupil with respect by using verbal 'put-downs'. This infringes a rule and there is a consequence for this choice. We have explored some of the thinking behind the idea of choices and consequences in Chapter 8. The language of choice:

- allows the teacher to focus on the behaviour rather than the pupil's character;
- puts the responsibility for the behaviour on the pupil;
- conveys the implicit message that a different choice was possible and will be possible in the future;
- focuses attention on the pupil's individual choices, separating them from the behaviour of others;
- depersonalises the interaction, conveying implicitly the message, 'This is not a personal attack, you have chosen not to follow the rules and I am applying the appropriate sanction'.

(adapted from Dix 2007)

Consequences will vary according to the circumstances, and might include working away from peers at a separate table, staying in at lunchtime to complete work not done in the lesson, a formal detention, exit to another class or area in the school or referral to a senior colleague. These can be expressed as a choice with the teacher saying, for example, 'If you choose to carry on talking then you will need to work by yourself.' It is debatable whether the actual words 'choose' or 'choice' need to feature within every interaction of this nature. Over used, these can sound rather clichéd and more about technique than relationships. Arguably, choice is conveyed just as well in a statement such as, 'You either need to finish the work now, or you'll need to stay in at break time to complete it.' To emphasise the point, this could be followed with, 'It's up to you', or 'It's your choice'. The key point is that the statement, whether specifically using the words 'choose' or 'choice' or not, conveys to the pupil that there is an alternative outcome that their behaviour can determine. These principles apply whether the consequence is an action such as moving to work in a different seat, a sanction or a referral to a senior member of staff.

Some further considerations

The preceding section outlined a range of strategies. There are a number of other points to consider when using these.

Relaxed vigilance

Relaxed vigilance (Rogers 2011) is similar in many ways to Kounin's (1970) concept of 'withitness' and is a more positive alternative to notions of 'zero tolerance'. The use of the word *relaxed* is important in reflecting that this is not about obsessive fault finding or identifying wrongdoing. Instead, 'relaxed vigilance' conveys the sense that the teacher is aware of what is going on within the classroom and is prepared to act on behaviour that infringes the class rules. In Behaviour for Learning terms, relaxed vigilance involves the teacher monitoring group relationships.

The least to most intrusive approach

Rogers (e.g. 1997, 2007, 2012) conceptualises the notion of starting at the lowest level necessary to settle the behaviour as the 'least to most intrusive' approach. Figure 10.1 depicts this approach in visual form linked to a number of strategies discussed in this section of the chapter. This is not meant to be prescriptive – it is, for example, debatable whether *tactical ignoring* is less intrusive than *proximity*. Rather, the example is intended to convey the idea that the teacher needs to consider a gradual and graded set of strategies that they might employ.

Neill and Caswell (1993) found that a lot of classroom behaviour fell into the category they defined as 'closed challenge'. This was behaviour that was relatively low level, typically occurred between a pair of pupils and involved no attempt to draw others into the interaction, as it was not intended to entertain the class or annoy the teacher (McPhillimy 1996). Neill and Caswell (1993) suggest that such incidents rarely evolve into disruption that carries a higher risk to the teacher's authority. Their video evidence showed that the majority of such incidents died away by themselves without the teacher intervening or even necessarily being aware. If the pupil did notice the

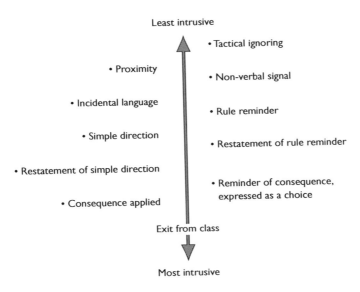

Least intrusive

• Tactical ignoring

• Proximity

• Non-verbal signal

• Incidental language

• Rule reminder

• Simple direction

• Restatement of rule reminder

• Restatement of simple direction

• Reminder of consequence,
  expressed as a choice

• Consequence applied

Exit from class

Most intrusive

Figure 10.1 Least to most intrusive approach.
Source: based on Rogers 1997.

teacher was aware of them this was usually sufficient to refocus them on their work (McPhillimy 1996). This supports the view that using the least intrusive strategy is likely to be the most appropriate approach.

Neill and Caswell (1993) also refer to 'open challenges'. These are more concerning as they are intended to involve other pupils or to annoy the teacher. Unlike a 'closed challenge', pupils engaged in 'open challenge' may show a high level of 'control checks', glancing frequently at the teacher to check whether they are being observed or otherwise trying to conceal their actions from the teacher in order to avoid detection. The assumption in Neill and Caswell's (1993) categorisation is that pupils have developed the necessary social, emotional and behavioural skills to behave in the manner required by the teacher. This is not always the case, even with secondary-aged pupils, and we should be wary of ascribing motive (e.g. an intent to annoy the teacher or disrupt the lesson) to *all* pupils who appear to demonstrate an 'open challenge'. Realistically, however, there will be some pupils whose behaviour does fall into the category of 'open challenge' and is underpinned by a conscious intent to disrupt and challenge the teacher. McPhillimy (1996) suggests that if the behaviour is not dealt with effectively, the pupil may become less concerned with attempting to conceal their actions and engage in open attempts to disrupt. The least to most intrusive approach is still appropriate for this type of behaviour, but teachers should be aware that an approach such as 'tactical ignoring' may reinforce to the pupil that the behaviour has gone undetected. Low key corrections using simple directions and rule reminders may be a more appropriate starting point within the least to most intrusive hierarchy in such situations.

Reflective Exercise 10.2

Ofsted's *Below the Radar* report (Ofsted 2014a) lists a range of low level behaviours encountered by teachers in all types and phases of schools it surveyed. These were:

- talking and chatting;
- disturbing other children;
- calling out;
- not getting on with work;
- fidgeting or fiddling with equipment;
- not having the correct equipment;
- purposely making noise to gain attention;
- answering back or questioning instructions;
- using mobile devices;
- swinging on chairs.

Select two or three behaviours from this list – or choose some that are more relevant to your setting. For each one:

- identify what you would do or say, ensuring this adheres to the principles of using the least intrusive strategy necessary and framing correction positively;
- identify what the next step in the least to most intrusive sequence would be if the pupil does not respond to the first strategy.

Use of 'thanks'

Readers will have noticed that in giving examples of how a strategy might be used we have often incorporated the word 'thanks'. It is a technique suggested both by Hook and Vass (2002) and Rogers (e.g. 2011). The use of 'thanks' after a request instead of the more usual 'please' conveys a stronger sense of expectation whilst still maintaining a polite tone. It helps the teacher to appear confident in two important ways. First, it conveys that when the teacher asks for something to happen they have no doubt that it will because they are confident in themselves and their authority. Second, it conveys that when the teacher asks for something to happen they have no doubt that it will because they are confident in the pupil's desire and ability to do the right thing. There may be some schools where either the word 'thanks' is considered to be too informal as a form of language to be used by teachers, or there is an insistence that pupils say 'thank you' rather than use this abbreviated form. In such cases, there is the option to use 'thank you' instead, but teachers would need to be aware that this potentially loses some of the relaxed, friendly quality because of the formality of the term.

'Take up' time

When directing or correcting a pupil it is important to allow 'take up' or thinking time (Rogers 1997, 2011; Hook and Vass 2002; Rogers and McPherson 2008). In a secondary school a teacher might say, 'Put your mobile away, thanks'. This brief interaction has significance in terms of the pupil–teacher relationship and the pupil's relationship with their peers. The pupil, in putting the phone away, is effectively showing the teacher and their peers that they are accepting the teacher's authority over them. For some pupils this may represent a loss of face. To remain standing over the pupil awaiting compliance can exacerbate this feeling as they need to comply under the teacher's gaze and, inevitably, with other pupils watching to see what will happen. Allowing take up time avoids this. It involves the teacher issuing the direction and then moving away to talk to another pupil or attend to something else. It gives the pupil the opportunity to process the request, which is important for some, and then to take the decision whether to comply or not, out of the spotlight of teacher and peer attention.

As well as the benefits for the pupil in terms of allowing them to save face by not having to comply so publicly, take up time is also beneficial for the teacher. When the teacher moves away they, of course, remain vigilant with regard to whether the pupil has complied with the direction or not. If the pupil has complied, then the teacher can decide when to go back and engage in a positive interaction about the task or behaviour to show that the relationship is still intact. If the pupil has not complied, then, having moved away from the interaction, the teacher is in a far better position to take a considered decision about the next action necessary than if they were standing over the pupil awaiting compliance.

Tactical ignoring of secondary behaviours

Secondary behaviours are behaviours that the pupil exhibits in response to teacher correction. Typically, these are behaviours that may be experienced by the teacher as irritating or provocative. They convey a degree of minor resistance, implying, 'I'm doing it, but grudgingly'. For example, a pupil told to put a toy away in their tray might comply but slide the tray under their desk in an unnecessarily noisy manner. A common form of secondary behaviour is a 'tut' or a mumbled comment. The recommended default position is to ignore secondary behaviours and keep the focus on the primary behaviour (Hook and Vass 2002; Rogers and McPherson 2008; Rogers 2011).

The primary behaviour is the behaviour that the teacher originally set out to address. Some pupils may be consciously or subconsciously using secondary behaviours as a way to deflect attention from the primary behaviour. By attending to the secondary behaviour the teacher is effectively both succumbing to this agenda and reinforcing the diversionary use of secondary behaviour as a successful strategy. Other pupils may be using it as a face-saving strategy to show either the teacher or their peers that although they are complying they are offering some resistance. Some readers may be wondering whether we should be concerned with allowing pupils to save face. If we are concerned with the pupil's relationship with self and relationship with others, then we should. Demanding total capitulation is not good for either of these relationships. If the secondary behaviour is of concern, then it is usually better to call the pupil aside at the end of the lesson 'for a quick word' and address the issue privately and calmly.

We have said that the *default* position is to ignore the secondary behaviour to capture the sense that there will be times when professional judgement, based on knowledge of the pupil and the context, determines a different response. The most obvious example is if the secondary behaviour is of a level that means that it assumes the status of a primary behaviour and has to be dealt with. There are other occasions however. For example, if a young child appeared to be trying out a phrase learned from a television programme or an adult or older sibling without realising it was an inappropriate response to adult direction, then the teacher might choose to act on it straight away.

The key point is that the teacher should not simply be *reacting* to secondary behaviours. When unsure, the default position is to ignore, keep the focus on the primary behaviour and follow up the secondary behaviour later if it is a cause of concern.

Partial agreement

Partial agreement (Hook and Vass 2002; Rogers 2011) is not a strategy that sits within a least to most intrusive sequence. Rather it is a technique a teacher can use in response when a pupil reacts to a positive correction strategy by attempting to argue back. Imagine that you say to a pupil, 'Ben, the writing needs to be finished by break. If you choose to carry on talking, then you will need to stay in and complete it.' This is a quite reasonable reminder of the consequence if the behaviour continues. However, as we have indicated, while we can use a good practice strategy to increase the likelihood of a positive outcome, we cannot guarantee the pupil response. Ben might respond with 'I wasn't the only one talking, why don't you tell them?'. Partial agreement involves framing a response that acknowledges the concern expressed but re-states the original message. For example, the teacher might say something like, 'Maybe you weren't the only one, but at the moment I need you to get on quietly. I'm keeping an eye on the others.'

For secondary colleagues in particular, there is the potential for conflict with pupils brought about by the inconsistent enforcement of school rules. For example, when directed to follow a seating plan a pupil might say, 'Mr Smith, lets us sit where we like'. Typically, this will not be delivered by the pupil as a casual observation of inconsistency in school, but accompanied by body language and tone of voice that challenges the teacher to justify their use of a seating plan. Partial agreement can be used here as a way of avoiding attempting to justify use of the seating plan, publicly criticising a colleague for not following school policy or reacting with an aggressive response such as, 'I don't care what happens in Mr Smith's class, in my class you sit where I tell you'. Using partial agreement, the teacher could instead say something like, 'Maybe he does … (small pause to allow the pupil to recognise that the teacher is not going to argue or confront), in our class we have a seating plan, so I'd like you to sit there.' Depending on the pupil and the situation it might be appropriate to add, 'If you are unhappy with where you are sitting then we can talk about it at the end of the lesson.'

Hook and Vass (2002) argue that it is better to frame partial agreement statements as 'Maybe … *and* …', rather than the more natural, 'Maybe … *but* …'. Their premise is that if the teacher says, 'Maybe you weren't the only ones talking but …', it immediately conveys a message that disagreement, discord or criticism is going to follow and thus invalidates the agreement in the first part of the sentence. It may also cause the pupil to turn their attention to defence against anticipated criticism rather than hearing what is actually said.

Hook and Vass's (2002) point is valid, but we would suggest the use of 'and' as opposed to 'but' may help rather than make the critical difference between a successful and an unsuccessful interaction. If teachers do use 'but', the key point we would take from Hook and Vass's observation is that it should not be emphasised within the sentence. The key parts that the pupil must hear are the partial agreement and the statement of the required behaviour.

Delivering blanket messages

Up until now the assumption has been that the behaviour to be addressed is restricted to a small number of pupils to whom positive corrections can be delivered individually. Sometimes, however, the behaviour is more widespread and it will be necessary to stop the class to reinforce the expectations of behaviour. This needs to be handled carefully because of two potential problems:

1   Having to talk to the whole class is a very serious step and implies that the teacher has been unable to stem the tide of individual behaviour (Kyriacou 1998). An unfocused catalogue of wrongdoings delivered in an aggressive or exasperated tone may serve to reinforce this to pupils.
2   The sizeable minority who were behaving appropriately may be alienated if they feel they are being included in a blanket critical message.

The teacher can address both of these problems by considering the language they use. The teacher might say, for example, 'Many of you were too noisy coming in today', because this allows those who came in appropriately to feel that they are not getting the blame. Other phrases might be, 'There are rather too many people …' or 'I know it wasn't everybody but some people…'. Delivered calmly, these sorts of phrases also convey the message to the class as a whole that the teacher has weighed up the proportions and taken a decision as to how to act. In all cases, the statement of the problem should be followed by a statement of the required behaviour, or a reminder of the appropriate class rules or routines. Contrast this approach with sentences that start, 'This class is far too noisy …', or 'How can anybody be expected to work with this noise …', or 'I will not have this noise….' These types of comment emphasise the global scale of the problem.

Resisting the temptation to use whole class sanctions

Situations in which it is difficult to identify specific individuals to positively correct present a considerable challenge for the teacher. This practical difficulty, coupled with a feeling of needing to do something, can lead teachers to consider resorting to the use of a whole-group or whole-class sanction. Reflective Exercise 10.3 provides an opportunity to explore some of the issues related to such a strategy from a Behaviour for Learning perspective.

The use of whole-class sanctions such as the one described in Reflective Exercise 10.3 is problematic. Previous government guidance has clearly stated that schools should 'avoid whole group sanctions that punish the innocent as well as the guilty' (DCSF 2009: 31). As the Elton Report (DES 1989) pointed out, such approaches are always likely to be seen as unfair by pupils and the resulting sense of grievance is likely to be damaging to the school atmosphere. More recently, in one of the case studies illustrating good practice in Bennett's (2017) report on behaviour in schools, the banning of whole-class detentions was listed as one of the ten actions contributing to the school's improvement.

From a Behaviour for Learning perspective, the use of whole-class sanctions is an approach that raises some additional concerns. We would see self-efficacy as an important component of an individual's relationship with self. Self-efficacy can be

---

Reflective Exercise 10.3

A Year 5 teacher has given her class several warnings because they are being too noisy. Unable to identify specific individuals who are contributing to the nose level, she writes on the board 'Whole class detention – 1 minute'. As the noise persists, she adds minutes. Eventually some pupils notice and start to 'shush' the others. By the time the teacher reaches '10 minutes' on the board the class is quiet. At lunch time she keeps the class in and makes them sit in silence for a period of ten minutes.

Reviewing the current strategy

1   What learning behaviours is the teacher trying to promote?
2   Are there any unhelpful behaviours that the teacher risks promoting implicitly?
3   Are there any predictable adverse effects on one or more of the three Behaviour for Learning relationships?

Considering alternatives

4   Why might the pupils be too noisy?
5   What could the teacher have done instead?

---

thought of as a person's estimate that a given behaviour will lead to certain outcomes, coupled with a belief in their ability to successfully execute this behaviour (Bandura 1977). The strategy used by the teacher in Reflective Exercise 10.3 potentially undermines the individual's sense of self-efficacy. Even if an individual chose to take personal responsibility (a positive learning behaviour) in order to get on with the task quietly and attempted to filter out distractions from others (a positive learning behaviour), this is neither rewarded nor recognised and still leads to the same negative outcome (i.e. staying in) unless sufficient others make similar positive choices. Such a strategy risks sending the unhelpful message that, as an individual, the child is able to exert little influence over what happens to them; it is the behaviour of others that determines whether the individual receives the sanction. We might also speculate on the potential damage to pupils' relationship with others. The inherent unfairness may be damaging to the pupils' relationship with the teacher but we can look further than this and consider what it might do to peer relationships. Although the assumption underpinning this strategy is often that it makes use of peer group pressure, it is essentially underpinned by a 'divide and conquer' (Kohn 1999: 56) principle. If the peer group pressure moved beyond the 'shushing' in class to take the form of the perceived culprits subsequently being socially isolated by their classmates, or even experiencing physical coercion, it would be a concern. There is, therefore, the risk that unhelpful behaviours are promoted.

In thinking about alternative strategies, question 4 in Reflective Activity 10.3 is of particular importance. For example, we might consider whether the problems result from pupils getting stuck and not knowing what to do. Unable to continue, they may become restless and find other ways of occupying their time. In this situation the priority might be to teach problem-solving strategies. These could be supported by a poster displaying the steps to take when stuck; the teacher can then remind pupils of this. The noise levels might also prompt a need to look at the level of challenge. It might be that pupils are getting stuck so frequently because the task is too difficult. Conversely, the level of challenge may be too low, meaning either that pupils can complete it and talk at the same time or it is experienced as boring so to relieve this they find other distractions. If the level of challenge is the issue, then differentiation strategies rather than behaviour management strategies may be the priority.

Assuming there are no significant issues related to curriculum and pedagogy that explain the noise levels, it is appropriate to consider alternative behaviour management strategies. Rogers (2011), for example, describes a noise meter based on a cardboard circle divided into red, amber and green segments. Green represents the desired noise level, amber is a warning that it is becoming too noisy and the level needs to be adjusted and red means it is too noisy. A cardboard arrow indicates the current noise level. The noise meter can be presented as part of a wider consideration of appropriate noise levels for different types of activity when learning in a group setting. Some teachers, for example, will distinguish between 'partner voices', 'table voices', 'classroom voices' and 'playground voices'. This encourages the class to take more responsibility for monitoring their own behaviour. It is a positive strategy that can be used throughout the lesson. A class reward could be linked to staying out of the red zone. This encourages a similar sort of peer group pressure to a whole-class sanction but directs it in a more positive manner. It also enables the teacher to direct positive feedback to those who have noticed the position of the pointer and adjusted their behaviour

Selecting and evaluating the strategies

Essentially, in the preceding sections we have gathered a range of positive correction strategies that we consider to represent a useful toolkit and fit with the principle that any strategy used to manage behaviour should promote, or at least not undermine, the development of positive learning behaviours and should not compromise any of the Behaviour for Learning relationships. Scenario 10.1 demonstrates how a combination of the strategies described could be used.

In scenario 10.1 the teacher is careful to avoid inflaming the situation and uses respectful language throughout. Although this ends up being a protracted interaction the teacher attempts to use the least intrusive strategy possible to address the behaviour each time and bides their time between individual interactions. In ending 10.1A the pupil complies and puts the phone away. In ending 10.1B, despite the teacher's best efforts, the situation erupts. This alternative ending is provided to illustrate the important point that we cannot predict every pupil's response. In making a strategy selection we are effectively making a prediction about how the pupil will respond. Knowledge of the pupil will clearly help in making a more accurate prediction. The strategies suggested in this chapter are those that we consider on *more* occasions stand a *greater* chance with *more* pupils of leading to outcomes of the type described in ending 10.1A. The same cannot be said of the strategies employed in Scenario 10.2. While the strategies in Scenario 10.2 may be successful in stopping behaviour on many occasions, when they do not succeed the failure is likely to be public and spectacular. The strategies in Scenario 10.2 are high risk strategies and, as we explore next, also contribute little to the development of learning behaviour.

Scenario 10.1

Situation	Commentary
Jason is texting on a mobile phone during the lesson and is spotted by the teacher.	**Relaxed vigilance/withitness** – the teacher notices the unwanted behaviour.
Teacher: *Teacher says nothing but calmly walks around to Jason's area of the room while still speaking to the class.* *Jason continues texting.*	The teacher starts with a **non-verbal** technique as this is the least intrusive strategy. Jason either does not notice or is unconcerned that his behaviour might have been spotted by the teacher.
Teacher: 'Jason.' *As Jason looks up, the teacher makes a non-verbal gesture pointing at own ear and then downwards to indicate the phone should be put away. Jason puts the phone down on his desk.* *After a few minutes Jason picks up his phone.*	The teacher cues the pupil in by name and then uses a **privately understood signal**. The teacher accepts this partial compliance.
	Relaxed vigilance/withitness – the teacher notices the unwanted behaviour.
Teacher: 'Jason, put the phone away, thanks.' *Teacher moves away and talks to another pupil about the task. The teacher looks over and sees Jason still has the phone in his hand.*	The teacher makes use of a **simple direction**, followed by **take up time** to give Jason the chance to comply.
Teacher: 'Jason, you either put the phone away in your bag or put it on my desk.'	The teacher offers a **choice** (with one option that the pupil is likely to find preferable).
Jason: 'OK, OK, I was just checking it was turned off.'	
Teacher: 'Maybe you were, but now I need you to put it away and get started on the writing.'	The teacher uses '**partial agreement**' rather than entering into an argument.
Ending 10.1A *Jason:* 'Tut' *(audibly). Slides chair back with unnecessary noise and puts the phone in his bag. The teacher makes no comment on this.*	The teacher chooses to **ignore the secondary behaviour**.
Ending 10.1B *Jason:* 'Why don't you just get out of my face? I don't want to do the stupid writing and you can't make me.'	The teacher, recognising a rapidly escalating situation, sends another pupil with a red card to the 'on call' member of the Senior Leadership Team.

Scenario 10.2

Situation	Commentary
Jason is texting on a mobile phone during the lesson and is spotted by the teacher.	Relaxed vigilance/withitness – the teacher notices the unwanted behaviour.
Teacher: *(Loudly)* 'Jason! … What on earth do think you're doing?!' Bring that here now.' *Jason gets up and takes the phone to the teacher at the front of the class.*	The teacher uses a highly intrusive approach that, by its volume, is arguably more disruptive to the class as a whole than the behaviour it seeks to stop.
Teacher: 'You obviously don't know what the school rule is about mobiles so you'd better stay in at lunch time and copy out the school's Code of Conduct. And you won't be seeing this again until the end of the day *(puts the phone in desk drawer)*. Now sit down … you've wasted enough of everyone's time already.'	The teacher uses this as an opportunity to demonstrate that they are in a position of authority and will not tolerate any challenge to this.
Ending 10.2A	
Jason goes back to his seat, the class is completely silent.	Based on compliance as the success criteria the teacher judges the strategy to be successful
Ending 10.2B	
Jason: 'You give that back! If anything happens to my phone my dad's going to be up here. D'you hear me?!'	The interaction ends in a publicly played out confrontation. Relationships are damaged and difficult to repair
Teacher: 'How dare you talk to me like that!? Get out!?' *Jason storms out, slamming the door.*	

The strategies used in Scenario 10.1 promote learning behaviour, or, at least, do not contradict the principles of the Behaviour for Learning approach by impacting negatively on relationship with self, others or the curriculum. This remains true whether the interaction results in ending 10.1A or 10.1B and provides the criteria by which to judge the effectiveness and the *appropriateness* of the strategy. Judging effectiveness simply by whether the behaviour stops places the teacher in a reactive position where they are trying and discarding strategies based on the response of the pupil which may be influenced by all manner of complex interacting factors.

In Scenario 10.1, the teacher's use of respectful language throughout recognises the need to avoid damaging either the relationship with the pupil or the pupil's relationship with self. The interaction seeks to re-focus Jason on learning, which currently the mobile phone is distracting him from. In contrast, strategies in Scenario 10.2 are focused on quelling a perceived challenge to authority and taking opportunities to demonstrate that any challenge of this sort will be dealt with in a similar manner. The strategies in Scenario 10.1 place the responsibility on Jason through choices and time to consider his actions. Moreover, the teacher models appropriate behaviours for dealing with a situation that is currently not as they would wish it to be. The teacher in Scenario 10.2, however, models that if someone is in a position of power through the authority conveyed by their role, and possibly also through other factors such as their physical size, strength, command of language or greater intellect, it is acceptable to use coercive means or disrespectful language to secure their desired outcome. In terms of self-regulation the teacher in Scenario 10.1 keeps the events in proportion and manages themselves well, recognising that although the behaviour needs to be addressed it does not warrant the disproportionate anger and aggression demonstrated by the teacher in Scenario 10.2. Again, this is a modelling issue. The teacher in Scenario 10.1 models effective management of their own frustration and irritation through the use of assertive language, calmness and persistence.

A final point to note is that in the case of ending 10.1B from Scenario 10.1 the teacher–pupil relationship may be strained but is readily recoverable. The same cannot be said of ending 10.2B in Scenario 10.2 where considerable effort is likely to be necessary to repair and rebuild the relationship.

Analysing individual interactions

Taking the Behaviour for Learning approach further, it is also possible to scrutinise individual statements to consider their likely contribution to the promotion of learning behaviour and their potential effect. Consider the following scenario.

Scenario 10.3

A pupil in the Reception class, Terry, is making a tower out of plastic building blocks. He has been working on this for some time and then it collapses. The teacher hears Terry swear and makes the judgement that this is out of frustration. Teacher A responds with a focus on the promotion of learning behaviour, whereas Teacher B responds with a focus on the challenge to authority:

Teacher A: 'Terry (*said calmly, with a pause to get attention*), we don't use language like that in our class. You know our rule … now what's the difficulty?'
Teacher B: 'How dare you use that language in my class! Go and sit on the naughty chair!'

If the intention is to remark upon the unacceptability of swearing then either response achieves this outcome. If the desired outcome is to remark on the unacceptability of swearing *and* promote learning behaviour, Teacher A's response is more likely to achieve this. Teacher A uses the pupil's name. This not only cues Terry into the fact that the teacher wants him to listen but also demonstrates that he is worthy of being spoken to with respect. A person's name is a central element of their identity and therefore an important element of relationship with self. Teacher A's pause after the pupil's name cues him in and avoids this becoming a 'thrust' (Kounin 1970). The intention is not to surprise the pupil, but to prime him to hear an important message. The statement, 'We don't use language like that in our class', does not seek to moralise. The phrasing allows for dual expectations to exist in the pupil's life. Such swearing may be viewed as acceptable in the pupil's home, but the teacher does not seek to pass judgement on this and just conveys clearly that a particular set of expectations apply in the classroom environment. Unlike Teacher B, who refers to 'my class', Teacher A's use of '*our* class' emphasises participation and collaboration. The reference to the rules by Teacher A supports the development of social learning behaviours by demonstrating to Terry that when living and working alongside others, in almost any context, there is a set of rules that apply. Teacher B misses this learning opportunity and moves straight to a sanction which is a period of time out on the 'naughty chair'. The use of the term 'naughty chair' conveys a label in the sense that presumably anybody who sits on it is naughty. The problems of labelling and self-fulfilling prophecy have been well documented. There is potential for a negative impact on the pupil's relationship with self if they continually receive the message that they are naughty. Although it has become something of a mantra within the field of behaviour management, it is worth restating that we should label the behaviour, not the child. The other criticism in Behaviour for Learning terms is that a title of 'thinking chair' would convey a better sense of the behaviours we want the pupil to engage in whilst there, such as reflecting on their own behaviour. Teacher A finishes the interaction with a focus on learning by asking, 'What's the difficulty?', and takes the opportunity to promote resourcefulness and resilience by conveying the message that it is recognised that a difficulty has occurred and that this is something to be tackled.

The suggestion is not that a teacher should seek to break down every interaction they have with pupils in this way. After all, as Watkins (2016) suggests, the teacher may be involved in 1,000 or more interactions over the course of a day. Rather, teachers should reflect generally on the sorts of language they use in their interactions. Neither is the suggestion that, in this case, Terry will be psychologically damaged by Teacher B's handling of the situation or that Teacher A's handling will have developed his learning behaviour dramatically. It is, of course, the cumulative effect that we are concerned with. If Terry's experience is *frequently* of Teacher B-type responses that focus on the challenge to authority, label and move rapidly to sanctions, this may have negative effects. If, however, Terry's experience is *frequently* of Teacher A-type responses that focus on the promotion of learning behaviour and have regard for the three relationships, then this is likely to have more positive effects.

Conclusion

This chapter has dealt with the very practical concern of what to do when a pupil misbehaves. As we indicated at the beginning of the chapter it is almost inevitable that this will happen. We have sought to provide teachers and trainees with a basic toolkit of strategies for positive correction when dealing with such situations. The strength of the approaches encouraged within this chapter lies in their focus on relationships. They provide a form of language that the teacher can use that is respectful and reduces any risk both to the teacher–pupil relationship and the three Behaviour for Learning relationships.

We are sure readers will already have ideas about which of these strategies are immediately applicable to their contexts, which have some utility if adapted and those that are likely to be of limited use. Readers will also want to expand the toolkit by accessing a variety of resources. Although we would warn against the indiscriminate pursuit of behaviour management strategies in the mistaken belief that a universally effective set exists, to professionally consider the utility of any new approaches and engage with the literature on the subject is something we would encourage. As a starting point, a more extensive list of strategies is provided in Appendix 3. As we indicated in Chapter 2, the Behaviour for Learning conceptual framework is intended to support teachers in the task of selecting and evaluating strategies for behaviour management. Any strategy that is selected should be based on its potential to contribute to the development of learning behaviour and, at the very least, carry no predictable risk of harm to the three Behaviour for Learning relationships.

Chapter 11

Dealing with more challenging behaviour

Introduction

This chapter invites the reader to consider what we might term more challenging behaviour and how this can be managed in a way that retains a focus on promoting learning behaviour and does not compromise the three Behaviour for Learning relationships.

From our experience working with schools, there seem to be two distinct categories of challenging behaviour that concern teachers. The first is behaviour exhibited with a high degree of frequency by certain individuals. In other words, the problem is not the seriousness of the behaviour itself but the fact that the pupil exhibits it a lot. The second is higher level behaviour, such as physical and verbal aggression, usually underpinned by anger. Although it focuses primarily on the latter, the chapter considers both forms of challenging behaviour.

High frequency behaviour

This section of the chapter is concerned with individuals who exhibit certain behaviours frequently. The behaviours are not especially serious or unusual; the problematic dimension is the fact that the pupil exhibits them often and may not respond to the teacher's prompts and corrections. There are some pupils whose behaviour does not abate; despite the use of a number of strategies they continue to exhibit the same or other similarly problematic behaviour. Others may temporarily moderate their behaviour when corrected, but repeat it or similar problematic behaviour later in the lesson. In both cases it is important to respond consistently and make use of school systems at the time when the behaviour occurs. To reiterate a point made earlier in the book, we should seek to employ strategies before sanctions. That is, we should employ a range of strategies, moving from least to most intrusive (see Chapter 10), in an attempt to moderate the behaviour. If the pupil moderates their behaviour in response to one of the least to most intrusive strategies employed, or when a sanction is issued, the immediate problem is resolved. However, as we have previously noted, this does not necessarily mean any learning behaviours have been developed as a result.

It is important to recognise that the use of least to most intrusive strategies is not a formulaic exercise; we should always be monitoring carefully the pupil's responses and gauging our next step accordingly. This should inform us when to pursue a particular line, perhaps by being more insistent with a re-statement of a rule or reminding of the consequence of a continuation of this behaviour, moving in closer for a quiet word or physically and metaphorically taking a step back.

Using the sorts of least to most intrusive strategies described in Chapter 10 will help to ensure that behaviour is managed in a way that does not compromise the three relationships that underpin the development of learning behaviour. What happens at the most intrusive level varies between schools and it is important for the teacher to be aware of, and confident in, the systems that are in place. Knowing the stage available next, including how to access support from a colleague, can give the teacher greater confidence in using the less intrusive strategies prior to this.

Typically, it is not the sort of sequence of events described previously that causes the teacher greatest concern. In simple terms, if the pupil responds to one of the least to most intrusive strategies or to a sanction that is imposed, the teacher no longer has a behaviour problem. The greater concern is when, despite using a sequence of least to most intrusive strategies and imposing a sanction, the behaviour that impacts significantly on the learning of others continues unabated. Many schools have systems in place for this sort of situation that involve summoning assistance from (usually) a senior colleague. It is important for teachers to know the system that operates in their school and expectations regarding its use. The latter point is important. For example, most schools would not expect assistance to be summoned for refusal to work unless this took the form of a behaviour that had a significant negative impact on other pupils' learning. Passive non-compliance of this sort can usually be dealt with later. Individual teachers have a responsibility not to over-use such a system; senior leaders have a responsibility to ensure that when requested such support is quick and effective, secure in the knowledge that it is based on a genuine need.

Colleague support in exiting a pupil

In thinking about colleague support when exiting a pupil there are a few guidelines we can consider:

- The supporting member of staff should be given a brief, quiet, factual account of the situation. The referrer should not use this as an opportunity to express their own frustrations or publicly list all the pupil's misdemeanours in front of the class. Typically, this should be a quiet conversation just inside the classroom door where at least one of the adults has sight of the pupil concerned and the rest of the class.
- The referrer should avoid comments to the colleague providing support such as, 'I'm not prepared to teach this pupil', 'he needs to be excluded', or 'I will not have him back in my class'. They are emotive and the reality is that the referrer does not have the power to make these decisions anyway. This fact will, of course, be abundantly obvious to the class and the pupil when they are not excluded and later return. Such comments also place the supporter in a difficult position because they cannot agree to any of these points on the spur of the moment. This kind of comment only serves to make the relationship with the pupil more difficult when they do return.
- The supporter should not question the referrer or start to suggest other strategies that should have been tried. If there are issues about how the referrer handled the situation prior to referral, or advice that can be offered on additional strategies, these should be discussed in a supportive environment later.
- As a general rule, the supporter should not engage the pupil in conversation within the classroom and should use a brief, respectful directive statement such as, 'I need

you to come with me now', and turn expectantly, conveying confidence that the pupil will follow. Placing one hand on the edge or handle of the open door whilst extending the other arm outwards as you might do in an 'after you' type gesture can add to this air of confidence. An exception to this principle of minimal dialogue is when the supporter's professional judgement is that this is an escalating situation and allowing the pupil to talk would be beneficial in diffusing a potentially more serious situation.

- The referrer needs to be given feedback later on concerning what happened to the pupil when they were removed from class. If this feedback is not forthcoming the referrer should take the initiative in requesting this.
- Consideration needs to be given to how relationships are repaired between the referrer and the pupil. This is especially important in a secondary school context where several days may elapse before the timetable brings the pupil and teacher together again. The central focus of any meeting with the pupil prior to the next lesson should be on what they can do differently next time and what might help them to do this rather than dwelling on events that led to their exit from the class the last time.

The out-of-class or after-class discussion

Pupils will sometimes need to be spoken to out of class. Teachers meeting one- to-one with a pupil need to be aware of the risk of malicious allegations. The general advice would be to make sure colleagues are aware of the meeting and that you can be easily observed, keeping a door open if necessary. However, readers would be well advised to check with their school's policy for further guidance on this issue. Frequently such meetings will be at break time but may also take the form of brief conversations just outside the classroom door. The latter approach raises issues in relation to the supervision of the rest of the class, so again readers should be clear on their school policy and expectations of the senior leadership team with regard to this.

The brief out-of-class discussion

We need to recognise the limitations of the brief out-of-class discussion. If the teacher is briefly seeing a pupil just outside the classroom during a lesson it clearly limits the scope of the conversation. Despite the briefness, the teacher's language needs to remain positive and respectful throughout so as not to impact negatively either on their relationship with the pupil or the pupil's relationship with self. Typically, there is opportunity for little more than a conversation that:

- summarises events that have led to this point, e.g. 'Jack, I've reminded you several times about the need to work quietly without disturbing the rest of the group';
- states the likely consequences of continuation of this behaviour, e.g. 'If you continue then you will need to stay in at break time and complete your work';
- states or offers any options available to the pupil that may help, e.g. 'Would it help if you moved seats and sat at the spare desk by the window?';
- ends positively, e.g. 'OK, let's go back into class and I'll come and see how you're getting on in a few minutes'.

Protracted conversations about what the pupil did and why they did it are neither possible nor desirable. Such conversations leave the class unsupervised, unless another adult is present who is capable of taking on this duty, and run the risk of arousing strong emotions or opening up issues that the teacher has insufficient time to deal with. If this kind of conversation is necessary, it is better that it is deferred until quality time can be devoted to it.

When returning to class from a conversation such as this, the teacher needs to be realistic in their expectations of the pupil's behaviour. For the pupil their relationship with others may be a key factor at this point and they may exhibit some secondary behaviours (see Chapter 10) to save face. It is important to recognise that it is difficult to return to the classroom with potentially 29 other pupils watching. Teachers should accept therefore that the pupil may grin at friends when passing, slump heavily into their seat or exhibit some other form of low level but potentially irritating behaviour. As we indicated in Chapter 10, the default position regarding secondary behaviours is to ignore them. Following the pupil into class allows the teacher to see their behaviour and lets them know that their behaviour can be seen. This can help to curb some of the more overt secondary behaviours that the pupil may be tempted to exhibit if they were following the teacher.

Used sparingly, the brief out-of-class conversation can be effective. It is a way of removing the pupil from the immediate environment and making a personal link. It takes the pupil away from an audience that may be reinforcing the behaviour, either through comments, looks or just their presence.

Follow-up discussions

Unlike the brief out-of-class discussion, the follow-up discussion takes place at a set time. For example, the teacher might have asked the pupil to see them at break or lunch time. In thinking about this meeting there are a few guidelines we can consider.

Distinguish between those who 'can't behave' and those who 'won't behave'

Before speaking to the pupil, consider their level of understanding of the behaviour. Age and level of development will inform this assessment. Your approach to a pupil who, due to age or stage of development, does not understand why a behaviour is unacceptable or problematic, will need to be different to the approach used when you are confident the pupil knows how to behave and is developmentally able to demonstrate the behaviour required. This issue is explored in Reflective Exercise 11.1 at the end of this section.

Allow sufficient time

It is important to allow sufficient time, free from interruptions, to talk with the pupil.

Label the behaviour not the pupil

A key principle when managing behaviour is to label the behaviour, not the pupil. This relates to the pupil's relationship with self, as the purpose is to avoid the behaviour becoming part of the pupil's identity. Therefore, the teacher would talk of the action as being unkind or disruptive rather than the pupil. This is a useful rule to adhere to but needs to be expanded a little. Sometimes, even when we label the behaviour, there is a strong connotation of what that makes the individual. Examples might include, 'What you did was bullying' or 'That is stealing.' Though such phrases are labelling the behaviour and as such are considerably better than, 'You're a bully' or 'You're a thief', the terminology is still emotive. Instead, describe what the pupil actually did. In the case of a younger pupil suspected of bullying the teacher might begin: 'I understand that you have been calling Sam names during break time. I know this is not the first time you have done this to Sam. When someone keeps making life unpleasant for the same person I take it very seriously....'

If the teacher feels it is appropriate to use the label then it can be used in an explanatory, educative way, such as: 'I understand that you have been calling Sam names during break time. I know this not the first time you have done this to Sam. When someone keeps making life unpleasant for the same person it is called bullying. I take that sort of behaviour very seriously.'

This confronts the pupil with the reality of what they have done in a manner that reflects back to them how others view the behaviour or collection of behaviours exhibited currently. The pupil is therefore encouraged to reflect on whether how they currently present is how they want to present, thereby showing them that choice is available and change is possible.

Recognise underlying feelings

If the teacher asks to see a pupil after a lesson or asks to see them for a moment outside the class, this carries a connotation that something is going to happen which is not going to be an entirely comfortable experience. There may be feelings of anxiety coupled with annoyance and irritation (Hook and Vass 2002), particularly if seeing the teacher involves loss of the pupil's time. Older pupils may refer to the practice as 'getting done', as in the phrase, 'You're going to get done', meaning that a reprimand or sanction is likely (Hook and Vass 2002). The fact that after-class follow-up discussions have this status should be reassuring to teachers when using deferred consequences, as it means that dealing with a situation later rather than confronting a pupil directly in class is not seen by other pupils as a weakness or a sign that pupils are 'getting away with it'. The other, more important message, however is that we need to recognise that we are dealing with a pupil who may already be feeling anxious, aggrieved or inconvenienced (Hook and Vass 2002). To adopt a heavy-handed approach by attempting to dominate through our body language, tone of voice or use of disparaging or belittling language, is therefore both unnecessary – as pupils already perceive the event as significant – and unhelpful, as it may be the trigger that causes an unnecessary escalation.

Recognise the implications for communication of a heightened emotional state

Be aware that any heightened emotional state will adversely affect the ability to take in and cognitively process information and instruction. For this reason, any communication needs to be clear, short and consistent.

Thank the pupil for staying behind or returning

Hook and Vass (2002) suggest thanking the pupil for staying behind, which may at first seem strange given that it is the teacher's decision that they have stayed behind, and the reason for this decision has been the pupil's misbehaviour. The strength of this approach is two-fold. First, it is a defusing strategy. It is harder to be angry with someone who has just thanked you. Second, it is a point of success from which to start. The pupil has already chosen to be cooperative by coming to speak with the teacher. Hook and Vass (2002) sum up the rationale behind thanking the pupil succinctly, suggesting, 'You are in effect, making a positive emotional deposit into the emotional account you have with the student before you make the inevitable withdrawal by discussing more difficult issues' (Hook and Vass 2002: 78).

Reflective Exercise 11.1

Jacob, aged 4, has taken another pupil's set of colouring pencils and is observed by a member of staff putting them in his own bag. You have had a number of reports from parents of their children's belongings going missing and unsubstantiated claims from other pupils that Jacob has taken them.

Kerry, aged 13, has taken another pupil's calculator and is observed by a member of staff putting it in her own bag. You have had a number of complaints from pupils about possessions going missing and a number of them have suggested that Kerry could be the culprit.

- In both cases what would be the purpose of your interaction with the pupil?
- How would the interaction be different?

Note: For the purpose of this exercise we have made the assumption that developmentally Kerry is functioning broadly in line with her chronological age. Individual knowledge of the pupil would determine whether this was a reasonable assumption.

Beyond managing behaviour

The fact that a pupil is frequently progressing though the range of least to most intrusive strategies and receiving sanctions, or perhaps on occasions needs to be collected from class by a colleague, is data that should be interpreted as an indicator of a need for other interventions. This is a point we highlighted through Figure 8.1 in Chapter 8. As we also suggested in that chapter, it needs to be recognised that sanctions often do little to *change* behaviour. A pupil who is regularly reaching the sanctions level is effectively providing proof of this point. Therefore, although the class teacher may still need to continue managing behaviour through consistent application of school policy, it should be recognised that it will be other interventions that change behaviour. In their future planning we would want the teacher to use their knowledge of the pupil and the incident to consider whether, in order to bring about behavioural change, it will be sufficient to target the development of some specific learning behaviours or one (or more) of the three Behaviour for Learning relationships needs to be the focus for intervention.

Behaviour as an expression of anger

When a pupil does not respond to directions and is non-compliant the temptation may be to dismiss the behaviour as attention-seeking, fun-seeking, pushing the boundaries or simply rooted in a desire to give the teacher a hard time. Although such an assessment may be accurate for some pupils, we need to be alert to the possibility that this behaviour is an indicator of physiological or psychological arousal. The pupil may be reacting to something they perceive to be an emotional or physical threat. In most cases it is possible to spot the signs of arousal before an angry or aggressive incident develops. Effective intervention at this point relies on the teacher not only spotting the signs but responding appropriately. Monitoring and responsiveness on the part of the teacher is the key to avoiding escalation.

Understanding the emotion behind angry and aggressive incidents

The Behaviour for Learning approach emphasises the importance of understanding how a pupil is experiencing and interpreting events. Applying this perspective to incidents involving angry or aggressive behaviour, it is necessary to recognise that the display of anger, and the surface emotionality associated with it, will often cover up very different eliciting emotional states (Bowers 2005), including feelings of frustration, anxiety, loss or affront. Davies and Frude (2000) provide a useful model that helps us understand why some people, when experiencing normal human emotions such as frustration, anxiety or anger, exhibit violent or aggressive behaviours. They put forward a five-stage process shown in Figure 11.1.

The *situation* is the triggering event. Davies and Frude (2000) suggest that there are typically three elements that may lead to anger. These are as follows:

1   irritants: these might be aspects in the physical environment (e.g. loud or repetitive noise, smells) or the irritating actions of others;
2   costs: personal loss (e.g. of money or goods), loss of status or 'face' and other forms of detriment;
3   transgressions: these involve a person breaking a rule (or doing something 'out of order').

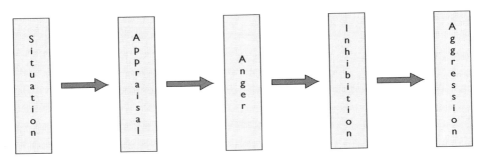

Figure 11.1 The aggressive incident model.

Source: based on Davies and Frude 2000.

However, it is not the situation in itself that produces the emotional responses but the *appraisal* an individual makes. For example, if two pupils happen to collide in the corridor, one may view this as an unfortunate accident while the other may interpret it as deliberate. The interpretation made by the individual will determine whether the resulting predominant emotion is anger. There are a number of influencing factors on the appraisal an individual makes, including the following:

- The way the individual usually views things. Do they usually put a negative slant on events?
- The individual's mood at the time. People who are already angry or pressured tend to view things in a more negative way.
- What other people are saying about the situation. Peers or others significant in the pupil's life may encourage a particular appraisal by, for example, suggesting that a particular act was underpinned by malicious intent or that not to interpret it as hostile is a sign of weakness.

Anger is an emotional state which can lead to aggression, although it does not necessarily do so in all individuals or on all occasions. It does, however, need some form of outlet because, while suppressing anger can be a useful and necessary strategy for all of us in certain circumstances, too much suppression can be problematic and lead to repressed anger that seeps out and influences our behaviour in ways we may not even be aware of (Faupel *et al.* 1998).

It is conceivable that two individuals may have been exposed to the same situation, made the same appraisal and experienced the same feeling of anger, yet only one reacts aggressively or violently. This difference can be explained in terms of an individual's *inhibitions*. In Davies and Frude's (2000) model, *inhibition* is used as a neutral phrase; it is not intended necessarily to imply a degree of suppression or repression. Inhibitions may be *internal* or *external* as shown in Table 11.1.

Inhibitions may be high towards the actual source of anger. The result may be displaced anger, where the pupil directs their anger at a target towards which their inhibitions are lower.

Table 11.1 Internal and external inhibitors

Internal inhibitors	External inhibitors
• Strong self-control • The individual is naturally disposed to – or has learned to – manage strong feelings. • Anticipated feelings of guilt, e.g. 'If I hurt this person I'll never be able to forgive myself'. • Moral inhibitions, e.g. 'I'm a pacifist – I don't believe in being physically aggressive'.	• Fear of physical retaliation, e.g. 'He's bigger than me – I could get hurt'. • Fear of social consequences, e.g. disowned by friends. • Fear of other consequences, e.g. school exclusion or police involvement. • Fear of embarrassment, e.g. 'I'll go red, my voice will go all squeaky and I'll just look silly'.

Source: based on Davies and Frude 2000: 21.

Aggression is the final stage of Davies and Frude's (2000) model. This term covers behaviours ranging from the verbal through to the physical. Physical aggression covers a wide range of behaviours from aggressive or intimidating posturing through to pushing, pulling, hair grabbing, biting, punching, kicking and, at the most extreme end, use of weapons.

It should be evident from Davies and Frude's (2000) model where there is scope for proactive intervention. For example, the teacher might work at the *situation* stage by:

- using activities that help the pupil to recognise triggering events ('What makes you angry?');
- using activities that help the pupil to recognise physiological changes that occur when they encounter this trigger ('What do you notice happens when you get angry?');
- identifying with the pupil strategies they can use when they encounter a triggering event;
- identifying with the pupil self-calming techniques they can use when they notice the physiological changes beginning.

Working at the *appraisal* stage the teacher might use activities that help the pupil to:

- recognise the causal explanations they make in relation to situations that currently act as triggers;
- identify feelings this causal explanation provokes;
- recognise other causal explanations they could make that engender less negative feelings.

There might also be scope to work on awareness of different forms of consequences to strengthen their external *inhibitions*.

Reflective Exercise 11.2

Think about an occasion where you experienced something as an *irritant, transgression* or *loss* (Davies and Frude 2000), but it did not result in you exhibiting aggressive behaviour. Use Davies and Frude's (2000) model to explain your response to this situation. For example, did you get angry or was there something about your appraisal of the situation that meant it did not provoke this emotion? If it did provoke feelings of anger, can you identify internal or external inhibitions that prevented this from resulting in aggression?

Although the focus of this chapter is not on proactive approaches to working with pupils for whom anger is a problem, it is important to recognise that incidents involving aggression should signal the need for this type of longer-term work with the pupil on managing emotions and the self-regulation of behaviour. As the class teacher, this may not be your responsibility; it may be, for example, that the pupil would benefit from inclusion in an anger management group or access to some individualised work. Even if not directly involved in the intervention, it may be that you are required to provide feedback on the pupil's performance in class or support particular strategies that have been put in place by, for example, the special educational needs coordinator (SENCO) or a member of the pastoral team working with the pupil.

Responding effectively to incidents

Breakwell (1997) presented the assault cycle (see Figure 11.2) as a way of understanding the process that occurs during a typical episode of physically aggressive behaviour. This understanding helps us to identify our priorities at each stage. The model has been presented in a more generic form as the anger mountain (Long 1999; Long and Fogell 1999), relating the process to other incidents in addition to those that involve physical aggression. Therefore, while originally presented as a way of understanding the process when an assault or other form of physical aggression is likely, the assault cycle is also relevant when considering events such as verbal aggression, panic attacks or any loss of control such as a pupil storming out of the room or off site. Within this chapter it is this broader perspective that is applied to the assault cycle.

The assault cycle links to the instinctive survival response of fight or flight. The fight or flight response has its origins long ago in human history, when our distant ancestors were faced with dangerous but not especially complex threats such as the approach of a sabre-toothed tiger or a member of another tribe. It is important therefore that we recognise the fight or flight response as both primitive and instinctive. It involves physiological changes as the body alters its priorities from long-term survival to emergency short-term survival.

Trigger phase

People have a normal baseline set of behaviours, and for almost everybody this normal behaviour is non-aggressive most of the time (Breakwell 1997). In the trigger phase something occurs that is *perceived* as a threat. It does not matter whether the teacher, another person or peers would perceive this as a threat, the important factor is that the individual concerned views it as such. The threat may be to physical or emotional well-being. Anger therefore is caused by the reaction to an event, not the event itself. During the trigger phase the fight or flight response is just beginning, the body has not yet become fully aroused physiologically (Faupel *et al.* 1998).

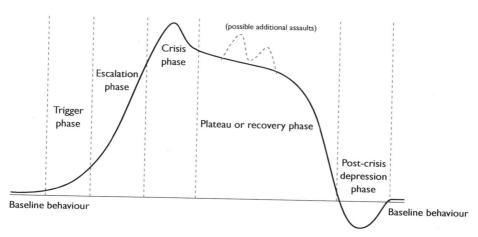

Figure 11.2 The assault cycle.
Source: Breakwell 1997: 43.

The priority during this phase is removing or distracting the individual from the trigger, or removing the trigger itself. At this stage it is often also possible to appeal to reason, suggest alternatives, remind of any 'calm down' techniques already taught (now is not the time to teach new ones!) and, if considered helpful, remind of the consequences of reacting to the trigger. The latter option should be used with caution. It is important to express this in terms and in a tone of voice that conveys that you are focused on the best interests of the individual concerned, not issuing a threat. For example, you might say, 'Callum, I can see you're angry. If you damage the chair you know you're likely to end up in detention. Leave it now, we can sort this out.'

Escalation phase

During the escalation phase the body is preparing itself physiologically for the fight or flight response. The release of hormones such as adrenaline cause blood pressure to increase and breathing to become more rapid as the body prepares itself for the muscular effort involved in making a fight or flight response (Faupel *et al.* 1998). The person may start to pace up and down and the speed and volume of their speech may increase (Breakwell 1997). There may also be more subtle physical movements signifying increased agitation such as drumming fingers on the table. As the escalation phase moves towards crisis the individual becomes increasingly unlikely to make rational judgements. The priorities at this stage are similar to those at the trigger phase; we are still trying to remove or distract the individual from the trigger, or remove the trigger itself if it is still present. Appealing to reason at this stage is likely to be less useful, but it is still relevant to offer clear alternatives and remind of any 'calm down' techniques that the pupil has *already* been taught or has used successfully before. It is also important to remember that the teacher's own presence may be acting as an ongoing trigger at this point. This is a real possibility if the incident started as a result of an interaction between the teacher and the pupil. In such cases it may be better if a colleague takes over the management of the situation.

Crisis phase

During the crisis phase the individual is unlikely to be able to think clearly, make rational judgements or respond to requests and instructions. They may, however, pick up on tone of voice or body language so it is important that the teacher does not signal additional threat by invading personal space, moving quickly or becoming highly animated or raising their voice. It is of little use – and potentially aggravating to the situation – to threaten with sanctions or the displeasure of senior staff who may need to be summoned.

The priority for the teacher at this stage is keeping the individual, others and themselves safe. Clearing the audience is important as it keeps these pupils safe and also removes additional stimulus for the individual who is in crisis. To do this sometimes requires removing the whole class. Many teachers we speak to are very anxious about this prospect. This is understandable as continually removing the class has a detrimental effect on teaching and learning. However if, at the point of crisis, the judgement is that removal of the rest of the class would reduce either the level of arousal or the danger, then it is a procedure that needs to be followed. The place for debate and deliberation is after the event when alternative approaches can be considered, in particular identifying where there is scope for earlier intervention before the crisis point is reached.

If it is safe to do so, remove any objects nearby that may endanger the individual, could be thrown or may lead to the individual being in more trouble if broken.

Plateau or recovery phase

For the teacher involved in managing the incident, it can feel like the hard work is complete once the crisis begins to subside. In practice, however, we need to give careful consideration to the final two phases of the assault cycle. The first of these is the 'recovery phase'. At this point the anger begins to subside but the individual is at a heightened level of susceptibility to triggers. Events that are quite minor in nature and which normally the individual would not react to may be sufficient to reignite the anger during this phase. It is not the time to start analysing the incident with the pupil or demanding explanations (Breakwell 1997). Breakwell (1997) suggests that this phase could last 30–90 minutes, while Faupel *et al.* (1998) suggests leaving at least 45 minutes but ideally an hour before discussing a major incident with a pupil. There will be differences between individuals and age and the severity of the incident are also likely to be factors, but the key message is that time needs to be allowed for the physiological and psychological arousal to subside. The implication, therefore, is that we need to have the facility for the pupil to calm down away from obvious triggers, including inquisitive passers-by who may ask questions.

Post-crisis depression phase

The 'post-crisis' phase is one of resting and recovering from the high state of arousal that the body has just experienced. The ability to think clearly and to listen begins to return at this stage. The pupil may become tearful, remorseful, guilty, ashamed, distraught or despairing. The pupil is quite vulnerable at this stage and so it is important that the teacher or adult managing this part of the process supports them in distinguishing between guilty feelings about themselves and remorse about the behaviour. Guilt directed at oneself may reduce self-esteem and impact negatively on the pupil's relationship with self. In contrast, remorse about the behaviour could lead to effective responses such as apologising and making amends which may help to rebuild relationships with others or lead to the generation of alternatives to this behaviour in the future (Faupel *et al.* 1998).

Non-confrontational approaches: Looking at our own behaviour

Hewett (1998) refers to the defusing style (Figure 11.3) to capture the idea that the adult needs to give consideration during an incident to both their outward presentation and their internal thought processes.

Voice

The teacher should adopt a calm but firm tone of voice (Long and Fogell 1999). Remaining unnaturally calm, or assuming what might be termed almost a clichéd calm tone, is not likely to help matters.

It is important for the teacher to listen more than talk. Usually, if the pupil is talking, even if this is a rant and/or contains language that on other occasions the teacher would

Voice

- Calm, even, not loud
- Monitor pace and pitch of own speech
- Listen more than talk

Body language

- Stay sensitive to personal space
- Avoid square on positions
- Adopt a relaxed stance
- Move slowly and predictably
- Don't stand on the other person's central line

Thoughts

- Stay calm
- Draw on mental structures
- Focus on effective outcomes rather than 'winning' or 'losing'
- Positive self talk
- Keep a sense of perspective

Face

- Careful use of facial expression, not changing frequently
- Avoid smiling unless sure it will defuse
- Give good, attentive eye contact but monitor intensity – don't stare, lower eyes if necessary

Hands

- In view
- Open, with palms visible
- In a low, relaxed position

Other issues

- Tune in to the other person for signals
- Be prepared to hand-over to a colleague

Figure 11.3 The defusing style.

Source: based on Hewett 1998.

attempt to limit, there is a greater chance that the situation will end without physical aggression. The adult needs to monitor the pace and pitch of their own speech. Increases in the pace of speech or a raising of the pitch are associated with emotional arousal and so do not convey calming signals to the pupil. Unless monitored, these changes in speech can inadvertently happen because the adult's state of emotional arousal increases when faced with a difficult situation.

Although a considerable percentage of the meaning communicated is conveyed not by the actual words we say but by tone of voice and body language, it is important to pay attention to the words used:

- Avoid phrases such as 'I know how you feel ...', and 'I understand how you feel ...'. The pupil may react angrily to this presumption on the part of the teacher. Instead, name the feeling that the outward display of behaviour conveys by saying, for example, 'I can see that you're angry/upset/frustrated ...'. A degree of judgement applies as to whether to use the term 'upset' because, for some older pupils, the fact that they have lost control and perhaps are tearful may be a source of embarrassment. To reinforce this with the word 'upset' may therefore be unhelpful, and 'angry' may be the better generic phrase. However, this is not an exact science and there is a counter-argument that 'upset' conveys sympathy, which is a good way of building a caring relationship (Long 1999). If applicable, the teacher could also name the source of the anger – for example, 'I can see that you are upset because you think I was unfair ...'.
- Avoid phrases such as 'Don't be silly ...', 'It's not worth getting upset/angry over it ...', 'Come on, it can't be that bad ...' and 'There's no need to get upset about it ...'. Whatever has triggered the incident *is* of significance to the individual and is not silly, so clearly at some level for them it was worth getting upset or angry over.

Phrases such as 'It sounds really awful ...', 'That must have been really difficult for you ...', 'I can see that this has made you angry ...' or 'I can see this is really important to you ...' help to demonstrate an understanding on the part of the teacher of the significance to the pupil.

- Phrases such as 'I hear what you're saying ...' and 'I can see where you're coming from ...' should be used in moderation. They can be useful but they have become somewhat clichéd to the point where they can appear as simply a form of jargon with little personal engagement. It would be far better to use phrases such as 'It sounds awful ...' or 'Yes, I see' (Braithwaite 2001).

- Prohibitions such as 'can't ...', 'mustn't ...' and 'shouldn't ...' should be avoided. Negative words such as these only add to the negative state of aggression being expressed (Braithwaite 2001). Phrases such as, 'I can help you if you can stop shouting ...' or 'We can work this out if you come and sit down ...', that suggest possibilities of what can be done are generally better than prohibitions.

- Avoid phrases such as 'Come on, let's see a smile ...', 'Cheer up' and 'Pull yourself together'. The individual is showing strong emotions and, as the assault cycle indicates, is likely to take a while to recover. To assume the individual can switch emotions is trivialising, patronising and ultimately unrealistic.

- Avoid phrases such as 'Well, this isn't going to achieve anything ...' and 'You won't get anywhere like that ...'. The implication of these phrases is that there is rationality behind the behaviour. The incident is a loss of control on the part of the individual so they are unlikely to be able to contemplate the pros and cons of this behaviour as an attempt to achieve something.

- The teacher can ask questions to check their own understanding of the situation by using a phrase such as, 'Let me see if I've got this right, you're angry because ...', or inviting more information by asking, 'I'm not sure I understand.... Could you tell me a little more?' (Long 1999). Checking for understanding serves to slow the pace down and encourages the pupil to articulate the difficulty. It is a useful de-escalation technique and also shows that the teacher is not just listening but is also keen to fully understand (Long 1999).

- Affirmations such as 'Yes', 'Right' and non-specific utterances (e.g. 'uh-huh', 'mmhmm') help demonstrate that the teacher is listening and also encourage the speaker to continue. These affirmations can be coupled with the use of occasional nods and appropriate subtle changes in expression to show surprise, disbelief, concern and so on.

- Use 'Sorry' sparingly but effectively. The teacher can be sorry even if they are not at fault through phrases such as, 'David, I'm sorry this has happened' (Braithwaite 2001), or 'I'm sorry you're feeling like this'. If there is an element of fault on the part of the teacher, this can be acknowledged by, for example, saying, 'I'm sorry I shouted at you'. It is also possible to use a token concession (Long 1999) such as, 'Yes, I admit I could have handled it better', as a strategy for diffusing current negativity within the relationship. Braithwaite (2001) advises that overuse of 'sorry' can cause it to lose its impact and risks misinterpretation as a manipulative tool.

Body language

Movements should be smooth and predictable. Rapid or big arm and hand movements may well be perceived as threatening gestures. Hewett (1998) refers to the avoidance of the other person's central line. This is an important consideration when both approaching the pupil and talking to them. The central line is an imaginary line extending directly out in front of the pupil. The teacher should approach the pupil at an angle, keeping to one side or the other of the central line (see Figure 11.4). This is less threatening than walking directly at someone. This is especially true if the teacher is physically bigger than the pupil.

When talking to the pupil, the same principle applies; the teacher should keep off the central line (see Figure 11.5). Standing square on to the pupil would be far more confrontational; it also means there's no 'flight' response available to the pupil to the front, which risks increasing the possibility of a 'fight' response.

A relaxed posture should be adopted – Hewett (1998) suggests relaxed neck, shoulders and arms, hands open and visible and weight distributed to one side, giving a relaxed, slightly leaning posture. However, it is important that in adopting a relaxed posture a balance is struck in order to appear calm while still conveying an appropriate level of interest, involvement and appreciation of the significance the source of upset has to the pupil. Braithwaite (2001) suggests hands in pockets can convey a lack of interest and thumbs stuck in belt loops or the top of a pocket can indicate arrogance or intransigence. Arms folded or hands on hips may convey similar messages.

Throughout the interaction, the teacher should have regard for the pupil's personal space. It is considered that a distance of 15–46 cm is the intimate zone into which people only allow those who are emotionally close, such as lovers, parents, spouses, children, close friends, relatives and pets (Pease and Pease 2004). The teacher should avoid straying into this zone because it is provocative and likely to be perceived as a threat. Outside the intimate zone is the personal zone, which extends from 46 cm to

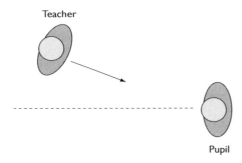

Figure 11.4 Approaching a pupil.

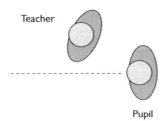

Figure 11.5 Talking to a pupil.

1.22 m. People tend to stand this distance from others at social functions and friendly gatherings (Pease and Pease 2004). As an approximate guide, the teacher should stand towards the outer end of this range. Braithwaite (2001) makes the suggestion that the average space requirement is about two arm lengths if standing and perhaps one-and-a-half arm lengths if sitting.

Hands

Hands should ideally be in view, open, with palms visible and held in a relaxed position by the sides. They can also be used either singly or together in a gentle palms down motion to accompany a 'let's calm down' message (Long 1999). Pointing or wagging the index finger at the individual is provocative and in close proximity is likely to encroach too far into the pupil's personal space.

Face

Eye contact should be established if possible but without staring because this may be perceived as a challenge (Braithwaite 2001). Eye contact should not be demanded (e.g. 'Look at me when I'm talking to you') because this is likely to escalate matters (Long and Fogell 1999). In a confrontation, the aggressor may stare, retaining eye contact for an unusually long period. The teacher needs to avoid matching this, lowering their eyes if necessary, because this would be conveying an aggressive signal back.

In the right circumstances, a smile may help to defuse but as a general principle smiling should be avoided because it may be interpreted as a smirk (Braithwaite 2001) or an indication that the situation, which is a cause of obvious distress to the individual, is not being taken seriously.

Thoughts

The type of incidents referred to in this chapter are likely to be unwelcome and difficult. The teacher's feelings may run from frustration that this is an interruption to the normal course of events through to fear of the harm the pupil might do to themselves or others. Thoughts will determine the teacher's behaviour during the incident and, of course, how any individual responds cognitively under pressure is, to a large extent, personal. However, there are a few considerations that may help:

- *Stay calm*: this is easier said than done when confronted with a significant incident. If the teacher takes a moment to assess and take in all the contextual information, it is likely to help in better informing their response and in slowing the pace. The other points listed below may further contribute to calmness.
- *Draw on mental structures*: Hewett (1998) uses the term 'mental structures' to refer to frameworks that help us to understand what is happening and/or inform decision making. Breakwell's (1997) assault cycle is one such structure. It is a way of conceptualising an incident as a sequence of stages in order to understand the priorities at each point. A specific behaviour management plan for the particular pupil could also be considered a mental structure.
- *Focus on effective outcomes rather than 'winning' or 'losing'*: if the teacher assumes that, as the adult, they have to 'win' or somehow 'come out on top' having stamped

their authority on the situation, it limits the options available to them and is likely to engender a behaviour based on achieving control and dominance. The focus needs to be on effective outcomes, which may be that the pupil calms down and nobody gets hurt.

- *Positive self-talk*: some people may find it helpful to have a phrase they repeat to themselves when confronted with a difficult incident. This might be something like, 'This is difficult but I've seen it before; I've got good technique and can handle it', or 'This is difficult but we have a sound policy so I know what to do next'.

- *Keep a sense of perspective*: like 'Stay calm' (above), this may appear as little more than a platitude rather than a practical consideration. In reality, an accurate under-standing of what is at stake will exert a significant influence over the adult's actions. Most incidents in school are unlikely to be life threatening. Once this is established, some perspective is introduced. The next consideration may be whether there is any real risk of physical harm. By going through this process it will often become clear that, although the situation is difficult, is impeding what the adult, the pupil and their peers should be doing and needs to be addressed, instant action is not necessary. This is not to diminish the significance of the situations teachers and others may face, but to convey the message that they can take a few moments to appraise and determine their response.

Other issues

As well as monitoring their own actions, it is important that the teacher monitors all possible communications from the pupil. This, of course, means listening to what they say and how they say it, but also looking at their face and body language for informa-tion about what they are thinking or feeling at that moment. This information should be used to inform the teacher's next action based on whether the pupil is, for example, becoming more aroused or giving signs of calming down. There are certain signs to look out for that indicate physical conflict may occur. These are:

- direct prolonged eye contact;
- pale, patchy or blushed skin;
- rapid speech;
- unusually loud or quiet speech;
- standing up if sitting, pulling themselves up to full height or other actions that have the effect of making them appear physically bigger;
- fists clenching and unclenching;
- feet spread for balance;
- forward movement, closing the space between you and them.

An important aspect of the defusing style is the acceptance by the adult that they may be contributing to the developing situation and that possibly their previous actions and demands of the pupil, however justified, acted as the trigger. As already suggested earlier in this chapter, the person who is present when the incident occurs is not neces-sarily the best person to work to resolve it. In any incident, an honest appraisal should be made by the teacher of whether their presence is contributing negatively to the situ-ation. Handing over to a colleague may be a better option in some situations.

Physical intervention

When dealing with more challenging forms of behaviour, there may be occasions where physical intervention is a consideration. This will always be a difficult issue for teachers. Over the years various guidance documents have been produced by government, often heralded by the claim that they clarify teachers' powers in this area. Such a claim may have been justified in relation to Circular 10/98 (DfEE 1998) as this played a significant role in clarifying teachers' powers in the wake of the Children Act 1989. In attempting to explain how the Act should be interpreted a range of non-statutory guidance had introduced confusion (Allen 1998a). Subsequent guidance has primarily re-explained essentially the same points set out in Circular 10/98 (DfEE 1998) in different ways. Teachers' powers in this area are clear but decisions in relation to the use of these powers will never be easy or beyond challenge. Although judgements regarding the 'reasonableness' of any force used will always be open to challenge, current government guidance makes clear that,

> Where a member of staff has acted within the law – that is, they have used reasonable force in order to prevent injury, damage to property or disorder – this will provide a defence to any criminal prosecution or other civil or public law action.
>
> (DfE 2013: 7)

Therefore, operating in line with school, local and national guidance offers teachers a degree of protection. Government guidance (DfE 2013) also now makes clear that suspension must not be an automatic response when a member of staff has been accused of using excessive force.

We use the generic term 'physical intervention' to cover those occasions when a teacher may consider it necessary to make physical contact with a pupil in response to the behaviour exhibited. Other terms commonly applied include 'positive handling', 'use of reasonable force' and 'physical restraint'. The latter is heard less often because it has connotations of a higher level of physical intervention than is typically employed. There is no requirement for schools to have a separate policy on the use of force, but current guidance advises that it is good practice to set out, in the behaviour policy, the circumstances in which force might be used (DfE 2013). The guidance also encourages the governing body to notify the head teacher that it expects the school behaviour policy to include the power to use reasonable force. It is specifically stated in the guidance that, 'Schools should not have a "no contact" policy' (DfE 2013: 6). The guidance makes clear that, 'All members of school staff have a legal power to use reasonable force' (DfE 2013: 5). It further specifies that:

> This power applies to any member of staff at the school. It can also apply to people whom the headteacher has temporarily put in charge of pupils such as unpaid volunteers or parents accompanying students on a school organised visit.
>
> (DfE 2013: 5)

The purpose of this part of the chapter is not to provide guidance on specific techniques or to replace national, local or school guidance but to highlight some key issues to consider. We would stress that readers should consult their own school's policy on physical intervention and seek guidance from senior colleagues regarding their responsibilities or any concerns this chapter raises.

The situations in which school staff can physically intervene

The current guidance (DfE 2013: 4) states that: 'Reasonable force can be used to prevent pupils from hurting themselves or others, from damaging property, or from causing disorder.' It then provides the following list of examples of situations where reasonable force could be used (DfE 2013: 5):

- removing disruptive children from the classroom where they have refused to follow an instruction to do so;
- preventing a pupil behaving in a way that disrupts a school event or a school trip or visit;
- preventing a pupil leaving the classroom where allowing the pupil to leave would risk their safety or lead to behaviour that disrupts the behaviour of others;
- restraining a pupil from attacking a member of staff or another pupil, or to stop a fight in the playground;
- restraining a pupil at risk of harming themselves through physical outbursts.

The list of examples above reflects a perennial problem with all guidance produced from Circular 10/98 (DfEE 1998) onwards. Coverage of physical intervention to address issues of discipline is always included alongside coverage of physical intervention to prevent harm or serious injury. It is unfortunate in the list of examples provided by the guidance (DfE 2013) that so many refer to disruption. While there may be a relatively high degree of consistency in judgements about physically intervening when a pupil is at serious risk of harming themselves or others, judgements over whether a pupil is 'causing disorder' (DfE 2013: 4) at a level to warrant physical intervention are likely to be highly subjective. The decision is likely to be influenced by a range of factors including the school's ethos and expectations, the context in which the behaviour occurs and the individual teacher's awareness of, and willingness to use, a range of alternative non-physical strategies. The guidance is non-statutory and an interpretation of the Education and Inspections Act 2006. The Act states:

> A person to whom this section applies may use such force as is reasonable in the circumstances for the purpose of preventing a pupil from doing (or continuing to do) any of the following, namely –
>
> (a) committing any offence,
> (b) causing personal injury to, or damage to the property of, any person (including the pupil himself), or
> (c) prejudicing the maintenance of good order and discipline at the school or among any pupils receiving education at the school, whether during a teaching session or otherwise.
>
> (Education and Inspections Act 2006: 74)

Previous guidance (e.g. DfEE 1998; DCSF 2007b, 2010) has directly quoted these categories and this has served as an important reminder that 'prejudicing the maintenance of good order and discipline' is only one of three. The repeated reference to disruption in the current guidance (DfE 2013) arguably gives this category undue prominence. It is the one where, we would suggest, teachers need to consider extremely carefully whether a physical intervention is appropriate or whether there are other better ways of managing the situation.

The reference to committing an offence within the Act relates to criminal offences. It includes pupils under the age of criminal responsibility, whose actions would be an offence if committed by an older pupil.

The concept of reasonable force

Government guidance produced in 2010 attempted to clarify how to determine whether the use of force was reasonable, stating:

> There is no statutory definition of 'reasonable force'. Whether the force used is reasonable will always depend on the circumstances of individual cases. Deciding on whether the use of force is justified will depend in part upon the context in which the misbehaviour takes place. The test is whether the force used is proportionate to the consequences it is intended to prevent. The degree of force used should be the minimum needed to achieve the desired result. Use of force could not be justified to prevent trivial misbehaviour.
>
> (DCSF 2010: 9)

It is interesting to note that this paragraph refers specifically to 'misbehaviour', which may imply a view that many of the challenges over the reasonableness of the force used are likely to concern physical intervention in relation to behaviour considered to be 'prejudicing the maintenance of good order and discipline' (DCSF 2010: 8). As suggested earlier in the chapter, it is the concept of reasonableness that can leave teachers and schools feeling that there remains a lack of clarity regarding their powers to physically intervene.

The decision to physically intervene

Although now superseded by a much shorter document (DfE 2013), the 2010 guidance (DCSF 2010) contained some general advice that remains helpful in outlining the considerations that need to be taken into account before taking the decision to physically intervene. It states that staff need to make the clearest possible judgement about the following:

- The chances of achieving the desired result by other means. The lower the probability of achieving the desired result by other means, the more likely it is that using force may be justified.
- The seriousness of the incident, assessed by the effect of the injury, damage or disorder which is likely to result if force is not used. The greater the potential for injury, damage or serious disorder, the more likely it is that using force may be justified.
- The relative risks associated with physical intervention compared with using other strategies. The smaller the risks associated with physical intervention compared with other strategies, the more likely it is that using force may be justified.

(DCSF 2010: 14)

Recording

The current guidance (DfE 2013: 7) merely states:

> It is good practice for schools to speak to parents about serious incidents involving the use of force and to consider how best to record such serious incidents. It is up to schools to decide whether it is appropriate to report the use of force to parents.

Clearly, records of any incidents of physical intervention, completed as soon as possible after the event, are important in responding to any query, complaint or allegation. The general advice (e.g. DfES 2002b) is that schools should keep detailed, contemporaneous, written reports of all incidents where staff have physically intervened. Individual schools will have their own systems and forms for recording incidents, often informed by local authority guidance.

Follow-up

From a Behaviour for Learning perspective, physical interventions would always be seen as a last resort option due to the way in which the act of the teacher putting their hands on a pupil in these circumstances potentially changes the teacher–pupil relationship. However, it is accepted that, while for situations related to 'prejudicing the maintenance of good order and discipline' there may be alternatives, if the pupil is causing injury to themselves or others options may be limited. Reflective Exercise 11.3 explores the issue of the impact on relationships.

Reflective Exercise 11.3

Physical intervention inevitably involves a teacher putting their hands on the pupil in some way and it will usually be against the pupil's will. In order to understand the significance of this action consider these points:

- In your day-to-day life as an adult, who would you allow to put their hands on you (e.g. your partner, a doctor, personal trainer)?
- What would be your expectations of them if you indicated that on this occasion it was unwelcome or you displayed signs of discomfort or distress?
- How would your relationship with this person be affected if they did not act in line with these expectations?
- What issues does your personal reflection on the three questions above raise in relation to a pupil's experience of a physical intervention by the teacher?

However necessary and justified, a teacher putting their hands on a pupil in the context of physical intervention needs to be viewed as a significant event that potentially changes both the relationship between the teacher and the particular pupil and also how the teacher–pupil relationship is understood by other pupils. Follow-up procedures are important, as it is at this point that there is an opportunity to attempt to assess and begin to address any damage to the three Behaviour for Learning relationships and mediate the learning that takes place as a result of the experience.

Obviously, if an incident results in injuries to a pupil or to staff, then access to first aid and other medical help that might be necessary is the priority. After this, consideration needs to be given to the support necessary for all involved. Serious incidents that involve the use of physical intervention can be upsetting and unsettling for the pupil, the adult(s) and observers. When considering the timing of any follow-up with the pupil and the form this takes, it is important to be mindful of the recovery and post-crisis depression phases of Breakwell's (1997) assault cycle described earlier in this chapter (see Figure 11.2). The adult's emotional state may have followed a similar cycle and schools should also recognise that after a significant incident it may be very difficult for a member of staff to simply turn their attention to their teaching duties. The follow-up for the pupil can just focus on a simple set of steps:

- the pupil explains what happened from their perspective;
- the adult explains what happened from their perspective;
- identification of alternative ways the pupil could respond in the future;
- if appropriate, consideration of any sanction or reparative activity necessary;
- identification of any further support necessary now to enable the pupil to return to the normal school routine and relationships.

If the teacher involved in the physical intervention is not conducting this meeting then an area for discussion would be how the resumption of a normal teacher–pupil relationship will be managed. A more elaborate framework for the follow up process is provided by the IESCAPE model, based on Fritz Redl's (1959) Life Space Interview. The letters in the IESCAPE acronym stand for each of the stages in a seven step process:

- *Isolate*
  Locate a quiet place where the amount of external stimuli is reduced.
- *Explore*
  Provide the pupil with the opportunity to explain their view of what happened. It is important that the adult listens rather than contradicting the account. However, they can use facilitating questions – for example, to support the pupil to recognise how one event led to another or encourage reflection on critical points where alternative choices might have been possible. The information the pupil provides may include important clues about the causal attributions they are making and inform priorities for future proactive interventions.
- *Share*
  The adult describes events from their perspective. Gibson and Smith (2000) suggest possible opening lines such as, 'Here is what I saw happening …', or 'I think you've told me nearly everything but there are some bits of information you've not mentioned yet'. The phrasing in the second example is important as it is intended to reduce the feeling that the adult is the person in possession of the definitive version of events.
- *Connect*
  At this point the adult attempts to support the pupil to make a link between internal emotional and cognitive reactions to events in the external environment (Gibson and Smith 2000). This may involve making suggestions based on what the pupil has said, for example: 'So you were feeling angry because you thought Mrs

Brown was unfair when she gave you a detention, that's why you left the class and tried to run off site?' Check with the pupil if this is an accurate assumption.

- *Alternatives*

  Discuss with the pupil what they might have done differently. These ideas should ideally come from the pupil, but it may be necessary to make suggestions initially. When a few alternatives have been selected, each should be discussed in terms of advantages and disadvantages (Gibson and Smith 2000). The pupil can be gently challenged to think about the barriers to any of the more unrealistic options they might suggest.

- *Plan*

  Move from generating a range of alternatives to identifying the specific options that will form a plan. Discussion should cover what support the pupil feels they need from staff and any opportunities that may be required to learn and rehearse new skills and strategies.

- *Enter*

  Thought needs to be given to how the pupil returns to class. In many cases the incident that led to the adult physically intervening is likely to have been very public and to have involved a visible loss of control by the pupil. Talk to the pupil about what they might say or do on re-entering and what it would be helpful for their teacher to do.

Although we have presented the Life Space Interview in the context of a follow-up meeting after a physical intervention, it can, of course, be used on other occasions if felt to be a useful way of working with a pupil.

Reflective Exercise 11.4

Consider these three points from Cornwall (2000):

1 'Physical restraint practices give out a very strong "enforcement" message to young people. Should we accept that it is the teachers' role to coerce and control young people to remain in the classroom against their will?' (Cornwall 2000: 22)

2 'Using physical control whilst at the same time motivating and socialising troubled children does not seem compatible.' (Cornwall 2000: 22)

3 'If challenging and physically aggressive behaviour is seen as a form of communication – then what is communicated to pupils when they are physically restrained by a group of adults? Might is right?' (Cornwall 2000: 20)

- What is your response to the points raised in quotes 1 and 2 regarding the teacher's role?
- What is your response to the point raised in quote 3 regarding what the pupil and others who witness it may learn from a physical intervention?
- Writing on the subject of physical intervention, Allen (1998b: 16) uses the word 'experts' pejoratively to suggest detachment from the realities of practice and states, 'practical day to day experience tends to act as a safety break on fanciful ideas'. Do you consider the quotes from Cornwall (2000) to be 'fanciful ideas' or important cautionary points regarding physical intervention?

Conclusion

The consistent message from national reports (e.g. DES 1989; DfES 2005b; Ofsted 2014a) is that it is low level persistent behaviour that teachers encounter frequently and concerns them the most. Nevertheless, there are occasions when more serious behavioural incidents do occur. This chapter has sought to provide some coverage of strategies relevant to behaviour of a more challenging nature. To reiterate a message from preceding chapters that is perhaps even more pertinent here due to the nature of the behaviours covered, what we are effectively providing is a set of strategies and approaches that increase the probability of a more favourable outcome for both pupil and teacher on more occasions. Teachers cannot realistically anticipate and prepare for the entire range of pupil responses they will experience in the classroom (Powell and Tod 2004) and behaviours driven by anger are, by their very nature, especially unpredictable. The assault cycle (Breakwell 1997) is a useful mental structure (Hewett 1998) that can help a teacher understand the stages involved in an incident and make a better prediction regarding strategies that are likely to be more or less effective at a given point.

Even when pupils engage in behaviour that is of a higher level or happens with such frequency that it has a damaging effect on the learning of the class, we should still aspire to manage this situation in ways that protect and maintain the three relationships that underpin the development of learning behaviour. Although this needs to remain the aspiration it may not always be possible, particularly if physical intervention becomes necessary. The Life Space Interview, or a similar process, can be used to increase the possibility of positive learning taking place and to repair relationships.

Chapter 12

Reframing special educational needs

Introduction

This chapter looks at how the Behaviour for Learning approach can support teachers to work effectively with those individual pupils who may experience particular difficulty, delay or difference in developing the relationships that underpin their learning in school. These pupils are likely to include, but are not necessarily restricted to, those who are described as having special educational needs (SEN).

The Behaviour for Learning approach supports the bio–psycho–social view of individual diversity. The individual is not viewed as the 'cause' of their learning difficulties. However, it is recognised that the individual pupil brings to their school learning a unique combination of skills and dispositions based on biological and psychological factors and their own environmental, social and cultural backgrounds. This unique combination of skills and dispositions influences, and is influenced by, the interactions and experiences available in the pupil's school environment. In seeking to identify strategies to develop a pupil's learning behaviour we need therefore to address this dynamic and changing interaction between the individual and their school environment. This leads to the view that schools and teachers need to be resourceful in developing environments that are responsive to individual diversity. There is also a need to develop in individual pupils the skills and dispositions required to increase their chances of becoming beneficiaries of the learning environment in which they are placed. For this to happen it is necessary to focus on promoting the learning behaviours in individuals that are required for the development and maintenance of positive learning relationships within schools and classrooms. This is irrespective of whether the individual has SEN or any other label or diagnosis.

Through a focus on relationships the Behaviour for Learning approach positions the learner as a contributing partner to their progress in learning. This places an emphasis on how the individual pupil is *experiencing* and *interpreting* classroom practice, including any 'additional or different provision' (DfE/DoH 2015: 25) intended to meet their educational needs.

Is there a need to reframe SEN?

Traditional thinking about SEN involves placing children into 'categories' or assigning descriptors or labels based on a judgement about how far their learning and behaviour deviates from a hypothetical norm or average. Often associated with this thinking is the belief that placing the child in a category or assigning a descriptor or label will determine the adaptations to standard practice, interventions and support that they need. This belief is indicative of the continuing influence of the medical model of disability and difference as it is essentially based on the idea of a diagnosis prescribing appropriate treatment. At the level of practice this type of belief would be reflected if, for example, a teacher was to say: 'Daniel is messing about in class and having trouble reading and writing – he seems quite bright, maybe he is dyslexic? Perhaps I should get him seen by the SENCO or suggest he gets referred to the educational psychologist. If he has dyslexia then I will need to find out how I should be teaching him.' It is a line of reasoning that potentially disempowers the classroom teacher and is at odds with the expectation in the SEND Code of Practice (DfE/DoH 2015: 99) that it is the classroom teacher who remains 'responsible and accountable for the progress and development of the pupils in their class, including where pupils access support from teaching assistants or specialist staff'. It relates to a broader argument put forward by Thomas and Loxley (2007: 27) that the field of special education 'has been so successful at continually devising more glossy and more elaborate forms of assessment and pedagogy that teachers have begun to lose confidence in their own ability to assess and teach all children in their charge'.

However, in looking at this line of reasoning and recognising its potentially detrimental effect if it becomes the default perspective for all children with SEN, it is also important to recognise that it is not without substance. Decisions about provision should be guided by assessment and investigation of individual learning and this will *sometimes* require the involvement of outside agencies.

When a pupil is described as 'having SEN' it tells us little other than that someone, hopefully drawing on a range of qualitative and quantitative data on the pupil's performance over time, has concluded that they have 'a learning difficulty or disability which calls for special educational provision to be made for him or her' (DfE/DoH 2015: 15). However, other labels and diagnoses may be more useful as they connect with a body of knowledge and accompanying strategies that have developed over the years. For example, as discussed later in this chapter, awareness of the triad of impairment (Wing and Gould 1979) can help us understand how a pupil diagnosed with autism might experience the classroom environment. We also know that visual timetables, social stories and comic strip conversations can be useful strategies for pupils with autism.

The problem with all labels, categories and diagnoses is that the pupils to whom these relate are not a homogeneous group. They will share a number of general characteristics but they will experience their own difficulty, need or condition differently. For example, when tested, a pupil with dyslexia may have a cognitive and attainment profile that is consistent with a particular label or diagnostic category, but they will not exactly match the overall learning profile of a hypothetical typical dyslexic individual. Even if the pupil's cognitive profile is considered typical, their social and emotional learning behaviours, which reflect their response to their dyslexia, will be different. Therefore, what a teacher can predict about the individual pupil's learning and behaviour from a label is necessarily limited.

The Behaviour for Learning approach reframes the pupil's SEN in terms of the three relationships – with self, with others and with the curriculum. This perspective does not deny the need for more specialised forms of assessment or the value of some labels, categories and diagnoses in signposting bodies of established knowledge and associated evidence-based strategies but these are not the starting point.

Starting with relationships

The social, emotional and cognitive aspects of learning that reflect the three Behaviour for Learning relationships are interdependent. Therefore, although a particular label, category or diagnosis might suggest that the pupil's difficulties relate primarily to one of these aspects, in promoting learning behaviour all three relationships remain important. Focusing only on the area of difficulty associated with the label, category or diagnosis may serve to restrict the choice of strategies. For example, if a pupil is identified as having a social, emotional and mental health difficulty, the teacher's first thought might reasonably be to concentrate on the emotional aspects of learning. However, while one individual with such a label may respond positively to having attention directly focused on their emotional difficulties, another individual with the same label may find emphasis on how they are 'feeling' too much to handle at that point in time. Such a pupil may benefit more from having the emotional aspects of learning 'detached' from cognitive aspects. For example, strategies could include those that promote the development of learning behaviours through the pupil's engagement in routine, structured cognitive tasks in non-competitive contexts.

As noted previously, pupils who share a particular label, category and diagnosis are not a homogeneous group. It is important to recognise and harness what the *individual* pupil brings to each of the three Behaviour for Learning relationships. This principle reflects the emphasis on a person–centred approach in the SEND Code of Practice (DfE/DoH 2015). Our use of the term relationship and the associated language is intended to emphasise that the pupil is not a passive recipient of provision. It serves to focus attention on the skills and dispositions that the individual pupil with SEN contributes to the relationship. Some of these skills and dispositions may be very similar to those of their peer group or they may be distinctive and different.

In the case of pupils with SEN and others who exhibit a particular and significant difficulty, delay or difference in developing the learning behaviours required for building positive relationships, it is likely that the cluster of behaviours currently exhibited have developed over a long period of time. It follows, therefore, that if the teacher successfully eliminates or reduces one specific behaviour (e.g. shouting out in class) the likelihood is that the pupil will simply replace this behaviour with another from their repertoire. For this reason, the teacher will typically need to employ what we described in Chapter 2 as extended use of the Behaviour for Learning conceptual framework. This requires the teacher to focus on the learning relationship itself rather than on one or a limited number of specific learning behaviours. For monitoring and evaluation purposes, it remains important to be clear about the types of learning behaviours that would indicate that the target relationship was developing positively. A relationship is evaluated over time and observed inconsistencies in responses (e.g. 'bad days') should be balanced with overall progress.

Thinking in terms of the three relationships helps the teacher to consider which one provides the most likely explanation for the cluster of behaviours exhibited by the pupil. The relationship, once identified, can determine the focus of any assessments and inform decisions regarding strategies, interventions, additional support and the need for any specialist input. For example, a screening test (e.g. Lucid Rapid,[1] Dyslexia Quest[2]) used to identify dyslexic traits might provide the teacher with a better understanding of the pupil's relationship with the curriculum. In the case of a pupil with autism spectrum it might be appropriate to use an augmentative/alternative communication intervention such as the picture exchange communication system (PECS) to develop learning behaviours associated with relationship with others.

Thinking in terms of the relative contribution of cognitive, social and emotional factors to the pupil's cluster of behaviours allows the teacher to recognise if any of three relationships are being overlooked. For example, many strategies for a pupil with dyslexia may be focused on their relationship with the curriculum but the importance of protecting and enhancing their relationship with self might be overlooked. Burden's (2008) review of previously conducted research led him to conclude that the bulk of evidence available was strongly indicative of a clear relationship between being dyslexic and having a low academic self-concept.

Where outside agencies are involved, a focus on the three relationships can help in recognising the distinctive and complementary roles of those involved, based on the shared aim of developing learning behaviour. For example, a counsellor or therapist may be directly targeting the pupil's relationship with self, whereas the teacher may be using their expertise in curriculum and pedagogy to target relationship with self indirectly, working via the pupil's relationship with the curriculum. Both the teacher and the therapist or counsellor would evaluate the impact through the emergence of specific learning behaviours that would indicate a positive change in the pupil's relationship with self.

Assess, plan, do and review

The current SEND Code of Practice (DfE/DoH 2015) endorses the use of an assess, plan, do, review approach when making provision for pupils with SEN. When this model is employed from a Behaviour for Learning perspective, the purpose of any assessment is to develop a deeper understanding of the three relationships and, from this, to identify a target relationship area to develop. Essentially, this involves looking at:

- how the pupil presents cognitively: their general ability as a learner and response (attitude and behaviour) when taking part in learning activities (e.g. What are they good at? What do they struggle with? How would you describe their rate of progress?);
- how the pupil presents socially: the skills and dispositions demonstrated when learning in the company of others (e.g. How would you describe their interactions with adults and with peers? How do they cope with the social demands of the setting? How do they respond in group activities?);
- how the pupil presents emotionally: mental health and wellbeing (e.g. How do they respond when presented with unfamiliar or difficult tasks? Do they appear confident? How well do they manage their emotions? How do they cope with setbacks and adversity?).

It is important to recognise that the positive learning behaviours a pupil currently exhibits, together with any problematic behaviours, are important indicators of the current quality of each relationship. Schools will have multiple methods of assessing pupils cognitively. Methods of assessing social and emotional development may not necessarily be as well developed, but examples include the Strengths and Difficulties Questionnaire (SDQ) (Goodman 1997), the Leuven Scale (Laevers 1994), the Boxall Profile (Bennathan and Boxall 1998) and the behaviour scales from *Supporting School Improvement: Emotional and Behavioural Development* (QCA 2001).

From this initial assessment, planning decisions can then be taken based on these key questions:

1   What is the relationship that I need to promote for learning in a group setting?
    a. Is it better for the individual pupil if I focus directly on the target relationship or seek to develop it via one of the other two relationships?
    b. Is there a relationship area that I feel more confident/competent to work in initially?
2   Which cluster of learning behaviours (or specific significant learning behaviour) do I need to promote in order to have a pervasive, positive effect on the relationship?
3   What knowledge, skills and understanding does the pupil bring to this relationship?
4   What knowledge, skills and understanding can I contribute to this relationship?
5   Do I need any additional advice, guidance and support from within my school or from multi–agency partners?
6   What adaptations to standard practice, interventions and support need to be put in place to promote the targeted relationship?
7   What are the assessable indicators that will show whether I am being successful in promoting the target relationship?

The planned adaptations to standard practice, interventions and support would be implemented at the 'Do' stage of the cycle. Review would be against the assessable indicators identified at the 'Plan' stage, although it is important to be open to the possibility of other unanticipated indicators. The assessable indicators are likely to include the cluster of learning behaviours (or specific significant learning behaviour) associated with the target relationship. In addition, it may be appropriate to repeat some of the assessments conducted at the 'Assess' stage to identify positive change.

The version of the assess, plan, do, review cycle presented here allows teachers to respond to the behaviour that is causing concern through their knowledge about teaching and learning in their classroom.

Practical application of Behaviour for Learning conceptual framework

In this chapter we have chosen three categories of SEN to explore from a Behaviour for Learning perspective. *Cognition and Learning* is explored with a specific focus on dyslexia; *Communication and Interaction* is explored with a specific focus on Autism Spectrum Disorders; and *Social, Emotional and Mental Health Difficulties* is explored as an overall category. We recognise, of course, that within each of these categories from the SEND Code of Practice (DfE/DoH 2015) there are many other forms of need. It is hoped that the examples we have selected will provide illustrations of how thinking about SEN can be reframed using the Behaviour for Learning conceptual framework.

Cognition and learning

Pupils who experience delays or differences in their *cognitive* development are likely to experience learning difficulties that directly affect their relationship with the curriculum. Such pupils are classified under the SEND Code of Practice (DfE/DoH 2015) as falling into the SEN category of *Cognition and Learning*.

As described in Chapters 4 and 5, a relationship with the curriculum can be understood in the same was as any other relationship even though we are dealing with a non-human component in the form of the curriculum. However, the relationship is distinctive in a school setting in that it is largely brokered by the teacher and typically has defined intended outcomes and purposes. As such this relationship requires the pupil to develop appropriate dispositions towards the curriculum and display learning behaviours that reflect 'willingness' and 'interest' along with some personal responsibility for maintaining this relationship. The skills needed by the pupil for this relationship are those that enable them to actively process information and monitor the efficacy of their activity in meeting curricular requirements.

Pupils who experience difficulty in cognitive processing

Some individuals will experience significant difference, delay or difficulty with the cognitive demands involved in accessing and processing the information required for making and sustaining a relationship with the curriculum. Some pupils have low levels of working memory and struggle to process, maintain and store information simultaneously (Alloway *et al.* 2005). Such pupils would include those who have an overall developmental delay, those with language difficulties and those who are categorised as having dyslexia. In the next section we consider what a pupil might experience if they have a difficulty with the interplay between the oral and written language systems that are used in school contexts to develop a relationship with the academic curriculum.

A closer look at dyslexia

In the SEND Code of Practice (DfE/DoH 2015) dyslexia is identified as a Specific Learning Difficulty (SpLD) and is included in the Cognition and Learning category. Although pupils who experience a specific difficulty with the interplay between oral and written language may share the label of dyslexia, their pattern of difficulties varies, as does their response. For this reason, it has been argued that as a group they are not distinguishable or different from others who exhibit delay and difficulty with written language (Elliott 2005; Elliott and Grigorenko 2014). However, the first tranche of *Inclusion Development Programme* (IDP) support materials (DCSF 2008a, 2008b) targeted dyslexia and Sir Jim Rose was commissioned by the government to review provision in schools for pupils with dyslexia (Rose 2009).

The British Psychological Society (BPS 1999) defined dyslexia as evident when accurate and fluent word reading and/or spelling develops very incompletely or with great difficulty. Rose (2009: 30) offered a different definition, stating that: 'Dyslexia is a learning difficulty that primarily affects the skills involved in accurate and fluent word reading and spelling. Characteristic features of dyslexia are difficulties in phonological awareness, verbal memory and verbal processing speed.' Despite differing definitions, within the literature on dyslexia there is some consensus that pupils who share this categorisation exhibit:

- a *discrepancy* within their cognitive profile with weaker performance in those areas that necessitate that the sound system of language is represented and processed in the written format;

- a *delay* or *deficit* in the development of phoneme: grapheme correspondence, which in turn reduces the efficiency of working memory;
- a *delay* in the development of automatic word identification;
- a *difficulty* in generating written (and sometimes oral) language in the sequence needed for accurate spelling and fluent communication;
- a *difference* in form and function of some areas of the brain.

(Tod 2000)

Pupils with dyslexia are reported to exhibit and experience a wider range of difficulties than those that specifically impact on their progress with literacy. However, it is clear from the above descriptors that their specific cognitive processing differences are likely to have a significant impact on their relationship with the curriculum.

Planning for relationship building

Knowledge about difficulties, delays and differences that are thought to characterise dyslexia can be useful when trying to understand how a pupil might experience some aspects of their relationship with the curriculum.

Individuals with dyslexia might experience a number of feelings in school settings, including:

- *Confusion* and *frustration* from knowing that they can achieve in some areas of school work but struggle in others. They may not understand why this is when peers seem to read and write more quickly, fluently and without so much effort.
- Feelings of *uncertainty*, *anxiety* and *annoyance* when having to manipulate information that requires changing it speedily from one format to another – usually oral to written. They may not be able to easily retain or make sense of such information – especially if a response is required within a given time frame.
- *Tired* from the effort it takes to cope frequently with written formats of language. It takes effort to copy from the board or when the teacher requires the pupil to simultaneously listen, read and write.
- *Enjoyment* and understanding of books and written information when listening to someone else reading them.
- *Frustration* at not being able to easily read *and* at the same time understand and retain this written information.
- *Cross* that it takes longer for them to read and write than others. It is hard to think what to write, put it in order, hold the words in your head, break them down and build them up again. Homework can take a long time and yet the teacher may not know this. Work can look scruffy with spelling errors even when effort has been given to the task.
- *Sad* when work is not as good as that of their peers and 'fed up' when it is so hard to achieve success at school, particularly at secondary school.
- *Happy* when with friends talking and discussing but *worried* that a difficulty with written language might be seen as being 'thick' or 'stupid'.
- *Great* when people understand things from their perspective and work with them to improve things.
- *Brilliant* when they get things right or receive good marks.

We have already noted that every individual will have different experiences of their dyslexia resulting in a different balance of positive and negative feelings. The above list only gives a flavour of how dyslexia might affect a pupil's experiences in the classroom.

Relationship with the curriculum and impact on the other two relationships

Pupils with dyslexia and others who experience difficulty with the sound system of written language will often have learned to use oral language in a meaningful social context. Typically, they will arrive at school with the ability to comprehend, reason and relate to others through the use of oral language. Much of the work in the classroom requires accessing, processing and reproducing language in a written form. To do this the pupil has to break down this *meaningful* language into what is for them *meaningless* sound components and then reformulate these in a sequence that reflects conventions for written communication, including correct spelling. It follows that the relationship between oral and written language needed for school learning is difficult to develop and sustain; this may lead to the individual pupil developing adaptive behaviours (e.g. task avoidance) that further impair their relationship with the curriculum and could result in them being reclassified as having a behavioural difficulty. This is illustrated in Scenario 12.1.

Scenario 12.1

Jack has been assessed as exhibiting some learning difficulties that are considered to be characteristic of dyslexia. He brings to the class literacy task a negative view of himself as a learner of literacy. The class teacher, with Jack's best interests at heart, allocates him some additional support from a teaching assistant. At the end of the lesson Jack is publicly praised for his effort. This makes him a focus for attention and he feels that his peers are making judgements about his lack of progress in literacy and generally about him 'being thick'. At the start of the next lesson he refuses to work with the teaching assistant, 'messes about' and is disciplined accordingly. This resistance to support develops into a pattern, with Jack exhibiting behaviours that effectively reject the very help the teacher feels he needs. Jack is referred to the school's SENCO due to having a possible behaviour problem and this becomes the focus of concern – thus affirming to himself what he perceives others think about him.

In Scenario 12.1, we can see that there is a dynamic interaction between Jack's relationship with self, relationship with others and relationship with the curriculum. He and others in the classroom, including the adults, are seeking to make sense of their experiences and feelings and behave accordingly. In this example, we can see behaviour changes that can occur within a relatively small space of time with all parties involved acting with purpose and 'making sense' of their ongoing experiences and actions:

* *The teacher*
  The teacher initially feels positive towards Jack, allocates support and praises his efforts. The teacher then disciplines Jack and feels that he now has a behaviour problem as well as a learning difficulty.

- *The teaching assistant*
  The teaching assistant offers support. Jack progresses well and the teaching assistant feels it appropriate to follow school procedures for 'reward'. The teaching assistant may then feel negative about Jack once he refuses to work with him/her.
- *Peers*
  We do not know what Jack's peers are learning. Some may feel that it is 'not cool' to be rewarded for good work and give some subtle negative feedback to Jack. Others may think it is fine to be rewarded and in fact are not thinking Jack is 'thick' – this perception is in Jack's head. Some may see Jack getting attention for refusing to work and be pleased by his interruption of the lesson, while others may be irritated and annoyed with him. They confirm Jack's own perceptions of his status among his peers through their behaviour towards him.
- *Jack*
  Jack feels he is not much good at literacy, then experiences some success when undertaking the task supported by the teaching assistant. He feels embarrassed when praised. He then feels angry that the class procedures have 'made' his peers judge him negatively. For Jack, his behaviour is a way of making sense of and confirming that he is no good at his work. His adaptive response is to avoid doing his work and, in so doing, he develops a revised identity as having a 'behavioural problem'. Jack's case illustrates that many pupils who exhibit behavioural difficulties in the classroom also have an underlying learning difficulty.

Implications for the classroom

Pupils with dyslexia experience particular difficulty in relating to the curriculum because the input to and output from this relationship frequently require different formats. For example, the teacher may be talking to the class with an expectation that the pupils will be making notes. In so doing, the pupil has to simultaneously cognitively process and comprehend the oral language *and* translate this oral input into a written output. This demand on cognitive capacity is normally addressed in primary settings through the teacher emphasising the need to focus on sequential rather than simultaneous processing. For example, the teacher might talk to the pupils and then invite questions that serve to secure an understanding of the oral input. The teacher might support this further with mind maps and writing frames. With these visual representations on hand, the pupil then only has to concentrate on generating their own written response. The teacher has adapted their input and response requirements in order to develop and sustain pupils' relationship with the curriculum. At secondary level, learners have typically automated the translation of oral to written language forms. Therefore, it is often assumed that they can apply their cognitive capacity to processing language, whatever its format. Clearly, for some pupils, including those with dyslexia, this is not the case. Teachers often require pupils to multitask, expecting them to read, listen, comprehend and write notes. This poses problems for pupils who have not automated the rapid interchange between oral and written language that is required in à school context. The production of written language for pupils who experience dyslexia typically takes longer and requires more effort.

Transition from primary to secondary school may, through a change of teaching strategy, highlight the difficulties experienced by some pupils with dyslexia and, for some, lead to the development of social, emotional and mental health difficulties that were not apparent in the primary setting. A key point is that although the individual's underlying cognitive difficulty may stay the same, their *experience* of this will be dependent on the context in which they are placed and the strategies they develop both independently and with support.

Knowing more about the processing differences of a pupil with dyslexia does not necessarily allow the teacher to generate and select strategies. It does however support the teacher in understanding how the pupil may be experiencing learning activities in the classroom. This understanding is an essential prerequisite in forming a relationship with the pupil. If a teacher understands more about the pupil's processing differences, they are less likely to attribute the pupil's response to the curriculum to a lack of effort, a behavioural issue or a lack of interest.

Understanding which strategies support relationships with the curriculum

There are many strategies available for pupils with dyslexia (e.g. DCSF 2008a, 2008b; Reid 2016; Montgomery 2017). These are typically designed to address characteristic aspects of dyslexia, such as poor organisational skills, automaticity and speed of process-ing, poor memory and sequencing skills (Kelly and Phillips 2016). Strategies to support the development of pupils' relationship with the curriculum fall into six main groups listed below.

Multisensory approaches

Typically, relationships require communication and active processing of information. Multisensory approaches involve stimulating two or more senses in order to provide the pupil with additional support and choice in developing ways that best enable them to synthesise, learn, retain and manipulate the oral and written components of language. Although multisensory approaches are regularly recommended (e.g. Kelly and Philips 2016) and used, there is a risk that some pupils may not experience these approaches as beneficial due to issues of cognitive load (see Chapter 5). It is important, therefore, to monitor closely the pupil's response to this strategy.

Meaningfulness

Effective relationships need to be meaningful if motivation is to be sustained. Pupils with dyslexia typically have relative strengths in comprehension and reasoning. Relating to the curriculum through written text initially involves breaking down meaningful lan-guage into *meaningless* sound components. Those with dyslexia experience specific diffi-culty with holding 'meaningless' material in their short-term working memory systems. Useful teaching strategies aim to allow individuals to give personal meaning to mean-ingless materials such as phonic sounds – thus the pupil may make a set of sound cards with, for example, the 'i' sound represented by their own picture memory (e.g. 'iguana'). Commercial schemes use similar approaches but it is important that pupils with dyslexia supply their own meaning as this supports active processing through personalisation.

Memory

A relationship with the curriculum requires information to be retained in order that it can be processed and used. The most common problem for pupils with dyslexia is cognitive overload simply because they have often not automated basic decoding skills and all of these require attentional space. Memory skills are enhanced by *active* processing and any activity that encourages this is useful for all pupils. To support processing to long-term memory, it can be helpful for teachers to ask pupils to re-process information in a different format to the one they have been given (e.g. through mind maps, flow diagrams, presentations, 'discuss and explain to a peer', role-play, etc.). In the case of pupils with dyslexia they usually need more practice and overlearning with phonics and additional support with generating their own written language, including spellings.

Metacognition

It is important that a pupil's relationship with the curriculum is reciprocal and that they play an active role. To do this, they need to develop self-knowledge about what has to be learned and how they are responding as a learner. The more understanding the pupil has of their own learning and the more they are able to adopt and/or develop the most effective strategies, the more resilience they will be able to develop. There are many strategies that encourage the development of metacognition through opening up discussion with pupils about the process of learning rather than just the product. For example, study skills programmes can be developed that cover areas such as time management, personal organisation, setting personal targets, self-assessment and monitoring, reading skills (e.g. skimming and scanning), listening skills, self-questioning, planning and revision strategies.

Manageability

As mentioned previously, if a skill or activity cannot be carried out automatically and still requires conscious effort then overload and breakdown of the processing system becomes a real threat. In the case of pupils with dyslexia who may not have automated activities involving written language, having to listen to the teacher, copy from the board and/or make notes and think at the same time is clearly very difficult. Work needs to be pre-structured and planned. More time needs to be given for the production of work – or less written work given. This is not because such pupils are lazy; it simply takes them longer. It should also be remembered that a generic strategy of giving extra time to all pupils with dyslexia may not, in itself, suffice to address the range of individual variability in processing that characterises dyslexia. Pupils might need to make use of visual planners and electronic organisers, and preparation for coursework and exams needs to be carefully structured if they are to complete on time. As we have indicated, thinking, reading, writing, spelling and checking is often done sequentially by pupils with dyslexia rather than simultaneously, and teachers need to be aware of this if they are to work with the pupil to identify and develop appropriate strategies. As an example, the use of revision guides at the start of the course, rather than at the end, gives the opportunity for pupils to gain an overview of the syllabus and areas to be covered, estimate time frames involved, identify high risk areas in relation to their difficulty and gauge the relative worth of different areas in contributing to the overall grade.

In reducing the cognitive load, any strategy that seeks to take information 'out of the mind' and transfer it into more permanent and accessible formats such organisers, lists and electronic formats will support pupils to manage their relationship with the curriculum.

Motivation

Any relationship requires motivation on both sides for it to be initiated and sustained (see Chapter 5). A pupil who experiences success at school and in personal relationships is likely to be more motivated and successful, which in turn enhances the likelihood of maintaining or increasing positive self-perceptions (Burns 1982; Blatchford 1992). In contrast, relatively negative feelings about self may result in less success and lead to reduced motivation and further impaired performance (Chapman 1998). Pupils with learning difficulties generally have been found to have lower self-perception (Lindsay and Dockrell 2000). Pupils tend to compare themselves with their peers and for those with dyslexia this comparison may lead to disaffection. There is a need to ensure that a required emphasis on skill development does not deprive pupils of balanced opportunities to access and engage with meaningful texts that are commensurate with their level of language and reasoning ability. This would involve parents/carers and teachers reading to their children in order to sustain interest, motivation, enjoyment and confidence in literature. Such an approach has been endorsed by research that has sought to improve teachers' knowledge and experience of children's literature in order to help them increase all pupils' motivation and enthusiasm for reading, especially those less successful in literacy (Cremin et al. 2009).

In looking at the key priorities for developing a positive relationship with the curriculum by using the example of dyslexia, it can be seen that the strategy groups above are entirely appropriate for building positive relationships with the curriculum for *all* pupils, including those with dyslexia. Responding to individual differences is likely to involve personalising these generic strategies through increasing the intensity and/or frequency of their use.

Which relationship should be prioritised?

In looking at the cluster of difficulties, differences and delays that characterise dyslexia, it is likely that in adopting the Behaviour for Learning approach the teacher would prioritise developing the pupil's relationship with the curriculum. In seeking to do this there is a particular need for teachers and parents/carers of children with dyslexia to make sure that the child's relationship with self and relationship with others are not compromised. Schools have traditionally placed high value on written recording as a means of both acquiring and demonstrating acquisition of knowledge, skills and understanding. It is a challenge for schools not to create the impression that written recording is a very important skill because, of course, it is. However, pupils who experience difficulty with written language, including those with dyslexia, are conscripts to an environment in which they are required to spend a considerable proportion of their time doing something that they are aware they struggle with.

Providing opportunities for success involves identifying alternatives to written language production both in accessing (e.g. being read to, having story tapes, films, etc.) and in responding through offering alternative forms of recording. A range of alternatives to written recording are provided in Figure 12.1. These have not been designed

Access to the curriculum

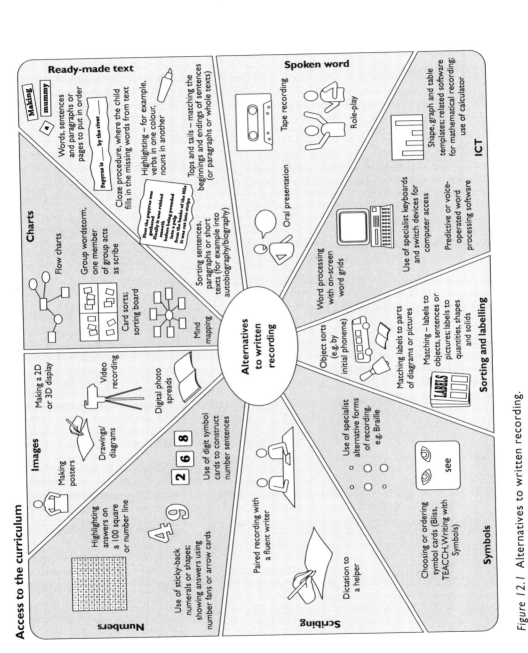

Figure 12.1 Alternatives to written recording.

Source: adapted from DfES 2004h: 43.

specifically for pupils with dyslexia but such pupils may find a number of them beneficial.

Building the pupil's relationship with self provides a powerful route for supporting curriculum-based strategies and this in turn can be enhanced by working on relationship with others. In the case of dyslexia, using the pupil's relative strengths in the area of relationship with others offers opportunities to improve relationship with self through group work (Gillies 2016). Parents/carers have an important role in supporting the development of the three relationships through their involvement with their child's academic work (Goler and Booth 2008) and in building their child's confidence and competence through participation in other extra-curricular pursuits.

Communication and interaction

Introduction

A pupil's relationship with others involves the social interactions that are linked to learning with others, such as listening, turn taking and joining in aspects of school life as a member of the school community. Pupils identified with a special educational need that falls within the Code of Practice (DfE/DoH 2015) category of Communication and Interaction are likely to experience barriers to learning and participation that relate to their relationship with others. The Communication and Interaction category within the Code of Practice (DfE/DoH 2015) is very broad, and includes those with speech, language and communication needs (SLCN) as well as those with an autism spectrum disorder (ASD). For the purposes of this chapter we have chosen to focus on those individuals who are categorised as having ASD. National statistics (DfE 2016e) published in 2016 indicated that ASD was recorded as the primary need for just over 30 per cent of pupils with SEN in mainstream schools.

A closer look at Autism Spectrum Disorders

Individuals with ASD have a lifelong developmental disability. The use of the word 'spectrum' is important in conveying that although pupils with ASD share certain characteristics, their needs may be very different. Some will be able to live relatively autonomous lives, while others may require a lifetime of specialist support. People on the autism spectrum experience difficulties in the areas of social communication, social interaction and social imagination. This is sometimes referred to as the 'triad of impairments' (Wing and Gould 1979). These three areas are defined in Table 12.1.

The information shown in Table 12.1 illustrates why a school represents a challenging environment for a pupil with ASD. They will typically experience particular difficulties in building the relationships with others needed for learning through interaction with teachers and peers in a group setting.

The Behaviour for Learning approach places emphasis on the building of positive relationships with the curriculum, with self and with others. In working with pupils with ASD it is therefore useful to give some thought to preparing for these relationships. Ideally, within any relationship, we seek a 'meeting of minds' so that we can be sensitive to the other person's needs, and they to ours. This is not easy for individuals with ASD as they find it difficult to understand what others are thinking, and those who do not have ASD can only surmise about the 'mind' of pupils with the condition.

Table 12.1 The triad of impairment

Area of difficulty	Description
Social communication	People with ASD often experience difficulties with both verbal and non-verbal language. Some may not speak or have fairly limited speech. Others may display good spoken language skills but experience difficulty processing language, understanding figurative speech and interpreting facial expressions, body language and tone of voice.
Social interaction	People with ASD often have difficulty recognising or understanding other people's emotions and feelings, and expressing their own. Consequently, they may appear withdrawn, aloof or uninterested in the people they meet, and experience difficulties in forming and maintaining social relationships.
Social imagination	People with ASD often find it difficult to understand and predict other people's behaviour, make sense of abstract ideas and imagine situations outside of their immediate daily routine.

Many writers (e.g. Baron–Cohen 1995) suggest that individuals with ASD have not developed theory of mind. Essentially, theory of mind refers to the ability of the individual to understand that another person is thinking differently from them. The inability to understand someone else's beliefs, thoughts and feelings leads to difficulties when attempting to communicate and interact with others (Brain and Mukherji 2005).

In thinking about the relationship issues within the classroom, both pupils with ASD and their neurotypical teachers and peers can be seen as being 'outside each other's culture' and unable or struggling to tune into the meanings that are embedded within each other's social world.

Preparing for a relationship with a pupil with ASD in the classroom

In this section we look at the experiences a pupil might have in a classroom environment that emanate from the triad of impairments. A number of writers, including some with ASD (e.g. Dumortier 2004; Sainsbury 2009) liken autism to coming from or being on a different planet. The analogy captures the sense that an individual with autism is living in an environment where all the other inhabitants know the rules, conventions and expectations but they do not. Viewed from this perspective we can think about how the three elements (i.e. social communication, social interaction, social imagination) that make up the triad of impairment might be experienced. Attempting to understand autism at this experiential level should support teachers and peers in preparing to relate to a pupil with ASD. However, it should be recognised that in the description below we are referring to a hypothetical person. Although, as a group, individuals with ASD may share diagnostic indicators, each individual will display different behaviours and have different experiences in their schools and classroom environments. Our use of terms such as 'happy' and 'confused' in the next section are intended to allow us some understanding of the nature – positive or negative – of the experience, although we acknowledge that the person with ASD may not share our understanding of those terms.

Experiences of social communication

As indicated in Table 12.1, people with ASD experience difficulties with both verbal and non-verbal language. For example, they may have a very literal understanding of language, think people always mean exactly what they say or find it difficult to express themselves emotionally and socially. The feelings associated with these difficulties could include:

- frustration and anxiety about others' reaction to their social and emotional behaviour;
- feeling confused and bewildered by seeing, but not understanding, the rapidly changing gestures and facial expressions of others;
- feeling under pressure when having to decide what to talk about and not easily knowing when to start or end a conversation;
- feeling perplexed when rules of language do not apply and meaning is changed by others, seemingly when they want to (an example is when people say 'pull your socks up': sometimes they want you to perform that action and sometimes it means 'work harder' or 'get moving' or something else – they do not tell you which one they mean, but other people seem somehow to just know);
- feeling lonely when other people are laughing at a joke or a remark that does not seem to be particularly interesting or different from other things they are saying;
- feeling scared when others keep making comments that include your name or say words to you that people refer to as 'swearing' or 'spiteful'.

Experiences of social interaction

Many people with ASD want to be sociable but have difficulty with initiating and sustaining social relationships. They may not understand the norms of different social contexts, which most of us recognise and adapt to with little conscious thought. In the case of a pupil with ASD this can lead to the following feelings and experiences:

- wanting to play with others but not knowing what to do: play seems to be something others like to do and so you have to do it if you want friends – it keeps changing all the time so it is difficult to learn what others want you to do;
- wanting to be with others but at the same time getting easily cross with people because they are annoying or because it takes a lot of concentration and effort trying to work out why they are doing what they are doing and how to get them to like you;
- feeling cross when the teacher asks a question and you tell them the answer but they are not pleased: the teacher asks you not to answer but lets other people answer first – they say this is 'waiting your turn' and if you do this they are pleased;
- being cross when others push you away or the teacher tells you off when you get very close to people or touch them when you are just trying to get their attention or be friends;
- having to do things that are not interesting but other people want you to do them;
- feeling anxious when the teacher says things like, 'How do you think John feels when you push him out of the way?', and you do not know the answer;
- feeling sad when the person who was your friend on Tuesday is now not your friend and you do not know why;

- feeling anxious when the teacher says, 'Now you can go out to the playground', but does not say if we are coming back.

Experiences of social imagination

People with ASD experience differences and difficulties with regard to *social* imagination. This can lead to the following feelings and experiences:

- feeling worried because of being unable to imagine and predict what people are going to do next;
- feeling inadequate when expected to guess what other people are thinking and feeling; others can make good guesses but you do not know how they do this;
- feeling anxious when you are prevented from following routines;
- feeling anxious when people stop you from doing what they call rituals and repetitions;
- having no idea what 'let's pretend' means and not knowing why other children make tea and cook in the play house when they do not end up with a cup of tea to drink or something to eat.

In addition to the triad of impairments, some individuals with ASD may also experience hypersensitivity to auditory, visual and kinesthetic features of their physical environment. This hypersensitivity may manifest itself in a range of behaviours that are seen by the teacher and others to be 'odd' and/or disruptive, particularly given that the teacher may often have no idea what the trigger was. For example, we recall one case of a pupil with ASD whose problematic behaviour in the period between break and lunchtime was due to hypersensitivity to the smell of certain foods being cooked in the school canteen.

In seeking to build a relationship with pupils with ASD it is necessary to try to understand what purposes their seemingly 'odd' behaviours are serving. This should result in a change of thinking that accepts that these behaviours, far from being odd, are *adaptive* and can be understood and discussed as such.

Strategies for building relationships in schools

In applying the Behaviour for Learning approach we have started by thinking about what a typical hypothetical pupil with ASD might experience in a classroom setting. From this we can be clearer about the core *purpose* behind our choice of possible strategies. These core purposes underpin the many strategies that are available in a variety of guidance and texts for use with pupils with ASD in mainstream and other settings. The core purposes are:

1   *To address the anxiety and uncertainty experienced from receiving too much stimulation and information.* Strategies are chosen to stabilise emotions and provide a more predictable environment within which the pupil can begin to develop independence.

2   *To recognise and build on particular strengths that the pupil brings to the relationship.* Such strategies aim to stimulate intellectual and cognitive growth through a broad and developmentally appropriate curriculum that allows for individual interests and talents to flourish and success to be achieved that is of value to the individual. In

selecting and implementing strategies, teachers need to take account of any individual adaptations necessary for each individual pupil.

3   *To promote communication necessary for relationships to develop with self and others.* This is likely to involve adaptations to existing strategies and contexts or the use of distinctive approaches for inter- and intra-personal communication that take account of the particular social differences that characterise pupils with ASD.

Teachers can select from existing strategies those that best meet the purposes outlined above for any particular individual in their class. Some of these (e.g. visual timetables, adjusting of communication style to make implicit instructions explicit, use of ICT to support learning, avoidance of exaggerated praise or positive touch to acknowledge success, working closely with parents/carers and others involved and acknowledging the need for personal space) can be used at whole-class or small-group level. For some individuals, there will be a need to make greater adaptations to teaching. Some specialist strategies for pupils with ASD consistent with the above generic purposes and useful for building relationships with self and others are listed below.

Visual timetables and First/Then boards

Visual timetables can help to reduce anxiety associated with the apparent unpredictability of the sequence of the school day. Typically, a visual timetable would take the form of a piece of card with a Velcro strip on it. Cards would be placed on the strip in a sequence that shows the order of the day. Depending on the pupil, the card may have a picture on it, words and a picture or just words describing the activity. Although photographs can be used, it should be noted that some pupils with ASD might over focus on other minor details in the picture (e.g. other pupils present in the background) rather than the activity depicted. The use of Velcro allows the teacher to change the timetable each day but also to use it as a visual tool if explaining an unexpected change that needs to occur during the day.

First/Then boards are based on the same principles but are a simpler form, just depicting the current activity and the next one. The pupil is able to see what is going to happen next by having the board close to them at all times. First/Next/Then boards are an extension of this.

Social Scripts (DfE 2017f)

Social scripts involve pre-teaching specific language that the pupil can use during social interactions. The pupil may be taught conversation starters, responses and ideas to connect conversations or change the topic. Kamps *et al.* (2014: 231) give a range of examples including: 'Check my work, please', 'May I have the …?', 'Help me', 'Let's play this game', 'My turn', 'It's your turn', 'This is a fun game' and 'Look at this book'.

Social stories (Gray 1994b; Rowe 1998; Smith 2003)

These 'stories' give pupils access to information about social activities and relationships in a clear format using a combination of descriptive, perspective and directive sentences (Gray 1994b). The pupil can then use the 'story' to guide them in real social situations. Working on relationship with others through explicit means such as the use of social stories could be a useful way of improving reference points for pupils with ASD as they construct and understand their relationship with self.

Comic-strip conversations (Gray 1994a)

Comic-strip conversations can be used to explore a pupil's understanding of a social interaction (Gray 1994a). Simple cartoon people (usually stick figures) are drawn depicting a social situation. Speech bubbles and thought bubbles are used to distinguish between the words a person is using and their feelings and intentions. It is possible to use different colours to reinforce the distinction. As well as being used proactively, comic-strip conversations can be useful when following up a social incident that requires the pupil to reflect upon and account for their actions. This activity can serve to reduce anxieties for the pupil and provide a shared medium for discussion with the teacher.

Ear defenders and workstations

The use of ear defenders and workstations is a response to hypersensitivity to aspects of the classroom environment. They attempt to reduce sensory overload. A workstation is typically a desk with plain screens to the front and sides. The purpose is to reduce the visual stimuli that may be a cause of anxiety for the pupil or simply distracting. In Behaviour for Learning terms, during the time the pupil is at the workstation the teacher is prioritising relationship with the curriculum by temporarily managing the physical and social aspects of the classroom for them.

Ear defenders or headphones are used to reduce or eliminate auditory stimuli. These should not be worn for extended periods of time. They would typically be used for periods of the school day that are particularly noisy when it is known that the individual is hypersensitive to this. Perhaps more than some other strategies listed here, ear defenders highlight the pupil as different to their classmates and potentially the rest of the school if, for example, worn into assembly or the canteen. We would suggest that their use is discussed with the pupil's parents and, at a developmentally appropriate level, with the pupil.

Picture exchange communication system (PECS)

PECS uses visual ways to enhance and facilitate communication for pupils with limited ability to communicate. The pupil is taught to approach another person and give them a picture of a desired item in exchange for that item. The initial aim is to promote functional communication (Liddle 2001) but PECS can be used to communicate a request, a thought or anything else that can reasonably be depicted on a picture card.

As a spectrum condition, it needs to be recognised that when we refer to pupils with ASD it is a description of a heterogeneous group. Although we can make some predictions regarding what they bring to the three relationships, and in particular relationship with others, their experiences within the classroom are likely to be very varied. For those working with the individual there will often be a need to make significant changes or adjustments to their own style of communicating and responding such that a 'meeting of minds and methods' needed for the relationship is developed.

Social, emotional and mental health difficulties

Introduction

In considering ASD and dyslexia we started from the perspective that pupils who are categorised in this way shared some characteristics in common with others in the same category. Effectively, to be placed in one of these categories requires the pupils to display a *cluster* of difficulties that potentially negatively impact on their learning in class contexts. Our argument was that the teacher, through being aware of some of these common characteristics, would have some knowledge of what the pupil brought to the relationship. Even if the teacher did not have experience in the area, just the awareness that the pupil may be viewing the world differently (in the case of autism) or processing information differently (in the case of dyslexia) would encourage a more responsive, reciprocal relationship.

As we considered in Chapter 1, there have been various attempts in policy and guidance to identify when behaviour exhibited by a pupil represents a special educational need. The current SEND Code of Practice (DfE/DoH 2015) has reduced the focus on the presenting behaviour through its introduction of a category entitled Social, Emotional and Mental Health (SEMH) difficulties. This replaced Behaviour, Emotional and Social Development (BESD) referred to in the 2001 Code (DfES 2001). Despite this, SEMH, like its predecessor, is an exceptionally broad category, stretching from becoming withdrawn or isolated through to displaying challenging, disruptive or disturbing behaviours, and also includes categories with a biological dimension such as Attention Deficit Hyperactivity Disorder (ADHD). There may be very little that pupils sharing the SEMH label have in common. All we might broadly be able to identify is that they do not relate to others in the manner generally expected, or required, in group settings. Arguably, this is true for those who exhibit withdrawn or isolated behaviours as well as those who are disruptive, aggressive or violent.

The SEND Code of Practice (DfE/DoH 2015) is predicated on a graduated approach based on the assess, plan, do, review model. The graduated approach involves drawing on more personalised approaches, more frequent review and more specialist expertise in successive assess, plan, do, review cycles in order to tailor interventions to meet the particular needs of the pupil (NASEN 2014). In the case of pupils with SEMH difficulties, their behaviour is particularly susceptible to changes in their school and home environment and as such their need is variable. This can make it difficult to apply a graduated approach effectively as there may be periods where the need for adjustments, interventions and support is greater than others. We might also speculate on how long a pupil has to go without any incident or episode to no longer be considered to have SEMH difficulties. Such considerations demonstrate the challenges posed for schools in determining whether a pupil has SEMH difficulties, identifying appropriate strategies and allocating necessary resources.

Using the Behaviour for Learning conceptual framework

As stressed throughout this book, the Behaviour for Learning approach is rooted in building relationships for learning. Of all the SEN categories, SEMH difficulties is perhaps the one that most reflects the interdependence of the three relationships for learning. The inclusion of the terms 'social' and 'emotional' should definitely not preclude teachers from paying due regard to the pupil's relationship with the curriculum as either a cause of, or a route to, addressing SEMH difficulties.

Relationship with the curriculum as the target relationship

Pupils with SEMH difficulties cover the full range of ability. However, their difficulties are likely to be a barrier to academic learning. There can often be a reciprocal relationship between learning difficulties and behaviour difficulties. For some pupils, behaviour difficulties may frustrate access to the curriculum; for example, if the presenting behaviour is such that it leads to exclusion from some classroom activities or from the school. For others, a learning difficulty may lead to or exacerbate behavioural and emotional difficulties. For example, a pupil who has difficulty in grasping the basics of literacy or numeracy may withdraw from lessons or try to divert attention away from their learning difficulty by exhibiting disruptive behaviour. The DCSF (2008c) suggests that difficulties in acquiring basic skills can also lead to low self-esteem and even depression, providing a salient reminder that difficulties with regard to the pupil's relationship with the curriculum may impact on relationship with self. By the time behaviour has reached the stage of being classified as a SEMH difficulty it can be hard to tell whether a deteriorating relationship with the curriculum preceded and contributed to difficulties in the pupil's relationship with self and relationship with others or vice versa. The interdependent nature of the relationships also means that even if a poor relationship with the curriculum was the cause, perhaps through an unrecognised learning difficulty, measures to address this may be frustrated by the difficulties that have developed with regard to relationship with self and relationship with others.

Relationship with others as the target relationship

The types of behaviour presented by many pupils with SEMH difficulties can act as barriers to the development of positive reciprocal relationships that underpin learning in group settings. Aggressive behaviour in particular is likely to alienate teachers and peers, especially those it is directed towards. The pupil's behaviour may also be experienced by the teacher as a personal or professional threat as the Teachers' Standards (DfE 2011b: 12) require teachers to 'manage behaviour effectively' and there is a general perception that 'one of the most essential characteristics of a good teacher is the ability to manage our students' behaviour' (Cowley 2003: xiii). The feeling that the pupil presents a threat to professional competence is not conducive to the development of a positive relationship.

The variability of some pupils' behaviour, often due to emotional factors, can also lead to the teacher feeling 'let down' or even betrayed. Sometimes headway is made in the relationship, often through compromise or considerable effort on the teacher's part, and the pupil then does something that undermines this. In short, the pupil's relationship with others, including that with the teacher, is frequently vulnerable. Because of the teacher's responsibility for the group they will also have to impose sanctions, often knowing that this will not change the pupil's behaviour, which again is not conducive to a good relationship. Peers' relationships with the pupil are likely to be strongly influenced by the presenting behaviour. Unpredictable behaviour, particularly that which is physically and/or emotionally hurtful to others, is unlikely to lead to durable positive relationships with others.

When considering relationship with others it is also important to recognise that a significant proportion of pupils experiencing behavioural difficulties also have communication difficulties (Cross 2004; I CAN 2006). As Cross (2004) debates, although these difficulties occur together we cannot necessarily conclude that the link is causal. However, teachers need to be aware of the association between speech, language and communication needs and behaviour problems. The behaviour exhibited may, for example, result from a pupil's difficulty in either constructing language to express themselves or understanding the language needed in order for them to respond to the teaching and learning opportunities on offer in group settings.

Relationship with self as the target relationship

Bowers (2005) conducted research looking at the Statements of Special Educational Need for 16 pupils with behaviour, emotional and social difficulties. He found plenty of descriptions of behaviour but only limited reference to emotions. Examples of emotions within the pupils' statements included 'low self-esteem', 'low self-confidence', 'anxiety', 'frequent mood swings' and 'anger'. It remains to be seen whether the renaming of the category as SEMH difficulties will lead to Education, Health and Care Plans that place more attention on underlying emotions. Within the Behaviour for Learning approach the term 'relationship with self' is used to encompass a range of constructs and concepts related to pupils' emotional health and wellbeing. For example, we would include self-esteem, self-confidence, self-efficacy, self-regulation, attributional style, locus of control, resilience, attachment disorder, anxiety and depression under this heading. A teacher reading this list might, with some justification, remark that they are not a psychologist or therapist. There is an expectation in policy and guidance (e.g. DfE 2016c) that schools and teachers support all their pupils to be resilient and mentally healthy and that they should employ various strategies to support any individuals who are experiencing higher levels of psychological stress or are at risk of developing mental health problems. However, there is also recognition that in cases where the difficulties are more significant, support would be provided by external agencies in terms of advice and guidance on school-based strategies and, where required, direct working with the pupil.

From a Behaviour for Learning perspective, knowledge of constructs and concepts related to emotional health and wellbeing can support understanding of how a pupil might experience teaching, learning and the classroom environment and of the purpose behind their behaviour. When considering the adjustments, interventions and support to employ to develop the pupil's relationship with self, this understanding will allow the teacher to make more informed decisions about those likely to have a beneficial effect. Because a pupil's relationship with self relates to what is going on inside their heads and we may often be attempting to bring about changes in dispositions, it is particularly important to devote time to identifying a clear set of assessable indicators of positive change. Often this will take the form of the emergence of particular learning behaviours that we associate with a positive relationship with self (see Appendix 1).

The skill and will behind learning behaviour

As stated earlier in this chapter, in seeking to improve a target relationship we would normally aim to identify and improve the cluster of learning behaviours that will have a pervasive, positive effect on it.

In Chapter 3 we noted that commonly cited learning behaviours reflect both skills and dispositions ('will'). It is significant that the 2009 guidance document on behaviour policies (DCSF 2009) distinguished between pupils who do not have the necessary understanding or skills, pupils who can behave but choose not to and pupils who have the necessary competences but 'are experiencing such stress that they are temporarily unable to make rational choices' (DCSF 2009: 54). While this is an artificial distinction as the categories themselves are not mutually exclusive, it acts as a reminder that for some pupils the issue may be one of disposition rather than a lack of skills. This has implications for strategy choice and reflects, in Behaviour for Learning terms, the important distinction between the 'skill' and 'will' components of behaviour as well as their interdependence.

Strategy selection

There are numerous strategies, approaches and interventions available for pupils with SEMH difficulties and many of these will already be known to readers and their schools. It is also salient to note Ofsted's (2005) observation that the most effective teaching for pupils with the most difficult behaviour is little different to the most successful teaching for others. Therefore, many of the strategies and approaches outlined in Chapters 8, 9 and 10 will continue to be applicable. As part of a continuum of teaching approaches, pupils identified as having SEMH difficulties will require greater levels of adaptation, involving variations in the frequency and intensity of intervention and subsequent monitoring of pupil response. This may involve additional staffing and support from multi-agency partners. Although there will be an overlap of elements of practice within and between these strategies we have sought to group them according to the core *purpose* against which they will be *evaluated*.

Strategies, approaches, interventions and support for pupils with SEMH difficulties typically fall into five main categories that reflect their overall purpose and address concerns about both 'will' and 'skill':

- bringing about changes in the school context and conditions;
- improving the skills of pupils with SEMH;
- changing the observable behaviour;
- changing the thinking associated with the behaviour;
- addressing deep-rooted, entrenched and sometimes subconscious emotional elements of behaviour.

Each of these categories is considered below.

CHANGING CONTEXTS AND CONDITIONS

This group of strategies involves bringing about changes to contexts and conditions. It is often referred to as a systemic approach (Davis and Florian 2004). We might, for example, seek to make changes to teaching approaches and learning activities, adult responses to the pupil's behaviour, the timetable or the physical environment (e.g. seating plans and pupil groupings). In Behaviour for Learning terms, any changes to contexts and conditions are evaluated against the extent to which they promote the development of learning relationships and improve the pupil's learning behaviour(s).

Changes to context and conditions should always be the starting point in preparing to improve any of the three Behaviour for Learning relationships. If a significant number of pupils present SEMH difficulties it is important to identify factors within the environment that serve to maintain or exacerbate these.

According to Watkins and Wagner (2000), when thinking about an individual pupil (or groups) there are two key questions to ask:

- In what situations does the behaviour occur? *In what settings/contexts, with which others?*
- In what situations does the behaviour NOT occur? *In what settings/contexts, with which others?*

In answering these questions it is important to think about all aspects – including the teacher, the peers who are present, the subject, the type of lesson and the physical environment. Essentially, the aim is to find out under what conditions the pupil behaves and learns better. The teacher can then seek to replicate these conditions across a range of lessons. In the case of a few pupils, the behaviour is serving such a significant purpose for them that it is for much of the time impervious to contextual changes.

IMPROVE THE SKILLS

In employing strategies that seek to improve skills, it is assumed that the problematic behaviour presented by some pupils can be attributed largely to a delay or difference in acquiring the skills expected of their age group for learning in group settings. Skill areas linked to SEMH difficulties that can usefully be developed or enhanced include:

- language and communication skills;
- essential curriculum skills (e.g. subject knowledge, study and organisational skills);
- social skills;
- conflict resolution skills.

For all of these areas there are either universal programmes such as SEAL (DfES 2005c, 2007b) or targeted programmes for groups and individuals such as social skills and anger management groups. These might be devised by schools, drawing on various sources, or be based upon published programmes (e.g. Rinaldi 2001; Wilson 2013).

Although such programmes are often structured around the development and rehearsal of *skills*, they also necessarily, and often intentionally, impact on how a pupil thinks and feels. As such they may influence both 'will' and 'skill' components of learning behaviour.

CHANGING THE OBSERVABLE BEHAVIOUR

This approach is rooted within behaviourist theory that, in its essence, seeks to minimise reference to the cognitive aspects of human behaviour. It is concerned with bringing about changes in observable behaviour through the use of different configurations of positive reinforcement, negative reinforcement and punishment. As discussed in Chapter 8, the use of rewards and sanctions by schools is underpinned by behaviourist theory. For pupils with SEMH difficulties an individualised approach may be used. For example, in a primary school a pupil might have their own sticker chart. The general principle is that a target behaviour is identified, taught and rehearsed if necessary, and then reinforced by a reward. The apparent simplicity of the behaviourist approach belies the skill required for its effective use.

Schools are usually very aware of the problem behaviour, but the element that is sometimes missed is the identification of antecedents and consequences. If the teacher can identify the antecedents, which may be in the form of people, events or environmental factors, it is possible to alter these or at least be aware of when a potential trigger situation is developing and intervene early on. The use of the term 'consequences' here simply refers to what happens after the behaviour. This might be, for example, that peers laugh, the teacher gives attention or work is avoided. This potentially gives the teacher an indication of what is serving to reinforce the behaviour. It might then be possible to change the consequences in some way to remove the reinforcement. The obvious example is where teacher attention seems to be reinforcing the behaviour. The teacher might make a point of withholding attention when the pupil displays the unwanted behaviour but giving attention when the required behaviour is demonstrated. A number of potential limitations associated with a behaviourist approach are identified in Chapter 8. This type of approach may have utility in promoting a specific learning behaviour but it should be recognised that the unwanted behaviour the teacher is attempting to target may be serving an important purpose for the pupil and so may be very resistant to change.

CHANGING THE THINKING ASSOCIATED WITH THE BEHAVIOUR

It is often possible and desirable to bring about improvements in the behaviour of pupils with SEMH difficulties through the systematic use of behaviourist approaches, combined with systemic changes. The combination of these approaches can be helpful in setting the scene for the individual to develop the thinking necessary to build their resilience to the many situational changes they experience in their school, family and community. However, for some pupils the internal processes and explanations they have developed around their behaviour serve to render them relatively impervious to systemic changes and behaviourist approaches. Whether we tackle this thinking explicitly or implicitly will depend on the extent to which, from the pupil's viewpoint, the presenting behaviour needs to be retained due to the valuable purpose it serves for them.

It is necessary to keep in mind that for some pupils with SEMH difficulties the behaviour is the solution, irrespective of whether for the teacher, or others, it is a problem. An example might be the pupil who disrupts lessons to avoid work and so protect themselves from the risk of failure and the uncomfortable feelings associated with this.

The collection of strategies designed to address the links between thinking and behaviour generally fall within the category of cognitive–behavioural approaches. When approaching behaviour from this perspective a teacher would be concerned with factors such as the pupil's attributional style, their perceived level of self-efficacy and whether they have an internal or external locus of control. Readers will note from Chapter 6 that these are all factors that predominantly relate to relationship with self. If the target relationship is 'self', then cognitive–behavioural approaches offer some scope for intervention. Emler (2002) suggests that those programmes that use a broad cognitive–behavioural approach seem to be particularly successful in bringing about changes in self-esteem.

ADDRESSING DEEP-ROOTED, ENTRENCHED AND SOMETIMES SUBCONSCIOUS EMOTIONAL ELEMENTS OF BEHAVIOUR

For some pupils the behaviours they exhibit may stem from unconscious conflicts, fears and anxieties originating from early childhood experiences (Ayers *et al.* 2000) that are influencing how they interpret and respond to experiences in the present. Because the behaviours are influenced by past events, they may not seem to the observer to be rational or proportionate responses to the current situation. Interventions need to tackle not only aspects of behaviour and ways of thinking that are in the pupil's conscious awareness, but also those that are influenced by factors that are not within their conscious awareness. Approaches employed to tackle behaviour influenced by these underlying factors range from forms of counselling undertaken by trained and supervised staff in school, through to psychodynamic interventions delivered by appropriately qualified staff, usually from outside agencies. Such approaches are often categorised as 'therapeutic'. As with all such interventions, ethical issues need to be considered and addressed.

Strategy selection where 'will' is the issue

From the broad strategy categories above, it should be clear that changing observable behaviours and improving skills are focused on targeting the skill element of learning behaviours. Cognitive-behavioural approaches explicitly seek to bridge the 'skill' and 'will' elements of learning behaviour, placing more emphasis on understanding the interpretation and sense making function for the pupil of their current behaviour. Given that the behaviour of many pupils with SEMH difficulties is likely to include a 'will' component, it is important to consider it in more detail. From a Behaviour for Learning perspective an issue of 'will' would typically suggest relationship with self as the target relationship.

Directly targeting relationship with self

When directly targeting relationship with self, the focus will often be on working with the pupil to identify, share and change the way in which they perceive or interpret events as a means of positively influencing their behaviours. Essentially, in using perspectives from attribution theory and constructs of self-efficacy and locus of control, the teacher is attempting to identify the extent to which the pupil is likely to take responsibility for changing their behaviour. (These terms are discussed in more detail in Chapter 6.) For the teacher, the aim is to critically explore with the pupil the validity of their causal explanations for events with a view to modifying these. The teacher might use proformas (see Ayers *et al.* 2000, for example) on which the pupil gives their own perspective on events. This form of self-reporting potentially provides the teacher with some insight into how the pupil is currently viewing particular situations. In the follow-up to any incident, care would be taken to allow the pupil to state their version of the events. The purpose is to attempt to understand the attributions the pupil makes. For example, if a pupil makes comments such as, 'He made me do it', or cites some minor provocation ('She was looking at me'), it is an indication that the pupil is attributing externally and taking little personal responsibility. Sometimes it is appropriate to talk this through and supportively challenge attributions in relation to the specific incident.

For some pupils concentrating on what they are thinking and how they are feeling simultaneously is problematic due to experience of overload. A depersonalised approach that reduces the emotional component may be more effective. Puppets could be used to act out a similar scenario. A young pupil may be quite happy to comment on what they think caused a puppet to behave in a particular way whereas they may be extremely resistant if required to talk about their own behaviour. Role-play or stories can also be used. Comic-strip conversations which, as we noted earlier, are often used with pupils with ASD, can also be helpful. In a depersonalised way, they let the pupil reflect on what they were thinking during the incident and offer their suggestion of what the other pupil(s) involved in the incident may have been thinking. The pupil might, for example, suggest that the other person in the cartoon has malicious feelings towards them. It may be this 'faulty' appraisal that then drives their behaviour. Rogers (2003) has made use of cartoons to reflect back to the pupil how they present behaviourally, and the reaction of others, in a given situation. The cartoon is used as a focus for discussion that draws out both the feelings of the pupil and the effect on others involved, including the teacher. The premise is that the pupil does not normally have opportunities to see what their own behaviour looks like or the effect it has on others.

When thinking about attributions it is also necessary to be alert to what, on the surface, appear to be internal attributions but place the locus of control outside the individual. For example, a pupil might say, 'It's my temper', as an explanation for a violent incident. The pupil is seemingly locating responsibility internally but, by presenting their temper as though it is something that is separate to themselves, they are still attributing externally. Essentially the message they are conveying is 'my temper made me do it'.

In this section we have primarily discussed the problems that occur when a pupil always attributes causes externally. It is important to remember that to attribute totally internally is also problematic. There may be some pupils within the broad category of SEMH difficulties whose behaviour is driven by feeling that every unfortunate event that befalls them is totally their responsibility.

Targeting self via relationship with others

The teacher may decide that targeting relationship with self via one of the other two Behaviour for Learning relationships is the better option. For example, it may be preferable to target relationship with self via relationship with others.

DEVELOPING THE TEACHER–PUPIL RELATIONSHIP

By necessity the teacher has probably had to positively correct the pupil, impose sanctions or ask for them to be exited from the class. Even supportive conversations with the pupil about their behaviour, such as those that might be undertaken to directly target relationship with self, may be experienced as 'going on about it'.

In targeting relationship with others the teacher is deliberately seeking to 'back off' from the behaviour, though of course keeping in mind the cluster of learning behaviours that would be indicative of an improving relationship with self. Many of the strategies designed to improve the teacher–pupil relationship are quite informal in nature. The teacher is essentially attempting to relate to the pupil through a shared interest that is *not* the pupil's problematic behaviour. The teacher might, for example, find out what interests the pupil and make a point of spending some time talking to them about it. For younger pupils, an activity like helping the teacher rearrange furniture or reorganise resources will also provide opportunities for non-behaviour-related conversations. For older pupils, there might be opportunities to help with painting scenery for a school production. Many teachers and other adults who work with pupils with SEMH difficulties in specialist settings will attest to the value of trips and extra-curricular activities in building relationships. The precise nature of the activity is not the important element. The aim is to form relationships with others that positively impact on relationship with self. Learning more skills, acquiring more confidence, having more good times with others, feeling part of the group and developing an identity that is not prescribed by behavioural problems all contribute to the pupil's bank of positive experiences against which they make judgements that inform their relationship with self.

As well as being a potential beneficiary of an improving relationship with others, relationship with self can impact negatively at times. Sometimes pupils will begin to build this positive relationship with others and then do something that threatens it. This can be disappointing for the teacher but should not be surprising. First, the new relationship may represent a threat to stability because it is different to the antagonistic relationship with adults that the pupil may be familiar, and even comfortable, with. The pupil may attempt to resolve this difference in favour of the familiar. Second, some pupils have, or perceive they have, been let down by adults in the past. Forming a close relationship runs the risk of being let down again. The pupil can protect themselves from this risk and exercise some control in their life by behaving in a way that wrecks the relationship before it starts to matter to them. Others will test the relationship through their behaviour to see just how serious the adult is about making this work.

BUILDING RELATIONSHIPS WITH PEERS

Even when a pupil begins to see that change is necessary it can be difficult because they have become locked into a role by the expectations of their peer group (McNamara and Moreton 2001). Effective use of pupil grouping and collaborative activities can help to change these expectations.

The teacher might monitor the target pupil's behaviour and identify whether when in the company of certain pupils the difficulties are less. Equally, there may be other pupils whose presence frequently exacerbates difficulties. Seating can be adjusted accordingly. This can be accompanied by increased monitoring to pre-empt problems. By recognising the first signs of tension or agitation the teacher can act to distract or divert the pupil before they embark on a familiar pattern of behaviour. The purpose of these approaches is to mediate the pupil's experience of peer relationships so that they are successful. By effectively keeping the pupil away from incidents, the teacher is avoiding situations where existing patterns of problematic behaviour can be reinforced. There is also the benefit that by minimising incidents other members of the class will develop a more positive view of the pupil as they will no longer be solely associated with trouble and upset.

Some pupils may be able to cope with paired work even though they present difficulties within a larger group. Setting up a paired activity, perhaps to research a topic within a particular curriculum area, can help both pupils to get to know each other better, encourage them to use communication skills and allow a relationship to develop (NcNamara and Moreton 2001). The common advice is that the other pupil should be a good role model, but in reality the main priority is that it is somebody the focus pupil has some chance of relating to. It should be remembered that the priority is not the task but to enable the focus pupil to form a relationship with a peer. McNamara and Moreton (2001) note Sullivan's (1953) research that pupils who had a 'best friend' had higher self-esteem. Coopersmith's (1967) work also showed that the regard of the peer group was important to self-esteem. As readers will be aware from Chapter 6, although we question the readiness of some teachers and others to ascribe all pupils' difficulties to global low self-esteem, a person's judgement about their own worth is an important element of their relationship with self. If we accept Lund's (1987) view that pupils exhibiting behavioural difficulties tend to have lower self-esteem then, in the light of Sullivan's (1953) and Coopersmith's (1967) findings, there is a rationale for targeting relationship with self via relationship with others.

Some pupils with SEMH difficulties respond well to either being tutored by a peer or being a peer-tutor themselves (McNamara and Moreton 2001). The latter approach, in particular, may be counterintuitive; the natural teacher tendency may be to restrict responsibility rather than give more, particularly where this may involve influence over younger pupils. Pupils with SEMH difficulties may have particular issues with those, such as teachers, who are in a position of authority. A well-trained peer-tutor may be able to work more effectively with the pupil because the power element in the relationship is significantly reduced. The peer-tutor can talk in the language the pupil understands, particularly if they, unlike many teachers, share the same cultural and social background (McNamara and Moreton 2001).

The pupil with SEMH difficulties may benefit from acting as peer-tutor to younger pupils. Pupils with SEMH difficulties can get locked into their role by the expectations of their peers (McNamara and Moreton 2001) and their teacher. Peer-tutoring places the pupil in a completely different context and allows them to try out a new role. Rather than their role as 'disruptive pupil' or 'class clown' they are placed in the role of responsible and more experienced peer. This requires them to draw on communication and social skills that are usually masked by a whole range of adaptive behaviours.

Targeting self via relationship with the curriculum

Relationship with the curriculum can be an effective route to strengthening relationship with self. If observations suggest that the behaviour is rooted in task–avoidance to protect the individual from failure, then there is certainly a rationale for this approach. Negative self-reference statements – such as 'I can't do it', 'I'm useless at Maths' or 'I'm thick' – may cue the teacher into strengthening relationship with the curriculum as a route to strengthening relationship with self. However, this is not the only type of pupil who might benefit from targeting an issue related to 'self' via the curriculum. Many pupils with SEMH difficulties who exhibit disruptive, acting-out behaviours, have what might be considered an anti–authority, anti–establishment attitude. They may appear to the observer to actively look for situations that bring them into conflict with the system, whether this is through uniform infringements, jewellery, unusual hairstyles or the behaviour they display in the classroom. As soon as the school acts by reprimanding or imposing a sanction this serves to reaffirm the pupil's view of authority.

If the teacher is able to build the pupil's relationship with the curriculum this can help to break the cycle. The pupil's SEMH difficulties should not detract the teacher from their particular area of expertise in brokering positive relationships through the curriculum in group settings. This expertise is a resource that can be brought to bear in developing adaptations to provision for pupils with SEMH difficulties. The priority is to achieve some shared interest and to secure motivation. This may be achieved through:

- *Content*
  This may involve identifying the pupil's area of interest and structuring learning activities around this or attempting to enthuse the pupil about the curriculum by enabling them to see the relevance.
- *Teaching style*
  This may involve varying how the task is introduced to the pupil and how they are expected to tackle it. Examples include reducing periods of extended listening, incorporating more kinesthetic elements, finding alternatives to written recording, use of ICT and breaking the lesson into smaller learning episodes with mini plenaries in between.
- *Groupings*
  Variations in this area have been touched on in discussion of relationship with others. The teacher can seek to develop shared interest and secure motivation by careful consideration of which peers work with the target pupil.
- *Assessment*
  The teacher can seek to secure motivation by involving the pupil in setting their own targets, providing feedback that helps the pupil to recognise what they need to do to take the next step towards the target, monitoring progress and recording achievements.

Some pupils will develop a positive relationship with an extra-curricular activity. This may be the only aspect of the curriculum with which the pupil has a relationship. The relationship with the person who runs it may also be the only positive relationship the pupil currently has with a member of staff. For this reason, we consider that schools that ban pupils from football club or some other extra-curricular activity due to behaviour in class may effectively be 'shooting themselves in the foot'. We can, of course, understand the school's rationale. The club matters to the pupil so banning them from this is a negative consequence. Because it matters to the pupil, the belief is that they will behave better to get this privilege back. Unfortunately, due to the attributions some pupils make, they are unlikely to share this logic. For them this action may simply act as further evidence that teachers, the school and possibly the world in general, are unfair, hostile and therefore 'deserve' the behaviour they get.

Evaluating against the target relationship

Readers will recall from Chapter 2 that when using the Behaviour for Learning approach in its extended-use form we evaluate based on improvements to the target relationship. This is assessed with reference to all participating members – the pupil, the teacher and peers. The approaches provided above involve changing peer and teacher responses in order to develop the pupil's relationship with self. Although they may not have the same reassuring feel as putting in a tangible, structured intervention, they are potentially very powerful in Behaviour for Learning terms. The teacher is trying all the time to place the pupil in situations where the social, cognitive and emotional experiences of school learning are improved. This prompts a need in the pupil to reappraise their relationship with self in terms of questioning the purpose behind their behaviour, their perceptions regarding the causes of their behaviour, their beliefs about their ability to change their behaviour and their view of self. If the teacher can engineer a gradual improvement in relationship with self they will have contributed to development of the responsibility and resilience needed to bring about longer-term change.

Specific strategies for pupils with SEMH difficulties

The strategies and approaches outlined in Chapters 8, 9 and 10 are relevant to pupils with SEMH, just as they are for all pupils. For example, the positive correction techniques provided in Chapter 10 are phrased in a way that protects the pupil's relationship with self and relationship with others and reduces the potential for the interaction to develop into a confrontation. An extensive list of strategies is also included in Appendix 3, ranging from general behaviour management strategies through to more personalised approaches. In looking at the more personalised approaches, it is useful to consider those that represent a 'normal' adaptation that can readily be made to class teaching and others that seem more 'specialist' in nature. These approaches might be deemed 'specialist' due either to the specialist knowledge required to implement them and/or the high level of adaptation necessary to incorporate them into class teaching. This way of thinking about strategies and approaches reflects Norwich and Lewis's (2001) notion of a continua of teaching approaches ranging from 'normal' adaptations to class teaching for most pupils through to greater levels of adaptation required for those with more significant difficulties in learning.

Given the broad range of needs covered by the SEMH label it is of particular importance to be clear regarding the focus and purpose of any strategy. It should be possible for any strategy to identify how it links with the development of learning behaviour and/or contributes to one or more of the three Behaviour for Learning relationships. Table 12.2 illustrates this point.

Reflective Exercise 12.1

Select three or four strategies from Appendix 3 that you think may be suitable for pupils you are working with. Write down or discuss with others how these link with the development of learning behaviour and/or potentially contribute to one or more of the three Behaviour for Learning relationships.

Conclusion

In this chapter, we have examined in more depth the case of individual pupils who exhibit differences and delays in development that result in them experiencing difficulties in school contexts. Many, but by no means all, are identified as having SEN. As we have outlined, it is possible to reframe the barriers to learning and participation experienced by pupils in terms of their relationship with self, others and the curriculum. We have illustrated this through the examples of pupils with dyslexia, ASD and SEMH difficulties.

Table 12.2 Some example strategies accompanied by a Behaviour for Learning analysis

Strategy	Behaviour for Learning analysis
Plan curriculum activities that incorporate a collaborative element that is initially within the pupil's capability. For example, create situations where the pupil is included in activities first with one other pupil, and then with a small group (ATL 2002).	This strategy is useful if the concern relates predominantly to underdeveloped skills related to relationship with others. It may also be useful where the issue is more one of 'will', if there are certain individuals the pupil appears more ready and willing to work with or where a small group context has been identified as a contextual factor that positively influences behaviour.
Provide opportunities to explore the attributional style of others and themselves in a non-threatening, safe setting. This could be through characters in stories, role-play or use of puppets.	The purpose of this strategy is to encourage the pupil to critically question their own current explanations and interpretations of their successes and failures in behaviour and learning. The key focus is relationship with self. However, it is also likely to benefit relationship with curriculum and relationship with others.
Teach and rehearse useful strategies that the pupil can use to either deal with or extricate themselves from social situations that they currently find difficult. This could include the sometimes vacuous, but socially useful, language and behaviour of apology. It might also include developing socially acceptable responses to criticism.	The purpose of this approach is to develop self-regulation and resilience by providing choice and alternatives to current response patterns. As such it targets relationship with self, but benefits are also likely to be accrued in the area of relationship with others as the pupil will be involved in less disputes. Readers will note that the strategy focuses initially on skills (i.e. making an apology, responding to criticism). This is to show the pupil that a different approach by them can lead to a different response from others.
Identify a 'safe' place or person that the pupil can go to as an alternative to a behaviour that would impact negatively and significantly on self and/or others.	This strategy targets self-regulation and so links with relationship with self. In this case self-regulation involves the pupil relocating themselves either in the classroom or to another identified area in the school. It would be hoped that the pupil could be supported to progress to using mental self-regulation strategies in situ rather than physical relocation. The use of a 'safe' person attempts to capitalise on an existing positive relationship with an adult.
Adopt a restorative approach to incidents, focusing on the key questions, 'What happened?', 'Who has been affected and how?', 'How can we put right the harm?' and 'What have you learned so as to make different choices next time?' (Hopkins 2004).	There is a focus on relationship with others through the emphasis on the effect on the other person. However, it also targets relationship with self by emphasising personal responsibility.

Table 12.2 Continued

Strategy	Behaviour for Learning analysis
Develop strategies to avoid conflict and confrontation. This involves trying to develop an awareness of anything that triggers unacceptable behaviour and intervening or distracting the pupil before a problem occurs. Relationships with peers and the teacher are likely to be much harder to repair after a major breakdown.	This strategy is rooted in preventing harm to the pupil's relationship with others and relationship with self. A public loss of control by the pupil is likely to adversely influence their relationship with peers who may subsequently perceive him/her as 'scary', 'dangerous' or 'weird'. The pupil's relationship with self is likely to be affected by the negative experience of the public loss of control. If successful, the strategy may impact positively on the pupil's relationship with self by increasing the proportion of successful days (i.e. days without incident) they experience.
Provide opportunities for the pupil to identify their existing effective self-regulation strategies and to explore socially acceptable strategies used by peers and others.	This strategy targets relationship with self. However, the development of greater self-regulation is also likely to benefit relationship with others as the pupil is less likely to come into conflict with and/or alienate peers and adults through unpredictable behaviour.
Identifying a particular role (e.g. leader, participant, reporter) with the individual pupil within a collaborative group work activity that seeks to address their particular behavioural and/or learning difficulty. Some may need a script to support them in the role.	This strategy is based on providing a structure to support and develop the pupil's relationship with others. Effectively, by allocating a role it sets some limits on the learning behaviours that the pupil is required to draw upon when working in a group.

Reframing SEN within the Behaviour for Learning conceptual framework allows the promotion of positive learning behaviours to be the focus of provision for all pupils. As such, all those involved in provision, including the pupil and their parents, have a shared purpose. The Behaviour for Learning approach explicitly recognises the inter-dependence between the social, emotional and cognitive factors involved in classroom learning. It follows that even if a pupil's core area of difficulty is perceived to be due primarily to emotional factors this will impact on the social and cognitive aspects of their learning. An approach that focuses on the relational aspects of learning offers a number of advantages:

- It is not susceptible to changes in SEN policy and guidance. The three relationships (with self, with the curriculum, with others) will have enduring relevance to learning in group settings.
- Labels and diagnoses are not seen as a prerequisite to effective working. Their utility is judged only in terms of their potential to signpost bodies of knowledge that help us to:
  - understand what the pupil might bring to the learning relationship;
  - identify evidence-based strategies and approaches thought to be beneficial to pupils with this label or diagnosis.
- It supports a person-centred approach as there is explicit recognition that any pupil assigned to a particular category or label will experience and respond to strategies associated with their category differently.
- It is applicable to all forms of educational setting and phases of education.
- Its focus on the pupil's experience and interpretation of provision encourages a responsive, personalised approach. Through their responses, the pupil contributes to and evaluates the efficacy of provision.

Our suggestion is that provision for all pupils should pay due regard to building relationships that support the development of positive learning behaviours as the route to improving educational outcomes.

Notes

1 www.gl-assessment.co.uk/products/lucid-rapid/ (accessed 3 January 2018).
2 www.nessy.com/uk/product/dyslexia-screening/ (accessed 3 January 2018).

Chapter 13

Transitions

Introduction

Pupils make educational transitions as they start school, as they progress through school, and as they move between schools. These transitions require pupils to acclimatise to new surroundings, to adapt to new ways of working, to make sense of new rules and routines and to interact with unfamiliar adults and peers (Sanders *et al.* 2005). Transitions therefore make intense demands on the three Behaviour for Learning relationships. It is important that we retain a focus on each of these relationships, but relationship with self assumes particular significance in relation to transitions. It is this relationship above all others that determines the pupil's ability to respond to the challenges of transition – and it is this ability that may influence the ways in which the pupil progresses and develops (Sanders *et al.* 2005). Experiences of transition in the early years are likely to affect the child and their capacity to adjust and to learn (Fabian and Dunlop 2002). Due to the significance of early transitions for young children it is important that 'parents, educators, policy makers and politicians pay close attention to young children's experiences in order to provide well for them' (Fabian and Dunlop 2002: 1).

In this chapter we concentrate on four transition points:

* Foundation Stage to Key Stage 1;
* Key Stage 1 to Key Stage 2;
* Key Stage 2 to Key Stage 3;
* Key Stage 3 to Key Stage 4.

We have used the term 'transitions' rather than making the distinction that is sometimes made between a 'transfer' as a move between two settings (e.g. from primary school to secondary school) and a 'transition' as a move within a setting, such as between year groups or from Key Stage 1 to Key Stage 2. We feel the term 'transition' better conveys the idea that what occurs is a process that starts before the change and finishes afterwards, rather than being a single event. Importantly, it is also a process that will occur irrespective of whether the school intervenes in any mediating role. This chapter is concerned with how schools can mediate the experience of transition in a manner that has regard for and maintains the three relationships that underpin the development of learning behaviour.

All transition points mark a progression, a 'moving on' not just in education, but through life, and it is entirely appropriate that within the new setting there are some differences and new experiences and challenges. Referring to the transition from

Relationship with self
Does the child have the dispositions and
attitudes that are likely to contribute to
better coping with the transition?
What are their feelings about the transition
and their perceptions of their own ability to
cope with change?

**Learning
behaviour**

Relationship with others
What skills does the child currently have
and what additional skills will be
necessary to form new relationships with
staff and peers and deal with increased
expectations of abilities to learn and
socialise in group settings?

Relationship with the curriculum
What skills does the child currently
have and what additional skills will be
necessary to deal with the differences in
the curriculum, teaching methods and
increased expectations of personal
organisation of learning?

Figure 13.1 The three Behaviour for Learning relationships at transition.

primary to secondary school, Galton *et al.* (2003) speak of the importance of *discontinuities* as well as continuities, challenging the dominant assumption that it is the *continuities* that need to be strengthened.

Change and difference are not inherently bad and are important elements of transition. The challenge for schools is to manage the process of change in a way that recognises that there is a need to attend to each pupil's relationship with self, with the curriculum and with others. Planning to support transition, at any age, involves thinking about the three key elements shown in Figure 13.1.

Continuity and progression in learning behaviour

Pupils start school and change schools according to age rather than developmental readiness. There is a practical logic to this as it would be difficult to predict class sizes, the physical space required to accommodate pupils and the number of required personnel if any other system was operated that allowed variable numbers to transfer. However, the choice of ages for the key transitions of starting primary school and transferring to secondary school is only based on historical assumptions about the right times for transfer for the majority of pupils developmentally.

The result of age-related transition is that there is a broad set of skills and dispositions that it is assumed pupils will have developed by each transition point. A major threat to successful transition is the adoption of age-related expectations of the learning behaviours that pupils bring with them. The issue of what teachers expect from pupils at particular ages has been explored by Bate and Moss (1997). An important finding was that in each Key Stage the teacher expected certain behaviours to have been taught the previous year, with secondary school teachers expecting the vast majority of behaviours to have been taught prior to the point at which they received the pupil. This research was revealing at a number of levels. It suggested that teachers were not adopting a developmental approach to the acquisition of these behavioural skills and instead connected them almost entirely with chronological age. In addition, the higher up the age-range the pupil moved the less the teachers saw it as their role to teach behavioural skills. It is also likely that teachers' attributions reflect these beliefs. Secondary school teachers may be more likely to attribute the misbehaviour to the pupil knowing how to behave but choosing not to, whereas teachers of younger pupils may be more likely to attribute the misbehaviour to the pupil not yet having acquired the necessary skills to behave. The former attribution inevitably leads to a system of behavioural consequences whereas the latter leads to a teaching response.

'Continuity' and 'progression' are terms frequently used in relation to transition (e.g. DfES 2004i). By 'progression' we mean that pupils' learning builds sequentially on what has been learned previously and shows an upward gradient in demand as they move from year to year (DfES 2004i). By 'continuity' we mean there are planned links and similarities to ensure that there are no unnecessary jumps and gaps or repetition in pupils' learning (DfES 2004i).

It is doubtful whether policy makers, schools or teachers view continuity and progression in the same way in relation to behaviour. In relation to learning, there is a strong sense of needing to look at what the pupil can do already and gradually increase that demand, ensuring that there are no sudden jumps in the expectations we have of them. We rarely adopt the same approach in relation to behavioural, emotional and social development. The transition from the Early Years Foundation Stage to Year 1 is a case in point. As the next section of this chapter illustrates, the Foundation Stage has some unique characteristics that distinguish it from other phases of education. The Foundation Stage curriculum is based on seven areas of learning and development that are considered 'important and inter-connected' (DfE 2017g: 7). Examining the language used in guidance (DfE 2017g) to describe the seven areas of learning and development, the Early Learning goals and the requirements for educational programmes reveals quite an overt focus on both the development of learning behaviour and the three Behaviour for Learning relationships. There is also explicit recognition that 'children develop and learn in different ways … and at different rates' (DfE 2017g: 6) based on the principle that 'every child is a unique child' (DfE 2017g: 6).

Having experienced the Foundation Stage curriculum, pupils then move on to the National Curriculum which is underpinned by a very different subject-based structure that places a higher value on subject-specific knowledge, skills and understanding. This neglects the obvious fact that the learning behaviours that are rightfully such a dominant focus within Foundation Stage teaching also need to be built on and developed as the pupil moves through their school career. The tendency may be to rely on these learning behaviours developing through incidental learning. The Behaviour for Learning approach seeks to encourage a more overt focus upon these skills and dispositions at all Key Stages.

Although Bate and Moss (1997) used an examination of the behaviours expected at certain ages to highlight a potential source of difficulty, an honest appraisal of the *learning* behaviours we expect at certain Key Stages is a valuable activity to undertake. This involves thinking carefully about the sorts of skills and dispositions necessary within the new learning environment, whether this is an early years setting or a secondary school, that the pupil is about to join. As we have already indicated, however, transition is a process that begins before the change, and so there is also a need for the pupil's current setting to consider the learning behaviours required by the receiving environment. It is not unusual to talk about continuity and progression with regard to the curriculum, and we are simply suggesting that the same consideration can be applied to the development of learning behaviour.

The Early Years Foundation Stage: An apprenticeship to the National Curriculum?

The Early Years Foundation Stage can be viewed as an apprenticeship that introduces the skills involved in learning in group settings. Even the regulations regarding staff ratios suggest this. At age two there must be at least one member of staff for every four children. By age three and over the requirement changes to one member of staff for every eight or 13 children, depending on the qualification of the staff member (DfE 2017g). In a Reception class in a maintained school or academy the ratio can be one teacher for 30 pupils (DfE 2017g). There is a sense in which the pupil is moving from forming a one-to-one reciprocal relationship with a parent or primary care giver at about 18–24 months (Berk 2003) to an expectation that they will function effectively socially, emotionally and academically within a class of 30 by, in some cases, as young as 48 months. Many schools, of course, recognise that there is a need to provide additional adult support in their Reception classes that reduces this ratio significantly. It is generally considered good practice in the Reception class to continue the approach used in early years settings of having a named key person for a smaller number of children. At some point in the day the child would be likely to be in a group with their key person. This approach contributes to a gentler transition from the high levels of adult support experienced in the early years setting to the 1:30 ratio that is likely to characterise the rest of their school-based education.

Many pupils cope with the Foundation Stage environment very well. Part of the reason may be the characteristics that it *does not* share with subsequent phases of education. These differences are highlighted in Table 13.1.

Without the restrictions of items in the second column of Table 13.1, it may be that Foundation Stage pupils (and their teachers) are more able to focus on developing their relationships with others. This is no small challenge. Accepted good practice is to *not* set limits on the number of pupils allowed on a particular activity, and consequently pupils need to be able to share equipment, negotiate and settle disagreements, all with the minimum of adult intervention. Some larger schools operate paired Foundation Stage classes with two teachers and two or more TAs and allow a free-flow of pupils both between the two classrooms and to the outdoor learning environment. Potentially, a pupil experiencing this arrangement has to interact and form relationships with up to 59 other children. This is in contrast to subsequent stages of their school career when they may only have to interact and form relationships with the pupils sitting either side of them for much of the day.

It is not just socially where Reception-aged pupils are challenged. Once taught where equipment is, what it is used for, how to use it and how to put it away, pupils

Table 13.1 Differences between the Foundation Stage and the rest of compulsory schooling

Foundation stage	Increasingly as the child progresses through the remainder of compulsory schooling
A significant amount of the pupil's time is spent engaged in child-initiated learning.	Most learning is teacher initiated and teacher directed.
Although there is a routine and structure to the day, time spent on many activities within this is not prescribed.	A timetable defines when activities are undertaken.
There is minimal restriction on movement between activities, including those in the outdoor learning environment.	Movement is restricted.
Assessment is ongoing, viewed as an integral part of the learning and development process (DfE 2017g). The Early Years practitioner observes children 'to understand their level of achievement, interests and learning styles, and to then shape learning experiences for each child reflecting those observations' (DfE 2017g: 13).	Assessment is an 'event' occurring at certain times, ranging from daily marking of work to national testing at set times.
The pupil moves between the areas of learning reflected in the classroom and outdoor learning environment.	The pupil may sit at a desk for the duration of a lesson.
Teacher-directed tasks are frequently supported by an adult in a small group.	Mainly pupils with SEN or those experiencing other barriers to learning receive this level of adult support.
There is the opportunity in the majority of schools for the parent/carer to talk to the teacher or a TA on a daily basis, allowing the teacher to discover any factors that may affect the child's learning and emotional wellbeing during the day.	Contact reduces as child moves through the age range.
The curriculum is thematic.	The curriculum is increasingly subject based.
Emphasis is placed on a range of skills.	Emphasis is increasingly placed on listening and written recording.

are expected to be able to access it independently. They need to learn how to make a choice between activities. This may be supported to a degree by, for example, each pupil, after teacher-led group discussion, putting a peg on their chosen starting activity. The peg is a means of focusing the pupil's thoughts at the start of the session; beyond this they would make the choice of when to move on from the activity and which activity to do next.

The Early Years Foundation Stage is therefore both a demanding and a comprehensive apprenticeship for National Curriculum learning. It is also potentially a frustrating one: having served this apprenticeship, these skills are never likely to be visited so explicitly again in most pupils' school careers. The main exception is some pupils with SEN who may experience specific programmes that target some of these skills. Not only might these skills not be visited so explicitly again, in some cases they may not even be used. Sanders *et al.* (2005) found that skills of independent learning, acquired during the Foundation Stage, were not always being capitalised upon in Year 1.

Strengthening the reception to Year 1 transition

Although the Foundation Stage to Key Stage 1 transition takes place within the same school, in terms of the extent of change in curriculum and pedagogy experienced, it is on a par with the transition from Key Stage 2 to Key Stage 3. There are a number of ways we can ease the transition:

- Year 1 teachers should use the Foundation Stage profile as a means of formative assessment. If pupils have completed the Early Learning Goals they should be working on the National Curriculum. However, there will potentially be a significant number of pupils, certainly during the first term, who should be provided with the opportunity to continue following the Early Learning Goals.
- The Year 1 teacher should *gradually* extend the length of time spent in whole-class teaching and teacher-directed tasks. There should still be time available for child-initiated learning.
- Retaining some of the physical aspects/arrangements of the Foundation Stage in Year 1 can help with transition. For example, it may be possible to have a library, role-play, art and writing area and access to the outdoor learning environment.
- Teachers should recognise that although the required staffing ratio at Foundation Stage is 1:30, in reality this will not have been the experience of many pupils. They will have been used to being supported in the majority of teacher-directed tasks by an adult. In Year 1 it may be possible to retain a similar ratio initially, gradually reducing the level of adult support over time. Where this is not possible, it will be important for the teacher to be aware that pupils have been used to working with this level of support and may find certain tasks daunting.
- Teachers need to recognise that there will be some pupils who are particularly vulnerable at this transition. These include those with SEN, pupils for whom English is an additional language, summer born pupils and those who have not spent a full year in the Reception class (i.e. 'late' transfers from a pre-school provider).
- If pupils have been used to coming into the Reception classroom with their parents, it is beneficial to maintain this routine at the start of Year 1 rather than moving straight to lining up in the playground or whatever routine is operated in the rest of the school.
- Ensure pupils are explicitly taught the routines for hanging up bags and coats, storing lunchboxes and going to the toilet. As far as possible, try to keep these the same or similar to arrangements at Foundation Stage, at least initially.
- If lunchtime and break times are different to those experienced in the Reception class consider what support will be necessary. In some schools, for example, Reception pupils will have had separate lunchtimes to the rest of the school or may have had their break times in the outdoor learning environment rather than in the main playground.
- Continue to use similar rules and routines for things like asking for help or using equipment. Retain familiar features from the Reception classroom such as visual timetables.

- Where staffing and finances allow it, consider the possible advantages of a TA from the Reception class moving up with the pupils for the first term of Year 1 – or even the whole year. In some schools it may be possible for the Reception teacher to move up to Year 1 with their class and the Year 1 teacher to move down to take the new Reception class. As well as continuity for the pupils in terms of their relationship with the teacher, this also aids curricular continuity and progression.
- Provide opportunities to visit the Year 1 classroom for 'taster' visits. However, think carefully about *what* the pupils will 'taste'. The main purpose is to build confidence by establishing some familiarity with the new teacher and the new environment; it is therefore advisable to organise activities that are not significantly different from those that pupils will be familiar with from the Foundation Stage. To place the pupils in the context of, for example, a structured English or Maths lesson is likely to dent confidence by stressing the enormity of the change.
- In the last term of the Foundation Stage the Reception teacher can seek to gradually extend the time the pupils spend on particular teacher-directed activities. We would stress, however, that this should be based on pupils' readiness and part of the natural progression through the Reception class that sees pupils increasingly able to sustain attention on an activity for a longer period of time. It should not be driven by the organisational imperative of preparing pupils to sit for extended periods by Year 1.

Reflective Exercise 13.1

To what extent do you think a Reception teacher should seek to make the summer term of Year R more like Year 1 by introducing elements of the Year 1 curriculum and increasing the amount of teacher-directed activity?

Unlike other transitions that we cover later, we have not emphasised the preparatory work that can be done by the Foundation Stage teacher. There is a good reason for this: the Early Years Foundation Stage in its entirety *is* the preparation for Year 1. Our view is that the priority is making the start of Year 1 more like the Foundation Stage. This view is supported by a number of recommendations in a research report by Sanders *et al.* (2005) pointing to the need to give attention to changes in Year 1. They recommended that:

- School managers should allocate resources to enable children in Year 1 to experience some play-based activities that give access to opportunities such as sand and water, role-play, construction and outdoor learning.
- Policy-makers should provide advice to teachers on how to continue elements of the Foundation Stage curriculum and pedagogical approach into Year 1.
- The amount of time children in Year 1 spend sitting still and listening to the teacher should be reduced. Year 1 teachers should be encouraged to increase opportunities for active, independent learning and learning through play.
- Guidance is needed to help reduce the emphasis given to children recording their work in writing at the beginning of Year 1.

(Sanders *et al.* 2005: v–vi)

Sanders *et al.* (2005) found that staff and parents/carers in their study were largely content with the quality of pupils' experiences of the Foundation Stage. The study also found that the pupils were largely content. The main difficulties were associated with the introduction of a more formal, subject-based and teacher-directed approach, with less time for child-initiated activities, choice and play in Year 1.

The transition from Key Stage 1 to Key Stage 2

The transition from Key Stage 1 to Key Stage 2 is likely to be less of an issue in primary schools where the pupil remains in the same school even though they are moving up a Key Stage. Nevertheless, it is important not to underestimate the possibility that 'becoming a junior' will be a daunting prospect in some pupils' minds even though they are not changing school. The following strategies will help to support the transition:

- Arrange visits to the Year 3 class.
- Arrange visits from the Year 3 teacher to the Year 2 class.
- Ensure the pupil knows the names of the class teacher and TAs who work in the receiving class.
- Plan circle time sessions exploring what pupils are looking forward to or worrying about. This can be depersonalised by using puppets and stories. Many pupils will find it easier to articulate the worries the puppet may have about the transfer than to talk about their own concerns.
- Practise skills such as asking for help and introducing yourself to someone you do not know through role-play, puppets and stories. Many pupils will feel more comfortable advising a puppet on strategies because it depersonalises the situation.
- Ensure transferring pupils know practical arrangements, such as the location of the toilets and their class's cloakroom, where to store lunchboxes and any changes to the procedures for entry to the school, such as a different place to line up or a different door to use. Make sure pupils know these arrangements *before* the summer holiday and are reminded on the first day of term in September. Such practical details can assume major significance for many young pupils.

The Key Stage 1 to Key Stage 2 transition takes on greater significance where it is from an infant to junior school. In this situation the pupil will be leaving familiar surroundings, familiar staff and on some occasions leaving friendship groups if the infant school feeds several junior schools. Because junior schools do not have infants on site, sometimes the ethos can feel very different to the pupil. Many of the strategies given for transition within the same school are applicable. In addition, the following strategies are advisable for transitions to a separate junior school:

- Arrange visits to the receiving school.
- Arrange visits by junior school staff, including the head teacher, to the infant school.
- During any visits by junior staff to the infant school, or infant children to the junior school, the emphasis should always be on the elements that will be the same and the elements that will be exciting and different. Going through a long list of rules or telling pupils that they will have to be a lot more grown up or that they will have to work a lot harder is unhelpful.

- Identify a 'buddy' at the receiving school.
- Plan farewell activities that celebrate past school experiences. This needs to be handled carefully so that it is upbeat, balancing 'What I will miss' and memories with plenty of 'What I am looking forward to'.

The Key Stage 1 to Key Stage 2 transition has historically (e.g. Ofsted 1999) been associated with dips in pupil performance in Year 3. A variety of reasons have been suggested for this. In a small-scale study Doddington *et al.* (1999) found that some teachers attributed the dip to the side effects of the Key Stage 1 tests in Year 2, including the intensive teaching of certain limited areas of the curriculum. One effect of this 'hot-housing' may have been a certain amount of inflated achievement and artificially heightened expectation. After the summer break pupils then dropped back to their 'natural' levels of achievement. Other teachers highlighted social reasons for the dip, suggesting that it reflected a phase of social curiosity and a preoccupation with friendships that could divert interest from classroom learning (Doddington *et al.* 1999). In Behaviour for Learning terms this reflects relationship with others taking priority for the pupil over relationship with the curriculum.

Doddington *et al.* (2001) pointed to a wider range of factors that could explain the Year 3 dip, including:

- different and heightened expectations, especially in relation to working more independently;
- increased curricular demands leading to feelings of pressure;
- new and unfamiliar ways of working;
- a fall-off in parental involvement;
- the organisation of staffing which may sometimes result in 'weaker' or less experienced teachers being given the Year 3 groups;
- the limited nature of Year 2/Year 3 'liaison' in the majority of schools, which could lead to problems of under-performance being overlooked as children are given time to adjust to their new setting.

The transition from Key Stage 2 to Key Stage 3

For many pupils the Key Stage 2 to Key Stage 3 transition will represent their first change of school since the age of four. The exceptions are those who have attended separate infant and junior schools. Even these pupils will have last changed school at a very different stage in their lives developmentally. The transition to secondary school not only represents a major change for the pupil in the terms of their educational environment, it also coincides with a major change in physical, mental and emotional terms as they move into adolescence. As we noted in Chapter 7, it has been suggested that changes occur in the adolescent brain that lead to heightened sensitivity to peer and other personal relationships (Blakemore 2008). Consequently, acceptance becomes fundamental to the experience of social relationships and self-worth (Somerville 2013).

The pupil moving from primary to secondary education encounters change in a number of different areas. Table 13.2 identifies a number of these.

In addition to these more overt differences there may be more subtle changes such as teachers' heightened expectations of pupils' capacity to collaborate in group work, sustain attention on particular tasks and generally cope with life.

Table 13.2 Differences between primary and secondary school

Primary school	Secondary school
Environment	
Typically smaller.	Typically larger.
Few specialist areas (e.g. ICT suite, hall for PE).	Numerous specialist areas (e.g. gym, dance studio, labs, art room, etc.).
Staff	
Typically one class teacher who teaches the majority of subjects.	Several subject teachers, as well as form tutor.
Limited number of adult roles.	Different adult roles and new terminology (e.g. 'form tutor', 'head of year', 'head of department', 'assistant head').
Most staff, including head, are likely to know students by name.	Staff not involved directly with the student are unlikely by to know them by name.
Personal organisation	
Equipment needed for most lessons is provided and kept in the room.	Students are expected to bring their own equipment and to remember which day they need to bring it. They are also expected to carry it around with them all day.
Timetable shows sequence of day; failure to understand or use it is of little consequence.	Timetable shows sequence and location. Student needs to use it to know where they should be, which lesson it is and what equipment is required.
Other pupils	
Year 6 are the oldest.	Year 7 are the youngest in the school.
All students in the school are children.	Population extends from children to young adults.
Many students in other year groups known, at least by sight.	Few students in other year groups known.
Pupil movement	
Lessons take place mainly in one room.	Students move to different rooms for different lessons.
Students usually move as a group to a different location accompanied by an adult.	Students move around the site independently, taking responsibility for arriving at the right time in the right place.
School is often in close walking distance; many pupils taken to school by an adult.	Students often have further to travel to get to school. They will often need to travel to school independently, using public transport.
Curriculum	
Subject-based but divisions less evident, some subjects incorporated within topic work.	Subject-based, emphasised by movement to different rooms and teaching by different teachers.
Homework set by one teacher, often on an occasional, informal basis.	Homework set by different teachers on a regular, more formal basis.

Source: Ellis 2010: 209.

When planning activities to support pupils in coping with these changes, the Behaviour for Learning conceptual framework helps us to keep in mind a clear purpose. This is illustrated by Table 13.3, which demonstrates how even activities undertaken for the purely practical purpose of familiarity with a new environment also link to the three Behaviour for Learning relationships.

A noticeable feature in Table 13.3 is the frequency with which the link is with relationship with self. Even where the primary purpose is linked to one of the other two relationships a secondary benefit is frequently in the area of relationship with self, due to increased confidence brought about by the experience. This highlights the importance of this particular relationship.

Is the pupil's relationship with self the most important relationship in transitions?

Jindal-Snape and Miller (2008) report that research on the primary to secondary school transition has found the primary transition to be a period of anxiety for many pupils, with a substantial decline in self-esteem, academic motivation and achievement. Jindal-Snape and Miller (2008) argue that both self-esteem and resilience are important factors in determining a pupil's experience of, and response to, the process of transition. A pupil's resilience is influenced by a range of factors (both within the individual and in their immediate environment). Their resilience will affect how well they cope with a period of adversity or threat. The primary–secondary transition is a period where the pupil is likely to encounter a range of challenges to their self-worth and competence (Jindal-Snape and Miller 2008). Self-worth and competence are the two components of the duality model of self-esteem discussed in Chapter 6. This model is based on the view that 'an individual's self-esteem is dependent upon two types of judgement: the extent to which one feels worthy of respect from others, and competent to face the challenges which lie ahead' (Jindal-Snape and Miller 2008: 218).

Resilience and self-esteem are important components of an individual's relationship with self – and it is this relationship that is under most threat during transitions and the one that we should strive to protect and maintain. The major transitions (e.g. primary to secondary school), involve moving pupils between settings that will lead them to encounter new forms of curriculum and pedagogy and new peers and adults. The element that stays with the pupil throughout the change is their relationship with self. It is the quality of this relationship that will play a key role in determining the relationship the pupil forms with others and with the curriculum in the new environment.

With any transition there is a strong emotional component. Cossavella and Hobbs (2002) outline a number of stages involved in transition. Their work is primarily related to the transition to secondary school, although the stages may be relevant to any transition point. Table 13.4 draws on and extends their framework.

It is important to recognise that not all pupils will respond to change in the same way as indicated in Table 13.4. There are a number of influencing factors, including:

- Existing relationships with adults and peers will affect how attached the pupil is to the current setting. Quite simply, it may be easier to leave people and places that you do not have a strong attachment to.

Table 13.3 Activities to support primary to secondary transition

Category	Activity	Behaviour for Learning relationship
Skills	Learning how to introduce yourself to an unknown pupil or member of staff.	**Relationship with others** Relationship with self
	Learning how to ask for help if lost or unsure of timetable.	**Relationship with self** Relationship with others
	Teaching pupils how to read timetable.	**Relationship with self**
	Targeting study skills, improving personal organisation.	**Relationship with the curriculum** Relationship with self
Familiarity	Providing 'taster' days where students visit new environment and guided tours.	**Relationship with self** Relationship with others
	Providing in advance welcome packs and opportunities to meet key personnel, Q&A session with current Year 7, etc.	**Relationship with self** Relationship with others
	Providing a map of the new school and teaching pupils how to use it.	**Relationship with self**
Curriculum and pedagogy	Teachers from current and future settings identify differences and similarities in learning and teaching styles.	**Relationship with the curriculum**
	Teacher passes on information regarding curriculum coverage and pupil achievement.	**Relationship with the curriculum**
	Introduce a more subject-based curriculum part way through Year 6.	**Relationship with the curriculum** Relationship with self
	Use subject specialists for some subjects in Year 6.	**Relationship with the curriculum** Relationship with self
	Reduce the number of teachers Year 7 pupils encounter, even if this means some lessons are not taught by subject specialists.	**Relationship with others** Relationship with self
Pastoral	Buddy/mentoring schemes.	**Relationship with others** Relationship with self
	Visits by Year 7 pupils to talk to the transferring Year 6 pupils. This is often most beneficial when it is Year 7 pupils who attended the primary school they visit.	**Relationship with self** Relationship with others
	Year 7 pupils start back in September a few days before the other year groups return.	**Relationship with self** Relationship with others
	Vertical tutor groups made up of pupils from Years 7–11.	**Relationship with others** Relationship with self

Note
Main purpose indicated in bold.

Table 13.4 Stages involved in transition

Stage and description	Children might feel	Outward signs that pupils may exhibit
Numbness The first phase is largely characterised by a degree of shock. It is the first recognition that the transition has started.	Overwhelmed. Unsure of what is happening. 'I don't know what to do.' Confused.	Expression of initial realisation – 'I can't believe it's my last year ...'. Recognition of timescales – 'This time next year I'll be ...' or, for a young child, 'How many "sleeps" until ...?'.
Minimisation/denial This stage is characterised by attempts to minimise the change by trivialising it and in some cases display bravado.	'It's nothing.' 'Everything can't change.' 'I'll carry on as if nothing is happening.'	Dismissive of the significance of the change. Reluctance to engage in activities related to the transition or to take these seriously. Dismisses discussion of the change by peers or teachers as 'going on about it'. Feigning enthusiasm for the change – 'Secondary school's going to be so great'.
Anxiety At this stage the realities of the change begin to become apparent. The pupil becomes more aware of the realities involved. This leads to many 'What if ...?' questions.	'What's going to happen?' 'Everything is going to be different.' 'How can I cope?' 'I'm not going to fit in.' 'Who will I know?'	Concern with detail – 'What if I miss the bus?', 'How will I find my way around?'. Concern with diminishing timescale – counting down the days. Expressions of self-doubt – 'I'll never be able to ...'. Sharing and believing myths about the unpleasant experiences they will face (Maines and Robinson 1988).
Sadness At this stage there is acceptance that the change is going to happen. In some cases this may be after the change, in the form of realisation that change has happened and there is no going back.	'I'm going to miss this place.' 'I'm going to miss these people (peers and staff).' 'I'm OK today, I wasn't yesterday.' 'Am I going to make any friends?'	'Clinginess', particularly in younger children. Expression of sadness – 'I'll miss this school ...' and promise to return to visit. Changeable moods. Changes in social groupings, including the end of some long-term friendships, as pupils align themselves with others moving to the same school.

Detachment

At this point the pupil is beginning to let go. The behaviour that sometimes occurs is difficult for staff in the current setting as it can feel like rejection after what has often been a long relationship.

'There's nothing for me here.'
'There's no point in making the effort.'
'I don't fit in here any more.'
'I've outgrown this school.'

Engaging in behaviour that alienates them from peers or teachers; damaging relationships so that the separation brought about by the change is less painful.

Denigrating current environment – 'I didn't like this school much anyway …'.

Generally appearing less motivated – conveying a recognition that they are in the last throes of this phase of their education.

Becoming withdrawn, not joining in activities that previously would have appealed.

Reorganisation

At this stage there is acceptance and, in many cases, some optimism. The change has transformed from being a threat to an opportunity, albeit one that still includes some challenging aspects.

'Some things will be the same, but many things will be different. These different things may not be so bad.'
'I'm going to learn new things and meet new friends.'
'It's time for a change.'

Talking more openly and positively about the new environment – 'In my new school …'.

Concerns and queries are expressed as rational requests for a specific piece of guidance.

Adaptation

At this stage the pupil begins to see themselves as a member of the new school.

'This isn't so bad, I can cope.'
'I'm in Mrs X's class.'
'It feels like I've been here ages.'
'I can find my way around.'
'I'm not alone here – others are new too.'

Clear friendship groups develop. Friendships begin to extend beyond those who transferred from the same primary school.

Pupil joins in some voluntary activities (e.g. clubs).

Pupil personalises (not always within accepted boundaries) uniform and equipment.

Pupil may begin to push boundaries with staff.

There may be conflict with other pupils as groupings and 'pecking orders' emerge.

Source: based on Cossavella and Hobbs 2002 and Hopson et al. 1992.

- Previous positive experience of a transition may help the pupil to recognise that even if the change appears daunting they have coped before. We should remember that younger pupils have fewer experiences of transition to draw upon.
- Sufficient social skills and communication skills can enable pupils to interact effectively with peers and adults in order to form relationships and to deal with any problems.
- An optimistic disposition can help the pupil to view setbacks and adversity as temporary and changeable.
- In the case of a child starting pre-school, prior experience of time away from their parent/carer will be important.
- Sufficient self-efficacy can allow the pupil to recognise that their actions can determine the nature of their experience. In other words, recognising that they are active participants in change rather than passive recipients.
- Sufficient self-awareness can help the pupil to recognise their own feelings associated with transition.
- The way in which the impending change is talked about by others who are significant in the pupil's life, including teachers, parents, siblings, other relatives and peers, will be influential.

Some of these points can be considered to be protective factors contributing to resilience in relation to transition. Therefore, the need is not just to think in terms of support as the transition becomes imminent, but to consider how, throughout the pupil's time in their current setting, they are being equipped with the skills and dispositions to deal with change and difficulty. We would suggest that, for example, the final term of Year 6 is far too late to introduce a self-esteem programme as part of a six session cross-phase project. Last-ditch rescue bids for self-esteem such as this will rarely be successful. It would be more beneficial at this late stage to focus on specific skills, such as rehearsing how to introduce yourself to someone you have not met before or how to ask for help when you are lost, learning how to read a timetable and about some of the different terminology used in a secondary school. Such activities may at least develop some confidence.

The other important consideration with regard to the sequence of stages outlined in Table 13.4, is that not all pupils will start on this sequence at the same time. Age and development will be factors in determining how far ahead the pupil looks, but equally there are some pupils who, as part of their personality, do tend to just focus on the here-and-now rather than getting anxious about future events.

For some pupils their first day in Year 6 will herald the start of the numbness stage as they recognise that they will never again be starting a new class in this school. For others it might be after the school Christmas party as they recognise that this joyful experience, shared with friends, will not be repeated again. For others it might be when their parents are officially notified of the school they will attend. The key point is that there is no fixed time – the calendar is no guide as to the stage the pupil will be at.

While we have highlighted the importance of relationship with self it is necessary to remember that all three Behaviour for Learning relationships are linked and exert influence on one another.

Are we pathologising transition?

Transition involves change and this may cause a degree of anxiety for all pupils. This is entirely natural and it is important that schools do not, in their well-intentioned attempts to support pupils, pathologise transition and the feelings associated with it. The ideas in Table 13.4 are useful in thinking about how pupils may experience transition and it provides some hypotheses about why pupils may display particular behaviours. However, it should not lead us to believe that all pupils will have problems. We should, for example, be open to the possibility that when, as described in Reflective Exercise 13.2, a pupil talks enthusiastically about aspects of the new school, this is because this is exactly how they feel about it. It is not necessarily a symptom of denial or minimisation.

Reflective Exercise 13.2

Think about some of the Year 6 behaviours you have observed. Which of the phases in Table 13.4 do they relate to? Examples of common behaviours include:

- clinginess and reverting to younger behaviours;
- behaving in an uncharacteristic 'too big for their boots' manner;
- refusing to engage with the change process;
- withdrawal;
- not bothering with work;
- being fascinated by rumours and myths about the new school;
- talking enthusiastically about aspects of the new school.

(based on DfES 2005f: 12)

Ecclestone and Hayes (2009) cite critically an article by Park and Tew (2007) that encourages schools to manage and ease the confused and ambivalent feelings associated with transition by 'eliciting and sharing feelings, encouraging "closure" of relationships that will be ending through activities such as exploring scenario cards, drawing storyboards, doing role-plays and asking children to write responses from agony aunts or problem pages' (Ecclestone and Hayes 2009: 35).

Such a list includes some useful strategies and activities for supporting transition, including a number that are similar to those suggested in this chapter. However, caution needs to be exercised when planning transition work as transition should not be constructed as a problem. This can be the result if schools place too much emphasis on activities that explore worries and concerns. Balance, of course, is important; we need to create an environment where pupils know that it is acceptable to talk about their natural and understandable worries and feelings about transition without, as we suggested earlier, pathologising it. Such an approach can be beneficial in allowing pupils to recognise they are not alone in experiencing concerns about change and it can positively influence their relationship with self.

The risk, if we get the balance wrong, is that pupils who are not worried come to believe they should be, effectively reconstructing themselves as vulnerable. The additional challenge is that although pupils go through transition as part of a group, they experience it as individuals. Some will therefore need different forms of support. A useful way of thinking about this is to apply the waves model, familiar to many teachers from National Strategy documents (e.g. DfES 2002a, 2005d), to transitions (see Figure 13.2).

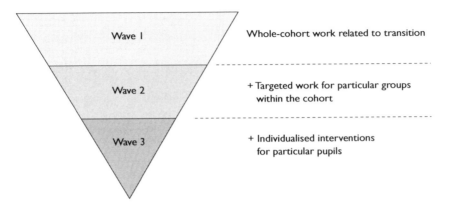

Figure 13.2 A 'waves' approach to transition.
Source: Ellis 2010: 203.

This model recognises that all pupils will benefit from some work to support them as they approach the change of school. Some groups within the class will need additional work and some individuals may need some focused individualised work.

Relationship with the curriculum

By the time most pupils arrive at secondary school they will have formed views of specific curriculum areas and their abilities within these. This can be considered as part of their relationship with the curriculum. As we have indicated, the transition brings its own anxieties for many pupils which can make their relationship with self vulnerable. A poor relationship with a particular curriculum area, especially Maths or English, which the pupil will know are highly valued, can impact on this already vulnerable relationship with self unless carefully handled. Consider Scenario 13.1.

Scenario 13.1

Jodie has learned through her experiences at primary school that numeracy is difficult. She has regularly been in 'catch up' groups during Key Stage 2 which, though bringing some improvements in attainment, have reinforced to her the idea that Maths is neither an enjoyable subject nor one that she is good at.

The Maths teacher at the secondary school who will be teaching Jodie is already starting with a pupil who has a fragile relationship with the curriculum. Table 13.5 demonstrates how this teacher could either help or hinder this situation.

With the type of approach outlined in Column A of Table 13.5 it is not only Jodie's relationship with the curriculum that is supported, and hopefully enhanced, but also her relationship with herself and her relationship with others, in the form of the teacher. With the approach in Column B, the risk is that what was originally an issue regarding relationship with the curriculum transforms into an issue pertaining to relationship with self.

Table 13.5 Approaches that could help or hinder the pupil's relationship with the curriculum

Column A: What would help	Column B: What would hinder
• Starting with familiar concepts, or new concepts that can be quickly understood, to build a sense of confidence and competence.	• Starting with unfamiliar, complex concepts. • Stressing that Maths gets a lot harder now the pupils are at secondary school.
• Making clear the procedure for asking for help and also that asking for help is welcomed.	• Making comments such as: 'If you were listening properly then you would know what to do.'
• Re-explaining new concepts patiently.	• Generally sounding irritated at having to re-explain.
• Using traffic light systems with the whole class for pupils to communicate their level of understanding: green means that the pupil is confident to get on independently, amber means that the pupil is not completely sure but can make a start and red means help is needed to get started.	• Making 'not understanding' a public event – e.g. 'Anyone who doesn't understand put your hand up now'.
• Making it clear to the whole class that learning involves making mistakes.	• Emphasising the importance of getting it right – e.g. 'Hands up who got them all right ... one wrong .... two wrong ....'.
• Marking work constructively.	• Using plenty of red ink.
• Giving the pupil the benefit of the doubt – assume that errors are due to conceptual understanding, not behaviour.	• Making comments that assume mistakes are linked to behavioural failings – e.g. 'Concentrate harder next time' or 'You need to pay more attention'.
• If you need to see the pupils, framing the request in a friendly manner that informs the pupil of the learning-related purpose of the meeting – e.g. 'Come and see me and I'll go over these with you to check you're OK with them'.	• Simply writing 'See me'. The pupil may worry that they are in trouble for not listening or not trying.
• Making it clear how additional help with homework can be sought, through, for example, attendance at a homework club.	• Over-emphasising the consequences of failing to hand in homework.

A complicating factor, however, is that Jodie's existing relationship with self may determine the effect of the teacher who adopts the approach in Column B, as illustrated in Figures 13.3 and 13.4.

This illustrates once again the importance of the pupil's relationship with self. If we can maintain this through any transition the pupil is more likely to be able to cope with difficulties in their relationships with others and in their relationship with the curriculum.

Reflective Exercise 13.3

We have indicated in Figure 13.3 that if Jodie was more resourceful she might recognise a number of *positive* actions to address her relationship with Maths. What are the less acceptable actions that pupils may take in such a situation that demonstrate resourcefulness?

- Copying somebody else's answers.
-
-
-

There are two points to draw out from Reflective Exercise 13.3. First, and as we highlighted in Chapter 3, a feature of a learning behaviour – in this case *resourcefulness* – is that it does not always meet the needs of schools or policy makers and is not always the same as compliant behaviour. Resourcefulness might, for example, take the form of internal truancy or causing sufficient disruption to be sent out of the class in order to avoid the task. Second, behaviour is adaptive. It will frequently be a response to a situation and will fulfil a need for the pupil.

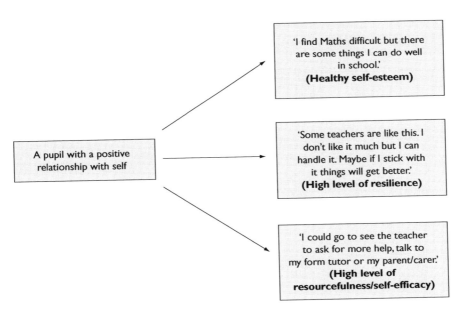

Figure 13.3 Possible interpretation by a pupil with a positive relationship with self.

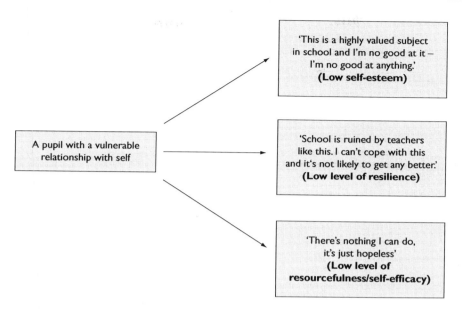

Figure 13.4 Possible interpretation by a pupil with a vulnerable relationship with self.

The transition from Key Stage 3 to Key Stage 4

The move from Key Stage 3 to Key Stage 4 is a significant transition within the pupil's journey towards adulthood. The choosing of subjects at age 14 represents the first real academic and career choices that pupils are required to make. The choices made at this point begin to map out longer-term opportunities, such as further study and future employment. Many pupils will approach this stage of their school career with enthusiasm and excitement, positively identifying subject options that will lead them on a path towards a future in further education, training or employment. There will be some pupils, however, who approach the transition with trepidation, concerned about factors such as their ability to cope with the demands of Years 10 and 11 and possibly also the impending end of the security of compulsory school-based education. Others may already see education as something that has little to offer and so view Years 10 and 11 as something to be endured.

The main support most pupils need at the transition to Key Stage 4 is of a practical nature related to the making of informed choices about future options. Examples of such activities include:

- involving parents/carers in the options process by holding open evenings and careers conventions to provide a forum for questions and concerns;
- producing written material in easily accessible formats to assist with discussions at home that cover Key Stage 4 courses, careers and coursework;
- arranging interviews where plans for future study, or job interests, are discussed in relation to options available now;
- ensuring form tutors and other key staff take an active role in talking through any worries or complications with the pupil before final decisions are made;

- providing taster sessions in subjects;
- providing group talks on career-related topics as part of the school's careers education and guidance programme.

Perhaps more significant in Behaviour for Learning terms, however, is the extent to which the three relationships have been maintained through Key Stage 3. Statistics (DfE 2017h) on school exclusion show that rates rise through Years 7, 8 and 9 before reaching a peak in Year 10. Summary information accompanying these statistics reported:

- Over half of all permanent and fixed period exclusions occur in national curriculum year 9 or above.
- Just over a quarter of all permanent exclusions were for pupils aged 14, and pupils of this age group also had the highest rate of fixed period exclusion, and the highest rate of pupils receiving one or more fixed period exclusion.

(DfE 2017h: 5)

This is a reasonably consistent pattern. Referring to statistics for the 2009–2010 academic year, the Department for Education (DfE (2012c: 21) reported that: 'The most common time for both boys and girls to be excluded is at ages 13 and 14 (equivalent to year groups 9 and 10). In 2009/10 52.8% of all permanent exclusions were of pupils from these age groups.' In data from the 1995–1996 academic year, presented by Parsons (1999) the peak for permanent and fixed term exclusion was in Year 10.

Barber (1994) analysed a database of 30,000 secondary pupils compiled by Keele University and concluded that, while 60 per cent or so of pupils in early secondary schooling were making reasonable progress, the rest split into three groups:

- 20–30 per cent who were bored – *the disappointed*;
- 10–15 per cent who were beginning to truant regularly and behave badly – *the disaffected*;
- 2–5 per cent who had given up school altogether – *the disappeared*.

More recently, research conducted by GL-Assessment (2016) identified the early years of secondary education as the point where there was a marked decline in pupils' positive attitudes towards school, teachers and attendance. The detail informing this general finding is interesting. The report notes that:

The scores from children who feel good about school declines from 94% in Year 3 to 84% in Year 9. Positive attitudes towards teachers fall from 93% to 84%, while positive attitudes to attendance decline from 90% in Year 3 to 82% in Year 9. The biggest declines in all of these factors occur after Year 7 not before.

(GL–Assessment 2016: 4)

The picture that emerges is of Key Stage 3 as a phase in schooling where there are 'casualties'. The vulnerability can begin in Year 8 as it often has none of the unique features that characterise either Year 7 or Year 9. Early Year 7 is a new and exciting experience for the majority of pupils. They are treated differently than in primary school and given more opportunities to take greater responsibility for their own learning (DfES 2004i). They may also be afforded more independence by both school and their parents than they have had before. By the start of Year 8 the excitement of starting secondary school may have diminished for some pupils and their relationship with the curriculum begins to suffer as they see Year 8 as 'just more of the same' (DfES 2004i: 2). This point is illustrated by two comments from pupils about Year 8 reported by Galton *et al.* (2003), from earlier work by Rudduck *et al.* (1996, 1998):

> You think, 'Oh god! I've got this today!' and so on. It gets really boring and you don't feel excited any more coming to school.
>
> (Rudduck *et al.* 1996)

> Year 7 you have just moved from a different school and in Year 8 you have already been there and you have nothing important to think about.
>
> (Rudduck *et al.* 1998, cited in Galton *et al.* 2003: 93)

For many pupils, Year 9 remedies this temporary lapse through its end of Key Stage status. It is the time when they begin to think about Key Stage 4 and the specific opportunities available to them through their subject choices and how these will impact on future life decisions (DfES 2004i). This can provide a 'pick-me-up' towards the end of Year 9 (Doddington *et al.* 1999) that rekindles the relationship with the curriculum and schooling generally.

For other pupils who experience a deterioration in their relationship with the curriculum, it is not a temporary lapse. Typically, these are pupils for whom this does not remain a relationship with the curriculum issue but begins to impinge on their relationship with self and relationship with others. If these pupils misbehave as an avoidance strategy or to relieve the perceived 'sameness' of the Year 8 curriculum, they may find their relationship with others is increasingly based on the behaviour they exhibit.

A number of pupils' responses in Galton *et al.*'s (2003) work illustrate the problem when this occurs:

> I think trouble with me were when I come to school I messed about from day one so people got me as a mess-abouter from day one so like if I didn't mess about, 'Oh, you're boring'. You know what I mean? (Year 11 girl).
>
> (Galton *et al.* 2003: 86)

> If you fall into a bad group of friends then ... I know one group; their kind of mission is not to do well, to mess around, to get told off.... One of them is extremely clever and always does well but.... It's part of her group to act like that (Year 10 girl).
>
> (Galton *et al.* 2003: 87)

> You mess around ... you get a reputation for yourself as a trouble-causer and you can't lose it – it's like there (Year 11 boy).
>
> (Galton *et al.* 2003: 86)

> Me personally I've brought a reputation upon myself. I'm known to be the class clown and that and it's got me in a lot of trouble. And so I've decided to change and it's just really hard to, like show the teachers that 'cos ... and when, like, I went on report, and I got, like, A1, A1, best, top marks. But there's been some

lessons where it's slipped and they're (saying) like, 'Oh, he's still the same.' I can understand how they feel about that (Year 10 boy).

(Galton *et al.* 2003: 86)

The first three quotes illustrate how by Years 10 and 11 the pupil's relationship with their peers is based on the behaviour they exhibit. The fourth quote is notable in demonstrating that, from this pupil's perspective, his relationship with his teachers is also determined by past behaviour.

Typically, the individual pupil will not be the only one exhibiting these behaviours and group norms may develop which further complicate their relationship with others. Galton *et al.* (2003) reported pupils finding it difficult to escape the norms of their anti-work peer group.

Implicit in each quote is also the impact on the individual's relationship with self. The notion of a 'reputation' involves a relationship with others in the sense that it is what others think of us, but there is also a relationship with self dimension if it becomes part of what we think of ourselves. The fourth quote is interesting because the pupil seems to be able to view his reputation as something separate to him. He recognises that he is capable of behaving in a manner that is different to his reputation. It would be reasonable to assume from this that his relationship with self is sound; he recognises his reputation is not *him*. We could speculate that because of the nature of this pupil's relationship with self, change may be more achievable. For many pupils however, their relationship with others becomes part of their self-image and impinges on their relationship with self. Galton *et al.* (2003) reported pupils wanting to change from 'dosser' or 'shirker' to 'worker' but not knowing how to do so. The labelling terminology used by these pupils reflects that the behaviour has become a part of their identity.

The message therefore is that Key Stage 3 'casualties' need to be minimised as anti-work identities, once established, are difficult to change. It is likely to be more productive to intervene in the early stages than to try to change pupils' identities as learners at Year 10 (Galton *et al.* 2003). Table 13.6 sets out a range of strategies suggested by the Department for Education and Skills (DfES 2004i) that contribute to the maintenance of a positive relationship with the curriculum and schooling. Although the table contains a number of specific terms related to the Key Stage 3 National Strategy that are no longer relevant, the strategies remain useful.

Conclusion

Although work to support transition needs to focus on the social, emotional and cognitive aspects, it is the nature of the individual pupil's relationship with self that is likely to be the key determinant in how successfully they make the transition. It will influence how they respond when, for example, they encounter new forms of curriculum and pedagogy and new peers and adults.

Transition can be viewed as a 'challenge of living' (Mruk 1999). Jindal–Snape and Miller (2008: 227) suggest that challenges of living are 'situations where individuals experience a series of significant events, find themselves in different and unfamiliar situations, and have to cope with new and sometimes difficult experiences'. As we remarked previously, we do not seek to pathologise transition. It is one of many challenges of living that people encounter in their lives and, retrospectively, it is unlikely to rank among the most significant. Nevertheless, it needs to be recognised that at

Table 13.6 Maintaining a positive relationship with the curriculum

Effective schools ...	Examples of how this can be achieved
regularly evaluate progress;	Develop whole-school policies on assessment that take account of transition. Ensure that all teaching staff are familiar with the prior attainment of their pupils and use this information in planning. Have systems for tracking pupils' progress in all subjects and ensure that outcomes of assessment are used to inform planning. Use diagnostic assessment at the start of new work.
make each year special;	Plan induction programmes for each new year. Make explicit, in schemes of work and to the pupils themselves, what is special about learning in each year.
recognise the increasing maturity of pupils;	Have reward systems that reflect increasing maturity. Provide opportunities for pupils to take additional responsibilities. Provide opportunities for pupils to benefit from more privileges as they get older. Ensure that schemes of work demonstrate higher learning demands and higher expectations, building on the Frameworks where appropriate.
ensure progression and continuity;	Ensure that the curriculum on offer across all subjects provides appropriate challenge, continuity and lack of repetition. Incorporate progression and continuity into schemes of work, using the Key Stage 3 Frameworks where applicable. Encourage all subject teachers to build a distinctive flavour into the schemes of work for each of the three years of Key Stage 3. Organise pupil groupings to allow pupils to move between groups without jeopardising their learning.
have systems that recognise and correct disaffection early;	Regularly monitor pupils' behaviour and attendance and ensure that the information collected and collated by pastoral staff is used to inform teaching. Provide structures for effective communication between teachers and pastoral staff. Monitor outcomes of any remedial actions.
have effective intervention plans;	Have systems for identifying pupils' needs that build on prior knowledge from Key Stage 2. Ensure that intervention is coordinated across the school and embedded in the school's planning cycle. Use a range of intervention activities to meet the profiled learning needs of individuals and groups of pupils. Use academic tutors or mentors for specific learning issues.
support pupils in their learning as well as their behaviour;	Involve pastoral staff in regular reviews of academic progress. Identify patterns of progress across the school and use any outcomes to plan interventions.
provide opportunities for a fresh start.	Allow pupils to reflect on past success and use the opportunity to plan for new learning. Recognise that whereas learning has to be carried forward, pupils can be helped to make a fresh start in relation to behaviour.

Source: © Crown copyright [2004] Department for Education and Skills (DfES 2004).

transition an individual's relationship with self is vulnerable. Pupils face a range of discontinuities and challenges and the potential impact upon feelings of worth and competence must be acknowledged (Jindal-Snape and Miller 2008). General resilience and reasonably healthy self-esteem are likely to enable the pupil to deal with new challenges and manage feelings of anxiety effectively. Resilience and self-esteem, like other factors that contribute to a positive relationship with self, develop over time. A challenge for schools and teachers therefore is to consider how, throughout the pupil's school career, their relationship with self can be protected and developed rather than viewing enhancement of self-esteem or the building of resilience as the focus for intervention when a transition point is looming.

Resource list of learning behaviours for the classroom

This list of learning behaviours should not be viewed as exhaustive or definitive. It is intended to provide a stimulus for thinking about the learning behaviours you want to promote in your classroom or develop in particular pupils. Some schools and teachers may like to develop their own preferred learning behaviours that may be specific to their subject curriculum or their pupils' social behaviour in school. Some of the broader learning behaviours may need to be promoted through smaller steps. Learning behaviours concerned with relationship with self are mainly dispositional in nature but some may necessitate some underlying skill development if they are to be enacted in the classroom.

Table A1.1 Learning behaviours associated with relationship with the curriculum

Learning behaviour related to motivation

Skills	*Will/disposition*
• Can self-direct attention in order to locate any personal interest in task or subject. • Pursues coherence, relevance and meaning. • Responsive to teacher's motivational strategies, e.g. asks questions, volunteers information. • Is able to get started on tasks without delay. • Can plan steps in task needed for successful completion. • Is able to persist and tolerate the discomfort of effort. • Has strategies for sustaining attention and effort. • Can sustain a focus on positive outcomes.	• Is willing to search for interest in task or subject. • Is willing to direct attention to the task in hand. • Is responsive and will ask questions and volunteer information. • Is willing to get started without complaining or moaning about having to get on with learning. • Gets started without using delaying tactics. • Is willing to imagine what it feels like to succeed.

Learning behaviours related to learning organisation

Skills	*Will/disposition*
• Brings correct materials to class. • Can select necessary equipment for the task. • Is able to share equipment. • Looks after own/others' property. • Keeps desk tidy, checks computer ready for use, etc. • Has a sense of time, punctual, is able to get started on tasks promptly, work at a reasonable pace, knows when to move on to the next activity or stage. • Sets appropriate goals, • Monitors own progress.	• Is willing to bring correct materials to class. • Is willing to share equipment with others. • Takes responsibility for looking after own/others' property. • Responds to requests and/or independently keeps desk organised and tidy. • Is willing to apply effort in such a way that tasks are started promptly, work is carried out at a reasonable pace and completed in allocated time frame. • Takes responsibility, when needed, to set own targets and goals. • Is willing to monitor own progress.

Learning behaviours related to learning in group settings

Skills	Will/disposition
• Can focus and sustain attention on learning. • Is able to work when others around them are talking at a reasonable level. • Can recognise interruptions and has a range of strategies to reduce or deal with these. • Is able to wait for teacher/adult attention when necessary. • Knows when it is appropriate to speak and follows group/class conventions for asking for help or expressing views. • Is able to work productively with others. • Is able to work independently when required. • Is able to respond to and use advice from peers.	• Is willing to self-direct attention towards what is required for curriculum learning – responds to requests to redirect attention towards learning. • Makes effort to concentrate, and is willing to respond appropriately to instructions that are required for successful task completion. • Is willing to make an effort to work when others around are talking at a reasonable level. • Is willing to use a range of strategies to reduce or deal with interruptions. • Will wait quietly for teacher/adult attention when necessary. • Is willing to follow group/class rules for asking for help, answering questions and expressing own views. • Is willing to work productively with others. • Is willing to learn alone and with others. • Is willing to have work fairly compared with that of others.

Learning behaviours related to dealing with difficulties when learning

Skills	Will/disposition
• Works independently unless a problem arises that cannot be solved without adult intervention. • Tells the teacher/other adult when they do not understand. • Uses a range of strategies to solve problems for themselves before asking for help. • Makes appropriate use of peer support. • Has the necessary language skills to ask teacher/other adult why/where they went wrong. • Knows how to refer to previous work before asking the teacher for help. • Persistent and tolerates the sometimes 'difficult' feelings associated with learning new things. • Knows own strengths and weaknesses in relation to curriculum learning. • Uses feedback to improve performance.	• Is willing to work independently unless a problem arises that cannot be solved without adult intervention. • Is willing to ask for help from the teacher/other adult when they do not understand what they are required to do. • Is willing to try to solve problems for themselves before asking for help. • Is willing to make appropriate use of peer support. • Is interested enough in their own learning to ask teacher/other adult why/where they went wrong, • Is willing to self-help by referring to previous work before asking the teacher for help. • Will persist and tolerate the sometimes 'difficult' feelings associated with learning new things. • Will tolerate aspects of lesson/subject perceived as 'boring'. • Is willing, and can cope with, making mistakes and learning from them. • Is willing to respond to feedback on learning and progress.

Learning behaviours associated with processing of information

Skills	Will/disposition
• Has the language and working memory skills needed to process information in pursuit of coherence, relevance and meaning. • Understands how, and is able, to think rigorously and methodically. • Looks for link with other subjects. • Is able to learn in different ways. • Can organise learning tasks so that they can be successfully completed.	• Is willing to get involved in learning and actively seek coherence, relevance and meaning. • Makes an effort to actively process information. • Is willing to put the required effort into thinking rigorously and methodically. • Actively and independently seeks links within and between tasks and subjects. • Is willing to learn by using different approaches and strategies. • Is willing to put effort into planning so that learning tasks can be successfully completed.

Learning behaviours linked to communication within group settings

Skills	Will/disposition
• Is able to talk about learning to adults and peers. • Is able to convey information clearly and knows when it is appropriate to speak. • Is able to alter voice pitch and tone appropriately and uses non-verbal signals effectively, e.g. eye contact, stance, distance. • Is able to organise communication in both individual and group situations. • Thinks through before offering an opinion. • Is able to justify what they have said. • Is able to act in a manner appropriate to the classroom situation and with due regard to teacher's expectations and 'class rules'. • Is able to work without seeking the attention of others. • Is able to control unauthorised talking to other pupils. • Is able to communicate with others without physical actions such as nudging or poking.	• Is willing to discuss own learning with adults and peers. • Is willing to turn take and speak when it is appropriate. • Is willing to alter voice pitch and tone appropriately and uses non-verbal signals effectively, e.g. eye contact, stance, distance. • Wants to communicate effectively and appropriately in both individual and group situations. • Is willing to monitor communication in a group and think through before offering an opinion. • Is willing to justify opinions and actions without undue resentment when asked. • Is responsive to rules and instructions about appropriate communication in the classroom. • Is willing to control unauthorised talking to other pupils. • Is willing to communicate with others without physical actions such as nudging or poking.

Learning behaviours associated with relationship with others

Skills	*Will/disposition*
• Is able to seek attention appropriately and control need for peer attention in class.	• Resists the impulse to interrupt and seek attention inappropriately.
• Can show concern and understanding.	• Is willing to think about how own behaviour has an impact on others.
• Is able to wait for his/her turn to speak.	• Is willing to respond to teaching aimed at improving social skills.
• Is able to listen to, understand and respond to the ideas of others without negative comment.	• Will show concern and understanding.
• Has developed appropriate strategies for resolving arguments and conflict.	• Will respond to requests to wait their turn to speak.
• Gives and defends own view without using 'put downs', verbal aggression or other coercive tactics.	• Will listen to the ideas of others and actively make an effort to control responding with negative comments.
• Is able to be responsive to school rules and conventions for communication with teachers and peers.	• Is willing to work on strategies for resolving conflict.
	• Is willing to give and defend own viewpoint without using 'put downs', verbal aggression or other coercive tactics.
	• Is willing to be responsive to school rules and conventions for communication with teachers and peers.

Learning behaviours associated with relationship with self

Skills	*Will/disposition*
• Is able to set realistic aspirations for self.	• Is willing to reconsider own perceptions.
• Can identify own positive attributes and achievements.	• Is willing to accept praise and positive comments.
• Makes positive self-reference statements.	• Is willing to postpone immediate gratification for long-term achievements.
• Can respond appropriately to criticism and praise.	• Is willing to listen to, and try, alternative ways of doing things.
• Is able to recognise and control mood changes.	• Accepts some responsibility for own actions.
• Can identify and apply different ways of doing things.	• Is willing to try and make an effort.
• Can work independently when necessary.	• Is willing to risk making mistakes.
• Is able to ask for help.	• Is willing to compare self with others.
• Can self-direct attention to task.	• Is willing to recognise the positive attributes of others.
• Can tolerate making mistakes.	• Is willing to share attention with others.
• Can make favourable comparisons with self and others.	• Will risk making decisions.
• Works to achieve success rather than to avoid failure.	• Will respond appropriately to school rules and discipline.
• Is able to make and sustain effort in order to successfully complete work.	• Will admit wrongdoings and is willing to learn from mistakes.
• Is responsive to school rules and routines.	• Is willing to accept that others can hold differing views from those that s/he holds.
• Can make decisions and weigh up options.	• Is willing to use strategies to control anger.
• Is responsive to but not overly influenced by peers.	• Is willing to attempt things that may be difficult.
• Has realistic belief in own ability.	• Is willing to self-assess own work against given criteria.
• Is able to take responsibility for own actions.	

Learning behaviours associated with relationship with self

Skills	Will/disposition
• Is able to predict and accept consequences of own actions. • Is able to postpone immediate reward for longer term goals. • Can adjust self-perceptions when appropriate.	• Has appropriate self-belief about what they can do in relation to the work that has been set. • Is willing to accept and follow advice from others about ways in which own learning can be improved.

Source: Ellis and Tod 2015.

Resource list of strategies to support the development of motivation in the classroom[1]

The strategies contained in this appendix are based on the section on *Motivation* in Chapter 5. In this chapter we suggested that all individuals will be motivated to meet their core needs (i.e. to achieve and succeed, to belong and be valued by others and to have some control and independence).

Many of the following strategies will be known and used by teachers reading this book. Not all of them can be used at any one time but it may be useful to refresh and renew those that are already in use, or to reflect upon which ones might be particularly relevant to the classes and pupils you currently teach. For ease of use, the strategies have been split simply into those to think about when planning and those to think about for your delivery.

As with previous strategy suggestions the following lists seeks to support you in identifying *what* strategies are likely to be most suitable for *which* particular pupils or class. It is not intended that you should try to apply all the strategies on a trial and error basis but draw on what you have learned about motivation and behaviour to make an informed choice.

Any strategies chosen will need to be rigorously evaluated against the purpose you want them to serve in bringing about changes to pupils' motivational learning behaviours. Otherwise, you will be continually searching for more and more strategies in the hope of finding the ones that will suffice. In spite of this pursuit, you will know that in reality no *one* strategy will suffice for all pupils. They own their motivation and have the power to direct it as they choose.

Table A2.1 Strategies for your planning

What?	Why?	Suggestion for how?
Meet pupils' core needs (see previous page) in your planning.	If there are aspects of the lesson that meet pupils' core needs they are more likely to be motivated.	Check that activities allow pupils to be able to succeed, to experience belonging and socialise with peers, and to have some control and independence.
Be organised and plan for transitions between tasks/ resources.	To maintain the flow of the lesson and leave no space or opportunity for unwanted behaviours.	Have all resources to hand or ensure pupils know where to find them through clear protocols for collecting them during transitions.
Carefully plan seating.	To reinforce positive learning relationships and ensure pupils are given the opportunity to bring out the best in each other.	Seat pupils where they will learn best and where they will behave best – sometimes you will sit a pupil where they will be quiet but this does not necessarily lead to learning.
Check the seating arrangements work practically for you and the pupils.	To ensure the environment does not add any barriers to learning or the development of learning behaviours.	Ensure you have clear pathways around the classroom, all pupils can see the front without discomfort and pupils have enough desk space to work comfortably.
Plan for routine and repetition.	To provide stability and security for pupils.	Have a repetitive structure to lessons and repeated protocols within those lessons with linked 'trigger' words and commands – within this structure you can then innovate and surprise pupils when needed.
Be clear with your *behavioural* objectives for the task.	To allow pupils to track their behavioural successes and next steps alongside their subject or topic-specific learning.	Replace non-specific instructions such as 'get on with your work' or 'focus' with specific instructions which include reference to the learning behaviours (see Appendix 1) that you wish to see.
Reduce teacher input during the opening of the lesson.	To increase pupils' active involvement in the lesson early; this gives you time to welcome pupils and provides an opportunity for early independent success.	Plan a task that is independently accessible, achievable, engaging and partly open-ended to allow for higher level thinking or challenge.

What?	Why?	Suggestion for how?
Manipulate conditions for assessment so that the pupil can experience some success.	To provide a sense of achievement – most pupils have made comparisons about themselves as learners relative to their peers but still need to experience personal success if their motivation is to be sustained.	Start tasks with activities and outcomes that everyone can achieve. Easier questions may come first or there might be varying assessment options. For example, 'recognition' responses (multiple choices) are easier than 'generative' responses (essays, written answers, etc.). In setting goals and giving feedback there is a need to distinguish between success that relates to *attainment* (as measured by externally prescribed age-normed levels) and success that represents *achievement* for the individual.
Provide starting helpers.	To avoid 'blank page syndrome' and remove low level barriers that stop pupils accessing the higher level learning.	Provide pupils with verbal starters, sentence starters, frameworks for laying out their work, etc.
Identify the motivational conditions.	To increase the chances of motivation in your lesson.	Use changes observed in the pupil's motivation between and within lessons to identify conditions under which they are most motivated – then try to recreate at least *some* of these conditions.
Establish whether it is a matter of 'can't' or 'won't' in relation to learning and behaviour.	To remove any barriers to success in learning and behaviour.	Liaise with your SENCO to explore whether the pupil has any underlying learning difficulty or difference such as speech, language and communication needs, dyslexia, ASD or other form of special educational need.
Reflect on the suitability of current rewards and sanctions.	To avoid sanctions being experienced as rewards and rewards being experienced as sanctions.	Within your sphere of influence, look at the impact of your current rewards and sanctions and adapt if needed. For example, removing a pupil from class may be seen as them escaping cognitive challenge or public praise may be seen as embarrassing.

continued

Table A2.1 Continued

What?	Why?	Suggestion for how?
Gain some one-to-one time	To give pupils opportunities to speak to you away from their peers and build relationships away from the formal structure of a lesson.	Use any duties, trips or time spent in the corridors to communicate with pupils one-to-one – this is mainly an opportunity to listen but also to carefully (and non-confrontationally) challenge their thinking about their motivational behaviours.
Keep your ear to the ground.	To provide you with the information you need to decide upon appropriate motivational strategies.	Listen out for pupils making statements that suggest negative self-worth, wobbly relationships with peers and historical failures in your subject or topic – this will help you pre-empt and address any behaviour that arises as a result.
Seek to tackle issues of personal motivation through non-emotional means.	To allow for objective discussion of motivation and behaviour issues through depersonalisation.	Use autobiographies/biographies and anecdotes about keeping motivated towards goals in the face of adversity, etc. – the pupil may be much better able to comment on, and address, a person's motivation if that person is not them.

Table A2.2 Strategies for your delivery

What?	Why?	Suggestion for how?
Model motivated behaviours to your pupils.	To convey enthusiasm for the topic, a sense of purpose and direction and anticipation of enjoyment and success.	Start and end the lesson with positive framing of what is about to happen and what has happened.
Take pupils through the school's behaviour system efficiently, quietly and with confidence.	To demonstrate that your main focus is on *learning*, not managing behaviour so that your use of the system does not distract you or your pupils from curriculum learning.	Ensure you have a thorough knowledge of the system so you can simplify it for your class and take students through the system privately as individuals, not as a public trial.
Provide formative feedback on ongoing appropriate behaviour.	To have a positive influence on motivation and self-esteem as well as providing models to the class of what 'good' behaviour looks like.	Link to the specific behavioural objectives for a task and comment on them throughout, being careful to give feedback publicly or privately depending on the pupil and situation. Encourage pupils to provide each other with similar feedback so that pupils focus on each other's positive behaviour as opposed to encouraging negative ones.
Prioritise non-verbal correction.	To avoid interrupting the flow of the learning activity and giving 'air-time' to undesirable behaviour.	Whilst providing positive feedback on the behaviours or learning you would like to see, address unwanted behaviours non-verbally (and thus privately) through tactical ignoring, a glance, a hand movement or standing behind/adjacent to the pupil.
Build an atmosphere of choice.	To allow pupils to feel they have control over how they direct their motivation.	Use phrases that inspire confidence in pupils to make their own choices such as, 'We all know what we are doing during this time so ...' or 'You may already know what to do here so feel free to ...' (even though these 'choices' have been carefully planned by you).

continued

Table A2.2 Continued

What?	Why?	Suggestion for how?
Share your plan and your process.	To provide pupils with the information they need to have confidence in you and your decision making.	Share a pupil-friendly version of the curriculum (long term plan) every lesson, along with the plan for the half term (medium term plan) and that lesson (short term plan) and show them their progress through it – this can also be done on a smaller scale by sharing strict time limits for tasks and tick sheets for what needs to be completed.
Openly question your own decisions.	To show pupils the thinking behind the decisions you make as their teacher so that they start to work alongside you as opposed to being dragged along behind.	When displaying the learning objective, lesson topic or plan, ask questions such as, 'Why do you think we are doing this now?', 'Why do you think we have our test during that week?' or 'Why did I think you would want to do this?'.
Harness pupils' knowledge about their own learning and behaviour.	To place emphasis on how learning behaviour differs between individuals, and getting pupils to apply their unique knowledge of their own learning so that they can better control issues such as goals, dispositions and attention.	If you ask them to explain why they think they did not succeed in a task and they reply 'because I am not clever enough' it is unlikely that they will be motivated to continue. If they can tackle this assumption about themselves and give a surmountable reason why they failed such as, 'I was messing about with my friends so I did not put enough effort in', they may be persuaded to try again.
Consider carefully 'public' versus 'private' assessment outcomes.	To ensure the pupils use feedback positively in order to build on prior learning as opposed to using it to reinforce negative feelings about themselves, others and the curriculum.	Pre-empt issues associated with giving back marked work to a pupil who has not done well, or those who do not want to be seen to have done well, by giving clear instructions for behaviour, e.g. 'You are going to get a grade ... you may feel ... do not share your grade or ask others to tell you theirs as this may make them feel ...'.

What?	Why?	Suggestion for how?
Model weakness and positive reframing.	To show pupils that they are not alone with issues of low self-esteem or making mistakes.	Share your experiences as a learner (including when you failed, or found something very difficult) and how you gained from it. Be careful not to over-share but, if you have an experience that is appropriate to share with a pupil then use your professional judgement as to whether they may benefit from hearing it.
Use language that creates positive self-belief.	To model appropriate language and create an environment conducive to positive behaviours.	Start the sentence with affirmation. For example, you might say, 'You can do this. Do you think the best way is …?' rather than 'If you work hard you will …'.
Give pupils responsibilities.	To allow pupils to experience your trust in their competence.	Give pupils a responsibility that allows them to feel useful and a vital member of the class – either through a practical task such as cleaning your board or handing out resources or something more challenging like supporting a weaker pupil.

Note

1 We are grateful to Kate Tod Forbes for her assistance in developing this list of strategies.

Resource list of strategies and approaches for maintaining and promoting positive classroom behaviour

The Behaviour for Learning approach is a way of thinking about behaviour rather than a specific set of strategies. However, this book necessarily contains references to a range of strategies spread across a number of chapters to illustrate how the Behaviour for Learning approach can be applied to practice. We recognise that for some readers it may be helpful to have these strategies, along with some others, collected in one place as an initial resource bank. The lists below distinguish between routine classroom strategies and those that might be considered to be more personalised. However, this is not a rigid distinction. There may be some personalised strategies that could usefully be implemented at whole-class level.

Strategies should always be selected based on their potential to protect or enhance the three Behaviour for Learning relationships and/or contribute to the development of learning behaviour.

Some general principles when responding to unwanted behaviour

- Through your language and behaviour maintain unconditional positive regard during any disciplinary interaction, making it clear that it is the behaviour that is the problem not the pupil. At the simplest level, it is the distinction between 'You are a naughty boy' (the individual as the problem) and 'That was a naughty thing to do' (the behaviour as the problem).
- Where possible, make use of positive feedback that provides information for the pupil (and others who may hear) on the behaviour that is gaining this recognition. For example, 'Kirsty, Raheem, I can see you're both taking turns nicely.'
- When addressing unwanted behaviour, aim to phrase your comments positively. For example, the teacher would say, 'Josh, facing this way, thanks', rather than, 'Josh, stop turning round'. Positively framed correction provides information for the pupil (and others who may hear) on the required behaviour.
- Follow behavioural directions with 'thanks' rather than 'please' (Hook and Vass 2002; Rogers 2011). The use of 'thanks' conveys a stronger sense of expectation whilst still maintaining a polite tone. For example, the teacher might say, 'Imogen … Amy … phones away now, thanks'.
- Although the emphasis should be on positive correction, for young children in particular, it may be appropriate to respond to more serious behaviours with a clear, 'No, we don't …' statement (e.g. 'No, we don't throw the toys' or 'No, we don't hit people'). On the occasions when this is necessary it will be more effective in an

environment where positive correction is generally used and it is not just one of the many 'No' messages the pupil hears.

- Plan your least to most intrusive approach for the class generally and, if necessary, for individual pupils. This simply means thinking about what the lowest level of intervention is that you might use to address the behaviour. For example, *tactical ignoring* would represent a lower level of intrusion than a *simple direction*. If the lowest level does not address the behaviour, what would you move to next? At what point would you move to imposing a sanction? When would you move from class-based strategies and sanctions to the whole-school system (e.g. referral to senior colleague)?

- After giving a behavioural direction, allow 'take up time' (see Chapter 10). Give the direction and then move away to give the pupil the opportunity to process the information and comply. This allows them to comply without your attention and that of the class focused on them. This approach also gives you thinking time – if, having moved away, you notice they have not complied you can consider what your next step will be. This will feel a lot less pressurised than if you are standing by the pupil with all the eyes of the class on you waiting to see how you are going to handle the non-compliance.

- *Tactically ignore* secondary behaviours. These behaviours (e.g. a 'tut' or something muttered under the breath) usually occur when the pupil is complying with the teacher's behavioural direction. This is important to note; the pupil is essentially *doing as required* but conveying a degree of minor resistance, possibly in some cases to save face in front of peers. The implication is, 'I'm doing it, but grudgingly'. Call the pupil aside at the end of the lesson to talk to them about the secondary behaviour if you feel it needs to be addressed.

Some general reactive behaviour management strategies

- For many classes, simply stating that they should stop what they doing and listen and waiting for attention will be sufficient. Where this is not the case, consider implementing a non-verbal method of gaining whole-class attention. For younger children a rain stick or tambourine could be used – it should be a soft sound rather than any instrument or device that adds to the noise levels. Alternatively, pupils can be taught a sequence of hand movements that they join in with as soon as they notice the teacher doing them. With older pupils various forms of visual count-down on the interactive whiteboard can be used.

- When waiting for whole-class attention, direct some positive feedback to those who are ready to listen. Once the number is down to the very few who are not ready, consider using a simple direction (e.g. 'John ... Sam, facing this way ready to listen now, thanks.').

- Use *tactical ignoring* for low level behaviours. Provide positive feedback as soon as the pupil corrects themselves and resumes the required behaviour. It is important to recognise that this is *tactical* ignoring – it is a positive strategy choice rather than done simply because you cannot think of anything else to do.

- Use *tactical ignoring* coupled with *proximity praise*. Ignore the 'target' pupil but praise a nearby pupil who is exhibiting the required behaviour. For example, you might say to a nearby pupil, 'Oh Kerry, I can see you're sitting quietly ready to listen.' If the target pupil changes their behaviour, praise them.

- Make use of *non-verbal cueing/privately understood signals*. The teacher supplies a cue that carries a clear (unspoken) message, reminder or direction. For example, if reading to the class from a text you might put the book down in response to a group talking to indicate you are waiting for their full attention. Some teachers will have their own particular 'waiting poses' or 'look' that they use to establish quiet.

  Privately understood signals can be generic such as a thumbs up or a circle made with thumb and index finger for 'OK', a rotational movement with the hand to indicate that a pupil needs to face the front or a finger to the lips to indicate that a lowering of the noise level is necessary. Other signals may need to be taught to particular individuals for particular circumstances.

- Make use of *incidental language*. The teacher directs or reminds the pupil without directly telling them, e.g. 'There's some litter on the floor and the bell is going to go soon....' The pupil is required to recognise the implied expectation (i.e. that they pick the litter up). Sometimes it will be appropriate to combine the description of reality with a behavioural direction: e.g. 'It's quiet reading time now (*the incidental element*). Read quietly inside your heads. Thanks (*the behavioural direction*)'. The strength of incidental language is that it is depersonalised – it does not feel like it is targeting or accusing anyone.

- Make use of *Prefacing*. The teacher focuses on a positive issue before addressing the behaviour. For example, if the teacher notices some minor giggling coming from one group during an English lesson, s/he might walk over and ask a general question such as, 'How are you getting on here?'. Although the interaction is focused on the task, it usually has the effect of also conveying to pupils that their behaviour has been noticed. As the teacher begins to move away, they might add quietly but firmly, 'Remember it's quiet, individual reading at the moment'.

- Use of *Simple Direction*. The teacher directs a group or individual by referring, directly, to the expected or required behaviour: e.g. 'Jason ..., Dean ..., facing this way, thanks'. Behavioural directions are appropriate for communicating the *required* behaviour, such as when pupils are talking while the teacher is talking and they need to be facing the front and listening.

- Use *Rule Reminders*. The teacher briefly reminds the class, group or individual(s) of what the rule is by saying, for example, 'We have a rule for asking questions' or 'Remember our rule for ...'. The teacher does not need to *spell out* the rule each time; a comment such as, 'Harry, remember our rule', may be sufficient. Rule reminders can also be given through a question such as, 'Olivia, what's our rule for ...?'. However, remember – do not ask any question unless you want an answer.

- Use *conditional directions* ('When ... then', 'After ... then', 'As soon as ... then'). For example, you could say, 'When you have finished your work, then you can go out', rather than, 'No, you can't go out because you have not finished your work'. This helps to place the control with the pupil – it is no longer the teacher prohibiting something; the pupil can affect the outcome through their behaviour (i.e. by finishing the work). Other examples include:
  - '*When* you've completed the writing *then* you can do the picture.'
  - '*After* you've completed this page *then* you can go to the sand tray.'
  - '*As soon as* we've finished this part of the lesson, *then* you can and have a drink.'

- Use partial agreement for pupils who attempt to argue. This can help to deflect confrontation with pupils by acknowledging concerns, feelings and actions.

Examples include: 'Yes, you may have been talking about your work but I would like you to …' and 'Yes, it may not seem fair but….'

- Make use of *distraction/diversion*. Distractions/diversions can take numerous forms. It could be talking to the pupil about something completely different to the problematic behaviour (e.g. you can see the pupil is getting distracted so you intervene with a friendly 'How are you getting on?' to re-focus on the learning and engage the pupil in conversation about this). It could be asking the pupil to do something that removes them temporarily (e.g. an errand, bringing something to you, etc.) from the situation that is developing.
- For very young children use a 5,4,3,2,1 countdown (or count up) in any situation where there is reluctance to comply with a request. This can be a useful distraction technique because it turns the situation into a game rather than a battle, e.g. 'Let's see if you can finish getting changed by the time I count to 5'.

Some proactive and more personalised approaches

- Use visual timetables (or, in its simpler form, 'now … next' boards) so that a sequence of activities is predictable. Visual timetables show the sequence of the day in visual form. A 'now … next' board uses just two pictures – what the pupil is doing now and what they are going to do. This can also help some pupils by showing that a preferred task will be following one with which they are less keen to engage.
- Provide pupils with a Task Planner (sometimes known as a 'Task Management Board') that sets out the different stages in a task so that they know step-by-step what they have to do.
- For pupils who fidget or fiddle at times when they are required to sit still and listen consider providing something legitimate to fiddle with (e.g. Blu-Tack, a fidget spinner or a stress ball). For others it may helpful to give them a particular role such as holding a pointer when the class is reading a shared text.
- For some pupils, it may be helpful to use individual reward charts with rewards (e.g. a sticker or tick on the chart) being given for demonstrating specified learning behaviours over a set period of time (e.g. a lesson, over playtime, etc.). When devising individualised reward schemes, identify rewards that have value and meaning for the pupil and deliver these with due regard for their preference for private or public recognition.
- Consider incorporating a social element into any individualised reward system. For example, if collecting a certain number of stickers leads to a pupil having additional time to use the computer they could choose another pupil to join in this activity with them. Through this strategy other pupils may be less inclined to view the pupil negatively and have a vested interest in supporting them to improve their behaviour.
- For pupils who find group work difficult plan curriculum activities that incorporate a collaborative element that is initially within their capability. For example, create situations where the pupil is included in activities first with one other pupil, and then with a small group. For some pupils it might be helpful to identify a particular role (e.g. leader, participant, reporter) for them within a collaborative group work activity. Some may need a script to support them in the role.
- Help the pupil to develop social skills (i.e. knowing how to join in, how to ask for things, how to express his/her point of view). Teach these and provide opportunities for rehearsal.

- Teach and rehearse useful strategies that the pupil can use to either deal with or extricate themselves from social situations that they currently find difficult. This could include the sometimes vacuous, but socially useful, language and behaviour of apology. It might also include developing socially acceptable responses to criticism.
- Use *social stories* to provide pupils with social information about situations they may find difficult. This can help them respond more appropriately in similar situations in the future or prepare them for new experiences (see Chapter 12)
- Use *comic-strip conversations* to help pupils recognise the thoughts and feelings that might be underlying their own and others' actions (see Chapter 12).
- Work with the pupil one-to-one or in a small group to identify the difference between designating a choice as 'good' because of its impact on them personally (e.g. they get an immediate sense of fun and excitement) and 'good' in relation to the effect on others.
- Provide the pupil with opportunities to take on responsibilities and provide positive feedback when these are carried out. This strategy shows the pupil that they are trusted and valued by another person and gives them an opportunity to strengthen their relationship with others and with self as it shows they are worthy of this.
- Use characters in stories, role-play or puppets to help the pupil to reflect on their own difficulties and possible alternative responses. This depersonalised approach is less threatening. For example, it may be easier for the pupil to advise a puppet or toy on how to have a happy playtime than to think about their own behaviour.
- Work with the pupil to analyse an incident (either real or from literature, a TV programme, etc.) in order to identify the key triggers, choice points, the efficacy of the responses and the outcomes for all involved. Write about, discuss or role-play alternatives.
- Provide opportunities to explore the attributional style of others and themselves in a non-threatening, safe setting (see Chapter 6). This could be through characters in stories, role-play or use of puppets.
- Identify a 'safe' place or person that the pupil can go to as an alternative to a behaviour that would impact negatively and significantly on relationship with self and/or relationship with others. Because at the time of need the pupil is likely to be in a heightened emotional state, the identified 'safe' place should be somewhere they can access without hindrance. It is often useful to seek the pupil's view on what would be a suitable safe place. The use of a 'safe' person as an alternative to a 'safe' place attempts to capitalise on an existing positive relationship with an adult.
- Implement an agreed (with the teacher) non-verbal system for conveying emotional state and necessary action (e.g. green card – 'I'm OK'; amber card – 'I need support'; red card – 'I'm going to my safe place'). The purpose of this strategy is to support the pupil to take responsibility for recognising and managing their feelings. Ultimately, the aim would be for the pupil to develop self-regulation strategies that enable them to remain within the classroom.
- Adopt a restorative approach to incidents, focusing on the key questions of 'What happened?', 'Who has been affected and how?', 'How can we put right the harm?' and 'What have you learned so as to make different choices next time?'.

References

Albert, L. (1996) *Cooperative Discipline*. Circle Pines, MN: American Guidance Service.

Alexander, S. (2017) 'No clarity around growth mindset'. Available at http://slatestarcodex. com/2015/04/08/no-clarity-around-growth-mindset-yet/ (accessed 31 March 2018).

Allen, B. (1998a) 'New guidance on the use reasonable force in schools 1998'. *British Journal of Special Education* 25(4): 184–8.

Allen, B. (1998b) *Holding back: Rarely and Safely*. Bristol: Lucky Duck.

Alloway, T.P., Gathercole, S.E., Adams, A. and Willis, C. (2005) 'Working memory abilities in children with special educational needs'. *Educational and Child Psychology* 22(4): 56–67.

Assessment Reform Group (2002) *Testing, Motivation and Learning*. Available at www.aaia.org. uk/content/uploads/2010/06/Testing-Motivation-and-Learning.pdf (accessed 2 January 2018).

ATL (2002) *Achievement for All: Working with Children with Special Educational Needs in Mainstream Schools and Colleges*. London: Association of Teachers and Lecturers.

Ayers, H., Clarke, D. and Murray, A. (2000) *Perspectives on Behaviour*. 2nd edn. London: David Fulton.

Baddeley, A. (1983) 'Working memory.' *Philosophical Transactions of the Royal Society of London*. Series B, Biological Sciences, 302(1110): 311–24.

Baddeley, A. (2002) 'Is working memory still working?' *European Psychologist* 7(2): 85–97.

Baddeley, A. and Hitch, G. (1974) 'Working memory', in Bower, G. (ed.), *The Psychology of Learning and Motivation: Advances in Research and Theory*. New York, NY: Academic Press.

Bandura, A. (1977) *Social Learning Theory*. Englewood Cliffs, NJ: Prentice Hall.

Bandura, A. (1986) *Social Foundations of Thought and Action: A Social Cognitive Theory*. Englewood Cliffs, NJ: Prentice Hall.

Barber, M. (1994) *Young People and Their Attitudes to School*. University of Keele, UK.

Baron-Cohen, S. (1995) *Mindblindness: An Essay on Autism and Theory of Mind*. London: MIT Press.

Bate, C. and Moss, J. (1997) 'Towards a behaviour curriculum'. *Educational Psychology in Practice* 13(3): 176–80.

Baumeister, R.F., Campbell, J.D., Krueger, J.I. and Vohs, K.D. (2003) 'Does high self-esteem cause better performance, interpersonal success, happiness or healthier lifestyles?'. *Psychological Science in the Public Interest* 4(1): 1–44.

Belbin, M. (1981) *Management Teams*. Oxford: Butterworth Heinemann.

Bennathan, M. and Boxall, M. (1998) *The Boxall Profile Handbook*. London: The Nurture Group Network.

Bennett, T. (2017) *Creating a Culture: How School Leaders Can Optimise Behaviour*. Available at www.gov.uk/government/uploads/system/uploads/attachment_data/file/602487/Tom_ Bennett_Independent_Review_of_Behaviour_in_Schools.pdf (accessed 23 June 2017).

Bergin, C. and Bergin, D. (2009) 'Attachment in the Classroom'. *Educational Psychology Review* 21(2): 141–70.

Berk, L. (2003) *Child Development*. Boston, MA: Allyn and Bacon.

Blakemore, S. (2008) 'The social brain in adolescence'. *Nature Reviews Neuroscience* 9(4): 267–77.

Blatchford, P. (1992) 'Academic self-assessment at 7 and 11 years: Its accuracy and association with ethnic groups and sex'. *British Journal of Educational Psychology* 62(1): 35–44.

Bonnell, J., Copestake, P., Kerr, D., Passy, R., Reed, C., Salter, R., Sarwar, S. and Sheikh, S (2011) 'Teaching approaches that help to build resilience to extremism among young people'. Available at www.gov.uk/government/uploads/system/uploads/attachment_data/file/182675/DFE-RR119.pdf (accessed 20 October 2017).

Bowers, T. (2005) 'The forgotten "E" in EBD', in Clough, P., Garner, P., Pardeck, J. and Yuen, F. (eds.), *Handbook of Emotional and Behavioural Difficulties*. London: Sage.

Bowlby, J. (1953) *Child Care and the Growth of Love*. London: Pelican.

Bowlby, J. (1969) *Attachment and Loss, Vol. 1, Attachment*. New York, NY: Basic Books.

BPS (1999) 'Dyslexia literacy and psychological assessment'. Report by a Working Party of the Division of Educational and Child Psychology of the British Psychological Society. Leicester, UK: British Psychological Society.

Brain, C. and Mukherji, P. (2005) *Understanding Child Psychology*. Cheltenham, UK: Nelson Thornes.

Braithwaite, R. (2001) *Managing Aggression*. London: Routledge.

Brand, R. (2007) *My Booky Wook*. London: Hodder and Stoughton.

Branden, N. (1969) *The Psychology of Self-esteem*. New York, NY: Bantam Books.

Breakwell, G. (1997) *Coping with Aggressive Behaviour*. Leicester, UK: British Psychological Society.

Burden, R. (2008) 'Is dyslexia necessarily associated with negative feelings of self-worth? A review and implications for future research'. *Dyslexia* 14(3): 188–96.

Burns, R. (1982) *Self Concept Development and Education*. London: Holt, Rinehart and Winston.

CACE (1963) *Half Our Future* (the 'Newsom Report') London: Her Majesty's Stationery Office.

Canter, L. and Canter, M. (1976) *Assertive Discipline: A Take-Charge Approach for Today's Educator*. Santa Monica, CA: Lee Canter and Associates.

Canter, L. and Canter, M. (1992) *Assertive Discipline: Positive Behavior Management for Today's Classroom*. Santa Monica, CA: Canter and Associates.

Carr, M. and Claxton, G. (2002) 'Tracking the development of learning dispositions'. *Assessment in Education* 9(1): 9–37.

Carter, A. (2015) 'Carter review of initial teacher training (ITT)'. Available at www.gov.uk/government/uploads/system/uploads/attachment_data/file/399957/Carter_Review.pdf (accessed 23 June 2017).

CESE (2017) 'Cognitive load theory: Research that teachers really need to understand'. Available at www.cese.nsw.gov.au/publications-filter/cognitive-load-theory-research-that-teachers-really-need-to-understand (accessed 1 January 2018).

Channel 4 (2005) 'Dispatches: Undercover Teacher' (originally broadcast by Channel 4, July 2005).

Chaplain, R. (2003a) *Teaching Without Disruption in the Primary School*. London: RoutledgeFalmer.

Chaplain, R. (2003b) *Teaching Without Disruption in the Secondary School*. London: RoutledgeFalmer.

Chapman, J.W. (1998) 'Learning disabled children's self concepts'. *Review of Educational Research* 58: 347–71.

Charles, C. (2002) *Building Classroom Discipline*. 7th edn. Boston, MA: Allyn and Bacon.

Children's Society (2015) *The Good Childhood Report 2015*. Available at www.childrenssociety.org.uk/sites/default/files/TheGoodChildhoodReport2015.pdf (accessed 23 June 2017).

Chivers, T. (2017) 'A mindset "revolution" sweeping Britain's classrooms may be based on shaky science'. Available at www.buzzfeed.com/tomchivers/what-is-your-mindset?utm_term=.foboLRaBB#.nsOxB1P77 (accessed 1 January 2018).

Chowdry, H., Crawford, C. and Goodman, A. (2009) *Drivers and Barriers to Educational Success: Evidence from the Longitudinal Study of Young People in England* (Research Report RR102). Nottingham: DCSF.

Clarke, S. (2001) *Unlocking Formative Assessment: Practical Strategies for Enhancing Pupils' Learning in the Primary Classroom.* London: Hodder & Stoughton.

Claxton, G. (1999) *Wise Up: The Challenge of Lifelong Learning.* London: Bloomsbury.

Claxton, G. (2002) *Building Learning Power.* Bristol: TLO.

Claxton, G. (2006) 'Expanding the capacity to learn: A new end for education?'. Opening keynote address, British Educational Research Association Annual Conference, 6 September 2006, Warwick University. Available at www.tloltd.co.uk/wp-content/uploads/2014/11/BERA-Keynote-Update-Feb10.pdf (accessed 28 March 2018).

Cochran, K., DeRuiter, J. and King, R. (1993) 'Pedagogical content knowing: An integrative model for teacher preparation'. *Journal of Teacher Education* 44(4): 263–72.

Coe, R., Aloisi, C., Higgins, S. and Major, L. (2014) *What makes great teaching?* Available at www.suttontrust.com/wp-content/uploads/2014/10/What-makes-great-teaching-FINAL-4.11.14-1.pdf (accessed 5 November 2017).

Coles, M. and Werquin, P. (2005) *The Growing Importance of NQS as a Resource for Lifelong Learning Policy.* Paris: OECD.

Cooper, G. (1998) 'Research into cognitive load theory and instructional design at UNSW'. Available at http://dwb4.unl.edu/Diss/Cooper/UNSW.htm (accessed 27 December 2017).

Coopersmith, S. (1967) *The Antecedents of Self-Esteem.* San Francisco, CA: W.H. Freeman.

Cornwall, J. (2000) 'Might is right? A discussion of the ethics and practicalities of control and restraint in education'. *Emotional and Behavioural Difficulties* 5(4): 19–25.

Corrie, L. (2002) *Investigating Troublesome Classroom Behaviour.* London: RoutledgeFalmer.

Cossavella, A. and Hobbs, C. (2002) *Farewell and Welcome.* Bristol: Lucky Duck.

Cowley, S. (2003) *Getting the Buggers to Behave 2.* London: Continuum.

Craig, C. (2007) 'The potential dangers of a systematic, explicit approach to teaching social and emotional skills (SEAL): An overview and summary of the arguments'. Glasgow: Centre for Confidence and Well-Being. Available online at: www.centreforconfidence.co.uk/docs/SEALsummary.pdf (accessed 23 June 2016).

Cremin, T., Mottram, M., Collins, F., Powell, S. and Safford, K. (2009) 'Teachers as readers: Building communities of readers' *Literacy* 43(1): 11–19.

Cross, M. (2004) *Children with Emotional and Behavioural Difficulties and Communication Problems.* London: Jessica Kingsley.

Curwin, R. and Mendler, A. (1989) 'We repeat, let the buyer beware: A response to Canter'. *Educational Leadership* 46(6): 68–71.

Damon, W. (1984) 'Peer education: The untapped potential'. Journal of Applied *Developmental Psychology* 5(4): 331–43.

Davies, W. and Frude, N. (2000) *Preventing Face-To-Face Violence.* 4th edn. Leicester, UK: Association of Psychological Therapies.

Davis, P. and Florian, L. (2004) *Teaching* Strategies *and Approaches for Pupils with Special Educational Needs: A Scoping Study.* Nottingham, UK: DfES.

Day, D. and Libertini, G. (1992) 'Profiles of children's learning behavior'. *Journal of Research in Childhood Education* 6(2): 100–12.

DCSF (2007a) *Safe to Learn: Embedding Anti-Bullying Work in Schools.* Nottingham: DCSF.

DCSF (2007b) *The Use of Force to Control or Restrain Pupils.* Nottingham: DCSF.

DCSF (2008a) *Initial Teacher Training Inclusion Development Programme Primary/Secondary: Dyslexia and Speech, Language and Communication Needs.* Available at http://webarchive.nationalarchives.gov.uk/20110202211342/https://nationalstrategies.standards.dcsf.gov.uk/node/175594?uc=force_uj (accessed 13 July 2017).

DCSF (2008b) *Inclusion Development Programme Primary/Secondary Dyslexia and Speech, Language and Communication Needs.* Available at http://webarchive.nationalarchives.gov.uk/20110202211152/

https://nationalstrategies.standards.dcsf.gov.uk/node/175591?uc=force_uj   (accessed   13   July 2017).

DCSF (2008c) *The Education of Children and Young People with Behavioural, Emotional and Social Difficulties as a Special Educational Need.* Available at http://dera.ioe.ac.uk/id/eprint/8410 (accessed 13 July 2017).

DCSF (2009) *School Discipline and Pupil-Behaviour Policies – Guidance for Schools.* Nottingham: DCSF.

DCSF (2010) *The Use of Force to Control or Restrain Pupils.* Nottingham: DCSF.

DES (1989) *Discipline in Schools* (the 'Elton Report'). London: Her Majesty's Stationery Office.

DfE (1994a) *Pupil Behaviour and Discipline* (Circular 8/94). London: DfE.

DfE (1994b) *The Education of Children with Emotional and Behavioural Difficulties* (Circular 9/94). London: DfE.

DfE (1994c) *Code of Practice on the Identification and Assessment of Special Educational Needs.* London: DfE.

DfE (2010) *The Importance of Teaching* (White Paper). Nottingham: DfE.

DfE (2011a) 'School discipline: New guidance for teachers' (press release). Available at www.gov.uk/government/news/school-discipline-new-guidance-for-teachers (accessed 23 June 2017).

DfE (2011b) *Teachers' Standards: Guidance for School Leaders, School Staff and Governing Bodies.* Available at www.gov.uk/government/uploads/system/uploads/attachment_data/file/301107/ Teachers__Standards.pdf (accessed 23 June 2017).

DfE (2011c) *Getting the Simple Things Right: Charlie Taylor's Behaviour Checklists.* Available at www.gov.uk/government/publications/behaviour-and-discipline-in-schools (accessed 23 June 2017).

DfE (2011d) *Support and Aspiration: A New Approach to Special Educational Needs and Disability.* Available at www.gov.uk/government/publications/support-and-aspiration-a-new-approach-to-special-educational-needs-and-disability-consultation (accessed 23 June 2017).

DfE (2011e) *Special Educational Needs in England, January 2011, Statistical First Release SFR 14/2011.* Available at www.gov.uk/government/uploads/system/uploads/attachment_data/ file/219086/sfr14-2011v2.pdf (accessed 29 June 2017).

DfE (2012a) 'Trainee teachers to get a better grip on managing behaviour' (press release). Available at www.gov.uk/government/news/trainee-teachers-to-get-a-better-grip-on-managing-behaviour-2 (accessed 23 June 2017).

DfE (2012b) *Behaviour and Discipline in Schools: A Guide for Head Teachers and School Staff.* Available at http://dera.ioe.ac.uk/14478/1/Behaviour%20and%20discipline%20in%20schools%20 -%20A%20guide%20for%20head%20teachers%20and%20school%20staff.pdf   (accessed   1 January 2018).

DfE (2012c) *A Profile of Pupil Exclusions in England.* Available at www.gov.uk/government/ uploads/system/uploads/attachment_data/file/183498/DFE-RR190.pdf (accessed 3 January 2018).

DfE (2013) *Use of Reasonable force: Advice for Headteachers, Staff and Governing Bodies.* Available at www.education.gov.uk/aboutdfe/advice/f0077153/use-of-reasonable-force (accessed 12 July 2017).

DfE (2014a) *The National Curriculum in England: Framework Document.* Available at www.gov.uk/ government/uploads/system/uploads/attachment_data/file/381344/Master_final_national_ curriculum_28_Nov.pdf (accessed 11 July 2017).

DfE (2014b) *Behaviour and Discipline in Schools: Advice for Headteachers and School Staff.* Available at http://dera.ioe.ac.uk/19446/1/Behaviour_and_Discipline_in_Schools_-a_guide_for_headteachers_ and_school_staff.pdf (accessed 23 June 2017).

DfE (2016a) *Behaviour and Discipline in Schools: Advice for Headteachers and School Staff.* Available at www. gov.uk/government/uploads/system/uploads/attachment_data/file/488034/Behaviour_and_Dis cipline_in_Schools_-_A_guide_for_headteachers_and_School_Staff.pdf (accessed 23 June 2017).

DfE (2016b) *Educational Excellence Everywhere*. Available at www.gov.uk/government/publica tions/educational-excellence-everywhere accessed 23 June 2017).

DfE (2016c) *Mental Health and Behaviour in Schools*. Available at www.gov.uk/government/ uploads/system/uploads/attachment_data/file/508847/Mental_Health_and_Behaviour_-_advice_ for_Schools_160316.pdf (accessed 23 June 2017).

DfE (2016d) *A Framework of Core Content for Initial Teacher Training* (ITT). Available at www.gov. uk/government/uploads/system/uploads/attachment_data/file/536890/Framework_Report_ 11_July_2016_Final.pdf (accessed 27 December 2017).

DfE (2016e) *Special Educational Needs in England: January 2016*. Available at www.gov.uk/government/ statistics/special-educational-needs-in-england-january-2016 (accessed 5 September 2017).

DfE (2017a) *Transforming Children and Young People's Mental Health Provision: A Green Paper*. Available at www.gov.uk/government/consultations/transforming-children-and-young-peoples-mental-health-provision-a-green-paper (accessed 24 December 2017).

DfE (2017b) *Special Educational Needs in England: January 2017* (SFR 37/2017, 27 July 2017). Available at www.gov.uk/government/statistics/special-educational-needs-in-england-january-2017 (accessed 29 September 2017).

DfE (2017c) *Primary School Accountability in 2017: A Technical Guide for Primary Maintained Schools, Academies and Free Schools*. Available at www.gov.uk/government/uploads/system/uploads/ attachment_data/file/666873/Primary_school_accountability_technical_guidance_2017__ December_update_.pdf (accessed 27 December 2017).

DfE (2017d) *Secondary Accountability Measures: Guide for Maintained Secondary Schools, Academies and Free Schools*. Available at www.gov.uk/government/uploads/system/uploads/attachment_ data/file/651158/Secondary_accountability_measures-Guide.pdf (accessed 27 December 2017).

DfE (2017e) *Preventing and Tackling Bullying: Advice for Headteachers, Staff and Governing Bodies*. Available at www.gov.uk/government/uploads/system/uploads/attachment_data/file/623895/ Preventing_and_tackling_bullying_advice.pdf (accessed 2 January 2018).

DfE (2017f) *SEN Support: Research Evidence on Effective Approaches and Examples of Current Practice in Good and Outstanding Schools and Colleges*. Available at www.sendgateway.org.uk/ resources.sen-support-research-evidence-on-effective-approaches-and-examples-of-current-practice-in-good-and-outstanding-schools-and-colleges.html (accessed 3 January 2018).

DfE (2017g) *Statutory Framework for the Early Years Foundation Stage*. Available at www.gov.uk/ government/uploads/system/uploads/attachment_data/file/596629/EYFS_STATUTORY_ FRAMEWORK_2017.pdf (accessed 5 July 2017).

DfE (2017h) *Permanent and Fixed Period Exclusions in England: 2015 to 2016*. Available at www. gov.uk/government/uploads/system/uploads/attachment_data/file/645075/SFR35_2017_ text.pdf (accessed 31 December 2017).

DfE/DoH (2015) *Special Educational Needs and Disability Code of Practice: 0–25 years*. Available at www.gov.uk/government/uploads/system/uploads/attachment_data/file/398815/SEND_ Code_of_Practice_January_2015.pdf (accessed 23 June 2017).

DfEE (1997) *Excellence for All Children*. London: DfEE.

DfEE (1998) *Section 550A of the Education Act 1996: The Use of Force to Control or Restrain Pupils* (Circular 10/98). London: DfEE.

DfEE/QCA (1999a) *National Curriculum: Handbook for Primary Teachers in England*. London: DfEE/QCA.

DfEE/QCA (1999b) *National Curriculum:* Handbook *for Secondary Teachers in England*. London: DfEE/QCA.

DfES (2001) *Special Educational Needs Code of Practice*. Nottingham: DfES.

DfES (2002a) *Including All Children in the Literacy Hour and Daily Mathematics Lesson*. Nottingham: DfES.

DfES (2002b) *Guidance on the Use of Restrictive Physical Interventions for Staff Working with Children and Adults Who Display Extreme Behaviour in Association with Learning Disability and/or Autistic Spectrum Disorders*. Nottingham: DfES.

DfES (2003a) *Advice on Whole-school Behaviour and Attendance Policy*. Nottingham: DfES.

DfES (2003b) *Key Stage 3 National Strategy Behaviour and Attendance Training Materials: Core Day 1*. Nottingham: DfES.

DfES (2003c) *Key Stage 3 National Strategy: Auditing Behaviour and Attendance in Secondary and Middle Schools*. Nottingham: DfES.

DfES (2004a) *Key Stage 3 National Strategy Behaviour and Attendance Core Day 2: Developing Effective Practice Across the School*. Nottingham: DfES.

DfES (2004b) *Every Child Matters: Change for Children*. Nottingham: DfES.

DfES (2004c) *Effective Lessons and Behaviour for Learning*. Nottingham: DfES.

DfES (2004d) *Behaviour in the Classroom: A Course for Newly Qualified Teachers: Course Notes*. Nottingham: DfES.

DfES (2004e) *Planning and Assessment for Learning: Assessment for Learning*. Nottingham: DfES.

DfES (2004f) *Unit 18 – Improving the Climate for Learning*. Nottingham: DfES.

DfES (2004g) *Creating a Learning Culture: Conditions for Learning*. Nottingham: DfES.

DfES (2004h) *Learning and Teaching for Children with Special Educational Needs in the Primary School*. Nottingham: DfES.

DfES (2004i) *Transition and Progression within Key Stage 3*. Nottingham: DfES.

DfES (2005a) *Higher Standards, Better Schools for All*. Nottingham: DfES.

DfES (2005b) *Learning Behaviour: The Report of the Practitioners' Group on School Behaviour and Discipline* (the Steer Report). Nottingham: DfES.

DfES (2005c) *Excellence and Enjoyment: Social and Emotional Aspects of Learning – Guidance*. Nottingham: DfES.

DfES (2005d) *Leading on Inclusion*. Nottingham: DfES.

DfES (2005e) *14–19 Education and Skills*. London: The Stationery Office.

DfES (2005f) *Transition at Key Stage 2–3: Supporting Positive Behaviour and Regular Attendance*. Nottingham: DfES.

DfES (2006) *Effective Leadership: Ensuring the Progress of Pupils with SEN and/or Disabilities*. Nottingham: DfES.

DfES (2007a) *School Discipline and Pupil Behaviour Policies*. Nottingham: DfES.

DfES (2007b) *Social and Emotional Aspects of Learning (SEAL): Guidance Booklet*. Nottingham: DfES.

DfES (2007c) *Practice Guidance for the Early Years Foundation Stage*. Nottingham: DfES.

DfES/TTA (2002) *Qualifying to Teach Professional Standards for Qualified Teacher Status and Requirements for Initial Teacher Training*. London: TTA.

Dix, P. (2007) *Taking Care of Behaviour: Practical Skills for Teachers*. Harlow, UK: Pearson.

Doddington, C., Flutter, J. and Rudduck, J. (1999) 'Exploring and explaining "dips" in motivation and performance in primary and secondary schooling'. *Research in Education* 61: 29–38.

Doddington, C., Flutter, J., Bearne, E. and Demetriou, H. (2001) 'Sustaining pupils' progress at Year 3'. Research report, Faculty of Education, University of Cambridge.

DoH/DfES (2004) *Promoting Emotional Health and Wellbeing through the National Healthy School Standard*. Available at http://webarchive.nationalarchives.gov.uk/20110227161902/www.education.gov.uk/publications/eOrderingDownload/DfES-0180-2005PDF3.pdf (accessed 1 January 2018).

Dreikurs, R., Grunwald, B. and Pepper, F. (1998) *Maintaining Sanity in the Classroom*. London: Accelerated Development.

Duckworth, A.L. and Seligman, M.E.P. (2006) 'Self-discipline gives girls the edge: Gender in self-discipline, grades, and achievement scores'. *Journal of Educational Psychology* 98(1): 198–208.

Dumortier, D. (2004) *From Another Planet: Autism from Within*. London: Paul Chapman.

Dweck, C. (2006) *Mindset: How You Can Fulfil Your Potential*. London: Robinson.

Ecclestone, K. (2015) 'Well-being programmes in schools might be doing children more harm than good'. Available at www.sheffield.ac.uk/news/nr/well-being-programmes-school-effect-comment-1.434283 (accessed 11 November 2017).

Ecclestone, K. and Hayes, D. (2009) *The Dangerous Rise of Therapeutic Education*. London: Routledge.

Education Act 2002, c.32. Available at www.legislation.gov.uk/ukpga/2002/32/pdfs/ukpga_20020032_en.pdf (accessed 9 April 2018).

Education and Inspections Act 2006, c.40. Available at www.legislation.gov.uk/ukpga/2006/40/pdfs/ukpga_20060040_en.pdf (accessed 7 November 2017).

EEF (2017) *Improving Mathematics in Key Stages Two and Three: Guidance Report*. Available at https://educationendowmentfoundation.org.uk/public/files/Publications/Campaigns/Maths/KS2_KS3_Maths_Guidance_2017.pdf (accessed 27 December 2017).

Elkin, S. (2004) *Top-performing School Starts by Managing Behaviour*. London: Specialist Schools Trust.

Elliott, J. (2005) 'Dyslexia myths and the feel-bad factor'. *Times Educational Supplement*, 2 September 2005.

Elliott, J. and Grigorenko, E. (2014) *The Dyslexia Debate*. Cambridge: Cambridge University Press.

Ellis, S. (2010) 'Managing transitions', in Soan S. (ed.), *The SENCO Handbook*. 2nd edn. London: Optimus.

Ellis, S. and Tod, J. (2015) *Promoting Behaviour for Learning in the Classroom: Effective Strategies, Personal Style and Professionalism*. Abingdon, UK: Routledge.

Ellis, S., Tod, J. and Graham-Matheson, L. (2008) *Special Educational Needs and Inclusion: Reflection and Renewal*. Birmingham: NASUWT. Available at www.nasuwt.org.uk/uploads/assets/uploaded/ddacdcb2-3cba-4791-850f32216246966e.pdf (accessed 1 January 2018).

Ellis, S., Tod, J. and Graham-Matheson, L. (2012) *Special Educational Needs and Inclusion: Reflection, Renewal and Reality*. Birmingham: NASUWT. Available at www.nasuwt.org.uk/uploads/assets/uploaded/fa1cbbdc-3cdb-4b2a-883d90defdfac493.pdf (accessed 1 January 2018).

Emler, N. (2002) *Self-Esteem: The Costs and Causes of Low Self Worth*. York, UK: Joseph Rowntree Foundation.

Evans, J. (2011) *Tough Love, Not Get Tough*. Ilford, UK: Barnardo's. Available from www.barnardos.org.uk/tough_love_report_2011.pdf (accessed 29 June 2017).

Fabian, H. and Dunlop, A. (2002) *Transitions in the Early Years*. London: RoutledgeFalmer.

Faupel, A., Herrick, E. and Sharp, P. (1998) *Anger Management: A Practical Guide*. London: David Fulton.

Finch, J. (1984) *Education as Social Policy*. London: Longman.

Fletcher-Campbell, F. and Wilkin, A. (2003) *Review of the Research Literature on Educational Interventions for Pupils with Emotional and Behavioural Difficulties*. Slough, UK: National Foundation for Educational Research.

Fogell, J. and Long, R. (1997) *Emotional and Behavioural Difficulties*. Tamworth, UK: NASEN.

Fordham, M. (2017) 'Should teaching methods be prescribed?'. Available at https://clioetcetera.com/2017/02/19/should-teaching-methods-be-prescribed/ (accessed 15 November 2017).

Froyen, L.A. (1993) *Classroom Management: The Reflective Teacher-Leader*. New York, NY: Macmillan.

Galton, M., Gray, J. and Rudduck, J. (2003) *Transfer and Transitions in the Middle Years of Schooling (7–14): Continuities and Discontinuities in Learning*. Nottingham: DfES.

Galvin, P. (1999) *Behaviour and Discipline in Schools 2*. London: David Fulton.

Gatongi, F. (2007) 'Person-centred approach in schools: Is it the answer to disruptive behaviour in our classrooms?'. *Counselling Psychology Quarterly* 20(2): 205–11.

Gibson, S. and Dembo, M. (1984) 'Teacher efficacy: A construct validation'. *Journal of Educational Psychology* 76(4): 569–82.

Gibson, J. and Smith, P. (2000) 'A good hearing? An application of the life space interview in residential child care'. *Child Care in Practice* 6(1): 39–52.

Gillies R.M. (2016) 'Cooperative learning: Review of research and practice'. *Australian Journal of Teacher Education* 41(3): 39–54.

GL Assessment (2016) *Pupil Attitudes to Self and School*. Available from www.gl-assessment.co.uk/media/2085/pass-report-2016_uk-edition.pdf (accessed 31 December 2017).

Glaze, B. (2016) 'Children as young as 4 expelled from school as bad behaviour soars'. *Mirror*, 31 March 2016. Available at www.mirror.co.uk/news/uk-news/children-young-4-expelled-school-7659190 (accessed 17 June 2017).

Goldacre, B. (2013) 'Building evidence into education'. Available at http://media.education.gov.uk/assets/files/pdf/b/ben%20goldacre%20paper.pdf (accessed 8 December 2016).

Goler, B. and Booth, J. (2008) 'Paired reading proves its worth'. *SENCO Update*, July/August 2008. London: Optimus.

Goodman, R. (1997) 'The strengths and difficulties questionnaire: A research note'. *Journal of Child Psychology and Psychiatry* 38(5): 581–86.

Gray, C. (1994a) *Comic Strip Conversations*. Arlington, TX: Future Horizons.

Gray, C. (1994b) *The New Social Story Book*. Arlington, TX: Future Horizons.

Gregory, A., Cornell, D., Fan, X., Sheras, P.L., Shih, T. and Huang, F. (2010) 'Authoritative school discipline: High school practices associated with lower bullying and victimization'. *Journal of Educational Psychology* 102(2): 483–96.

Gross-Loh, C. (2016) 'How praise became a consolation prize'. *The Atlantic*, 16 December 2016. Available at www.theatlantic.com/education/archive/2016/12/how-praise-became-a-consolation-prize/510845/ (accessed 1 January 2018).

Guardian (2014) 'Michael Gove urges "traditional" punishments for school misbehaviour'. Available at www.theguardian.com/education/2014/feb/02/michael-gove-traditional-punishments-school-misbehaviour (accessed 1 January 2018).

Haggarty, L. (2002) 'What does research tell us about how to prepare teachers?'. Paper presented to the ESCalate PGCE Conference held at the University of Nottingham, 9 July 2002. Available at www.escalate.ac.uk/downloads/1860.rtf (accessed 25 October 2017).

Hallam, S. and Rogers, L. (2008) *Improving Behaviour and Attendance at School*. Maidenhead, UK: Open University Press.

Halpin, T. and Blair, A. (2005) 'Schools crisis as discipline standards fall in classrooms'. *The Times*, 3 February 2005. Available at www.thetimes.co.uk/tto/education/article1800374.ece (accessed 13 June 2017).

Hardin, C. (2008) *Effective Classroom Management*. Upper Saddle River, NJ: Pearson.

Hargreaves, D., Hestor, K. and Mellor, J. (1975) *Deviance in Classrooms*. London: Routledge and Kegan Paul.

Harris, S. (2015) 'Unteachable! Schools struggle to cope with unruly pupils who are suspended up to 50 times a year'. *Mail Online*, 26 September 2015. Available at www.dailymail.co.uk/news/article-3249713/Unteachable-Schools-struggle-cope-unruly-pupils-suspended-50-times-year.html (accessed 13 June 2017).

Harris, S. (2017) 'The badly behaved pupils kept hidden from Ofsted: Heads cover up problems by removing troublesome students from school premises during inspections, government adviser warns'. *Mail Online*, 25 March 2017. Available at www.dailymail.co.uk/news/article- 4347726/The-badly-behaved-pupils-kept-hidden-Ofsted.html (accessed 23 June 2017).

Harrison, J. (2004) *Understanding Children: Foundations for Quality*. 3rd edn. Melbourne: ACER.

Hattie, J.C. (2009) *Visible Learning: A Synthesis of Over 800 Meta-Analyses Relating to Achievement*. London and New York: Routledge.

Hayes, D. (2012) *Foundations of Primary Teaching*. 5th edn. Abingdon, UK: Routledge.

Hayles, N.K. (1991) *Chaos and Order: Complex Dynamics in Literature and Science*. Chicago, IL: University of Chicago Press.

Hewett, D. (1998) 'Managing incidents of challenging behaviour – practices', in Hewett, D. (ed.), *Challenging Behaviour: Principles and Practices*. London: David Fulton.

Higgins, S., Baumfield, V. and Hall, E. (2007) 'Learning skills and the development of learning capabilities'. Report in *Research Evidence in Education Library*, EPPI-Centre, Social Science Research Unit, Institute of Education, University of London.

Hirsch, E.D. (1987) *Cultural Literacy: What Every American Needs to Know*. Boston, MA: Houghton Mifflin.

Hirsch, E.D. (2006) *The Knowledge Deficit: Closing the Shocking Education Gap for American Children*. Boston, MA: Houghton Mifflin.

Hohnen, B. and Murphy, T. (2016) 'The optimum context for learning: Drawing on neuroscience to inform best practice in the classroom'. *Educational and Child Psychology* 33(1): 75–87.

Hook, P. and Vass, A. (2002) *Teaching with Influence*. London: David Fulton.

Hopkins, A. (2008) 'Classroom conditions to secure enjoyment and achievement: The pupils' voice. Listening to the voice of *Every Child Matters*'. *Education 3–13* 36(4): 393–401.

Hopkins, B. (2004) *Just Schools: A Whole School Approach to Restorative Justice*. London: Jessica Kingsley.

Hopson, B., Scally, M. and Stafford, K. (1992) *Transitions: The Challenge of Change*. Didcot, UK: Mercury Books.

House of Commons Education Committee (2011) *Behaviour and Discipline in Schools*. First Report of Session 2010–11 (Vol. I). Available at www.publications.parliament.uk/pa/cm201011/cmselect/cmeduc/516/516i.pdf (accessed 23 June 2017).

I CAN (2006) *The Cost to the Nation of Poor Communication*. I CAN Talk Series – Issue 2. London: I CAN.

James, W. (1890/2007) *The Principles of Psychology – Volume 1*. New York, NY: Cosimo.

Jindal-Snape, D. and Miller, D. (2008) 'A Challenge of living? Understanding the psycho-social processes of the child during primary–secondary transition through resilience and self-esteem theories'. *Educational Psychology Review* 20(3): 217–36.

John-Akinola, Y.O., Gavin, A., O'Higgins, S.E. and Gabhainn, S.N. (2014) 'Taking part in school life: Views of children'. *Health Education* 114(1): 20–42.

Johnson, D.W., Johnson, R. and Stanne, M.B. (2000) 'Cooperative learning methods: A meta-analysis'. Available at www.researchgate.net/profile/David_Johnson50/publication/220040324_Cooperative_learning_methods_A_meta-analysis/links/00b4952b39d258145c000000/Cooperative-learning-methods-A-meta-analysis.pdf (accessed 2 January 2018).

Jude, R. (2014) 'Is using running as punishment the right message?'. Available at www.sportsgazette.co.uk/section.php?aid=1121&sid=36 (accessed 31/1/17).

Kamps, D., Mason, R., Thiemann-Bourque, K., Feldmiller, S., Turcotte, A. and Miller, T. (2014) 'The use of peer networks to increase communicative acts of students with autism spectrum disorders'. *Focus on Autism and Other Developmental Disabilities* 29(4): 230–45.

Katz, L.G. (1988) 'What should young children be doing?'. *American Educator* Summer: 29–45.

Katz, L.G. (1993) 'Dispositions: Definitions and implications for early childhood practices'. Perspectives from ERIC/ECCE: A monograph series, No. 4. ERIC Clearinghouse on Elementary and Early Childhood Education, Urbana, IL.

Kelly, K. and Phillips, S. (2016) *Teaching Literacy to Learners with Dyslexia: A Multi-sensory Approach*. 2nd edn. London: Sage.

Kilbride, D. (2014) 'Recognising self-esteem in our pupils: How do we define and manage it?'. *Research in Teacher Education* 4(2): 17–21.

Kohn, A. (1999) *Punished by Rewards*. New York, NY: Houghton Mifflin.

Kohn, A. (2001) *Beyond Discipline*. Upper Saddle River, NJ: Prentice Hall.

Kohn, A. (2015) 'The perils of "Growth Mindset" education: Why we're trying to fix our kids when we should be fixing the system'. Available at www.salon.com/2015/08/16/the_education_fad_thats_hurting_our_kids_what_you_need_to_know_about_growth_mindset_theory_and_the_harmful_lessons_it_imparts/ (accessed 31 March 2018).

Kounin, J. (1970) *Discipline and Group Management in Classrooms*. London: Holt, Rinehart and Winston.

Kreidler, W. (1984) *Creative Conflict Resolution: More Than 200 Activities for Keeping Peace in the Classroom*. Glenview, IL: Scott, Foresman and Co.

Kuypers, L. (2011) *The Zones of Regulation: A Curriculum Designed to Foster Self-regulation and Emotional Control*. San Jose, CA: Social Think Publishing.

Kyriacou, C. (1998) *Essential Teaching Skills*. 2nd edn. Cheltenham, UK: Nelson Thornes.

Kyriacou, C. and Issitt, J. (2008) 'What characterises effective teacher-initiated teacher–pupil dialogue to promote conceptual understanding in mathematics lessons in England in Key Stages 2 and 3: A systematic review'. Technical report. In *Research Evidence in Education Library*, London: EPPI-Centre, Social Science Research Unit, Institute of Education, University of London.

Kyriakides, L. and Creemers, B.P.M. (2013) 'Characteristics of effective schools in facing and reducing bullying'. *School Psychology International* 34(3): 248–368.

Laevers, F. (1994) *The Leuven Involvement Scale for Young Children* [manual and video]. Leuven, Belgium: Centre for Experiential Education.

Lawrence, D. (2006) *Enhancing Self-Esteem in the Classroom*. 3rd edn. London: Paul Chapman.

Lemov, D. (2015) *Teach Like a Champion 2.0*. San Francisco, CA: Jossey-Bass.

Lepper, M., Greene, D. and Nisbett, R. (1973) 'Undermining children's intrinsic interest with extrinsic reward: A test of the "overjustification" hypothesis'. *Journal of Personality and Social Psychology* 28(1): 129–37.

Li, Y. and Bates, T.C. (2017) 'Does mindset affect children's ability, school achievement, or response to challenge? Three failures to replicate'. Available at http://mrbartonmaths.com/resourcesnew/8.%20Research/Mindset/Mindset%20replication.pdf (accessed 27 January 2017).

Liddle, K. (2001) 'Implementing the picture exchange communication system (PECS)'. *Journal of Language and Communication Disorders* 36(1): 391–95.

Lindsay, G. and Dockrell, J. (2000) 'The behaviour and self-esteem of children with specific speech and language difficulties'. *British Journal of Educational Psychology* 70(4): 583–601.

Lloyd, S.R. and Berthelot, C. (1992) *Self-Empowerment: How to Get What You Want from Life*. London: Kogan Page.

Long, R. (1999) *Challenging Confrontation: Information and Techniques for School Staff*. Tamworth: NASEN.

Long, R. and Fogell, J. (1999) *Supporting Pupils with Emotional Difficulties*. London: David Fulton.

Lord, P. and O'Donnell, S. (2005) *Learner Motivation 3–19: An International Perspective*. Slough: NFER/QCA.

Lund, R. (1987) 'The self-esteem of children with emotional and behavioural difficulties'. *Maladjustment and Therapeutic Education* 5(1): 26–31.

Maines, B. and Robinson, G. (1988) *The Big School*. Bristol: Lucky Duck.

Maloney, J. (2007) 'Children's roles and use of evidence in science: An analysis of decision making in small groups'. *British Educational Research Journal* 33(3): 371–402.

Marsh, H. and Martin, A. (2011) 'Academic self-concept and academic achievement: Relations and causal ordering'. *British Journal of Educational Psychology* 81(1): 59–77.

Martin, A. and Dowson, M. (2009) 'Interpersonal relationships, motivation, engagement, and achievement: Yields for theory, current issues and educational practice'. *Review of Educational Research* 79(1): 327–65.

Marzano, R., Marzano, J. and Pickering, D. (2003) *Classroom Management that Works: Research-based Strategies for Increasing Student Achievement*. Alexandria, VA: Association for Supervision and Curriculum Development.

McCorkell, A. and Greig, R. (2010) 'Seven out of 10 teachers want to quit, survey shows'. *The Independent*, 2 October 2010. Available at www.independent.co.uk/news/education/education-news/seven-out-of-10-teachers-want-to-quit-survey-shows-2096257.html (accessed 29 September 2017).

McGrath, H. and Noble, T. (2010) 'Supporting positive pupil relationships: Research to practice'. *Educational and Child Psychology* 27(1): 79–90.

McLean, A. (2009) *Motivating Every Learner*. London: Sage.

McNamara, S. and Moreton, G. (2001) *Changing Behaviour: Teaching Children with Emotional and Behavioural Difficulties in Primary and Secondary Classrooms*. London: David Fulton.

McPhillimy, B. (1996) *Controlling Your Class: A Teacher's Guide to Managing Classroom Behaviour*. Chichester, UK: Wiley.

Miller, D. and Daniel, B. (2007) 'Competent to cope, worthy of happiness? How the duality of self-esteem can inform a resilience-based classroom environment'. *School Psychology International* 28(5): 605–22.

Miller, D. and Moran, D. (2005) 'One in three? Teachers' attempts to identify low self-esteem children'. *Pastoral Care in Education* 23(4): 25–30.

Miller, D. and Moran, D. (2012) *Self-esteem: A Guide for Teachers.* London: Sage.

Ministry of Education (1955) *Report of the Committee on Maladjusted Children* (the 'Underwood Report'). London: Her Majesty's Stationery Office.

Minton, S.J. (2017) 'Why aren't we beating bullying?'. *The Psychologist* 30, March: 41–3.

Montgomery, D. (2017) *Dyslexia-friendly Strategies for Reading, Spelling and Handwriting: A Toolkit for Teachers.* Abingdon, UK: Routledge.

Mortimore, P., Sammons, P., Stoll, L., Lewis, D. and Ecob, R. (1988) *School Matters.* Wells, UK: Open Books.

Mosley, J. (1996) *Quality Circle Time in the Primary Classroom.* Wisbech, UK: LDA.

Mosley, J. and Sonnet, H. (2005) *Better Behaviour Through Golden Time.* Wisbech, UK: LDA.

Moyers, B. (1989) *A World of Ideas: Conversations with Thoughtful Men and Women about American Life Today and the Ideas Shaping Our Future.* New York, NY: Doubleday.

Mruk, C. (1999) *Self-esteem: Research, Theory and Practice.* London: Free Association Books.

Mueller, C.M. and Dweck, C.S. (1998). 'Praise for intelligence can undermine children's motivation and performance'. *Journal of Personality and Social Psychology* 75(1): 33–52.

Muncey, J. and McGinty, J. (1998) 'Target setting and special schools'. *British Journal of Special Education* 25(4): 173–8.

Murphy, C., Kerr, K., Lundy, L. and McEvoy, L (2010) *Attitudes of Children and Parents to Key Stage 2 Science Testing and Assessment.* Available at https://wellcome.ac.uk/sites/default/files/wtx062721_0.pdf (accessed 29 November 2017).

NASEN (2014) *SEN Support and the Graduated Approach.* Tamworth: NASEN.

NASUWT (2012) *The Big Question.* Birmingham: NASUWT.

Neill, S. and Caswell, C. (1993) *Body Language for Competent Teachers.* London: Routledge.

Nelsen, J., Lott, L. and Glenn, H. (2000) *Positive Discipline in the Classroom.* 3rd edn. Roseville, CA: Prima Publishing.

Nelson, J. and O'Beirne, C. (2014) *Using Evidence in the Classroom: What Works and Why? Research Summary.* Slough, UK: NFER.

Newby, M. (2005) 'A curriculum for 2020'. *Journal of Education for Teaching* 31(4): 297–300.

NFER (2012) *Teacher Voice Omnibus February 2012 Survey: Pupil Behaviour.* Nottingham: DfE.

Nichols, D. and Houghton, S. (1995) 'The effect of Canter's Assertive Discipline programme on teacher and student behaviour'. *British Journal of Educational Psychology* 65(2): 197–210.

Norwich, B. (1994) 'Predicting girls' learning behaviour in secondary school mathematics lessons from motivational and learning environment factors'. *Educational Psychology* 14: 291–306.

Norwich, B. and Lewis, A. (2001) 'Mapping a pedagogy for special educational needs'. *British Educational Research Journal* 27(3): 313–29.

Norwich, B. and Rovoli, I. (1993) 'Affective factors and learning behaviour in secondary school mathematics and English lessons for average and low attainers'. *British Journal of Educational Psychology* 63: 308–21.

O'Brien, T. and Guiney, D. (2001) *Differentiation in Teaching and Learning.* London: Continuum.

Ofsted (1999) *Standards and Quality in Education 1997/98 – The Annual Report of Her Majesty's Chief Inspector of Schools.* London: Her Majesty's Stationery Office.

Ofsted (2003) *Handbook for Inspecting Secondary Schools.* London: Ofsted.

Ofsted (2004) *Special Educational Needs and Disability: Towards Inclusive Schools.* London: Ofsted.

Ofsted (2005) *Managing Challenging Behaviour.* London: Ofsted.

Ofsted (2011) *The Annual Report of Her Majesty's Chief Inspector of Education, Children's Services and Skills 2010/11.* London: Ofsted.

Ofsted (2013) *The Report of Her Majesty's Chief Inspector of Education, Children's Services and Skills: Schools*. Available at www.gov.uk/government/publications/ofsted-annual-report-201213-schools-report (accessed 23 June 2017).

Ofsted (2014a) *Below the Radar: Low-level Disruption in the Country's Classrooms*. Available at www.gov.uk/government/publications/below-the-radar-low-level-disruption-in-the-countrys-classrooms (accessed 23 June 2017).

Ofsted (2014b) *Maintained Schools and Academies Inspections and Outcomes – January to March 2014 (Final)*. Available at www.gov.uk/government/statistics/latest-official-statistics-maintained-schools-and-academies-inspections-and-outcomes (accessed 1 January 2018).

Olsen, J. and Cooper, P. (2001) *Dealing with Disruptive Students in the Classroom*. London: Kogan Page.

Park, J. and Tew, M. (2007) 'Emotional rollercoaster: Calming nerves at times of transition'. *Curriculum Briefing* 5(3): 21–8.

Parsons, C. (1999) *Education, Exclusion and Citizenship*. London: Routledge.

Parsons, C., Maras, P., Knowles, C., Bradshaw, V., Hollingworth, K. and Monteiro, H. (2008) *Formalised Peer Mentoring Pilot Evaluation*. Nottingham: DCSF.

Pavlou, V. and Maria Kambouri, M. (2007) 'Pupils' attitudes towards art teaching in primary school: An evaluation tool'. *Studies in Educational Evaluation* 33: 282–301.

Pease, A. and Pease, B. (2004) *The Definitive Book of Body Language*. London: Orion Books.

Pellerin, L. (2005) 'Applying Baumrind's parenting typology to high schools: Toward a middle-range theory of authoritative socialization'. *Social Science Research* 34 (2): 283–303.

Penney, C. (1989) 'Modality effects and the structure of short-term verbal memory'. *Memory and Cognition* 17(4): 389–422.

Perkins, D. (1995) *Outsmarting IQ: The Emerging Science of Learnable Intelligence*. New York: The Free Press.

Peterson, L. and Peterson, M. (1959) 'Short-term retention of individual verbal items'. *Journal of Experimental Psychology* 58(3): 193–8.

Pollard, A., Triggs, P., Broadfoot, P., McNess, E. and Osborn, M. (2000) *What Pupils Say: Changing Policy and Practice in Primary Education*. London: Continuum.

Porter, L. (2007) *Behaviour in Schools*. 2nd edn. Maidenhead, UK: Open University Press.

Pound, L. (2005) *How Children Learn*. London: Step Forward Publishing.

Powell, S. (1993) 'The power of positive peer influence: Leadership training for today's teens'. *Special Services in Schools* 8(1): 119–36.

Powell, S. and Tod, J. (2004) 'A systematic review of how theories explain learning behaviour in school contexts'. EPPI-Centre, Social Science Research Unit, Institute of Education, University of London.

QCA (2001) *Supporting School Improvement: Emotional and Behavioural Development*. Sudbury, UK: QCA.

Redl, F. (1959) 'Strategy and techniques of the life space interview'. *American Journal of Orthopsychiatry* 29(1): 1–18.

Reid, G. (2016) *Dyslexia: A Practitioners' Handbook*. Chichester, UK: Wiley.

Revel, P. (2004) 'Winning the war on classroom terror'. *Times Educational Supplement*, 2 July 2004.

Rienzo, C., Rolfe, H. and Wilkinson, D. (2015) 'Changing mindsets'. Available at www.niesr.ac.uk/sites/default/files/publications/Changing_Mindsets.pdf (accessed 1 January 2018).

Rinaldi, W. (2001) *Social Use of Language Programme – Revised*. Windsor, UK: NFER-Nelson.

Roberts, N. (2017) *The School Curriculum in England* (House of Commons Briefing Paper). Available at http://researchbriefings.files.parliament.uk/documents/SN06798/SN06798.pdf (accessed 14 November 2017).

Robinson, C. (2014) 'Children, their voices and their experiences of school: What does the evidence tell us?'. Cambridge Primary Review Trust Research Report. Available at http://cprtrust.org.uk/wp-content/uploads/2014/12/FINAL-VERSION-Carol-Robinson-Children-their-Voices-and-their-Experiences-of-School.pdf (accessed 1 January 2018).

Robinson, C. and Fielding, M. (2014) 'Children and their primary school: Pupils' voices'. Cambridge Primary Review Trust Research Briefing. Available at http://cprtrust.org.uk/wp-content/uploads/2014/06/Primary_Review_5-3_briefing_pupils__voices_0711231.pdf (accessed 1 January 2018).

Roffey, S. (2010) 'Content and context for learning relationships: A cohesive framework for whole school development'. *Educational and Child Psychology* 27(1): 156–67.

Roffey, S. (2016) 'Building a case for whole-child, whole-school wellbeing in challenging contexts'. *Journal of Educational and Child Psychology* 33(2): 30–9.

Roffey, S., Williams, A., Greig, A. and Mackay, T (2017) 'Mental health and wellbeing in schools: Concerns, challenges and opportunities'. *Educational and Child Psychology* 33(4): 5–7.

Rogers, B. (1990) *You Know the Fair Rule*. London: Pitman.

Rogers, B. (1997) *The Language of Discipline*. 2nd edn. Plymouth, UK: Northcote House.

Rogers, B. (2002) *Classroom Behaviour*. 1st edn. London: Paul Chapman.

Rogers, B. (2003) *Behaviour Recovery: Practical Programs for Challenging Behaviour and Children with Emotional Behaviour Disorders in Mainstream Schools*. 2nd edn. Melbourne: ACER Press.

Rogers, B. (2007) *Behaviour Management: A Whole-School Approach*. 2nd edn. London: Paul Chapman.

Rogers, B. (2011) *Classroom Behaviour*. 3rd edn. London: Sage.

Rogers, B. (2012) *You Know the Fair Rule*. 3rd edn. Harlow, UK: Pearson.

Rogers, B. and MacPherson, E. (2008) *Behaviour Management with Young Children*. London: Sage.

Rose, J. (2009) *Identifying and Teaching Children and Young People with Dyslexia and Literacy Difficulties: An Independent Report*. Nottingham: DCSF.

Rosenberg, M. (1965) *Society and the Adolescent Self-image*. Princeton, NJ: Princeton University Press.

Roseth, C., Johnson, D. and Johnson, T. (2008) 'Promoting early adolescents' achievement and peer relationships: The effect of co-operative, competitive and individualistic goal structures'. *Psychological Bulletin* 134(2): 223–46.

Rotter, J. (1954) *Social Learning and Clinical Psychology*. Englewood Cliffs, NJ: Prentice Hall.

Rowe, C. (1998) 'Do social stories benefit children with autism in mainstream primary schools?'. *British Journal of Special Education* 26(1): 12–14.

Rudduck, J., Chaplain. R. and Wallace, G. (1996) *School Improvement: What Can Pupils Tell Us?* London: David Fulton.

Rudduck, J., Wilson, E. and Flutter, J. (1998) *Sustaining Pupils' Commitment to Learning: The Challenge of Year 8* (a report for Lincolnshire LEA). Cambridge: Homerton Research Unit.

Rutter, M. (1985) 'Resilience in the face of adversity. Protective factors and resistance to psychiatric disorder'. *British Journal of Psychiatry* 147: 598–611.

Rutter, M., Maughan, B., Mortimore, P. and Ouston, J. (1979) *Fifteen Thousand Hours: Secondary Schools and Their Effects on Children*. London: Open Books.

Sainsbury, C. (2009) *Martian in the Playground: Understanding the Schoolchild with Asperger's Syndrome*. 2nd edn. London: Sage.

Sanders, D., White, G., Burge, B., Sharp, C., Eames, A., McEune, R. and Grayson, H. (2005) *A Study of the Transition from the Foundation Stage to Key Stage 1*. Nottingham: DfES.

Schon, D. (1983) *The Reflective Practitioner: How Professionals Think in Action*. New York, NY: Basic Books.

Seligman, M. (1975) *Helplessness: On Depression, Development, and Death*. New York, NY: W.H. Freeman.

Shavelson, R.J. and Bolus, R. (1982) 'Self-concept: The interplay of theory and methods'. *Journal of Educational Psychology* 74(1): 3–17.

Shavelson, R.J., Hubner, J.J. and Stanton, G.C. (1976) 'Self-concept: Validation of construct interpretations'. *Review of Educational Research* 46: 407–41.

Silber, E. and Tippett, J.S. (1965) 'Self-esteem: Clinical assessment and measurement validation'. *Psychological Reports* 16 (3): 1017–71.

Sisk, V.F., Burgoyne, A.P., Sun, J., Butler, J.L. and Macnamara, B.N. (2018) 'To what extent and under which circumstances are growth mind-sets important to academic achievement? Two meta-analyses'. *Psychological Science* 29(4): 549–71.

Slavin, R.E. (2004) 'When and why does cooperative learning increase achievement?', in Edwards, A. and Daniels, H. (eds.), *Reader in Psychology of Education*. London: RoutledgeFalmer.

Smith, C. (2003) *Writing and Developing Social Stories: Practical Interventions in Autism*. Bicester, UK: Speechmark.

Smith, C., Dakers, J., Dow, W., Head, G., Sutherland, M. and Irwin, R. (2005) 'A systematic review of what pupils, aged 11–16, believe impacts on their motivation to learn in the classroom'. In *Research Evidence in Education Library*, EPPI-Centre, Social Science Research Unit, Institute of Education, University of London.

Smithers, R. (2005) 'Tough love'. *Guardian*, 21 June 2005. Available at www.theguardian.com/education/2005/jun/21/classroomviolence.schools (accessed 25 December 2017).

Somerville, L.H. (2013) 'The teenage brain: Sensitivity to social evaluation'. *Current Directions in Psychological Science* 22(2): 121–27.

Sroufe, L.A. and Siegel, D.J. (2011) 'The case for attachment theory: The verdict is in'. *Psychotherapy Networker* 35(34–39): 52–3.

Sullivan, H.S. (1953) *Interpersonal Theory of Psychiatry*. New York, NY: Norton.

Sweller, J. (1988). 'Cognitive load during problem solving: Effects on learning'. *Cognitive Science* 12(2): 257–85.

Sweller, J. (2010) 'Element interactivity and intrinsic, extraneous and germane cognitive load'. *Educational Psychology Review* 22(2): 123–38.

Swinson, J. (2017) 'Evidence based practice, classroom behaviour, the importance of feedback'. *Debate* 164: 17–20.

Swinson, J. and Cording, M. (2002) 'Assertive discipline in a school for pupils with emotional and behavioural difficulties'. *British Journal of Special Education* 29(3): 72–5.

Swinson, J. and Melling, R. (1995) 'Assertive discipline – four wheels on this wagon – a reply to Robinson and Maines'. *Educational Psychology in Practice* 11(3): 1–8.

TA (2012) 'Improving teacher training for behaviour'. Available at http://dera.ioe.ac.uk/14683/7/improving%20teacher%20training%20for%20behaviour%20without%20case%20studies.pdf (accessed 23 June 2017).

Tafarodi, R.W. and Milne, A.B. (2002) 'Decomposing global self-esteem'. *Journal of Personality* 70(4): 443–83.

TDA (2007) *Professional Standards for Teachers*. London: TDA.

Teacher Support Network (2010) *Teacher Support Network and Family Lives Behaviour Survey 2010*. London: Teacher Support Network.

Thomas, G. and Loxley, A. (2007) *Deconstructing Special Education and Constructing Inclusion*. 2nd edn. Buckingham, UK: Open University Press.

Thompson, F. and Smith, P. (2011) *The Use and Effectiveness of Anti-Bullying Strategies in Schools*. Available at www.gov.uk/government/uploads/system/uploads/attachment_data/file/182421/DFE-RR098.pdf (accessed 2 January 2018).

Tod, J. (2000) *Individual Education Plans: Dyslexia*. London: David Fulton.

Treasury Office (2003) *Every Child Matters*. London: The Stationery Office.

TTA (1998) *National Standards for Qualified Teacher Status*. London: TTA.

Wallace, B. (2000) *Teaching the Very Able Child: Developing a Policy and Adopting Strategies for Provision*. London: David Fulton.

Wallace, B. (2001) *Teaching Thinking Skills across the Primary Curriculum*. London: David Fulton.

Watkins, C. (2016) *Managing Classroom Behaviour*. 5th edn. London: ATL.

Watkins, C. and Wagner, P. (2000) *Improving School Behaviour*. London: Paul Chapman.

Weare, K. (2004) *Developing the Emotionally Literate School*. London: Paul Chapman.

Weare, K. (2010) 'Mental health and social and emotional learning: Evidence, principles, tensions, balances'. *Advances in School Mental Health Promotion* 3(1): 5–17.

Weare, K. (2015) *What Works in Promoting Social and Emotional Well-being and Responding to Mental Health Problems in Schools?* London: National Children's Bureau. Available at www.mentalhealth.org.nz/assets/ResourceFinder/What-works-in-promoting-social-and-emotional-wellbeing-in-schools-2015.pdf (accessed 23 June 2017).

Weare, K. and Nind, M. (2011) 'Mental health promotion and problem prevention in schools: What does the evidence say?'. *Health Promotion International* 26(S1): i29–i69.

Weiner, B. (2000) 'Interpersonal and intrapersonal theories of motivation from an attributional perspective'. *Educational Psychology Review* 22(1): 1–14.

Werner, E. and Smith, R. (1992) *Overcoming the Odds: High-risk Children from Birth to Adulthood.* New York, NY: Cornell University Press.

Wheldall, K. and Glynn, T. (1989) *Effective Classroom Learning.* Oxford: Blackwell.

White, R. and Mitchell, I. (1994) 'Metacognition and the quality of learning'. *Studies in Science Education* 23(1): 21–37.

Whitehead, T. and Riches, C. (2005) 'Discipline in schools is worst ever: And no wonder if our football idols set such a bad example'. *Daily Express*, 3 February 2005.

Wilby, P. (2008) 'Ain't misbehaving' (interview with Sir Alan Steer). *Guardian Education*, 23 September 2008.

Wilson, Y. (2013) *Taming your Temper.* Syresham, UK: Small World.

Wing, L. and Gould, J. (1979) 'Severe impairments of social interaction and associated abnormalities in children: Epidemiology and classification'. *Journal of Autism and Developmental Disorders* 9(1): 11–19.

Woods, S., Hodges, C. and Aljunied, M. (1996) 'The effectiveness of assertive discipline training: Look before you leap'. *Educational Psychology in Practice* 12(3): 175–83.

Young, T. (2017) 'Schools are desperate to teach "growth mindset". But it's based on a lie'. *The Spectator*, 21 January 2017. Available at www.spectator.co.uk/2017/01/schools-are-desperate-to-teach-growth-mindset-but-its-based-on-a-lie/ (accessed 1 January 2018).

Ziegler, A. and Stoeger, H. (2010) 'Research on a modified framework of implicit personality theories'. *Learning and Individual Differences* 20: 318–26.

Index

Page numbers in **bold** denote tables, those in *italics* denote figures.

Printed in Great Britain
by Amazon